Richard and Adolf

DID RICHARD WAGNER INCITE ADOLF HITLER
TO COMMIT THE HOLOCAUST?

Christopher Nicholson

gefen publishing house
JERUSALEM ◆ NEW YORK

Copyright © Christopher Nicholson
Jerusalem 2007 / 5767

All rights reserved. No part of this publication may be translated, reproduced,
stored in a retrieval system or transmitted, in any form or by any means,
electronic, mechanical, photocopying, recording or otherwise, without
express written permission from the publishers.

Typesetting: Jerusalem Typesetting, Jerusalem
Cover Design: S. Kim Glassman, Jerusalem

ISBN 978-965-229-360-2

1 3 5 7 9 8 6 4 2

Gefen Publishing House, Ltd.　　　　　　　　　　Gefen Books
6 Hatzvi Street, Jerusalem 94386, Israel　　　　600 Broadway, Lynbrook, NY 11563, USA
972-2-538-0247 • orders@gefenpublishing.com　　1-516-593-1234 • orders@gefenpublishing.com

www.israelbooks.com

Printed in Israel　　　　　　　　　　　　　　　*Send for our free catalogue*

"For me Wagner is a god, his music is my religion. I go to his operas as others go to church".[1]

– Adolf Hitler

---

1. Köhler, *Wagner's Hitler*, 137.

Table of Contents

Foreword: 1
Chapter one: The Final Assault. 13
Chapter two: The Dung from Which It Grew 19
Chapter three: Son of a Vulture. 25
Chapter four: Seeds of Anti-Semitism 41
Chapter five: Full-Blown Racism 73
Chapter six: A Royal Patron 97
Chapter seven: Ideological Lunacy 145
Chapter eight: The Hagiographers 179
Chapter nine: The Widow Spider 197
Chapter ten: Nearly Schickelgruber 211
Chapter eleven: Opera Lover and Aspirant Composer 217
Chapter twelve: Soldier and Anti-Semite 233
Chapter thirteen: Bayreuth Spectator 247
Chapter fourteen: Sexual Depravity 301
Chapter fifteen: Absolute Power 325
Chapter sixteen: The Holocaust 385
Chapter seventeen: Last Will and Testament 407
Chapter eighteen: Denazification 419
Chapter nineteen: Wagner in Israel 433
Select Bibliography: 451
Index: 459

Foreword

My early writing career saw me publish two books about the effect that Apartheid had on the lives of two very different people. The first addressed the killing of the Cradock Four and traced their killers to the highest echelons of the Nationalist government including the then president of South Africa. The second book dealt with the struggle of an Indian golfer with the Apartheid laws prohibiting him playing against white golfers. He eventually was allowed to and was given his prize in the rain while other golfers were allowed into the clubhouse. He also beat Gary Player in a wonderful match that I believe is the most significant game of golf ever played.

I have often wondered what induced me to put pen to paper on the subject of Richard Wagner and Adolf Hitler. Love of the music of Wagner led me on a voyage of discovery into the life of the composer. When I raved to friends about the music there was a general disapproval expressed, initially to the music. These friends were in good company.

Writing in the October 1896 number of the magazine *Cosmopolis*, Professor Max Müller wrote that though he had "passed through a long school he could never learn to enjoy Wagner except now and then *in one of his lucid intervals*." Others had harsher comments to make. "Wagner's music is better than it sounds," said Mark Twain, who visited the Bayreuth Wagner festival.[1] The length of his works distressed even his fellow composers. "Wagner has wonderful moments, but…long half hours" said Gioacchino Rossini.[2] "Wear comfortable shoes" was the advice legendary singer Birgit Nilsson gave to aspiring Wagnerian sopranos.[3] Elizabeth Schwarzkopf was highly regarded in her early career but somewhat rebellious and found it more comfortable to perform barefoot in Tannhäuser in October 1939 in Berlin.[4] Finally one noted critic damned him with faint praise. Oscar Wilde loved Wagner's music "better than anybody's; it is so loud, one can talk the whole time without other people hearing what one is saying."[5]

As to the music I was quick to defend the hypnotic effect of the style. There were also criticisms of the man Wagner and his ideology, and, more pointedly, a charge that he was a Nazi. The more I read the more I saw a link between his thoughts and those of Adolf Hitler. The links became fascinating and I read wider and wider on the topic. I decided to write a book because, as Nietzsche once said, "I did not know any other way of getting rid of my thoughts."

It is now more than fifty years since the horror of the Holocaust. While the measurement of crime and criminality is not an exact science, few would quibble with the stigmatization of Adolf Hitler as mankind's most evil man. Under his megalomaniac dictatorship the world was plunged into a war that cost more than fifty-five million lives. Six million Jews, all non-combatants and many Slavs, gypsies, communists, political opponents and mentally deficient persons were deliberately murdered in an insane attempt at establishing a purified nation and expanding German territory. One writer has even written a fictionalized account of an imaginary trial of Hitler for crimes against humanity.[6]

Although Hitler did not achieve this alone his iron rule made his tyranny the achievement of a personal agenda. What circumstances drove him to this goal? This book seeks to examine his personality and find some answers to this riddle. Above all it seeks to investigate Hitler's idolization

---

1. Bentley and Esar, *Treasury of Humorous Quotations*, 200.
2. Ibid., 161.
3. Weiner, *Richard Wagner and the Anti-Semitic Imagination*, 261.
4. Kater, *The Twisted Muse*, 62.
5. Bentley and Esar, *Treasury of Humorous Quotations*, 212.
6. van Rjndt, *The Trial of Adolf Hitler*, 268.

of the great German composer Richard Wagner and the influence of the latter on Hitler.

"The canonization of Saints which the heathen called apotheosis" was the way Thomas Hobbes described the process involving the deifying of mortals, in his seminal political study *Government and Society*. Views on the links between the composer and the dictator are not harmonious. The subject is also controversial as some reckon that the composer had little effect on the dictator. "To see Wagner through the eyes of Hitler is historically unacceptable and morally indefensible, since there is no direct path that leads from Wagner to Hitler." Thus spoke Dieter David Scholz in his doctoral thesis *Richard Wagner's Antisemitismus*. An immediate rebuttal or rejoinder can be found in Hitler's own words uttered to a journalist in 1942: "For me Wagner is a god, his music is my religion. I go to his operas as others go to church."[7]

In 1993, Gottfried Wagner, the great-grandson of the composer, wrote a book in which he stated that: "Wagner himself misused music as a vehicle of propaganda. Where arguments about Wagner are concerned, Germans quickly lose their sense of humor. With Wagner the German soul becomes exalted! Woe betide anyone who questions Wagner."[8] He went on to place the blame fairly and squarely on his famous forebear. "Richard Wagner, through his inflammatory anti-Semitic writings, was co-responsible for the transition from Bayreuth to Auschwitz."[9]

Joachim Fest wrote an outstanding biography of Hitler and pointed to a number of factors that pointed to Hitler's idolatry of Wagner. In the first place he pointed out how "the theatricality of the Third Reich…found its basis in Wagner's operas."[10] The vast spectacles during the annual Nazi Party meetings in Nürnberg with the great Cathedrals of Light gave splendor to policies that were opportunistic, racist and totalitarian.

Secondly Fest points out that the master of Bayreuth was not only "Hitler's great exemplar, he was also the young man's ideological mentor." As a young man Hitler read voraciously and nothing fascinated him more than the race stereotypes and calls for a national savior in Wagner's prose. "Wagner's political writing was Hitler's favourite reading and the sprawl-

---

7. Köhler, *Wagner's Hitler*, 137.
8. Wagner, Gottfried, *The Wagner Legacy*, 240.
9. Ibid., 256.
10. Fest, *Hitler*, 56.

ing pomposity of his style was an unmistakable influence on Hitler's own grammar and syntax."[11]

On other occasions Hitler linked the political ideology of his party with the Bayreuth Master. "Whoever wants to understand National Socialism must know Wagner."[12] There is substantial proof that Hitler read everything that Wagner wrote and Fest states unequivocally that "the political writings together with the operas form the entire framework of Hitler's ideology." The Wagner of the late regeneration writings advocated a form of social Darwinism in terms of which the most powerful politically earned the right to rule. Fest also identified the rampant anti-Semitism ("I hold the Jewish race to be the born enemy of pure humanity and everything noble in man") as a central pillar in the ideologies of both.[13] Wagner refused to credit the Jews with what Nietzsche called their greatest achievement – namely as the inventors of Christianity. Hitler of course had little respect for either the New or the Old Testament, calling the latter "Satan's Bible."[14]

The horror of the new thinking was the total abdication of reason and toleration and what Fest calls "the adoration of barbarism and Germanic might." The elevation of the Aryan race to the top of the totem pole of culture gave justification for aggression and land grabbing. In a flurry of damning metaphors Fest catalogs the irrational and emotional features in Wagner, which appealed to the young down-and-out Adolf Hitler.

"[T]he mystique of blood purification expressed in *Parsifal* and the general histrionic view in which good and evil, purity and corruption, rules and the ruled stand opposed in black and white contrast. The curse of gold, the inferior race grubbing underground, the conflict between Siegfried and Hagen, the tragic genius of Wotan, this strange brew compounded of bloody vapours, dragon slaying, mania for domination, treachery, sexuality, elite paganism and ultimately salvation and tolling bells on a theatrical Good Friday were the perfect ideological match for Hitler's anxieties and needs."[15]

Fest concludes that Hitler imbibed recklessly of this deadly broth and

---

11. Ibid.
12. Suirer p. 133.
13. Fest, *Hitler*, 56.
14. Gutman, *Richard Wagner*, 594.
15. Fest, *Hitler*, 56.

"found the granite foundation for his view of the world."[16] Not only did the young politician worship the man and his ideas, he also posited himself as the ideological heir apparent. Fest identified the kinship Hitler felt for Wagner and comments that one of his favorite ideas to which he returned frequently concerned Wagner's towering importance "for the development of German Man." He admired the courage and energy with which Wagner exerted political influence "without really wishing to be political" and Fest records how on one occasion he admitted that a "literally hysterical excitement" overcame him when he recognized "his own psychological kinship with this great man."[17] Hitler truly saw himself as a political son of the composer.

Writing in the late 1930s Pieter Viereck said that "Wagner's warped genius [is] the most important single fountainhead of current Nazi ideology."[18] In his role as the heir of Wagner, Hitler took great pleasure in finding similarities in their background and nature. As Fest has pointed out: "Hitler was stimulated by gods and heroes; gigantic aspirations of horrendous superlatives helped to mask the banality of his circumstances. In music Richard Wagner brought him to bright flames. Wagner was his idol during his years as a young man, not only in music."[19]

Frederic Spotts, in his masterful account entitled *Bayreuth: A History of the Wagner Festival,* maintains that "With the apotheosis of Wagner and the glorification of Bayreuth as Germany's supreme cultural showpiece, it is easy to see why there took root in the public mind a symbiotic relationship: Wagner – Bayreuth – Hitler – National Socialism – Third Reich." Others were even more outspoken. Leonard Woolf in his memoirs says that "Wagner was both cause and effect of [the] repulsive process which ended in the apogee and apotheosis of human bestiality and degradation, Hitler and the Nazis."

Na'ama Sheffi has written an excellent account of the vehement opposition to the reception of Wagner's music in Israel. She concludes that "I do not believe the shape of that memory should be determined by a musical boycott. Both the Nazi and the Israeli perceptions of Wagner essentially followed the same process by which Wagner created his mythical

---

16. Ibid.
17. Ibid., 49.
18. Viereck, *Metapolitics*, 91.
19. Fest, *Hitler*, 49.

world of the Nibelungs. In each case a ring of myths was created, though for widely different purposes. The Nazis' artistic aim was to revive the glory of Teutonic legend by apotheosizing Wagner's artistic work and political thought; the Israelis sought to condemn them."[20]

If Hitler felt depressed as to his humble circumstances or failure in his early years he consoled himself with the notion that he was following in another's footsteps. As Fest goes on to say: "In fact Hitler saw Wagner's early disappointments, lack of recognition and obstinate faith in his own vocation in life flowing into the glory of world fame as a prototype of his own destiny. Hitler himself in fact later declared that with the exception of Richard Wagner he had no forerunners and by Wagner he meant not only the composer but Wagner the personality…the greatest prophetic figure the German people has had."[21]

The roots and causes of Hitler's anti-Semitism have mystified several eminent writers. Professor Percy Schramm concluded that "we must be satisfied with the realization that there is about Hitler's…anti-Semitism an unknown factor."[22] An early and very eminent historian on the Third Reich, Karl Bracher, also concluded that "Hitler's fanatical hatred of the Jews defies all rational explanation; it cannot be measured by political and practical gauges."[23]

The predominant view that emerges is that Hitler's ideology was based largely on the anti-Semitism of the writings and to some extent the artistic works of Richard Wagner, reckoned by many to be the greatest composer of all time. The lineage spawned by his works includes ideological as well as physical descendants. Also examined in this book is the development of the seeds of anti-Semitism in Wagner and the cross-pollination via the eccentric Englishman Houston Stewart Chamberlain, who married Wagner's daughter Eva, and others to Hitler.

Nietzsche commented on one occasion that once people abandoned religion they elevated artists into gods. Hitler regarded Wagner as a god and made the fulfillment of Wagner's anti-Semitic ideas his life's mission. Wagner's personal life, and especially his philandering and sponging, showed that he was anything but a god. This book explores not only the

---

20. Sheffi, *Ring of Myths*, viii.
21. Fest, Hitler, 49.
22. Langer, *The Mind of Adolf Hitler*, 222.
23. Ibid., 223.

tortured political and social ideology but also the seedier side of Wagner's personal life to illustrate his absence of godliness. Major biographers, including Ernest Newman, have shrunk from probing too deeply into the darkness that such an enquiry requires. The coexistence of great genius and moral depravity appears to have been an insuperable obstacle to them.

In a strange quirk of literary heredity this trait of biographical abstinence has passed on to those relating the life of the Führer. A topic shunned by the authentic biographers of Hitler is the depravity of his personality. The dark and uncertain world of psychiatry is not for the untutored traveler but some light is thrown on the anti-Semitism of Hitler by considering his sexual perversions. As Freud himself said, "manifest abnormality in the other relations of life can invariably be shown to have a background of abnormal sexual conduct."[24] Throughout this study I will be making fairly frequent reference to Freud. Although many of Freud's theories have been questioned and redefined in modern psychiatry, he remains a towering figure in the history of psychoanalysis and it is interesting to note what he said in the context of the times. And Freud is very much in context here: he lived in Vienna at the same time that Hitler lived there – in fact only a few blocks away.

The notion that one man attempted to wipe out a whole religious group is so alien and incongruous to the ordinary reader that every aspect of his personality has to be examined in search of answers. For this reason some details are provided of the private life of Hitler – and specifically of the depraved practices in his relationships. There are vast differences in the approach of the major biographers to this side of his life. Alan Bullock in his study of Hitler described a man who was thoroughly in his element with women but was probably syphilitic and impotent.[25] Fest described a man of great loneliness and sexual frustration whose public appearances were substitutes for sex, his only great love being the tabooed Tristanesque uncle/niece incestuous relationship with his niece Geli Raubal.[26]

Ian Kershaw saw Hitler as a man obsessed by politics without any personal life and what Kershaw saw was more abhorrent than what previous research had indicated.[27] Waite, Langer and Infield paint a picture

---

24. Freud, *On Sexuality*, 75.
25. Machtan, *Hidden Hitler*, 5.
26. Ibid., 8.
27. Ibid., 13.

of a sexual pervert who performed strange acts with women and Lothar Machtan constructs a mostly convincing argument that he was a homosexual. Hitler's press chief Putzi Hanfstaengl, a bohemian bon vivant who appears to have had personal knowledge of the subject, talks of Hitler inhabiting what he calls very appropriately a "sexual no-man's-land."[28]

So you can take your pick. Hitler's sexual dalliances, peccadilloes and perversions are related to shed light on what sort of personality embraced the Wagnerian oeuvre. Only after such an enquiry is it possible to tentatively suggest that the sole personality capable of carrying out the ideas propagated by Wagner was one so warped and deranged that it contemplated such sexual practices.

Once Hitler became chancellor and was more or less permanently in the public eye, the contemporary morality meant that his sexual activities had to be subjugated to a large extent. This may well have contributed to the growth of neuroses and megalomania in him. We know that from the time when Freud first recognized the importance of sexuality in human life, he tended to think of psychic disturbance as the sequel, or as the potential sequel to any large-scale sexual abstinence: this is seen strikingly in the actual neuroses.[29]

Another central theme explored in this book is the relevance of an artist's ideology and personal life to any appreciation of his art. Normally the ideology of the artist matters little as long as the art remains uncontaminated. With Wagner the question is more simply answered because the anti-Semitism permeated the ideological writings as well as the operas or music dramas as he preferred to call them.

Much has been written about the two principal protagonists in this book. Biography is at best an inexact record but in the hands of deliberate falsifiers such as Cosima Wagner and her lieutenants Glasenapp, Chamberlain and Praeger the life of Wagner might well have been elevated to a gigantic fraud on history. Konrad Heiden observed that "with Richard Wagner in mind, Chamberlain foreshadowed a whole school which falsifies facts and calls the result higher truth."[30] All is not doom and gloom on that

---

28. Machtan p. 277.
29. Wollheim, *Freud* (London: Fontana Collins, 1971), 142.
30. Gutman, *Richard Wagner*, 10.

front as a most unlikely writer rescued posterity from the machinations of the Bayreuth brigade. The indomitable English Wagnerian Mary Burrell did much to preserve the primary materials that ensured that most of the truth about Wagner would be told. Her struggle to find the materials and counteract the intrigues of Cosima and others from Wahnfried, ancestral home of the Wagners, makes a fascinating story on its own. The world had to wait many years before these primary sources were made available to historians and biographers. The materials she hunted down and purchased lay in a dusty Victorian vault until after the Holocaust and the fury of the Second World War.

These papers exposed a Wagner who was completely different from the oracle held out by Hitler to be the prophet of the Third Reich. While it is always difficult to speculate on cause and effect, an exposé of the sordid details of Wagner's life might well have tempered Hitler's enthusiasm for the Bayreuth Master and prevented the disastrous slide to fascism, National Socialism and the Holocaust. For our purposes, an examination of the private lives of Wagner and his contemporaries demonstrates the pervading mores – or lack thereof – in the artists' society of the day, and gives us a glimpse into the personality of the great composer whose views were so formative for the Führer he presaged.

This book is based on well-documented facts. To enable interested readers to follow up the background to various events footnotes and a select bibliography are provided. There are numerous recordings of Wagner's music and all his operas have been recorded. For the less adventurous, excerpts from the operas exist and many recordings include orchestral passages without the singing. It is not necessary to know the music intimately well to appreciate the book, though a thorough knowledge will enhance a proper appreciation of some of the less obvious themes.

Those disinclined to spend hours poring over the biographies or listening to the music could do a lot worse than watch Tony Palmer's biography, *Wagner*, made for television in 1983. Richard Burton plays Wagner to perfection and Vanessa Redgrave brings richness to the role of Cosima. The music includes chunks of the great composer's best conducted by Sir Georg Solti. That great trio of doyens of theatre, Sir Laurence Olivier, Sir John Gielgud and Sir Ralph Richardson play wonderful cameo parts as the Bavarian ministers who conspired to overthrow the powerful alliance forged between Wagner and King Ludwig II. The composer William Walton is harnessed to briefly depict an aged and very infirm Friedrich August II of Saxony.[31]

The idea of this book arose from the lengthy experience of the music of Wagner, commencing with early exposure as a nine-year-old boy to *The Ride of the Valkyries*, played at an agricultural show in Pietermaritzburg, South Africa, while stunt vehicles rocketed up ramps and through fiery hoops. Further contact with better-known passages, such as the bridal music from *Lohengrin* and the Pilgrims' chorus from *Tannhäuser*, led to an exploration of the orchestral suites compiled from the operas. Gradual exposure to the early operas *Tannhäuser* and *Lohengrin* stimulated a keen interest in the mature works.

On a trip around Europe in a camper van with the family in 1987, acquaintance was made with Wagner's only comedy, *Die Meistersinger von Nürnberg*. Recently (April 2005) an article in the *Financial Times* has drawn attention to a production of that opera in 2002 at the Hamburg State Opera where the singers halted in their singing in the last act just as Wagner spoke of honoring German masters over "foreign vanities." This is sometimes regarded as a jibe at Jews. They were instructed by the director to provoke comment on what Wagner was trying to achieve with his words and music. A lively discussion resulted on Wagner's anti-Semitism with members of the audience participating.[32] Andrew Clark, the music critic responsible for the article, then said, "Peter Konwitschny's staging had a simple but provocative message: given all we know about Wagner's ideology and the way it guided Hitler to the Final Solution, can we really allow Hans Sachs's call for racial purity to pass without a comment?"

Certainty of the greatness of Wagner, as a musician, came as a result of an encounter with compact disc recordings of *Parsifal* and the awesome tetralogy *Der Ring des Nibelung* (*The Ring of the Nibelungs*). A trip to the Bayreuth festival during 1992 stimulated interest in the darker reaches of the race problem in Wagner. The trip also enabled the author to explore the vast resources available for research. Further opportunities presented themselves with a trip to the Amsterdam production of the Ring cycle in

---

31. See Conrad, "He's Tricky, That Dicky."
32. See Andrew Clark's article "A Redeemer Tainted by Purity," *Financial Times*, April 2, 2005.

2000. A recent visit to Bayreuth provided a further opportunity to plunder the materials there, including the wonderful books with photographs of the Wagner family.

Throughout the musical experience, a lurking suspicion existed that, to fully understand the poorly articulated horror people expressed at the mention of Wagner, and the prohibition of the music in Israel, a full understanding of the man had to be acquired. The result of my curiosity was a devouring of the existing biographies of Wagner, including the four-volume version by the monumentally erudite Ernest Newman and the fascinating account by Robert Gutman. The latter account must rank as one of the greatest single-volume biographies of any time.

The road signs erected by Gutman led inexorably to a dark journey through the literature on the Third Reich, from its early vague National Socialism to its final sinister and murderous racism. Friedelind Wagner's account of Bayreuth between the years proved to be as invaluable as did Trevor-Roper's account of Hitler's table talk.[33] Also invaluable in the search for the truth has been the immense scholarship of Joachim Köhler whose book *Wagner's Hitler: The Prophet and His Disciple* probes the relationship between the two figures. Other recent publications have also been invaluable, including Brigitte Hamann's biography of Winifred Wagner.

While it is understood that many still feel sensitive about even listening to the music of Wagner, it is important that the roots of racism and anti-Semitism should be explored and exposed. If this book does nothing else, it will have achieved much if it exposes the dangers of racism, anti-Semitism and intolerance. It was the great novelist and poet Thomas Mann, himself a great Wagnerian, who said, "Wagner's art is the most sensational self-portrayal and self-criticism of German character that is conceivable."[34]

Should one continue to listen to the music? Marc Weiner justifies listening on the basis that "our culture is not Wagner's [and] may constitute our redemption…from the Wagnerian agenda and may allow us to experience his breathtakingly beautiful and stirring musical-dramatic accomplishments as works that can be enjoyed *despite* their initial, intended message of racial exclusion."[35] I agree and yet still feel some guilt at enjoying

---

33. See Trevor-Roper, *Hitler's Table Talk*.
34. See Spotts, *Bayreuth*, viii.
35. Weiner, *Richard Wagner and the Anti-Semitic Imagination*, 29.

those intoxicating and narcotic moments. If our defense mechanisms are in place are we not safe from all dangers?

It was Nietzsche who said that the music had the power to "charm the spinal marrow" and "persuade even the bowels."[36] If some stout hearts have fallen victim should we not consider an embargo on his works? That alternative was suggested by Dr Carl Engel, the editor of the American *Musical Quarterly* of April 1941, when he reviewed the third volume of Ernest Newman's monumental biography of Wagner. Engel developed a morbid hatred for Wagner because Hitler was his most enthusiastic supporter and believed that Wagnerism and Nazism were identical. We should realize, the good doctor submits, that to give up Wagner's music would merely be to give up "the music of Klingsor who for one hundred years has numbed our senses with his witchcraft" and "allowed to grow up round us a garden of gorgeous flowers that at last have revealed themselves as poisonous and death-dealing." The solution suggested is that "we should retaliate…we should ban and burn every scrap of Wagner's music and writings, and every book written about the amazing wizard…"[37]

---

36. Gutman, *Richard Wagner*, 9.
37. Newman, *Life of Richard Wagner*, vol. 4, 720.

Chapter one
The Final Assault

During the last days of the Second World War Adolf Hitler ordered that the city of Nürnberg be defended to "the last drop of blood" but after a tremendous battle with immense casualties on both sides the city was taken. A secret tunnel in the street called Blacksmith's Alley led to heavy steel doors with dialing devices as locks. Two Germans were interrogated at length and eventually gave up the codes that allowed the doors to be opened with the use of dynamite. At 2:10 P.M. on April 30, 1945, the most important weapon in the world in the mind of the mad dictator fell into the hands of the American 7th Army under General Patton.[1]

What sort of missile or warhead was this that so much blood had to be spilled to enable it to be recovered? The soldiers found no v1 or v2 rocket nor any missile of any nature, but resting on a red cushion an ancient spear. On January 6, 1946 the spear and the other regalia were handed over to the mayor of Vienna by General Mark Clarke for temporary housing in the vault of the Austrian Postal Savings Bank.[2] Today it awaits the next megalomaniac, supine on its faded red velvet cushion in the treasure room museum of the Hofburg Imperial Palace of Vienna where it was seen by Richard Wagner, Friedrich Nietzsche, Houston Stewart Chamberlain and Adolf Hitler.

---

1. Ravenscroft, *Spear of Destiny*, 346–48.
2. Ibid., 353.

This spear held quite a fascination for Hitler, who was intrigued by occult legends. By some accounts, especially that of Dr Walter Stein, while living in Vienna Hitler undertook a very thorough study of the occult meanings underlying Wolfram Von Eschenbach's thirteenth-century grail romance, *Parsival*. This was the main source of Wagner's last opera of the same name. Stein had frequent contact with Hitler and was satisfied he was deeply involved with the occult and that his more than infamous necromancing mentor had close links to the infamous Blood Lodge of Guido von List.[3] List had written a book, *The Invincible*, in which he spoke of a "strong man from above," a German prince whose appearance had been predicted in the Icelandic Eddas on which Wagner based his *Ring of the Nibelungs*. Hitler believed that he was that person and had read the book avidly according to his Munich bookseller.[4]

Another book by List, *The Secret of the Runes*, was also a favorite. In it the author had an illustration of a swastika which Hitler told his young buddy Kubizek was the "sort of military badge or symbol needed to show that they were Germans." In *Mein Kampf* he states that the swastika means "the mission of the struggle for the victory of the Aryan Man."[5] In earlier books List says the swastika is the sign of the "invincible one" and the "strong one from above."[6]

Hitler even made footnotes to the edition of *Parsival* and it soon became clear how he interpreted the work. Alongside the script where the Knights of the Grail enter the grail sanctuary Hitler wrote, "these men betrayed their pure Aryan Blood to the dirty superstitions of the Jew Jesus – superstitions as loathsome and ludicrous as the Yiddish rites of circumcision."[7]

Hitler later wrote in *Mein Kampf* that during these times he learned all he needed to know to lead the Nazi Party. Of more relevance was the allegation by Stein that Hitler shared a mutual interest in the Spear of Destiny – the relic on display in the Hapsburg's treasury at the Hofmuseum in Vienna.[8] The spear was said to have phenomenal talismanic power and

---

3. Ibid., 71.
4. Hamann, *Hitler's Vienna*, 213.
5. Ibid., 210.
6. Ibid., 209.
7. Ravenscroft, *Spear of Destiny*, 49.
8. Ibid.

The Spear of Longinus as portrayed in The Mark of the Beast by Ravenscroft and Wallace-Murphy, page 120. As the authors point out it has often been called the Maurice Spear, and now consists of two parts, held together by a silver sheath. They also mention that a nail from the Cross of Christ has been inserted into the blade. Kunsthistoriches Museum, Vienna.

legend decreed that possession of it would bring its owner the power to conquer the world, but losing it would bring immediate death.

The origins of the "holy" spear are steeped in mystical history; the weapon is generally reckoned to have been used by the Roman soldier Longinus to pierce Christ's side on the cross. This spear was also known as the Spear of Herod Antipas, the king of the Jews, and therefore was considered a symbol of Jewish authority. The spear had originally been made by Phineas the ancient prophet and represented the might of the Chosen People; it had been used by Joshua when he raised the shout that brought the walls of Jericho tumbling down. It had been hurled by King Saul at the young David when the former was in a fit of jealous rage.[9]

The relic had been in the hands of powerful European rulers down the ages, including Hitler's favorites, Friedrich Barbarossa and his grandson Friedrich II, and ended up with the Austrians. Prior to arriving in Vienna it had been kept in the Free Reich city of Nürnberg and was invariably sent to Aachen or Frankfurt for coronations. During the Napoleonic era

---

9.   Ibid., x.

the spear and other imperial treasures were brought to Vienna to protect them from the French. In 1906 a motion was instigated in the Austrian Parliament that these be returned to Nürnberg on the occasion of the hundredth anniversary of the dissolution of the Roman-German Reich.[10] The motion was brought by Harald von Jostenoode and his article "The Imperial Insignia Back to the Reich," in a booklet called "Ostara" which Hitler is known to have read, and which advocated that the time was right for the spear to go back to Germany.

Hitler told Stein that the first time he saw the spear he felt his destiny being foretold. "The air became stifling so that I could barely breathe. The noisy scene in the treasure house seemed to melt away before my eyes. I stood alone and trembling before the hovering form of the Superman – a spirit sublime and fearful, a countenance intrepid and cruel. In holy awe, I offered my soul as a vessel of his Will."[11] That Superman was the man of which Nietzsche spoke in *Also Sprach Zarathustra*: "I love those who do not seek behind the stars for a reason to go under and be a sacrifice, but who sacrifice themselves for the earth, that the earth may some day be the Superman's."[12]

Friedrich II had reigned in a time when royalty had an immense influence on history. A rare genius who spoke six languages, a lyric poet who inspired his Minnesangers to sing of the mysteries of the Holy Grail, he was a patron of the arts who showed great courage on the battlefield. He was nurtured in Sicily and spoke Arabic with his Saracen soldiers; he wrote a thesis on hawking, dabbled in alchemy and the occult and possessed a harem. He engaged in innumerable battles with the Italian states and Papal armies and always carried with him and relied on the sacred spear. The famous St Francis of Assissi obtained the spear on loan and used it on a mission of mercy.[13] This was its subsidiary role in Wagner's opera *Parsifal* where the Knights of the Grail refreshed themselves spiritually before rescuing damsels in distress, treating the poor and fighting holy wars against the infidels and Jews.

Wagner had told Chamberlain of the significance of the Holy Spear and when the latter went to live in Vienna he often visited the museum

---

10. Hamann, *Hitler's Vienna*, 109.
11. Ravenscroft, *Spear of Destiny*, 38.
12. Ibid., 31.
13. Ibid., 18.

where it was housed and made an intensive study of the history and power of the sacred weapon. Chamberlain told the German Kaiser that he had received a message from beyond the grave from the German Emperor Sigismund that it was a crime against God for the weapon to remain outside German territory.[14] After a number of subterfuges and ruses the Kaiser tried to persuade the elderly Austrian Emperor Franz Joseph to attend an exhibition of German Art in Berlin and bring the sacred artifacts, including the spear, on loan to the Germans. The Kaiser was a blabbermouth and soon his entire retinue and entourage understood that his sudden interest in art was to secure possession of the spear and never return it. It was only the intervention of General von Moltke that saved the day as he wrote to the Austrian Emperor explaining the plot and elucidating his fear that the German Kaiser wanted the weapon to incite a war that all Christian and God-fearing people shrunk from.[15]

What the Kaiser failed to do by stealth Hitler achieved by force of arms. On March 12, 1938, when Germany annexed Austria, he first laid a wreath at his mother's grave in Leonding. He reviewed the troops in Vienna and made a speech saying how he had felt "the call of Providence…to unite my homeland with the German Reich." Once inside the city one of his first missions was to recover the spear that pierced Christ's side – sometimes referred to as the Spear of Destiny – where it was housed in a museum in Vienna.

After midnight that same evening he went straight to the Hofmuseum with Himmler; von Sievers, the head of the Nazi Occult Bureau; Kaltenbrunner ss Führer Austria; and others to reclaim the Spear.[16] Hitler spent an hour or more alone with the sacred talisman while his Gauleiters – regional leaders, a special rank Hitler had invented to bestow on his high-ranking officers – hovered anxiously outside. History does not tell us what happened in that time but no doubt it was a triumphant reverie for the tyrant.

Soon thereafter he sent it to Nürnberg, to be secreted away where no one would ever find it. With that weapon in his hands what need he fear from the world? The occasion and circumstances of its subsequent discovery seven years later were as fascinating as its long and mysterious

---

14. Ibid., 121.
15. Ibid., 122–23.
16. Ibid., 316.

journey from ancient times to its sepulchral tomb in the Blacksmith's Alley in Nürnberg, the cultural capital of Nazism.

No disciple of Richard Wagner would choose a site that was not closely associated with the great composer to place the spear on display. The venue of the singers' contest in his opera *Die Meistersinger von Nürnberg* – the ancient Hall of St Katherine's Church – now became the repository of the talisman of German greatness. On October 13, six months after the annexation of Austria, an armored train guarded by the SS made the journey to carry it to its new home. A national holiday was proclaimed. Only the military importance of the city ensured that it became a target for Allied bombing and secured the move of the spear to the tunnel under the Blacksmith's Alley behind the comforting strength of two huge metal doors.[17] That was where the US Army demolition corps found it.

The spear Hitler stole is now stored once more in the Hofburg Museum in Vienna. What was it about this spear that made it so important for Adolf Hitler and his ambitions for world conquest? Why did he vow to have it in his hands if he ever came to power? What significance did it have in his attempt to destroy European Jewry? In order to properly investigate this fascinating question we have to go back to 1813 and the birth of the great German composer Richard Wagner. Only by investigating his full and adventurous life and his operas and polemical writings can we discover why the German dictator was so anxious to possess and retain the Spear of Longinus. It will also help us to understand why he instigated a process that resulted in the Holocaust – his attempt to exterminate the whole of European Jewry.

---

17. Ibid., 331.

Chapter two
The Dung from Which It Grew

Many regard Richard Wagner as the greatest composer of Western music of all time. W.H. Auden called him "the greatest genius that ever lived," though on other occasions he decried the efforts of the hagiographers and called Wagner "the greatest of the monsters" because of his manifold weaknesses including megalomaniac conceit, his racial bigotry, his sexual treachery and financial dishonesty.[1] Recognition of him by T.S. Eliot can be found in his epic poem *The Waste Land*.[2] In that masterpiece appear from time to time deep undercurrents and allusions to the operas and hints that the citizens of England have been ravaged by their passion for Wagner.[3] Many great writers prided themselves in being his most ardent admirers, including D'Annunzio – who wrote a Wagnerian novel, D.H. Lawrence, Zola, Shaw, Renoir, Joyce, Thomas Mann, Gauguin, Degas and of course Nietzsche – until his discovery of the real man and his subsequent tragic disillusionment.[4] Prominent musicologist Brian Magee reckons he made a "greater contribution than any other single artist

---

1. See Conrad, "He's Tricky, That Dicky."
2. Waite, *The Psychopathic God*, 103.
3. See Conrad, "He's Tricky, That Dicky."
4. Ibid.

on the culture of our time."[5] Ernest Newman, who wrote the wonderful four-volume biography, said, "more has been written about this man…than about anyone else in the history of art." He reckons that "Wagner was one of the three or four genuinely original spirits in the entire history of music."[6]

Frederic Spotts, author of the leading book on the Bayreuth festival, called him "the most controversial artistic figure of all time."[7] His greatest work, *The Ring of the Nibelungs*, took some twenty-five years to create and runs for some fifteen hours or more on four separate evenings. It ranks with Michelangelo's Sistine chapel ceiling as a monument to Western art at its best. Gerhart Hauptmann called it "the mightiest work of art of the last millennia."[8] Some reckon he is the third most written-about public figure after Jesus Christ and Napoleon, with forty-five thousand titles.[9] More recent assessment puts Adolf Hitler with one hundred twenty thousand publications in poll position.[10] Karl Marx would be green with envy. Popular opinion still elevates Richard Wagner to the pantheon of composers though Max Nordau called him the "last mushroom on the dunghill of romanticism."[11] Nordau was a pioneer Zionist and published his magnum opus *Degeneration* on the question of cultural decline having a kinship to biological degeneration. The degenerates had to be mercilessly crushed, in his view, as they were "anti-social" vermin.[12]

Because of the accusation of anti-Semitism and the use of his music by the Third Reich, Wagner has been outlawed in concerts in Israel. What is it about the music of Richard Wagner, who died six years before the birth of Adolf Hitler, that causes such strong feelings amongst modern Jews and Israelis? That Hitler loved the music of Wagner is without doubt but is that enough to blame Wagner for the Holocaust? Was Wagner a racist and anti-Semite?

Is it possible that racism in the form of anti-Semitism could have insinuated its way into the mind of Hitler via the music? There seems to be

---

5. Ibid.
6. Richard Wagner Museum brochure, "About Richard Wagner."
7. Spotts, *Bayreuth*, vii.
8. Richard Wagner Museum brochure, "About Richard Wagner."
9. Poliakov, *History of Anti-Semitism from Voltaire to Wagner*, 445.
10. Machtan, *Hidden Hitler*, 2.
11. Viereck, *Metapolitics*, 93.
12. See Spotts, *Hitler and the Power of Aesthetics*, 23.

much to be said for such a view. In one of his endless monologues around the dinner table, which he decreed should be recorded, so that nothing of his wisdom would be lost to posterity, Hitler said, "when I listen to Wagner I hear the rhythms of a bygone world."[13] That world was one created by Wagner out of Nordic myths depicting gods, giants, incest, murder and bloody conquest. It was a universe portraying the centrality of the lust for power and the quest for a hero who knew no fear and would lead his nation to greatness.

The names of his military headquarters were invariably given Wagnerian epithets, the lupine variety predominating as a result of Wotan's "Wolf" alter ego in *The Valkyries* and his own nickname, reserved for exclusive use by the Wagner descendants. On this occasion, after the defeat of the German armies before the gates of Moscow in 1942, at the aptly named Wolf's Lair, he went on to say "that one day science will discover in the waves, set in motion by the music of *Das Rheingold*, a stream of consciousness evidencing secret mutual relations, connected with the order of the world and the pulse of the universe."[14] What the Führer was hinting at was that the music subconsciously conveyed the ideology, without the mediation of the reasoning faculties. That this music would show the world the way to go forward – via a subliminal racist text – was the wisdom of the fanatical man, with the cold light blue eyes, the shaking left hand and nervous tick in his eye, locked up in his snowbound hideout, before a circle of yawning generals.

Other more reputable sources were later to echo the danger in the subconscious message. "Music is demonic territory" said the great German writer Thomas Mann, who was exiled from Germany after writing an article about Wagner.[15] He went further to say, "I find an element of Nazism not only in Wagner's questionable literature; I find it also in his 'music'."[16] On previous occasions he had been more positive. "[Wagner's was] a wonderful, astonishing, eternally fascinating life," he said on one occasion, and on another, "what a vital magic must have emanated from this man."[17] If Wagner was a rabid anti-Semite is it possible that his hatred for the Jews permeated

---

13. Köhler, *Wagner's Hitler*, 56.
14. Windell, Hitler, "National Socialism and Richard Wagner," 237.
15. Köhler, *Wagner's Hitler*, 2.
16. Viereck, *Metapolitics*, 92.
17. Richard Wagner Museum brochure, "About Richard Wagner."

his music and subconsciously entered the distorted and depraved mind of the psychopathic mass murderer Adolf Hitler? In an article in the *Financial Times* on April 3, 2005 the music critic Andrew Clark hinted at this when he said: "People who love Wagner do so in a different way from those who love Mozart. It's almost a sickness: something in his makeup that compels idolatry. Like his texts, his music is full of dark desires and impulses, often of a sexual nature, touching parts of our subconscious. Played out on stage, his dramas provide release, a way of simultaneously expressing and sublimating those desires."

If the answer to the above question is in the affirmative, a number of important considerations follow. The first posits the inherent danger in the music, especially to the least well balanced of our citizenry. The second question examines the improbability of a sequence of musical notes played on ordinary musical instruments having such a devastating effect on social interaction. Is it not possible to listen to and watch operas depicting myths and legends without assuming that they incite us to kill persons of a religion that is not ours?

How much responsibility must an artist or writer bear for the consequences of painting a picture, telling a story or creating an opera? The great German novelist Goethe wrote a romance entitled *The Sorrows of Young Werther* about a hero who killed himself when his great love Charlotte rejected him. The book was a best seller and the bookstores in Germany could not keep up with the demand for the story. Jules Massenet translated the story into one of the greatest operas every produced. Goethe's heroine Charlotte had promised her mother on her deathbed that she would marry her current beau, one Albert. Werther and Charlotte met and fell in love but she stuck to her promise with the disastrous consequences to which I have alluded. The publication of the work resulted in every lovesick loon aping the mode of dress of Werther – blue trousers and a yellow swallow-tailed coat – and his mode of death. The public blamed the author and pointed fingers at Goethe who was incensed at receiving blame for merely recounting a tale.

In *Towards a Genealogy of Morals* the German philosopher and writer Friedrich Nietzsche[18] posed the question whether the artist was not "after all

---

18. Friedrich Nietzsche was born at Rocken in Saxony in 1844. From 1889 he suffered a mental and physical breakdown and died insane at Weimar after a syphilitic infec-

only the presupposition of his work, the womb, the soil, at times the dung and manure on which and out of which it grows and accordingly, in most cases, something one must forget if the work itself is to be enjoyed…".[19]

Can one not watch Wagner's magical opera *Lohengrin* without fretting that the composer might have harbored anti-Semitic thoughts when he composed it? How many millions of wedding guests have not thrilled to "Here Comes the Bride" from that magical opera, without realizing its sinister origins? Do we in fact need to know anything about the composer at all? When we look at the Mona Lisa do we need to know about Leonardo da Vinci?

The great philosopher provided a partial answer to his fascinating question. In *The Gay Science* Nietzsche stated that the artist's philosophy was of little importance if it remained only a "supplementary" element, leaving the work uninjured.[20] The enquiry should therefore be a subjective one and every reader would have to determine if the message of the work is one that foments rebellion or incites evil. In the context of this book the question can be narrowed down. If Wagner was anti-Semitic was that "supplementary," or did it permeate his work? Is it fair to burden him with the guilt of the machinations of his most ardent fan fifty or more years later?

Marc Weiner sums up his views of the relationship between Wagner's musical works and his polemical writings:

> Indeed, his mature, post-revolutionary music dramas, written and composed in conjunction with diverse social-aesthetic anti-Semitic tracts, constitute dramatic representations of the ideas found in his writings. Many Wagner scholars have been at great pains to dissociate his theories from the dramatic works for which he is largely remembered today, and especially to disavow any connection between his racism and his most celebrated Total Works of Art, but comparison

---

tion on August 25, 1900. His main writings include *The Birth of Tragedy from the Spirit of Music* (1872), *Untimely Meditations* (1873–76), *Human, All-too-Human* (1878), *Thus Spoke Zarathustra* (1883–84), *The Dawn* (1881), *The Gay Science* (1882), *Beyond Good and Evil* (1886), *The Genealogy of Morals* (1887), *The Will to Power* (1906), *The Wagner Case* (1888) and *The Anti-Christ* (1888).

19. Cited in Gutman, *Richard Wagner*, 12.
20. Ibid., 13.

of these works with motifs and arguments in Wagner's prose writings demonstrates that the former are dramatic enactments of Wagner's theories concerning the preservation of the German community threatened by the Jew in the modern world.[21]

The views expressed in this book are but one possible cause for the madness that was the Holocaust. It does not pretend to be all-encompassing. It explores the relationship of Adolf Hitler with Richard Wagner and considers the extent to which the sexual perversions and depraved worldview of the former led to a distortion of views expressed by the latter. The causes of all great tragedies are many and various. No single view can ever explain everything. Any proffered analysis suffers from the dangers of oversimplification and soon enough critics mutilate the logic and undermine the reasons. Hopefully something survives out of the frenzied hacking and the search for objectivity continues – the errors of limited perspective are lessened.

In examining the justifiability of this view it is necessary to examine the lives of Richard Wagner and Adolf Hitler to determine whether the Israelis are right in proscribing his work in their country. Such an investigation will concentrate on those aspects in the lives of the two which impact most profoundly on the central enquiry. Those in search of other biographical detail should consult the plethora of excellent material available. Some of the texts are set out in the bibliography. Attention is also directed – mostly en passant – at the early biographers who recorded the details of Wagner's life. Certain of them determined to hide any details of his life that did not measure up to the stature of his works. Of interest in this regard are the facts that relate to his political and racial views and the background to them. The importance of that question relates to the reading material available to the man who was the executioner of the composer's plans.

---

21. Weiner, *Richard Wagner and the Anti-Semitic Imagination*, 65.

Chapter three
Son of a Vulture

Richard Wagner was born on May 22, 1813 in Leipzig and died on February 13, 1883 at Venice after nearly seventy years of a very full life. His favorite aphorism was that he did not want to die until he had *lived*. By that he meant that he wanted to enjoy life in its fullness. He was a dramatic composer and theorist whose operas and music had a revolutionary influence on the course of Western music. There are many who count his major works *The Flying Dutchman* (1843), *Tannhäuser* (1845), *Lohengrin* (1850), *Tristan und Isolde* (1865), *Die Meistersinger von Nürnberg* (1867), *Parsifal* (1882), and his great tetralogy *The Ring of the Nibelungs* (1869–76) as the finest art on the planet.

In a town in Bavaria that was to become synonymous with his name – Bayreuth – the poet and philosopher Jean Paul Richter foretold of his coming.[1] It was uncanny – almost biblical. "And behold it came to pass in the little town of Leipzig. For unto us a child is born and his name shall be revered amongst nations. Richard Wagner."

Prior to the advent of Wagner, with some limited exceptions, musicians had composed operas to the words of poets and playwrights. Frequently plays were taken and adapted for the purposes of an opera and formed the basis of the *libretto* – Italian for a little book. The great works of literature

---
1. For an account of the prophecy of Jean Paul see Richard Wagner Museum brochure, "About Richard Wagner," para. 1.

have provided a rich vein for operas and numerous Shakespearian works have been set to music including *Othello, The Merry Wives of Windsor, Hamlet, Macbeth* and *Romeo and Juliet*.

Jean Paul went on to say that Apollo had given the gift of poetry with his right hand and that of music with his left, to two widely separated people. The gift of poetry was that of the great writers and playwrights whose works fascinated the reading public over the years. The ability to compose music was reserved for another team of artists. This last-mentioned group composed operas by utilizing the poetry and tales of the dramatists. Doubtless he was thinking of the early German composers including Carl Maria von Weber, Wolfgang Mozart and the Italian masters of the eighteenth century.

Jean Paul was looking for a man who would compose both the text and the music for a genuine opera.[2] Wagner responded to the call and Hector Berlioz fashioned Virgil to the same purposes – notably in his greatest work *Les Troyens* – as Wagner adapted the old myths and legends of the northern climes. The partnership in both instances must have been invigorating as it bequeathed on a hushed world some of the greatest musical masterpieces ever composed. The internationally acclaimed and controversial Israeli conductor Daniel Barenboim summed it up as follows: "Although Wagner wrote the libretto first and then the music, he was looking for an art form that unified them. And he made a unity of sound and words going absolutely and indivisibly hand in hand. And the expression doesn't come only from the fact that there are very important sentiments expressed, whether it is love, death, or whatever it is, but it occurs almost onomatopoeically, when somehow the sound of the syllable, joined with a certain sound that comes in the music is already part of the expression."[3]

The Leipzig into which Wagner was born was a thriving town of 33,000 inhabitants in the Protestant kingdom of Saxony and counted amongst its industries activities as widespread as the manufacture of locomotives, musical instruments, bookselling and publishing.[4] At the time of his birth there was a strong music tradition in the town and it continues to this

---

2. Harding, *Magic Fire*, 16.
3. Guzelimian, *Parallels and Paradoxes: Daniel Barenboim and Edward W. Said*, 50.
4. Taylor, *Richard Wagner*, 16.

Johanna Wagner – the mother of the composer, Gregor-Dellin, page 17. Nationalarchiv der Richard Wagner-Stiftung/Richard Wagner Gedenkstätte, Bayreuth.

day. *Blüthner* pianos are still lovingly crafted in workshops that go back hundreds of years.

Of particular interest to us in this account of the growth of anti-Semitism is the fact that Martin Luther fought with Eck in 1519 over the supremacy of the Roman Pontiff in that very city. His views on Jews were so extreme that they were to have a profound influence on Wagner and Hitler. Goethe spent time there as a student and his writings were to set standards of writing seldom subsequently equaled in the whole region.

Wagner's origins are locked up in much mystery and conjecture. His mother Johanna was thought to be the illegitimate daughter of Prince Constantin, brother of the Grand Duke of Weimar. Prince Constantin, who had a decided talent for music, fathered her by Dorothea, the baker's wife, in his sixteenth year. In fact it transpires that she was his mistress.[5]

---

5.   Köhler, *Wagner's Hitler*, 32.

There are two candidates for the position of his father: Ludwig Geyer, an actor, playwright and tenor, and Friedrich Wagner, a registrar in the police department.[6] It was a good year for composers, as two day's journey to the south in the small town of Le Roncole near Parma in Italy a boy child was born, who was considered by many to rival his genius – Giuseppi Verdi.[7]

Wagner was thought to be illegitimate and some even suggested he was partly Jewish. Friedrich had married Johanna and she bore him nine children in the first fifteen years of marriage.[8] So the probabilities favor him as Richard's father. Some indomitable researcher, however, has been at great pains to seek out the truth of the real origins of the composer. A perusal of certain hotel registers in Leipzig, in September 1812, some nine months before Richard Wagner was born, revealed a number of very interesting facts.[9] The hotel was a simple and modest one and the room contained little more than a washstand with mirror, a wooden cupboard and large double bed. The persons who temporarily occupied the room were deeply in love. They had entered the names of Ludwig and Johanna Geyer in the hotel register.

Ludwig had come to know the Wagner family while still a student at the university in Leipzig and he had stayed thereafter with the family when he was in that city.[10] He was part of the *Seconda* theatrical group and was engaged with them in a tour of an opera by Mehul entitled *Joseph*. Ludwig was the lead tenor and had dabbled in writing plays himself, including a play on *The Child Murders in Bethlehem*, which had been well received. Johanna's infidelity with the man of the stage was largely the result of a number of unsatisfactory features in her relationship with her husband Friedrich. Apart from cruelty and neglect he was engaged in an affair with a woman by the name of Hartwig. Johanna had learned of his infidelity but was even more incensed with his attitude. His deception was so transparent that she developed contempt for him. He would tell her stories that he

---

6. Taylor, *Richard Wagner*, 16.
7. Harding, *Magic Fire*, 16.
8. Taylor, *Richard Wagner*, 18.
9. The possibility of Wagner being the son of Geyer is further mentioned in Viereck, *Metapolitics*, where he refers to an article by Henri Malherbe whose book *Richard Wagner: Révolutionnaire* has a hotel register for the time before Wagner was born.
10. Taylor, *Richard Wagner*, 21.

Reputed father of Richard Wagner – Ludwig Geyer. Gregor-Dellin page 16. Nationalarchiv der Richard Wagner-Stiftung/Richard Wagner Gedenkstätte, Bayreuth.

was staying late at the office working on his police papers and held up his fingers to give proof of his labors. Unfortunately he had not even bothered to substantiate the duplicity by putting ink on them.[11]

There are further reasons for believing that Ludwig Geyer was the father of Richard Wagner. Johanna took the baby to see Ludwig in Teplitz two months after he was born. Geyer was staying in a small room in that town as his theatre company was on tour there and she braved the long distance to take the child to him. Her husband Friedrich was not pleased with the birth and refused to have him baptized. Richard's elder brother Albert had been baptized five days after birth and the church elders were asking questions.

The reason for the delay was of great concern to Friedrich Wagner as he believed that his son Richard was Jewish and could not, therefore, be baptized. Subsequent research, mostly at the instance of Adolf Hitler, who feared for the origins of his idol, has revealed no Jewish relatives in Geyer's past. Gottfried Wagner, great grandson of the composer has, however, unearthed Jewish Wagners from Leipzig and Frankfurt am Main,

---

11. Ibid., 19.

but that alone does not assist in determining his origin.[12] Richard Wagner also nursed a secret fear that he was Jewish and subsequent writers have attributed his anti-Semitism to the teasing he had to endure at the hands of his peers.

The probabilities favor that the visit by Johanna Wagner to Ludwig Geyer had only one purpose, namely, to show a father his new son. What other reason would have induced a woman to bring her newborn son to Teplitz, which was 150 miles from Leipzig where she was living? Again a fastidious researcher – a Swiss journalist – has found the records of the inn – *The Three Pheasants Hotel* – in which they both stayed on July 21, 1813 less than three months before the Battle of Leipzig.[13]

The times were hard and there was a war on. The roads were dangerous at that time with soldiers wandering around raping and killing – Napoleon's armies were everywhere. Johanna was a desperate woman who found little respect in her own home. Friedrich refused to end his relationship with the Hartwig woman, and she left to spend three weeks with her lover. Perhaps the most convincing proof lies in the fact that the baby was named Richard Geyer. Ludwig often visited the household while Friedrich was alive and Wagner in his autobiography suggests rather tongue in cheek that he "took over the father's role."[14]

Friedrich died some six months after Richard's birth and Geyer married Johanna some nine months after Friedrich's death, the earliest time allowed in Saxon law. The reason for the stipulation of nine months was simple enough. In case of any doubt posterity would know who the father of any children was. That Johanna and Ludwig Geyer did not wait for the benediction of marriage to engage in relations is plain to behold. A further child, after Richard, was born to Johanna and Geyer six months after the marriage.

In later life Richard Wagner commented on the resemblance of his son Siegfried to the portrait of Geyer that hung in Wahnfried, Wagner's home in Bayreuth.[15] When Wagner came to write his autobiography he insisted that the emblem on the cover be that of a vulture as the word Geyer has that meaning in German. Over the main entrance of Wahnfried were

---

12. Wagner, Gottfried, *Twilight of the Wagners*, 227.
13. Gal, *Richard Wagner*, 15–16.
14. Taylor, *Richard Wagner*, 22.
15. Gal, *Richard Wagner*, 15 and Taylor, *Richard Wagner*, 22.

Wagner's family crest for the first edition of Mein Leben, 1870, showing the Geier (vulture), a hint from Wagner himself that his father was Ludwig Geyer. Nationalarchiv der Richard Wagner-Stiftung/Richard Wagner Gedenkstätte, Bayreuth from Weiner, page 4.

two painted coats of arms including the distinctive figure of a vulture – a touching but somewhat belated acknowledgment of Geyer's paternity.[16]

Friedrich Nietzsche maintained that the first edition of Wagner's autobiography commenced with the declaration that Wagner was the son of Ludwig Geyer and that the composer's insistence that a vulture be boldly embossed on the cover was further proof of that fact. Nietzsche was convinced that Wagner was of Jewish origin and later seriously questioned whether his anti-Semitism was not a betrayal of his roots. In German an *Adler* is an eagle and the surname is very common among the Jewish community. Hinting at Wagner's Semitic origins Nietzsche said that a Geyer is almost an Adler.[17]

The artistic and theatrical background of Wagner's early years is of considerable importance in his development. His elder brother became an opera tenor and his two elder sisters Rosalie and Luise became opera singers or actresses; he was consequently steeped in the world of the

---

16. Richard Wagner Museum brochure, "About Richard Wagner."
17. Taylor, *Richard Wagner*, 23.

theatre from a young age. In his autobiography he was to describe his excitement and he maintained that "everything connected with a theatrical performance had for me a mysterious, intoxicating attraction."[18] That same excitement was to permeate his life drawing him close to a number of passionate women.

When Richard was one year old Ludwig Geyer took the family to Dresden as his theatre company was based there.[19] Nicknamed Cossack, the young Wagner was impulsive, self-willed and failed to make a lasting impression as a scholar at the Kreuzschule, Dresden, which he attended from 1822 to 1827. At the age of eight he lacked the precocious talents of Mozart and others but there was some promise; his parents noted with considerable interest that he picked out nursery rhymes and folksongs on the piano.[20] As Geyer lay dying he overheard Richard playing on the piano and his last recorded comments were a prediction that "his place, his whole life, will be music."[21]

There were some signs of a man of the future. His teacher Silling inspired him with enthusiasm for Greek history and mythology; as a thirteen-year-old he translated the first three books of the *Odyssey* into German.[22] He later attended the Nikolaischule in Leipzig with a level of indifference that worried parents and teachers alike. Sixty years later when King Ludwig of Bavaria urged him to write about his life he used the opportunity to stigmatize the "deadly, false education" that the school provided.

Both Leipzig and Dresden had rich musical traditions. Johann Sebastian Bach was appointed the cantor of the nearby Thomasschule in Leipzig in 1723 and spent the rest of his life in the town.[23] Few could ever match the fecundity of his musical invention. Asked by a young admirer, "Papa Bach, how do you think of all these new tunes?" Bach is reputed to have answered: "My dear fellow, I have no need to think of them. I have the greatest difficulty not to step on them when I get out of bed in the morning and start moving about my room."[24]

---

18. Newman, *Life of Richard Wagner*, vol. 1, 39.
19. Taylor, *Richard Wagner*, 25.
20. Ibid., 27.
21. Harding, *Magic Fire*, 18.
22. Richard Wagner Museum brochure, "About Richard Wagner."
23. Taylor, *Richard Wagner*, 16.
24. Frank, *Quotationary*, 159.

In later life when engaged in the "agonizing birth" of his mature works Wagner was to call Bach "the most wondrous enigma of all time." He linked his own method of composition with that of Bach and referred to the process as "continuous melody." His opera *Meistersinger* was the logical conclusion of his long idolatry of the Master of Leipzig and he termed the mode of his composition "applied Bach." In 1864 in his largely pompous and polemical essay "What Is German?" he was to refer to Bach as a composer whose greatness lay in the pursuit of the beautiful and noble innate in national culture, not as a means to acquire fame and fortune.[25] There is reason to believe that Bach taught organ lessons to Geyer's grandfather.[26]

Wagner grew up in Am Brühl, the Leipzig Jewish Quarter and the center of the thriving fur trade.[27] Given his later rampant anti-Semitism it is not without interest to note that his first girlfriend was a Jewish girl, Leah David, and his best school chum at that time was Lippert Levy, whose parents attended the synagogue in the city. The Jewish community was small and his perceived origins and the company he kept earned him taunts from the other schoolchildren, which were to rankle for the remainder of his life. He was referred to in jeering fashion as a "Jew-boy."

Of interest to aspirant composers and musicians were the views of his instructors at school. Whereas legend would have it that, at the tender age of seven, Mozart was refused further tuition by his teacher ("Wolfgang, I cannot teach you any more"), matters were different with Richard Wagner. An early music teacher, Robert Sipp, described Wagner as one who "caught on quickly but was lazy and unwilling to practice. He was my very worst pupil." Sipp loved to joke about his "once small and later great pupil." Despite this the composer did not forget him when he reached the pinnacle of his fame. In 1876 Wagner invited him to attend the first Bayreuth festival, which was established to play his operas exclusively. (That in fact was obeyed to the letter until the Allies entered Bayreuth in 1945 and the Festspielhaus was subject to the sacrilege and desecration of hosting Italian operas, operettas, musicals and the solid brass of Glenn Miller and other big band favorites.)

An acting career was never in the cards though in later life singers

---

25. Taylor, *Richard Wagner*, 293.
26. Newman, *Life of Richard Wagner*, vol. 1, 15.
27. Taylor, *Richard Wagner*, 18.

commented on his ability to portray any scene or emotion. At the age of seven he played the part of William Tell's younger son Wilhelm in Schiller's great drama. Geyer played Gessler. Klara, Wagner's elder sister, played Walther, the older son of Tell. At the point in the story when Tell bids farewell to his wife, taking Walther with him, Wilhelm was supposed to cling to his mother's skirts and say "Mother, I stay with you!" But when the less than intrepid Richard saw Klara leaving with Tell he cried, "Klara, if you are going I'm going too." He then ran after her to the great amusement of the audience. Geyer was not in the least put out and commented on Richard's gift for improvisation.[28] Little did he realize how the little rapscallion would turn the world of theatre upside down and sow ideological seeds that would later breed monsters.

The death of Ludwig Geyer from tuberculosis when Richard was eight years old was a great blow to the family and in his dying moments he heard the youngster picking out the Huntsmen's Chorus from Weber's opera *Der Freischütz*. The composer of that masterpiece lived in Leipzig at the time and visited the house from time to time.[29] For weeks little Richard was inconsolable but his was a hardy soul. The early onset of vicissitudes of every sort was to develop in him a robust optimism that was to stand him in good stead in the years to come.

A performance later that year of the very opera I have just mentioned was to have a wonderful response. His clear blue eyes shone with wonder as he lived through the troubled times of the hero. Max the huntsman enters into a compact with the devil to forge a magic bullet that will enable him to win the shooting contest and the hand of the beautiful heroine. Not for him did the fascination of that great work lie in the happy choruses or stirring arias. He loved the evil and the horror of the forging of the magic bullets. In the days that followed the performance he spent every waking moment recreating the Wolf's Glen – the venue of Max's meeting with the devil – in his toy marionette set. That opera with its stream of melodies and sinister themes was to influence his choice of subject in the future. Indeed, perhaps this was the origin of the fascination with wolves that Hitler would later pick up on.

The two principal protagonists in this account shared another char-

---

28. Newman, *Life of Richard Wagner*, vol. 1, 41–42.
29. Richard Wagner Museum brochure, "About Richard Wagner."

acteristic, Wagner in his youth and Hitler in his mature years: a paranoid fear of the dark and sleep. Hitler's fear arose from specters of those he had killed, visiting him – principally his erstwhile comrade-at-arms and lover Ernst Röhm – while Wagner's stemmed from his vivid imagination. In his autobiography Wagner tells us, "even in my latest boyhood years not a night passed without my waking out of some ghostly dream and uttering the most frightful shrieks, that could be put an end to only by the sound of some human voice…"[30]

Wagner's fourteenth year saw the ripening of a talent that was to stand him in good stead when he transformed the old myths and legends into prose and poetry – he won first prize for a poem on a dead school friend.[31] Whatever speculation might have existed as to his religious origins his mother determined during that year that he was to enter the Christian faith; he was confirmed in church as Wilhelm Richard Geyer. His most influential biographer Ernest Newman was later to describe him as a man who "thought in continents." Never to blanche at the immense, he regarded the impossible as an interesting challenge.

Some of that explosive optimism was to manifest itself in his teens. Wagner's love of music and literature was evident from an early age and he frequented concerts, taught himself the piano and composition, and read the plays of Shakespeare, Goethe and Schiller. These sources were the inspiration for his first literary effort, which shocked his Uncle Adolf Wagner, a scholar and translator with an extensive library that the youngster pillaged.[32] He immersed himself in the creation of a sprawling five-act play, *Leubald und Adelaide*, in which no less than forty-two characters live and then die in dramatic fashion. Their disappearance presented problems for the narrative so he devised the simple expedient – not entirely unknown in theatre (see, for example, *Giselle*) – of resurrecting them later as ghosts.[33] The play has interest only for the love quartet that looks forward to the drama of *Tristan und Isolde*, but shows a limitless appetite for the large scale, a feature of his mature works.

He enrolled at Leipzig University for the wrong reasons – he thought the life was all beer and skittles, a view held by many others – but had

---

30. Newman, *Life of Richard Wagner*, vol. 1, 38.
31. Richard Wagner Museum brochure, "About Richard Wagner," item 2l.
32. Taylor, *Richard Wagner*, 29.
33. Ibid., 33.

inferior privileges because of his lack of success at his preparatory schooling. He joined a dueling fraternity and narrowly got away with his life after a number of serious encounters with notorious opponents. His gambling exploits saw him gamble away his mother's pension one evening and win it back the next. These events led him to believe that he was to lead a charmed life and he was right. He was dogged by good luck.[34]

There was, however, to be one great change in the youth whose early teachers had castigated for laziness and lack of application in his music studies. The wild social life that he led contrasted starkly with his devotion to the enormously important rules of composition. He was impatient with academic techniques, and spent only six months acquiring the groundwork of musical theory with Theodor Weinlig, cantor of the Thomasschule. That is how conventional biographies would have it but if the truth be told – an echo of the Mozart story but at more than twice the age – the cantor told Wagner that he could teach him nothing more and could only assist him with the "advice of a friend." He refused payment and said: "it would be improper of me to accept payment for the pleasure of having taught you. Your industry and my hopes are recompense enough."[35]

Shortly before he turned sixteen Wagner heard the legendary Wilhelmina Schröder-Devrient singing the lead role in Beethoven's *Fidelio* and as he blinked back the tears of emotion he determined that he would bend his will to music.[36] He shyly walked up to the great soprano and handed over a letter written in his neat calligraphy in which he explained "that from now on my life had received its meaning." He went on to explain that "if she should one day hear my name mentioned with praise in the world of art, she should remember that on this evening she made me that, which I herewith swear to attempt to become."[37] Little did he realize that his idol was to sing the lead soprano role of Adriano in his first real operatic success (*Rienzi*) thirteen years later. A performance of that opera was to so inspire Hitler that he was to date his political program from the occasion.

His adoration of Wilhelmina was not to last indefinitely. Sixteen years later disillusionment set in when Wagner saw her in *Tannhäuser* in 1845; the rather portly Wilhelmina represented the ravishing, incandescent beauty

---

34. Richard Wagner Museum brochure, "About Richard Wagner," item 2l.
35. Ibid., item 3l.
36. Ibid., item 35.
37. Ibid., item 3u.

of Venus, a tradition followed on numerous occasions thereafter in the world of opera. A sylphlike figure is not an absolute requisite for an opera singer – indeed there is much in that form of art that requires the audience to suspend belief in reality. Was it this that urged Wagner to counsel a friend to close his eyes at the premiere of the Ring cycle in Bayreuth in 1876 and surrender to the music?

The real merit of his education was that he had an opportunity to make a close personal study of the scores of the masters, notably the quartets and symphonies of Beethoven. Although concerts were few and far between he remembered one with particular vividness – in fact he saw it as his musical awakening. "I heard one evening a symphony of Beethoven's. I thereupon fell ill of a fever, and when I recovered I was – a musician." The first steps to achieving his own style were those of every eclectic. He wrote a piano transcription of Beethoven's Ninth Symphony, which was no mean achievement for a student a few months shy of his eighteenth birthday. That masterpiece was to represent for him the highest point in symphonic writing.

Once he reckoned he had sufficiently understood the methods of his compositional mentors he commenced composing; his own Symphony in C Major was performed at the Leipzig Gewandhaus concerts in 1833, when he was twenty years of age. Promise there certainly was but the symphony shows its roots deeply anchored in Beethoven and Mozart's Jupiter Symphony. Absolute music momentarily held his attention but what excited him the most was the theatre and he longed to compose an opera.

On leaving the university that year, he was engaged for the summer in the position of operatic coach at Würzburg, where he became acquainted with the operas of a large number of composers, including Giacomo Meyerbeer, who is to play an important part in our tale. He coached the chorus in the opera *Robert le Diable* which had been a huge success in Paris two years previously. Wagner found it flat and lacking in melodic inspiration.[38]

He then set to work and composed his first opera, *The Fairies*. Writing the opera was difficult but achieving a production proved impossible at that time. Instead he became conductor to a provincial theatrical troupe from Magdeburg, having fallen in love with one of the actresses of the troupe, Minna Planer, whom he married three years later in 1836. In his

---

38. Taylor, *Richard Wagner*, 52.

Minna Planer, the first wife of Richard Wagner. Barth et al., 24. Burrell Collection, Philadelphia.

autobiography he described her as being "very graceful and [having] a fresh appearance, the young actress distinguished herself through great deliberation and serious assurance in movement and behaviour, which lent the friendliness of her facial expression a pleasantly attractive dignity."[39] The world at large believed that prior to her marriage Minna lived with her eight-year-old "sister" Natalie but if the truth be told she was Minna's daughter as her mother had been raped at the age of fifteen by Captain Ernst von Einsiedel of the Royal Saxon Guards.

Despite his obsession with music and opera, even at that young age Wagner's wide-ranging mind still sought further stimulation. More is the pity of it as his contribution to political and racial theory was to have disastrous consequences for Europe. Wagner embarked on the first of his essays in a lifelong passion for ideology and rhetoric. In 1834 he wrote as an internationalist and prayed "that the master will come who writes in neither Italian, French, nor German fashion…[art's mission] is to rise above

---

39. Richard Wagner Museum brochure, "About Richard Wagner," item 4l.

national vanity to a feeling of universality."[40] In the years to come his views were to change so dramatically that it would not be unfair to describe his journey as having come full circle.

---

40. Viereck, *Metapolitics*, 94.

Chapter four
Seeds of Anti-Semitism

While employed as conductor and stage director for the Magdeburg opera company Wagner undertook an extensive journey looking for artists for the company in 1835. As he traveled he came to Bayreuth, a town in which he was to settle thirty-five years later and establish the famous music festival. "The journey through Eger, through the Fichtelgebirge, with the arrival in Bayreuth, which was charmingly lighted by the evening sun, has been a pleasant recollection even in most recent times" was how he described it in his autobiography.[1]

Wagner continued with composition but his second opera, *The Ban on Love*, after Shakespeare's *Measure for Measure*, was a disaster. He was allowed two performances by the impresario of the Magdeburg opera company at the end of the season. At the first performance on March 29, 1836, the tenor forgot his part and resorted to snatches from the other operas *Fra Diavolo* and *Zampa*. The second performance, which was for Wagner's benefit, the proceeds of the first accruing to the company, commanded the attention of only three spectators, all Jews: a Madame Gottschalk, who had befriended him, her husband and a "Polish Jew in full dress."[2] In the middle of the performance there was a huge commotion on the stage when the young tenor in the opera was attacked by the husband of prima donna

---

1. Richard Wagner Museum brochure, "About Richard Wagner," item 4l.
2. Osborne, *World Theatre of Wagner*, 15–16.

Karoline Pollent, who suspected that they were having an affair. The cast joined in and the performance was cancelled.[3]

Wagner was always a man whose tastes exceeded the depth of his pocket and he borrowed or sponged off friends to finance his extravagant lifestyle. During 1837 he was employed as music director for a while at Königsberg where Minna had obtained a position. The management went insolvent and he left the city with a string of debts. Riga was to be the next venue for his work and his two years there saw a commencement of his opera *Rienzi*. In later years his treatment of his wife Minna was to cause much shaking of conservative heads but in the early days of the marriage he was at the receiving end of the deception. Minna left Wagner on two occasions for other men and this left him deeply depressed.

Music in the cold and inhospitable Hanseatic port of Riga was to have at least one advantage for a young and ambitious conductor. The opera house with its sunken pit and steeply rising auditorium was to so impress the musician that he was to copy many of its features in later years at Bayreuth. After arguments with the director of the theatre he fled in a small ship – the *Thetis* – via Norway to England and thereafter to France. Something must have occurred in that headlong flight as Minna's barrenness was attributed to the harsh journey and the inclement weather that accompanied it. At one stage the heavy vehicle they were traveling in overturned and his hapless wife had to spend a long painful night in a peasant's cottage.[4] His experiences during the stormy voyage were to stand him in good stead when he composed *The Flying Dutchman*. On the boat Wagner had met a Jewish woman who gave him an introduction to the composer Giacomo Meyerbeer. The latter was the son of a Berlin banker and his operas had dominated the opera scene in Paris since the first production of *Robert le Diable*.

Wagner had written from Riga to Meyerbeer and after mentioning his early adulation of Beethoven moved on to deal with dramatic music. The rivalry between the two composers was to be a significant cause of the growth of anti-Semitism in Wagner. It is important, therefore, to note the sycophantic and opportunistic praise in the missive:

---

3. Ibid.
4. Newman, *Life of Richard Wagner*, vol. 1, 248.

Wagner's great rival, the Jewish composer Giacomo Meyerbeer. Gregor-Dellins, page 49. Archiv für Kunst und Geschichte, Berlin.

Since then, and especially since I came into contact with the actual life and practical aspects of music, my views about present-day conceptions have altered drastically, above all as far as the dramatic side is concerned. Should I deny that it was particularly *your* works which have given me the pointer to a new direction? In any case it would not here be fitting to indulge in uncouth flatteries as regards your genius. *May I just say that in your music I saw the perfect solution of the true German, who absorbed the best aspects of the Italian and French Schools in order to give the creations of his mind a universal import.*[5]

"In your music I saw the perfect solution of the true German" – these were words that would be anathema to an irate Wagner fifteen years later. At that time Paris was the cultural capital of the world and every artist longed to enjoy success there. Wagner hailed it as "the capital of free France,

---

5.   Gal, *Richard Wagner*, 21.

where a press exposes all wrongs, where only merit wins applause."[6] In 1839 Wagner fled from his creditors in Riga to that city, but success was not easily achieved and his three years there produced nothing of note.

Initially he had landed at Boulogne where he worked on the score of *Rienzi* and showed parts of it to Meyerbeer.[7] Initially all went very well, according to Wagner's autobiography; Meyerbeer "confirmed the reports I had heard about his generosity and kindness and made a very favourable impression on me in every respect."[8] Meyerbeer looked at the libretto and the first two acts and made all the right noises, though the real question was whether he would assist Wagner in the bullring that was the Paris opera.

Before he had completed *Rienzi* he made a further attempt to have an earlier work performed. He wrote sycophantic letters to Meyerbeer on January 18 and February 15, 1840 calling himself the latter's "protégé" and said that he looks forward to "salvation from all evil through God and you; if you remain well disposed towards me, then God too is near me" and he is confident of the French composer's favor, "for your kindness has already been too deeply engaged on behalf of one so necessitous as myself."[9] Wagner acknowledges he cannot "pick up a pin" in Paris without Meyerbeer's help. Wagner borrowed money in the expectation that he would have his opera *The Ban on Love* produced at the Theatre de la Renaissance but it was turned down despite an encouraging introduction to the director by Meyerbeer.[10] Life was a day-to-day struggle to meet the most basic needs. Politically he fell in with a group called "Young Germany" which included the poets Heinrich Heine and Ludwig Börne, Jewish exiles, who readily joined Wagner in wittily challenging the conservative patriotism they had escaped in their Motherland.[11]

Of special interest was Heine, whose life spanned the turbulent years from 1797 until 1856. A German Romantic, he turned his literary lance and vehemently challenged the literature of conquest and carnage then much in vogue. Exiled to Paris since 1831, he was to spend the rest of his life in

---

6. Viereck, *Metapolitics*, 94.
7. Taylor, *Richard Wagner*, 80.
8. Ibid.
9. Newman, *Life of Richard Wagner*, vol. 2, 603.
10. Taylor, *Richard Wagner*, 84.
11. Ibid.

that city and was to have a significant impact on Wagner.[12] At a dinner at Brocci's restaurant Wagner met Heine and his pretty wife Mathilde where the poet showed his brilliant and witty style and conversation.[13] His story of the Dutchman who sailed the seas forever was to be the basis of Wagner's great opera and his trenchant political analysis was to be the foundation of the composer's views at that time. He criticized the violence advocated by other German writers and his prophetic words were to be realized by the most fervent Wagnerian admirer of all time – Adolf Hitler. Speaking of the incipient fascism of the then current German authors Heine wrote that "these doctrines have developed revolutionary forces which only await the day to break forth and fill the world with terror and astonishment."[14]

Heine also saw through the shallow crude display of Meyerbeer's music – he coined a brilliant epigram: "Meyerbeer will be immortal during his lifetime, and perhaps for some years afterwards, for he pays in advance."[15] Despite his strong roots in Judaism Heine saw merit in the pacifism advocated by the spread of church doctrine in Europe at that time. He maintained that Christianity had restrained the German's "brutal joy in battle" for many centuries but "should the subduing talisman, the Cross, break, then will come roaring forth the wild madness of the old champions, the insane Berserker rage of which the Northern poets sing. That talisman is brittle, and the day will come when it will pitifully break. The old stone Gods will rise from the long-forgotten ruin and rub the dust of a thousand years from their eyes; and Thor, leaping to life with his giant hammer, will crush the gothic cathedrals."[16]

Oh that the political world had but taken note of what that Parisian oracle was saying from the abject poverty of the dingy suburb. How did he guess the use Wagner would make of the northern myths – and that Thor the God of Thunder and Might would appear in *Das Rheingold*, complete with his hammer? What prescience gave the poet in 1834 the foreknowledge that Adolf Hitler would take the subliminal and, indeed, overt message of the operas and the writings, still lying nascent in Wagner's restive imagination, and put them to effect with such catastrophic consequences? Did

---

12. Ibid., 86.
13. Newman, *Life of Richard Wagner*, vol. 1, 275.
14. Waite, *The Psychopathic God*, 261.
15. Newman, *Life of Richard Wagner*, vol. 2, 135.
16. Ibid., 261.

Heine know that *his* own works would be some of the first to be thrown on the great fires of the Nazi auto-da-fé when the nation threw its soul at the devil?

Mention has been made of Wagner's first meeting with the doyen of French composers Giacomo Meyerbeer and the positive impression it made on him. Wagner had further meetings with the influential musician and received some assistance but was not able to break into the closed circle at the Opéra. The lack of success exacerbated his chilly prospects and he wrote a pathetic letter to Meyerbeer: "I have arrived at the point where I must sell myself to someone. I realize I must become your slave, with my mind and my body."[17] The form his enslavement was to take became immediately apparent. Poverty ruled his life there in the colony of poor German artists, and his meager income accrued from musical journalism and hackwork, turning Meyerbeer's orchestral scores into vocal ones.

Heine's work on the legend of the Flying Dutchman has been mentioned and the young composer adapted the story for use as an opera libretto. Wagner's enslavement to French opera and its practitioners was to witness further degradations. Perhaps the greatest indignity he ever had to face was to hand over his prose draft for *The Flying Dutchman* to the Grand Opera for five hundred francs and see an opera composed from it – *La Vaisseau Fantôme* – that ran for ten performances.

The irony of the indignity was that though Wagner nursed a grudge against Paris and all matters French forever – witness his exultation at German victories against the French in 1870 – there was an unexpected benefit. With the money from the sale of his libretto he composed his own version of *The Flying Dutchman* that was to stun the musical world and hold opera lovers in thrall to this day. Sir Thomas Beecham was later to marvel at the beauties of the work and witness the "winds tearing at the sails" when he opened the score.

But the success of that masterpiece was only to accrue much later. Grinding poverty was a constant companion in those days. On one occasion he walked from where he was staying in Meudon outside Paris into the city to beg a few francs, but came home depressed and empty-handed. "Pity us artists for we are the raw material of the world spirit" was his trenchant comment. He was also homesick for his Saxony and the first hints

---

17. Richard Wagner Museum brochure, "About Richard Wagner," item 61.

of the future nationalism became apparent when he wrote in the journal *Europa*, "it is wonderful to be German, if one is at home, where one has comfort, Jean Paul and Bavarian Beer."[18] Little did he know how he was to fulfill the prophecy of the philosopher of Bayreuth – the poet and musician were forging an immortal partnership.

Apart from Heine and Börne he also made friendships with Ernst Kietz, a painter, and Samuel Lehrs, a Jewish philologist who was ill with a terrible chest complaint. They helped him whenever possible and he remained in their debt all his life. Another painter and friend, Friedrich Pecht, left a lively description of Wagner at that time: "only twenty-six years old, he already possessed such experience of the ways of the world and such inexhaustible resources, as I have never again seen; in addition, a magical power of attraction and an inborn nobility of nature, which never allowed him to become common or trivial, even in moments of great passion or exuberant wit. I always had to admire the inexhaustibleness and the will power of this man, whom no distress could depress, except for a short time, and whom no misfortune could cause to waver in his confidence in his own talent."[19]

He was also described as having "an arresting figure, with piercing blue eyes set in a large head, severe and initially of a reserved manner."[20] Mention will be made en passant to some of Wagner's sexual peccadilloes and one of his amours, Judith Gautier, described his eyes as "blue as the lake of Lucerne" and again as "beaming eyes, where blended the most beautiful shades of sapphire."[21] A young disciple from Cologne, August Lesimple, met Wagner in 1854 and spoke of them: "Whoever has looked once into his eyes will never again forget the deep and mysterious expression which shone there. There was something marvelous about his eyes."[22] By some malign stroke of cultural heredity his most fervent admirer, Adolf Hitler, was also to be complimented on his arresting eyes.

Others were to describe Wagner in less charitable terms. His stature meant that he narrowly escaped being a dwarf; his enormous head perched on narrow shoulders, with a prominent nose and jutting jaw. That was the

---

18. Ibid.
19. Ibid., item 7l.
20. Wallace et al., *Intimate Sex Lives of Famous People*, 457.
21. Newman, *Life of Richard Wagner*, vol. 1, 36.
22. Newman, *Life of Richard Wagner*, vol. 2, 429.

opinion of Mary Burrell, a courageous English biographer of Wagner, to whom we owe a great debt of gratitude for rescuing the story of his life from a succession of mendacious hagiographers.[23] The degradations of Parisian life were too much for him and he determined to leave the country. He returned to Germany on April 7, 1842, and, with great emotion, cried as he crossed the border, "impecunious musician that I was I pledged unswerving loyalty to my German Fatherland from that moment."[24] The great nationalist was born, and how the nations of Europe would suffer.

From home he wrote to his friends back in Paris and told them what had made him leave. "How your Paris appeared to me! This great den of murderers was the sort of place where without naïve and simple striving we are driven to death silently and without notice." And yet the years of poverty had forged a mindset and genius that would produce incomparable musical beauty. Appreciation was to be expressed in later years when he finally came to acknowledge the creative process inspired by his misery: "long live the pains of Paris, they bore magnificent fruits."

The internationalist liberalism that characterized his earlier days in Paris evaporated and he was later to say that he was "the most German man" in the history of the nineteenth century.[25] All that can be said of his years in the galleys was that they taught him the scores of other composers and he developed a poetic style that was to stand him in good stead for his music dramas. His indomitable spirit could never be tamed and in November 1840 he completed his opera *Rienzi* (after Bulwer-Lytton's novel) and wrote to the king of Saxony requesting him to arrange a performance in Dresden.

Given the enmity that was to follow between the two composers it is interesting to note that Meyerbeer wrote a letter of recommendation to Baron von Lüttichau, the director of the Royal Saxon Opera.[26] Meyerbeer supported the production of *Rienzi* in Dresden and said, "this interesting young German composer deserved his success in every respect."[27] The next year Wagner completed his first masterpiece, *The Flying Dutchman*, based on Heine's version of the legend about a ship's captain condemned

---

23. Newman, *Life of Richard Wagner*, vol. 1, 3.
24. Köhler, *Wagner's Hitler*, 32.
25. Ibid., 4.
26. Taylor, *Richard Wagner*, 91.
27. Köhler, *Wagner's Hitler*, 34.

A depiction of the Wandering Jew. Rose cover. The Mary Evans Picture Library drawing by Gustave Doré.

to sail forever. When it was later produced in France journalists in Paris advised their readers to boycott the work – it ought to carry a health warning, they wrote, because its tempest-tossed overture induced a nauseating seasickness.[28]

Into this story Wagner ingeniously wove the legend of Ahasuerus, the Wandering Jew, the origins of which are not entirely clear. Some maintain that it commenced with the account of Cain and Abel in the Old Testament. Cain brought Jehovah (the Christian reading of the Jewish name for God) fruit and vegetables but Jehovah preferred the meat brought by Abel. In a fit of jealous rage Cain killed Abel and as punishment Jehovah put a mark on him. "The mark of Cain" became a metaphor for a damned person and Jehovah's sentence also decreed that he would be an eternal vagabond on the earth; he would never die and never be killed. In a strange racist distortion many anti-Semites, including Wagner, ate vegetables alone as a reaction to the Jewish God Jehovah who preferred meat.[29]

A second less probable source of the story relates to the Persian King Ahasuerus of whom mention is made in the Old Testament Book of Esther in chapters 8 and 9. King Ahasuerus had ordered the massacre of the Jews

---

28. See Conrad, "He's Tricky, That Dicky."
29. Poliakov, *History of Anti-Semitism from Voltaire to Wagner*, 448.

but the Hebrew prophetess Esther persuaded him to reverse the decision and kill the Persians instead. This deliverance is celebrated in the Jewish feast of Purim and the benign nature of Ahasuerus makes him an unlikely candidate for his role as the tortured wanderer.[30]

A final and more probable source of the legend of the Wandering Jew involves Christ's last days on earth. When he was on his way to be crucified at Gethsemane he paused at the shop of a certain shoemaker, Ahasuerus, so myth has it, and asked permission to rest for a moment before he moved on to his death by crucifixion on Good Friday. Ahasuerus looked up and indicated that he could not give him permission to rest, as he was a condemned criminal.

Given the precedent imposed by his father Jehovah, Jesus imposed a similar sentence. After a sign of benediction, according to the legend, Jesus told him in a tone of great sadness that he would have no children, and would forever be a traveler who did not know his destination. Some versions added a few gratuitous sufferings; they maintain that Ahasuerus always had five farthings in his purse and his sleep never exceeded a quarter of an hour. The future of the poor man was not assured; Ahasuerus would seek death but it would not come until Christ returned to earth again. The story of the Wandering Jew became firmly entrenched in folklore for many centuries. During the next two thousand years there were regular sightings in Europe of the bearded, shambling figure of the Wandering Jew and many claimed that he had boarded with them.[31]

That the legend of the Wandering Jew was the basis for the main theme of *The Flying Dutchman* is apparent from Wagner's autobiographical essay *A Communication to My Friends*. "The Christian, without a home on earth, embodied this trait in the figure of the Wandering Jew: for that wanderer, forever doomed to a long since out-lived life, without an aim, without a joy, there bloomed no earthly ransom: death was the sole remaining goal of all his strivings; his only hope, the laying down of being."[32] This theme of "laying down of being" was to be a theme of Wagner's from that point on, culminating in his proposal of a "great solution" to the Jewish question which Hitler was to take up so enthusiastically eighty years later.

---

30. Waite, *The Psychopathic God*, 109.
31. See Hasan-Rokem and Dundes, *The Wandering Jew*, for a general discussion of the concept.
32. Osborne, *World Theatre of Wagner*, 30.

In Wagner's opera the story line assumes a more practical theme; the Dutchman has made a foolish vow to go round a certain cape – mostly reckoned to be the Cape of Good Hope in South Africa – or sail the seas until Judgment Day.[33] The devil overhears his vow and condemns him to wander forever – all that can save him is the love of a faithful woman. Wagner's choice of his décor – blood red sails and black masts – was to serve the Nazis well when they pondered colors for their swastika flag. The Dutchman seeks death vainly in order to find repose. On one occasion he confronts a pirate who "signs the cross and straight was gone, nowhere a grave, no way to death."

The Dutchman sings of his impending death and hopes for any end – "endless destruction be my lot." Little did he know how a fervent admirer of the composer would take up that call – literally – for the Wandering Jews of the world. In Wagner's opera when the Dutchman lands on the Norwegian coast he is introduced to Senta, who promises to be the woman who can save him by keeping faithful until death.[34] Speaking of her as his "angel" he prays for his "redemption" when she will become his "savior." When he is preparing to leave there is a confrontation between his own sailors and the Norwegians. That the Dutchman's crew are also Wandering Jews is clear from the method used by the Norwegians to silence them. "The Norwegians try to drown the song of the Dutchman's crew with their own song. After vain efforts the raging of the sea, the roaring, howling and whistling of the unnatural storm, together with the ever wilder song of the Dutchman's crew silence them. They fall back *making the sign of the cross and quit the deck; the Dutch crew, seeing them, burst forth into shrill, mocking laughter.*" The same laughter that condemned Ahasuerus to his eternal wanderings has returned; one day (in Wagner's last opera *Parsifal*) it will be the turn of the temptress Kundry – also a female representation of the Wandering Jew – to tell how she laughed at Christ's anguish on the cross.

The Dutchman overhears her previous lover Erik reminding her of their previous love and departs thinking that she, too, cannot be faithful to him. As he leaves in his ship she leaps into the sea singing "Praise me – I am your angel until you breathe your last! Here stand I, faithful unto death!" The last ditch attempt at proof of her fidelity persuades the Dutchman

---

33. Newman, *Wagner Nights*, 45.
34. Ibid.

and he is released from his curse; he and Senta are glorified and rise to heaven in each other's arms.[35] The Wandering Jew has been sanctified by a Christian angel.

Wagner's own analysis bears out the central role played by the Wandering Jew. "As an end to his anguish, he longs, like Ahasuerus, for death, this form of release, denied to the Wandering Jew, may be vouchsafed to the Dutchman through a *woman* who sacrifices herself to him out of love; yearning for death thus drives the Dutchman to search out this woman; this woman, however, is no longer the Penelope of Odysseus, wooed by him in ages past and caring for him at home, but it is womankind in general, a woman who does not yet exist, who is longed for and foreseen, the woman who is infinitely womanly, in short, *the woman of the future*."[36]

Some of Wagner's duplicity became evident in his acknowledgement of the sources of his opera. Despite the great privations he shared with Heinrich Heine and his debt to the latter's account, the march of time dimmed his memory. He had earlier praised the poet as the "great awakener of the German mind, this dominating talent…who might become equal to the greatest names in literature," but later regarded him as the Mephistopheles of modern German culture.[37] In his *Autobiographical Sketch* in February 1843 Wagner speaks of the genesis of *The Flying Dutchman* as follows: "Heine's truly dramatic treatment – *his own invention* – of the redemption of this Ahasuerus of the sea gave me all I needed to utilize the legend for an opera subject."[38] Wagner takes away the words "*his own invention*" in the reprint of 1871 and places instead: "*borrowed from a Dutch play bearing the same title.*"[39] Another explanation for the change in credit is that the rise of his anti-Semitism made it difficult for him to give credit to a Jew for the success of his opera.

Wagner never made friends amongst his peers, either as musicians or writers. He would invariably surround himself with sycophants and toadies who supported his endeavors and, more importantly, hated his enemies with his own undisguised venom. It was the French writer Romain Rolland, who had reason many years later to comment on the ideology built into his

---

35. Ibid., 57.
36. Jackson, "Baudelaire and Wagner," 45.
37. Rose, *Wagner: Race and Revolution*, 34.
38. Newman, *Wagner Nights*, 20.
39. Newman, *Life of Richard Wagner*, vol. 1, 21.

mature works, who identified this feature of great minds. "A deplorable law governing genius," he said, "seems to decree that, with the superior mind, a strong dose of mediocrity in the other is required to satisfy the needs of friendship. A genius will form only a passing friendship with his peers."[40]

The musical success did not go hand in hand with religious toleration and Wagner developed a brand of anti-Semitism that came to dominate his life. The source has already been hinted at and may well have derived largely from his rivalry with the composer Meyerbeer. The last mentioned came from noble stock and his parents were highly thought of as persons of culture and refinement. Heine had already written of the generosity of the latter's mother Amalie Wulf, a woman of rare intellectual gifts and noble character of whom Heine said "she could not lie down in peace unless she had done some generous deed."[41]

Wagner was not alone in his attacks on Meyerbeer. Already in 1836 the composer Robert Schumann had written a devastating critique of Meyerbeer's most popular opera *The Huguenots* – at the end of his review he concluded that the composer should be removed from the scene. For good measure he throws in an accusation of musical plagiarism. "It is easy to identify Mozart, Rossini and other composers in Meyerbeer's music. What is peculiar to him, however, is that persistent, nagging, unpleasant rhythm that runs through almost all the themes in the opera…Vulgarity, distortion, perversity, immorality" are the main features of the "un-music." He continues: "Nothing worse than this can be imagined, unless one were to turn the stage into a gallows. Then the cry of terror from the mouth of a tormented talent would be followed by the hope that things would soon get better."[42]

The roots of Wagner's *own* anti-Semitism are difficult to penetrate but some suggest that it all began with the disastrous performance of Wagner's overture *Columbus*, conducted by Henri Valentino in February 1841. Wagner believed that Meyerbeer had orchestrated his downfall, so to speak. That overture had been composed to a play written by his schooldays friend Theodor Apel in 1835 and was roundly booed on being presented

---

40. Ibid., 81.
41. Hussey, *Jakob Liebmann Meyerbeer*, 191.
42. Köhler, *Wagner's Hitler*, 260.

to a knowledgeable audience.[43] At a concert in Riga on an earlier occasion the overture had also not been appreciated.

Wagner himself wrote a letter in February 1840 to Meyerbeer thanking him for achieving a rehearsal of the work: "this would be the first and a really weighty success, for which I should have no one to thank but you. But why thank you for it? May heaven only grant that some opportunity may arise for me to render you even a thousandth part of what thank I owe you. I can hardly hope, however, that Heaven will be so generous to me; on the contrary, I see that I shall follow you from aeon to aeon stammering my thanks, until in the end, exasperated at not being able to get any peace from me even in heaven, you will consign me to hell."[44]

Already in 1841 Wagner had fired the first rounds in a battle that would finally provoke a racist war unequalled in the history of the world. Writing as V. Freudenfeuer he composed an essay entitled *"Parisian Fatalities for the German"*; the title alone bespoke his nightmares in the French capital as he watched Meyerbeer drink and feast on the proceeds of his mediocrity. "[If the German musician] attains a higher level of achievement, for instance if he becomes a composer who sets precedents at the Grand Opera, like Meyerbeer, he will have achieved this only as a banker; for a banker can do everything in Paris, even compose operas and have them produced…Yet the German bankers, of whom there are many here, no longer count as Germans; they are above all nationality, and therefore above all national prejudices; they belong to the universe and the Paris stock exchange…In the eyes of the French, Rothschild is more a universal Jew than a German."[45]

It was a theme that would recur again and again much as the curse motif in the great Ring cycle; Meyerbeer was not worthy of his financial success – Jews were leeches on society who sucked it dry. Wagner carried the battle further on his own behalf and wrote a vicious article in the *Neue Zeitschrift* in February 1842. Too cowardly to acknowledge his own authorship again he used the initials of Valentino (H.V.) to compromise the conductor and stated that Meyerbeer was a pickpocket. He was clearly following up on Schumann and his criticisms were a thinly veiled attack

---

43. Taylor, *Richard Wagner*, 48.
44. Newman, *Life of Richard Wagner*, vol. 2, 604.
45. Weiner, *Richard Wagner and the Anti-Semitic Imagination*, 52.

of plagiarism. From those early shots a war developed which was to have devastating consequences.

The failure of the overture was not the end of Wagner's career and he was to enjoy a wonderful success with *Rienzi*. The irony of the early stages of the war between the composers was that his success with that opera was probably an appreciation by the audience of a Wagnerian work that imitated the work of Meyerbeer. Many stigmatize the opera, as did Hans von Bülow – who was required later to sacrifice his wife Cosima, daughter of Franz Liszt, to Wagner – as Meyerbeer's finest opera, for Wagner had composed it in the same manner.

In 1842 Dresden saw *Rienzi* triumphantly performed on October 20, "which drove Dresden wild," according to Clara Schumann, wife of the more famous Robert.[46] Wagner was no less enthusiastic about his success. "I must tell you that never yet, as everyone tells me, was an opera received in Dresden for the first time with such enthusiasm…There was excitement, a revolution throughout the city…Triumph! Triumph…day has dawned."[47] His friend Ferdinand Heine has left a most amusing account of how Wagner responded to the fear and trepidation – and finally adulation – the occasion brought to him:

> He looked like a spectre; he laughed and wept at the same time and embraced everybody who came near him, while all the while the cold perspiration ran down his forehead. When he was first called for he did not want to go on the stage, and I had to give him a huge push; he flew out of the wings, but not an inch further than the shock of the kick carried him; then he recoiled again before the roar of the audience. Fortunately he has so famous a nose that at any rate the left half of the spectators could refresh themselves with the sight of the point of it.[48]

That famous landmark has become an infallible way to determine whether anyone in the future generations had inherited the right admixture of genius. For the women it did little to enhance their beauty.

Minna added a nice touch – she hid laurel leaves under his sheets – so

---

46. Köhler, *Wagner's Hitler*, 35.
47. Richard Wagner Museum brochure, "About Richard Wagner," item 10u.
48. Newman, *Life of Richard Wagner*, vol. 1, 343.

that when he returned from the great triumph he could literally and figuratively rest on them. There was a double blessing for the composer in that wonderful time; his own recognition and what he perceived as the end of his enemy. The success of his opera, claimed Wagner in a letter to two friends on November 6, 1842, had resulted in Meyerbeer taking flight.[49] He had not in fact taken flight but been appointed music director in Berlin, though he still spent much of his life in Paris.[50]

Rienzi had set the tongues wagging in Dresden but for the paranoid Wagner there was always the depressing shadow of Meyerbeer, enveloping him in a cloud of gloom. Some of the admiring voices pointed out the debt he owed his rival and that rankled more than anything else. Three months later Wagner wrote to Schumann saying that to mention him in the same breath as Meyerbeer was like a sentence of death on his creative powers and that the allegation that he had borrowed from the rival composer was a "remarkably perverse quirk of nature if I were to borrow from a source whose very smell I find repulsive."[51] The vehemence of the language showed the passion Wagner felt and this was to grow in intensity with the years.

Posterity can be partly grateful that humility did not prevent the young composer from recognizing that his future was bright. He commenced with an account of his life, a venture that was to receive the blessing and support of King Ludwig II, and continue until his death. Throughout he maintained that such scribblings had no merit but their "unadorned veracity," a virtue later biographers were to find in rather short supply. Wagner continued with his onslaught on French composers – whom he accuses of "making music only for gold" – in his first venture in that direction, the *Autobiographical Sketch* in 1843.[52]

His venom for Mendelssohn was not reciprocated by the other composer. Wagner acknowledged as much when he wrote to Minna on January 8, 1844, "Mendelssohn, with whom I dined once, gave me great pleasure; after the performance [of *The Flying Dutchman*] he came on the stage, embraced me, and congratulated me most heartily."[53] The winter of 1844 was to see a visit by the Italian composer Spontini, who had dominated

---

49. Köhler, *Wagner's Hitler*, 36.
50. Taylor, *Richard Wagner*, 80.
51. Köhler, *Wagner's Hitler*, 36.
52. Viereck, *Metapolitics*, 97.
53. Newman, *Life of Richard Wagner*, vol. 1, 437.

the Berlin opera scene for some twenty-two years. Wagner was to find an ally in the famous musician. His long reign made it difficult to accept the successes of Meyerbeer and Mendelssohn and he told Wagner "there was some hope for Germany, when I was Emperor of music in Berlin; but since [the new King of Prussia Friedrick Wilhelm IV] has abandoned his music to the disorder brought into it by the two Wandering Jews [Meyerbeer and Mendelssohn] the last hope had been lost."[54]

Despite his apparent rancor Wagner was never averse to the use of duplicity to achieve his own objectives. He wrote to Meyerbeer on December 26, 1844 sycophantically and hypocritically congratulating him on his latest opera *Ein Feldlager in Schlesien*, praising his "mastery" and stating that he would have gone to Berlin for the performance but he had learned from the composer himself that there was little prospect of him obtaining seats. Wagner went on to enquire whether there were any prospects of obtaining a production of *Rienzi* as a heroic tenor had to be found.[55]

The success of Wagner's work was recognized and Wagner was appointed Saxon Kapellmeister for life by the king Friedrich August on February 2, 1843 with a salary of 1,500 thalers.[56] No lesser composer than his childhood idol Carl Maria von Weber, whose works had been such an inspiration to him, had worn the boots he was filling. Minna was in raptures – her Richard had secure employment and two of his operas had been produced.

The next year *The Flying Dutchman* was produced at Dresden but was less successful. The new mode of composition baffled the audience, who were looking for more in the style of Meyerbeer. After the second performance he went to a wine bar with his friend Heine to drown his sorrows and imbibed too liberally for his own sake. Staggering home he found a young pale man, dressed in black, who wanted to shake his hand and tell him how deeply shattered he was by the performance. Struggling to concentrate Wagner asked the man to write down his name – Professor Werder – as he feared his own script might be too slurred. The personality of this man must have made a considerable impression on him. When he was fleeing, after taking part in the Dresden uprising, he took that name as

---

54. Ibid., 392.
55. Newman, *Life of Richard Wagner*, vol. 2, 604.
56. Köhler, *Wagner's Hitler*, 36.

an alias when he went to stay at Magdala, near Weimar. Friends of Wagner had to sacrifice a lot for the composer.[57]

Minna was of the view that when Wagner became conductor of the court opera at Dresden that was a position he should cling to as it commanded an adequate income and considerable status; but his plans were much grander than that. For a while he bided his time and bent his creative energies to the struggle between physical and spiritual love. In October 1845 his next masterpiece *Tannhäuser* received a lukewarm reception but the critics were not able to suppress its merits indefinitely. There is something of the Wandering Jew in that hero as well and he describes his fate: "onwards I am driven forever and will never find rest on earth. The past is closed to me always and I am doomed to roam alone unblessed."

There were problems with this production as well. The Dresden press spread the rumor that the Catholic party had bribed him. It is difficult to understand why they would have done so as the opera did little to enhance the reputation of that institution and the appearance of Venus in a love grotto in the first act would have shocked the straitlaced clerics. There was also patriotism sufficient to have later fired the susceptible heart of Adolf Hitler. The Landgrave of Wartburg talks of the "sword of strife that was recently drawn in the battle and victory to secure our German land against the southern foe."

Fellow composers were divided in their opinions. Robert Schumann initially had reservations but then professed to have been "very much moved" by the performance.[58] An amusing story did the rounds at the time and referred to Wagner's insufferable and unceasing monologues, when speaking to friends. Schumann spoke sadly of his colleague's "devastating fluency of speech, that allowed of no one else getting a word in, while Wagner, when asked his opinion of Schumann, complained that you could get no further with a man who never opened his mouth!"[59]

Few listeners have ever been able to resist the charms of the opera including the stirring Pilgrims' chorus, the music heralding the entry of the guests in act 2 and the Venusberg music. Rossini was asked his impressions after hearing the opera and retorted in his usual acerbic manner, "it

---

57. Newman, *Life of Richard Wagner*, vol. 1, 379.
58. Richard Wagner Museum brochure, "About Richard Wagner," item 11u.
59. Newman, *Life of Richard Wagner*, vol. 1, 439.

is too complex to be judged at a first hearing; and I certainly shall not give it a second!"[60]

On December 27, 1845 Wagner again wrote to Meyerbeer trying to get a footing in Berlin for his operas – particularly *Rienzi* – as Wagner regarded his successes in Dresden as being flattering but to all intents and purposes he regarded it as a provincial town.[61] A week later he again wrote to Meyerbeer, sending him a copy of the poem of *Lohengrin* hoping that the French composer would persuade the King of Prussia to commission the opera for his Court Theatre. He ended the letter as hypocritically as usual by trusting that Meyerbeer would continue to show sympathy for him and he remains his "for ever greatly beholden Richard Wagner."[62]

Despite the venomous attacks on his rival, the eternal sponger had the gall to approach Meyerbeer in November 1846 for a loan of 1200 thalers: the equivalent of Wagner's yearly salary. Meyerbeer confided in his diary on November 26 the smug comment that he had declined the request.[63] It was clear that perfection had also eluded him. The troubles with Meyerbeer continued in Berlin in the autumn of 1847 after performances of *Rienzi* in that city. After hearing a performance of the opera in Dresden some two or three years previously Meyerbeer had promised to produce it in Berlin. Wagner did not believe that Meyerbeer meant him any ill will at that stage and said, "I don't yet doubt the honesty of his disposition towards me."[64]

Wagner arrived in Berlin on September 18, 1847 and tried to persuade Meyerbeer to assist with the production. By that stage Meyerbeer was a very successful composer with a number of operas in the repertoire of the major companies including *Les Huguenots* and *Le Prophète*. On October 3 Wagner wrote to his wife Minna: "today, I am dining with Meyerbeer. He is leaving Berlin soon – so much the better."[65] When Wagner visited him to discuss his woes he found the French composer in a house with luxurious hangings, paintings and ornate furniture. Meyerbeer told him he believed that a good tenor was essential for *Rienzi* – the dress rehearsal and the premiere were well received on October 23 and 26 respectively. Wagner was

---

60. Bedford, *Schumann*, 20.
61. Newman, *Life of Richard Wagner*, vol. 2, 605.
62. Ibid.
63. Rose, *Wagner: Race and Revolution*, 202.
64. Ibid., 46.
65. Ibid.

convinced that Meyerbeer was afraid it would be a success, as had been his experience in Dresden.[66] Wagner and Minna spent time in the city while the composer helped with the production. Thereafter very few attended the performances and Wagner was deeply depressed about the failure.

Wagner was mystified by the fact that he had sought an audience with King Friedrich-William but that had been denied. Despite this, Wagner hoped the king would attend the production but the public and press noted his absence. It was a tremendous snub for Wagner, who hoped for success in a cultural center such as Berlin.

There were more disasters to follow. Wagner learned from his friend Eduard von Bülow that the Court Intendant Küstner would not be able to pay for the expenses of producing *Rienzi* in Berlin. In addition Küstner refused to pay for the rehearsals as well. Finally came the news Wagner had suspected ever since his previous experience with his overture *Columbus*. Von Bülow discovered from a conversation he overheard in a coffee shop that Count Redern, a great friend of Meyerbeer, was responsible for the king not attending *Rienzi* and not giving him an audience. In a mind tortured with bitter jealousy and chagrin such as that of Wagner, there could only be one conclusion: Giacomo Meyerbeer had orchestrated the whole fiasco.[67] Wagner set this all out in a letter and added "I also found out that the press…completely subservient to Meyerbeer immediately slandered *Rienzi*…I have proof of this."[68]

Meyerbeer was not as pure as the driven snow and the French tenor Roger wrote in his diary in 1848: "I have passed the evening with Meyerbeer, who received me with open arms. His conversation is charming; he has a way that is all of his own of saying the most biting things in the sweetest style, his eyes full of tenderness, his lips pursed as if for a kiss."[69] While time is reckoned by many to be the great healer it was not to heal the rift between the two rival composers. What compounded the feud was the realization in May 1849 by Meyerbeer that the author of the article under the initials H.V. calling him a pickpocket was Wagner.[70]

There is no real clarity as to whether Meyerbeer caused Wagner's

---

66. Ibid., 202.
67. Ibid., 46.
68. Ibid.
69. Newman, *Life of Richard Wagner*, vol. 2, 606.
70. Rose, *Wagner: Race and Revolution*, 45–48 makes mention of this incident.

downfall in Berlin but once the French composer discovered Wagner's duplicity there was no further reason for him to carry on supporting Wagner or his cause. The French composer – whose origins were in fact German – would not have taken attacks on him lightly and he might well have felt some guilt about his own borrowings. His deficiencies were recognized in other quarters. Weber himself, a friend of Meyerbeer, had written to him several years before bemoaning how a "composer of creative power stoop[ed] to become an imitator in order to win favor with the crowd."[71]

The sins of Meyerbeer were never to be forgiven by his competitor. Ironically the French composer had anticipated this when he told Heine in 1839 that as Jews they would be pilloried unmercifully: "Ninety-nine percent of readers are Jew-haters, that is why they relish Jew-hatred, and always will, as long as it is administered to them with a little skill."[72] Wagner's weapon of choice was the blunderbuss. In June 1949 Wagner wrote to Liszt and said – referring to Meyerbeer – "I have a tremendous desire to practice a little artistic terrorism. Come here and lead the great hunt; we will shoot; and the hares shall fall right and left."[73] From these petty beginnings the anti-Semitism in Wagner grew alarmingly.

Writing at the end of the year to his friend and violin player Uhlig he again invoked the ghastly metaphors of armed conflict when he said, "I am not concerned to bring about a reconciliation with the contemptible world of the theatre, but to declare absolute, pitiless war…it is not a question of convincing or persuading but of destroying."[74] It was clear whom he regarded as the victims of his vengeance. Wagner or "the plenipotentiary of destruction"[75] as he liked to call himself, vowed revenge on the Jews – "one cannot declare allegiance both to Jesus and to those who nailed him on the Cross"[76] – whom he regarded as having wrought unutterable misery against the German people. What had commenced as an artistic rivalry deteriorated into a campaign or vendetta against the whole religion.

From the particular to the general was a small step for the composer and he became a crusading zealot in his quest. He did not care whose

---

71. Goldman and Sprinchorn, *Wagner on Music and Drama*, 17.
72. Rose, *Wagner: Race and Revolution*, 37.
73. Poliakov, *History of Anti-Semitism from Voltaire to Wagner*, 435.
74. Köhler, *Wagner's Hitler*, 58–59.
75. Ibid., 61.
76. Ibid., 16.

assistance he enlisted and his comments became more and more outrageous. Ludwig Schemann, a friend, recorded the following concerning the vehement state of mind of the composer as he tried to articulate the agricultural areas occupied by Jewish landowners: "His laments at the unutterable misery wrought by the Jews against our people culminated in the description of the fate of the German peasant who would soon no longer own a square inch of his own soil... I have never seen him exhibit such a flare-up of holy wrath after his last word, quite beside himself, he flung himself out into the winter night, and only returned after an interval, when the paroxysm had died down, together with his Newfoundland dog who had in the meantime wearied him into a state of mad repose."[77]

The "holy wrath" wreaked such havoc with his temper that biographers have recorded that Wagner was in the habit of biting the carpet in his rages. True to form the Austrian corporal who admired his music more than any one else indulged in the same tantrums. The madness grew with time and the hatred increased. It soon became clear what the "artistic terrorism" was to be. He needed a leader to fight his war and he sought aid from the instrument reckoned to be mightier than the sword. With mighty slashes of his pen, in the finest calligraphy, he called forth a redeemer to purge the Germans of their worst enemy – the Jews.

In his essay on the *Wibelungen* – the Ghibellines of history, not to be confused with the Nibelungs – he created Siegfried as that redeemer, who like Jesus, died, was mourned and eventually avenged, "as we today are taking our revenge on the Jews."[78] Siegfried, the man who knew no fear, was to be the hero of his mighty four-part music drama (tetralogy) *The Ring of the Nibelungs* and he was to slay the dragon Fafner. His death by a stab in the back was also to provide rich imagery some seventy years later when the National Socialists were looking for culprits for the loss of the First World War and prestige in Germany.

In this seminal essay Wagner reckoned that, although Siegfried was a creature of myth, he had shaken off the dust of ages much as Heinrich Heine had described, been reborn and found human form. The death of Siegfried from the perfidious stab in the back had not seen the end of the superman. His successor-in-title was of Teutonic origin; the hero who

---

77. Poliakov, *History of Anti-Semitism from Voltaire to Wagner*, 439.
78. Köhler, *Wagner's Hitler*, 213.

sought the Holy Grail in the Holy Land during the Crusades was the German Emperor Friedrich Barbarossa, the reincarnation of Siegfried.

The mention of Barbarossa in the writings of the composer was to have a profound effect on Adolf Hitler, who named his campaign against Russia after that emperor. Despite a death worthy of a hero Barbarossa was not gone forever and he was believed to be in a magic sleep in the area of Berchtesgaden in the Obersalzberg. In the declining years of Wagner's political decay he was to develop this theme when he called for a Führer to rescue Germany. Adolf Hitler assumed the mantle of that redeemer and opportunistically established the very same area as his holiday home.

In further rambling and turgid prose in the *Wibelungen* Wagner cried out in desperation for a return of this figure, be it the mythological Siegfried, or his reincarnated form in Barbarossa, to carry out his holy mission – to slay "the dragon that is tormenting mankind."[79] The "dragon" in his sprawling four-piece play was a giant called Fafner but no one was in any doubt which religious group was the real target of his attack. No piece of prose ever written by Richard Wagner had more impact than did this essay – bolstered even more when he developed the main themes in his music dramas and his further political diatribes of the last quarter of the nineteenth century.

Lest we surmise for a moment that Wagner's generalized attack on Jews meant that he had abandoned his private vendetta against Jewish composers, such a notion was one that his fecund pen would soon dispel. His old enemy Meyerbeer – who was now joined by Mendelssohn, for reasons not entirely clear, apart from his Jewish origins – was to be the subject of a most venomous attack.

The personalized anti-Semitism spawned an article on "Jewry in Music" in 1850 in which Wagner bemoaned the extension of male suffrage to Jews. He said that "the granting of social and political rights to the Jews was stimulated by a general idea and not by any real sympathy." From those vague generalizations he moves on to plain insults. "The Jew is repulsive…he rules and will continue to rule as long as money remains the power before which all deeds and actions must pale into insignificance…In ordinary life, the Jew – who, as we know, has a God unto himself – strikes us first and foremost by his outward appearance, which, regardless of the

---

79. Ibid.

European nationality to which he belongs, has something about it which is foreign to that nationality and which we find insuperably unpleasant."[80]

He berated their music and stated: "The Jew, incapable in himself of communication artistically with us by means of his outward appearance or language and least of all through his singing, has nonetheless come to dominate public taste in the most widely disseminated of modern artistic genres; music…the Jew has never had an art of his own, and therefore never led a life that was capable of sustaining art. We are bound to describe the period of Judaism in modern music as one of total uncreativity and degenerate antiprogressiveness."[81]

He cannot resist a dig at the commercial success of the Jews. He boldly states the public has to examine the causes why it is impossible "to further create natural, necessary, and true beauty without completely changing the level to which art has now advanced." The decay has been caused since "the public taste in art [came] under the mercantile fingers of the Jews."[82]

Wagner continued by launching what came perilously close to incitement to the destruction that would indeed later be attempted. Jews, he continued, dominated a degenerate society and if emancipation from Judaism was the greatest necessity, "the most important thing is to prove our forces for this war of liberation." No suggestion is made that he is speaking in metaphors.

The depth of his hatred was manifest when he wrote, "Society's body is dead and the Jews lodge in it like a swarm of insects corrupting it…the cultured Jew has denied his Jewishness by even taking baptism, but this has not helped. He is still the most heartless of human beings."

The awful metaphor of insects corrupting the body of society was to find a resonance in the ideology of the Third Reich with tragic consequences. The article does little to spare the feelings of Jewish people and continues, "Whoever has observed the shameful indifference and absentmindedness of a Jewish congregation throughout the musical performance of divine service in the synagogue may understand why a *Jewish opera composer* feels not at all offended by encountering the same thing in a theatre audience

---

80. Wagner, Gottfried, *The Wagner Legacy*, 65.
81. Ibid.
82. Weiner, *Richard Wagner and the Anti-Semitic Imagination*, 53.

and how he can cheerfully go on labouring for it; for this behaviour must really seem to him less unbecoming than in the house of God…"

That Wagner is attacking his old enemy Meyerbeer becomes abundantly clear when he proclaims, "In general, the uninspiring, the truly laughable, is the characteristic mark whereby *this famed composer* shows his Jewhood in his music. From a close study of the instances adduced above, which we have been able to discover by seeking to justify our indomitable objection to the Jewish nature, a proof emerges for us of the ineptitude of the present musical epoch."

He concludes with a muttered threat. "Judaism is the evil conscience of our modern civilization," and he evokes the specter of the Wandering Jew, who has no salvation to expect except the grave. Adopting an ominous tone he urges the Jews, "one thing only can redeem you from the burden of your curse the redemption of Ahasuerus – going under."[83] That he is inciting their destruction is clear from an earlier passage in the article: "…on one thing I am clear; just as the influence which the Jews have gained upon our mental life – as displayed in the deflection and falsification of our highest culture-tendencies – just as this influence is no mere physiological accident, so also must it be owned-to as definitive and past dispute. Whether the downfall of our Culture can be arrested by violent ejection of the destructive foreign element, I am unable to decide, since that would require forces with whose existence I am unacquainted."

In a letter to Ferdinand Heine of September 14, 1850 – the same year as his article – he expressed his "terrible disgust over the banker-music whoring," a further nasty aside aimed at the financially successful Meyerbeer.[84]

Joachim Köhler, who has written a wonderful book in which he examines in detail the links between Wagner and Hitler, says that the fact that Wagner was the first writer "to have incited the destruction of the Jews is a boast that nobody is likely to challenge."[85] The character of the mythical wandering Jew Ahasuerus has been mentioned in connection with *The Flying Dutchman* and will engage our attention again when his last opera *Parsifal* is discussed. The fascination of that personality will emerge from

---

83. Poliakov, *History of Anti-Semitism from Voltaire to Wagner*, 436–37. A summary of "Jewry in Music" appears in Goldman and Sprinchorn, *Wagner on Music and Drama*, 51.
84. Weiner, *Richard Wagner and the Anti-Semitic Imagination*, 53.
85. Köhler, *Wagner's Hitler*, 65.

the period of development of the anti-Semitism of the composer when his views permeated not only his political tracts but also his art – above all his librettos and music.

A source very close to the composer was not happy with his campaign and did not share his view that Meyerbeer was responsible for his woes. Wagner's wife Minna wrote to him on May 8, 1850 to criticize his racist views: "As for our spiritual development, I was happy in the knowledge that you were close to me while you created all the beautiful things…You always made me so happy when you sang and played almost every new scene for me *but since two years ago when you wanted to read me that essay in which you slander whole races which have been fundamentally helpful to you*, I could not force myself to listen; and ever since that time you have born a grudge against me and never again let me hear anything from your works."[86]

He sought justification and support from his friends but little of that was forthcoming from his future father-in-law Franz Liszt. Writing to him in 1851 Wagner said: "I felt a long repressed hatred for this Jewry and this hatred is as necessary to my nature as gall is to the blood. An opportunity arose when their damnable scribbling annoyed me most, and so I broke forth at last…"[87]

Liszt was different and would not join the great hunt. Wagner, however, started his lifetime quest to wreak vengeance. He was the supreme egoist, and yet he wanted no status apart from recognition of his work. Offers of titles and degrees meant nothing to him and he was satisfied with being referred to as plain Richard Wagner.

Wagner embarked on a number of administrative and artistic reforms in the theatre and with the orchestra. He proposed taking control of the opera away from the court and placing it in the hands of a national theatre, whose productions would be chosen by a union of dramatists and composers. This caused such an upheaval with the authorities that they refused to stage his next opera *Lohengrin*, the magical music of the swan knight. What bride has not entered the church to the famous march "Here Comes the Bride" in the third act of this opera? The irony of this will not be lost on the brides who have left the church to the music of the famous wedding

---

86. Rose, *Wagner: Race and Revolution*, 49.
87. Poliakov, *History of Anti-Semitism from Voltaire to Wagner*, 439.

march from the incidental music to *A Midsummer Night's Dream* by one of his arch rivals – the Jewish composer Felix Mendelssohn.

Lohengrin makes mention of a Führer who will lead the way to glory and success – a refrain that was to have particular resonance seventy years later. Lines from the opening scene of the first act were also not without a dangerous sort of nationalism – and the acquisition of Austria, Danzig and the Sudetenland in the next century was a response to the call for the military to intervene where Germans farmed the land.

> *Now is the time to guard our Reich's honor.*
> *From east and west, all men count equal in this.*
> *Place armies wherever there is German land.*
> *So that none shall disparage again the German Reich.*

History informs us that he took part in the German revolution of 1848–49 by writing a number of articles advocating revolution and other more physical acts in the Dresden uprising of 1849. He made a speech to 3,000 persons at the Fatherland Society and his attacks on Jewish banking interests and other capitalists were somewhat veiled. "Like an evil, nocturnal spirit this demonic concept of money will disappear from us with all its despicable train of public and secret usurers, paper swindling, interest and bank speculations. That will be the emancipation of the pure doctrine of Christ." He advised the King of Saxony to relinquish the throne and receive it back at the hands of the people as the "first and freest republican of all." He called for a "free Folk with universal adult suffrage, a Folk army, free and flourishing trade" so that Saxons might become "the noblest of children, like unto Gods." He also parodied and pilloried what he called "a standing Army and a recumbent Communal Guard" to such a degree that he was challenged to a number of duels.[88] None of this endeared him to the powers that be.

The socialism is very apparent but he rejected what he called "crude and insipid communism." His friend August Röckel, the new conductor in Dresden – "the only person who really appreciated the singular nature of my position" – ran a People's Paper in which Wagner wrote an

---

88. Newman, *Life of Richard Wagner*, vol. 2, 11.

editorial promising to "break the power of the mighty, of the law, and of property."[89]

That they were insistent on a total overthrow of the existing order by violence is apparent from the veiled threats in the rhetoric. Röckel wrote a letter asking when "will we take our clenched fist out of our pocket?" The response was almost immediate as the most revolutionary wing of the Saxon parliament seized Dresden.[90] The upshot was that they were charged with treason, which warranted the death penalty. Röckel was alleged to have conspired with Richard Wagner, Michael Bakunin and Gottfried Semper to overthrow King Friedrich II of Saxony.

While Röckel was the mastermind, Wagner arranged with Semper to erect the barricades, and supplied hand grenades to the revolutionaries. The grenades were capable of killing upwards of twenty loyal subjects. Wagner was part of secret meetings with Russian agitator Bakunin and the signal for the commencement of the revolt was a typical Wagnerian touch – the burning of the royal palace.[91] Wagner had urged Röckel to achieve a thorough arming of the people and arranged for hunting rifles from the singer Joseph Tichatschek, the first singer of the lead roles in *Rienzi* and *Tannhäuser*, to be given to the rebels.

A great friend of Wagner by the name of Theodor Uhlig was the first violinist in the court orchestra at Dresden. He had helped with the piano score of *Lohengrin* and attempted to stage *The Flying Dutchman* and *Tannhäuser*. They shared the same political and musical ideas and Uhlig's daughter was called Elsa after the heroine of *Lohengrin* and her brother Siegfried. One of Uhlig's letters written at the time tells a colorful tale of the part Wagner played. The letter illustrates the role of the artist in war and the cunning steps taken by Minna to remove Wagner from the action. Mention is made of the Kreuzturm – a high tower in the town that commanded a fine view over the city:

> On the Monday Wagner again sent a letter from the Kreuzturm to his wife with a request for two bottles of wine. Frau Wagner became alarmed and asked the messenger whether Wagner was by himself

---

89. Richard Wagner Museum brochure, "About Richard Wagner," item 12u.
90. Viereck, *Metapolitics*, 99.
91. Köhler, *Wagner's Hitler*, 44.

up in the Kreuzturm. When this was denied and names like Bakunin were mentioned, she sent neither wine nor tobacco but a letter that Wagner should come home at once, otherwise she would leave him. At once Wagner abandoned his observation post and returned to his house where his wife kept him imprisoned through a wise concealment of the door key.[92]

Ever the emotional witness to life, the composer expresses his feelings while in the midst of a war. While in the watchtower as described above Wagner felt a "spiritual intoxication" of ecstasy and "experienced a strange sense of extravagant delight in playing with something so serious."[93]

Wagner attempted to reform opera in Dresden, and overthrow law and order. Furthermore he kept watch while under fire from Prussian sharpshooters from the tower of the Church of the Cross and passed on messages to the accused Röckel. In addition Wagner and Röckel incited the Saxon troops to desert and fight against the Prussians. "Are you with us against these foreign troops?" Wagner asked in a pamphlet he distributed. August Röckel was found guilty by the court of treason and was sentenced to death by firing squad. Kirchmeyer said, "That Wagner would have been sentenced to death, if they had captured him, may be considered certain."[94]

When the Prussian troops crushed the uprising, a warrant was issued for his arrest and he fled from Germany, winding up with Franz Liszt in Weimar who gave him money and a false, expired passport. Weimar was named the cultural capital of Europe in 1799 and had a rich tradition of music and literature – associated proudly with Goethe, Schiller, Liszt and Bach, who had all lived there. Was it intentional that the awful extermination camp at Buchenwald was established in the vicinity?[95] From Weimar Wagner beat a hasty retreat to Paris in June 1849 where he skulked in hiding for some nervous months. On one occasion he bumped into his old enemy Meyerbeer in Schlesinger's music shop in the city. That his hatred of the Jews had not abated was clear from his description of the new owner. He

---

92. Poliakov, *History of Anti-Semitism from Voltaire to Wagner*, 560. For an account of Wagner's part in the revolt including a sketch of one of the hand grenades see the Richard Wagner Museum brochure, "About Richard Wagner," para. 12.
93. Viereck, *Metapolitics*, 100.
94. Richard Wagner Museum brochure, "About Richard Wagner," item 12l.
95. Guzelimian, *Parallels and Paradoxes: Daniel Barenboim and Edward W. Said*, 6.

called the successor who had been appointed "a much more pronounced type of Jew named Brandus, of very dirty appearance." Wagner maintained his rival had been hiding behind a screen to avoid seeing him because of "his guilty conscience at his intrigues in Berlin." Wagner went to draw him out and found him at a loss for words and left the music shop in high dudgeon. "I had had enough after my strange encounter with this strange apparition."[96]

The financial success of his rival rankled and the barometer of his jealous outrage rose to dangerous heights. In November of the same year he wrote to a Dresden friend: "in recent decades under the money influence of Meyerbeer, the condition of opera in Paris has become so ruinously horrible that it is useless for an honest man to devote himself to it…Meyerbeer holds everything in his hand, that is, in his money-bag."[97] Wagner was back in Paris after a brief visit to Zurich in January 1850 when he stormed emotionally out of a performance of Meyerbeer's new opera *Le Prophète*.[98]

He moved then to Zurich in Switzerland and to his great regret was unable to attend the first performance of *Lohengrin* at Weimar, given by Liszt on August 28, 1850. There is a sad account of Wagner staring silently from his exile in Switzerland, imagining every note as it was played. Liszt wrote about the performance: "your *Lohengrin* is a sublime work from one end to the other: the tears have come into my eyes at many a passage. As a pious churchman underlines word by word the whole Imitation of Christ, I may easily come to the point of underlining note by note your *Lohengrin*."[99]

Wagner says he escaped to further the struggle outside Saxony; but if the truth were told he deserted his friends Bakunin, Röckel and others to rot in jail. Flight saved Wagner from execution and the musical heritage survived, alongside the tawdry philosophy.

At that time his political views would have pleased the left wing radicals of Europe. He managed to mix a heady broth of pseudo-socialism, anti-French hatred and anarchism: "What actually is the essence of socialism? Its sole content is to eliminate luxury and want. There is no longer any other movement than the radical social movement…I do not believe in

---

96. Rose, *Wagner: Race and Revolution*, 75.
97. Ibid., 76.
98. Ibid.
99. Beckett, *Liszt*, 42.

any revolution that does not begin with the burning down of Paris. Strong nerves will be needed and only real men will survive. Let us see how we shall find ourselves after this fire-cure. Our saviour destroys everything that is in our way with lighting speed. I only know that the next storm will surpass all the preceding ones just to the same degree as the revolution of 1848 surpassed all the expectations of 1847."

Wagner was beginning to sound like Karl Marx and yet he was mortally offended when the revolutionary referred to him as the "government bandmaster." In a strange turn of events their paths were to cross, albeit somewhat tangentially some quarter century later, when his career had been resurrected, thanks to a most improbable sponsor. In later life he was to spend large sums of money on satins and ribbons – so much so that it provoked copious literature from psychologists attempting to divine his sexuality. But the times were different in 1848 – idealism was in the air and his empty stomach provoked a poem entitled *Want*. It was a clarion call to the proletariat to liberate themselves and take down the capitalist classes.

> *Those who lived on the toil of others are now without wealth –*
> *They must learn to find their daily bread and*
> *Want shall be their teacher.*
> *For though all be ruin, life will spring anew;*
> *Humanity is freed of chains;*
> *Nature and man are restored – as one!*
> *What separated them is destroyed!*
> *The dawn of liberty has been kindled by – Want!*

Not that everything he said or wrote was couched in ringing socialist metaphors – his sharp tongue also engaged the hypocrisy of the churches when he accused the Sabbath Christians of never stinking when they fart! His writings at that time also included attacks against wealth and avarice, leavened as always by an unhealthy dose of anti-Semitism. A theme that he was to return to in his regeneration writings was touched on in those early days – to emancipate humanity he demanded the abolition of money, which he described as a "demoniac idea."[100]

Despite this attack on money he was never averse to sponging off

---

100. Viereck, *Metapolitics*, 101.

anyone and his letters are replete with examples of the most shameless begging. Wagner needed his creaturely comforts – soft materials, perfumes and fancy living quarters were luxuries he felt he deserved. A disarming honesty characterized his acknowledgement of these vices and he explained in a letter to Liszt in 1854 what he needed to create his art. In a sense he was arguing the case for state sponsorship of musicians or extreme license in the depredations he made on his friends' goodwill and pockets. "I cannot live like a dog; I cannot sleep on straw and drink bad whisky. I must be coaxed in one way or another if my mind is to accomplish the terribly difficult task of creating a non-existing world."[101]

---

101. Poliakov, *History of Anti-Semitism from Voltaire to Wagner*, 431.

Chapter five
Full-Blown Racism

After his flight from Dresden Wagner was to present no new works for the next fifteen years. Until 1858 he lived in Zurich, composing, writing treatises, and conducting the rather inadequate orchestra there. This was a period of deep introspection and for a while prose predominated. Not that he was ever idle; his feverish mind ransacked the public libraries where he plundered the Siegfried legend and the Norse myths to create the libretto for a new music drama, *Siegfried's Death*. The gestation period that was to see the birth of his greatest work – the Ring cycle – had begun. Social and artistic revolution next engaged his fermenting mind and he produced his basic prose works: *Art and Revolution*, *The Art Work of the Future*, *A Communication to My Friends*, and *Opera and Drama*.

The second-mentioned work he dedicated to Ludwig Feuerbach, who had endeared himself to the composer with his theory that true immortality was only possible through a noble deed or a spirit-infused work of art. In the second to last of the essays he planned to produce the Ring cycle at a festival in the future. "At a festival intended solely for that purpose I hope one day to perform these three dramas with a prologue in the course of three days with a preliminary evening."[1] Gone was the old form with arias,

---

1. Richard Wagner Museum brochure, "About Richard Wagner," item 13l.

duets, trios and choruses – Wagner was working on a new, revolutionary type of musical stage work. Music would never be the same again.

In his essay on *Opera and Drama* he developed his ideas about a return to the Greek drama as the public expression of national human aspirations in symbolic form. Woven into that ancient ideal was a new theme: by enacting racial myths and using music not as entertainment or pleasure but for the full expression of the dramatic action, the complete artwork was born.

But it was not "all work and no play" for the adventurer. In a telling remark Wagner once explained how the creative process was accomplished. "Mine is a highly susceptible, intense, voracious sensuality, which must somehow or other be flattered if my mind is to accomplish the agonising labour of calling a non-existent world into being."[2] Jessie Taylor had lived for a while in Dresden with Frau Ritter, mother of Wagner's great friend Karl, and had attended the first performance of *Tannhäuser* in 1845. The beautiful musically talented woman had met Wagner in 1848 when she was nineteen years of age. Wagner wrote that she had shyly expressed her admiration for him "in a way I had never experienced before. It was with a strange new sensation that I parted with this young friend…I experienced again that sympathetic tone that came as it were out of an old sympathetic past."[3] A lovely ally in the creative process had been identified.

Nietzsche later identified the fascination that women had for Wagner. "Wagner is bad for youths; he is fatal for women" he said in *The Case of Wagner* (1888). He developed this theme in identifying an adoration bordering on parasitism in them. He also saw dangers for Wagner himself. "The danger for artists, of geniuses…lies in women; adoring women are their ruin. Hardly one of them has character enough not to be corrupted – 'saved' – when he finds himself being treated as a god…in many cases of womanly love, and perhaps precisely in the most famous, love is merely a more refined parasitism, a creeping into the being of a strange soul. Sometimes even of a strange body, and ah! at what expense always to the 'host'!"[4]

Jessie was a fellow student of Hans von Bülow, who was to marry

---

2. Cooke, Deryck, "The Symbolism of *Parsifal*," notes to Philips recording, 13.
3. Newman, *Wagner as Man and Artist*, 55.
4. Newman, *Life of Richard Wagner*, vol. 4, 327.

Cosima Liszt, and the following year she had married Eugene Laussot, a wine merchant. The Laussots and the Ritters conceived of a plan to pay Wagner an allowance to permit him to compose without hindrance. At the time he was working on the prose draft of a libretto of *Wieland the Smith* that was to be taken over by a most prestigious follower with a Charlie Chaplin moustache and an insatiable appetite for power and racial purity sixty years later.

In March 1850 Wagner was invited by the Laussots to spend time in Bordeaux and he and the lovely Jessie shared a lot in common as she was cultured and musical. A passionate affair seems to have developed. Wagner's description is apt. "I soon discovered the gulf which separated myself, as well as her, from her mother and her young husband. While that handsome young man was attending to his business for the greater part of the day, and the mother's deafness generally excluded her from most of our conversations, our animated exchange of ideas upon many important matters soon led to great confidence between us. It was inevitable that we should soon feel the people around us irksome to us in our conversation."

"The great confidence" as the composer so slyly described his passionate affair, soon spawned grandiose plans of an elopement together. He felt he ought to tell his wife of the latest developments as she still hoped for reconciliation. The letter written by Wagner to his wife was duplicity personified. "I am on the point of taking an English boat to Malta and thereafter to Greece and the East. I have gained a new protector, one of the most eminent English lawyers, who in return for cession of the rights to my works will give me his support." The "eminent English lawyer" was the father of Jessie Laussot, who had been dead for some years! His daughter and Wagner had made plans to elope to Greece and Turkey. Wagner wrote to his wife Minna to tell her the marriage was over.

In a letter to Frau Ritter he spoke of "a love of which I shall never be ashamed, and which, even if bodily dead, will perhaps fill me to my dying day with the gladdest memories and an afterglow of happiness."[5] He went on to reveal a passion that was to find its finest articulation in *Tristan und Isolde* – "to the god of love we dedicated ourselves and despised all the idols of this miserable world…had you seen the jubilation of love that broke through from every nerve of the rich-souled woman as she not so much

---

5. Newman, *Life of Richard Wagner*, vol. 2, 149.

confessed as let me see, through herself, through the involuntary, clear and naked revelation of love, that she was mine!"[6]

In his Ring cycle Fricka says of her husband Wotan, "Your faithful wife you've always betrayed; down in the caverns, high on the mountains, your glance searched and lusted for love, where your raving fancy might lead you."[7] Jessie confided in her mother, who told her husband (Eugene) who then threatened to shoot Wagner. The composer then rather lost interest. Always a bad loser, he was rather scathing about her decision to remain with her husband: "the woman who wanted to bring me redemption proved herself to be a child."[8]

Wagner wrote in describing the failure of his elopement with Jessie: "He is mine who rebels through the power of love, though rebellion spell his ruin. And, if this love be for me, then it could only content me if it worked my ruin as well." The episode means little in the great scheme of things but shows a philanderer and a man with a passion for life and women. What is of greater interest is what subsequent biographers, under the influence of his second wife Cosima, would make of the episode that threatened to darken the image of the great man.

By 1852 he had added to the poem of *Siegfried's Death* three others to precede it, the whole being called *The Ring of the Nibelungs*, *Das Rheingold*; *The Valkyries*; *Siegfried* and *Götterdämmerung*. Continuing his socialist views he foresaw the disappearance of opera as artificial entertainment for the elite and the emergence of a new kind of musical stage work for the people. "Music drama" was born with a continuous vocal-symphonic texture, woven from basic thematic ideas, which Wagner called "motifs" (motives). Arising naturally as expressive vocal or orchestral phrases they would be developed by the orchestra as "memories" to express the reappearance of the motif or for further dramatic and psychological development.

Opera would never be the same again. The complete artwork had been created – a vast tapestry of interwoven themes, richly overlaid with the harmonies that a composer at the peak of his powers commanded. Writing to his niece Klärchen in 1854 he described his vision in apocalyptic terms: "…with the Nibelungen it will be different; this I am writing not for the

---

6. Ibid., 149.
7. Wagner, Richard, *The Ring of the Nibelungs*, German text with English translation by Andrew Porter. Faber Paperbacks, 1977, 100.
8. Richard Wagner Museum brochure, "About Richard Wagner," item 14u.

theatre but – for us! But I will perform it anyway: I have set this for myself as the only and last goal of my life. I will build the stage for it myself, and I will educate my performers myself; how many years it costs me does not matter to me, if I only achieve it some day. After the performance I will throw myself with the score on Brünnhilde's pyre, so that everything will be burned up…"[9] Death by fire was a theme that caught the imagination of Hitler as a youth, when he prophesied his own career path, and it would finally be the weapon of choice when his end came in Berlin, with the full arsenal of Russian artillery to provide the musical accompaniment.

Apart from the prose and political writings, and these became more rabid and fanatical as time went on, the anti-Semitism also infiltrated the art. Normally it matters little that artists lead dissolute lives or espouse outlandish views. It is often expected of them. Paul Johnson echoed these sentiments in his book *Intellectuals* when he argued that you couldn't entirely separate the private and public works of writers, who put forward proposals to transform the nature and condition of mankind. Mention has been made of the remarks of Nietzsche concerning the relevance of ideological views that are central to the art. Unfortunately the philosophy of Wagner did not remain supplementary and it plays such a central role in his last opera *Parsifal* and the mighty tetralogy *The Ring of the Nibelungs* that the works *themselves* do not escape the charge of anti-Semitism.

In order to properly appreciate the significance of the political and racist views of the Ring cycle it is necessary to consider in the barest outline the tale that unfolds in *Das Rheingold*. It commences in the depths of the river Rhine. In music depicting the beginning of time and the slow march from innocence to sin the great chords of E flat deep down in the double basses portray three lovely Rhine maidens swimming around. They are guarding the Rhinegold that is glistening in the depths. Slowly one by one the music motifs are introduced to represent characters, emotions and objects. One of the first to establish itself is the motif depicting the Rhinegold.

Throughout the tetralogy of the *Ring of the Nibelungs* these themes are interwoven like some great tapestry. The Rhine maidens are naked and free and are singing a beautiful song. Their breasts are whiter than snow and their nipples are a wonderful Nordic pink – Aryan nipples no doubt.

---

9. Ibid., item 14l.

They are so happy, these creatures of the deep: Woglinde, Flosshilde and Wellgunde.

Alberich the Nibelung, a horrid-looking man, is looking lustfully at them and they are teasing him. What is this gold that the Rhine maidens are guarding so zealously? Any person who turns the gold into a ring will be master of the world. There is one prerequisite to achieve world domination – whoever fashions the gold into a ring must foreswear love. The chances of Alberich foreswearing love seem to be pretty slim given his reckless pursuit of the maidens. The water boils with his unavailing attempts at satisfying his concupiscence.

But the maidens are teasing poor Alberich who determines to foreswear love as no one returns his affections. One by one he makes overtures to the slippery creatures who elude his lustful grasp. Their scorn at his unavailing grappling finds its expression in their girlish laughter. Alberich fails to seduce the Rhine maidens but steals the gold. Piqued and frustrated beyond endurance, Alberich the Nibelung shakes his stubby fist and raising his hoarse nasal voice he foreswears love. With the aid of his Nibelung blacksmith brother Mime he makes the ring of absolute power and the rest of the cycle describes the machinations of the gods, especially Wotan, to regain it.

Mention has been made of Wagner's views in his article on "Jewry in Music" that society's body was dead and the Jews lodged in it like a swarm of insects. The same ghastly image emerges when he describes the Nibelungs in his music dramas. The main Nibelung characters in *Das Rheingold* are Alberich and his brother Mime, whom he described as follows in the sketch of 1848: "Out of the womb of night and death there came into being a race dwelling in Nibelheim, i.e., in gloomy subterranean clefts and caverns. They are known as the Nibelungs, feverishly, unrestingly they burrow through the bowels of the earth *like worms in a dead body*. They anneal and smelt and smith hard metals."

Alberich, a gnomelike creature, is the dominant Nibelung and the Rhine maiden Flosshilde describes him in the following terms: "Oh your piercing gaze, your bristly beard, your wiry hair, your toad-like form, your croaking voice…" Barry Millington, author of the *Master Musicians* volume on Wagner (J.M. Dent, 1984), pointed out that in describing the Jew in his article on "Jewry in Music" Wagner uses exactly the same terminology. Mahler, himself a Jew, recognized Mime as a caricature of the Jew. In his

Karl Hill as the Nibelung Alberich in the first Ring cycle in Bayreuth in 1876. Wagner insisted on this character wearing a long black beard to portray the Jewish stereotype. In this regard see the photograph on page 369 of the exhibition in Berlin. The goal of this anti-Semitic show was to teach Germans how to identify Jews. See Barth et al., 219. Photograph by Joseph Albert, Bayreuth, 1876.

biography of Mahler, Henry-Louis de La Grange quotes the great composer as follows: "No doubt with Mime Wagner intended to ridicule the Jews (with all their characteristic traits – petty intelligence and greed – the jargon is textually and musically so cleverly suggested)..."[10] Mahler went on to say that the Jewishness of the role should never be overdone and even suggested that he himself could have played the part to perfection. "But for God's sake it must not be exaggerated and overdone as Julius Spielmann does it...I know of only one Mime and that is myself...you wouldn't believe what there is in that part, nor what I could make of it."[11]

In a masterpiece of musicological detection a French Wagner

---

10. See Cooke, *I Saw the World End*.
11. Solomon, "Wagner and Hitler," 2.

scholar – Jean-Jacques Nattiez – suggested that Flosshilde's music in *Das Rheingold* when she sings to Alberich is a parody on a Meyerbeer melody. The articles and venomous letters were insufficient to satiate the composer's desire for vengeance against his old rival; Wagner was now using his art to attack his *bête noire*. There are other indications that he intended Alberich and Mime to be portrayed as Jews. In his directions for performances of the *Ring*, Wagner desired the Nibelungs to speak a sort of Jewish German (Yiddish) and the overall impression is that Wotan and his family, the gods in the Ring cycle, are of Aryan stock and racially superior to the Nibelungs.[12]

Adorno and Edward Said conclude that Mime and Beckmesser in *Meistersinger* are caricatures of Jews although as characters they do not purport to be Jewish. "Wagner uses Jewish caricatures to represent characters who themselves are not Jewish."[13] Marc Weiner has recorded that Jews who witnessed productions at that time immediately seized upon what they believed to be their invidious representation by Wagner, especially after his freshly published essay "Judaism in Music" in 1850. They rose up in protest when they identified Wagner's Beckmesser as a mocking depiction of Jews at the premiere performances of *Meistersinger* in Vienna and Mannheim.[14]

Wagner wrote to Liszt on February 11, 1853 and drew an analogy between the story in the *Ring* and the downfall of the Jews. "Would that I could perish in the flames of Valhalla! Take heed of my words – they embrace both the creation and the destruction of the world! I shall soon set about composing the work for the Jews of Frankfurt and Leipzig – it is designed entirely with them in mind!"[15]

Any doubt about the correct interpretation of the mighty Ring cycle as a battle between good (the Aryans) and evil (the Jews) was removed in 1881 when he was to explain it to King Ludwig II of Bavaria as the "most Aryan work of art imaginable. No people on earth has ever had its origins and its national character demonstrated with such clarity."[16] The Walsungs – Siegmund, Sieglinde and their incestuous son Siegfried – have

---

12. Gutman, *Richard Wagner*, 235.
13. Guzelimian, *Parallels and Paradoxes: Daniel Barenboim and Edward W. Said*, 96–97.
14. Weiner, *Richard Wagner and the Anti-Semitic Imagination*, 123.
15. Köhler, *Wagner's Hitler*, 298.
16. Ibid., 61.

Friend and financial supporter of Wagner, the famous composer Abbe Fransz Liszt. Barth et al., 88. Oil painting by Miklọs Barabas 1846, National Gallery, Budapest.

the pure Aryan blood, of course, and the first mentioned Siegmund specifically calls out in the opera *The Valkyries* for the blood of the family to be perpetuated.[17]

In his essay "Know Thyself" Wagner wrote:

> [I]f the Jew comes tinkling with his bell of paper [money], (our nation) throws its savings at his feet, and makes him in one night a millionaire.... Clever though be the many thoughts expressed by mouth or pen about the invention of money and its enormous value as a civiliser, against such praises should be set the curse to which it has always

17. Ibid.

been doomed in song and legend. If gold here figures as the demon strangling manhood's innocence, our greatest poet shows at last the goblin's game of paper money. The Nibelung's fateful ring has become a pocket-book, and might well complete the eerie picture of the spectral world-controller. By the advocates of our Progressive Civilisation this rulership is indeed regarded as a spiritual, nay, a moral power; for vanished Faith is now replaced by "Credit," that fiction of our mutual honesty kept upright by the most elaborate safeguards against loss and trickery. What comes to pass beneath the benediction of this Credit we now are witnessing, and seem inclined to lay all blame upon the Jews. They certainly are virtuosi in an art at which we but bungle.

There will always be those with a different view. Dieter Borchmeyer was to write in the last decade of the twentieth century, despite a plethora of reliable authority to the contrary, that:

[I]n all of Wagner's innumerable commentaries on his own works, there is not a single statement which would entitle us to interpret any of the characters in the music dramas or any of the details of their plots in anti-Semitic terms, or even to interpret them as allusions to the Jews. The attempt to interpret the Nibelungs, and especially the figure of Mime, as mythic projections of the Jews – an interpretation based on Wagner's description of the physical appearance and speech patterns of Jews in his 1850 essay – is no more than an unverifiable hypothesis.[18]

Wagner's embodiment of his racial views in his music works illustrated the depths of his passion. The war between him and Meyerbeer continued albeit more sporadically. In the fall of 1852, during the creation of the *Rhinegold* poem, Belloni, Liszt's secretary, sought out Wagner to discuss a French premiere of *Tannhäuser*. Wagner thought highly of the French tenor Roger and mentions in a letter to his niece Franziska "that the possibilities of a really good performance" would have an additional advantage of a tilt against his old foe. "What attracts me…in addition is the prospect of a

---

18. Borchmeyer, Dieter, "The Question of Anti-Semitism," in *Wagner Handbook*, Ulrich Müller and Peter Wapnewski, eds. (Boston: Harvard University Press, 1992), 183.

terrific and yet momentous and uncommonly successful fight with Meyerbeer – call it malice if you like."[19]

All of this would be possible, Wagner continues, if his niece Johanna (her sister) "would enter the lists for me energetically and completely emancipate herself from Meyerbeer." Wagner's brother Albert informed him of a possible contract binding Johanna to sing Meyerbeer operas *exclusively*. Anything more likely to kindle the old flames of resentment is difficult to imagine. In this case it was the spark that lit the powderkeg of his rage. He writes to Albert that it is a great sorrow that Johanna, "who means so much to me, should have to sell herself to the greedy Jew; she could surely have found a nobler task for her youthful powers than sacrifice herself to that rotting carcass."[20] After discussions with Liszt they concluded that the time was not ripe.

There were difficulties with the project as a campaign had been under way in the Paris press for some time against Wagner. Belloni believed Meyerbeer to have been behind the contemptuous comments of the critic Fetis in a pamphlet serialized in the *Gazette Musicale* during the summer. It accused Wagner of creating by system rather than inspiration – a reprise of the criticisms leveled at Meyerbeer by Schumann, Weber and Wagner himself. The wheel had come full circle. In his autobiography we are left in no doubt as to what Wagner believed the true position to be; he states emphatically that Meyerbeer bribed Fetis to write articles against him.[21] Clearly Meyerbeer was seeking vengeance for the attack on him.

Despite the animosity that subsequently developed between the two composers Wagner learned much from Meyerbeer's instrumentation, which had been highly praised by the composer Gevaert. We cannot dismiss the caustic comment of the German composer that the scoring was so highly developed so that it would camouflage a poverty of musical thought; posterity has borne out the truth of the assertion. In other respects Wagner acknowledged the influence of Giacomo Meyerbeer – the organization of the opera in Paris became an example for Wagner for Bayreuth and the realism in décor inspired by Ciceri, designer of *Robert le Diable*, became the Bayreuth ideal.[22]

---

19. Newman, *Life of Richard Wagner*, vol. 2, 319.
20. Ibid.
21. Newman, *Wagner as Man and Artist*, 8 note.
22. Gutman, *Richard Wagner*, 113.

During a journey through Italy he went to La Spezia where he fell into a feverish illness. "I succumbed to a trance-like condition in which I suddenly had the emotion as though I were sinking into rapidly flowing water. Soon the rushing sound of this water was transmuted in my ears into the musical sound of an E flat major chord…the orchestral prelude to Rheingold."[23] The origins are somewhat more prosaic and eclectic – in all probability plain plagiarism. Wagner must have been dreaming of the opening bars of Mendelssohn's overture *The Fair Melusina* with "their remarkable foretaste of Wagner's Rhine music in *The Ring of the Nibelungs*."[24]

In 1855 Wagner set sail for England to conduct a set of subscription concerts at the invitation of the Philharmonic Society.[25] One member of the small German community there was Ferdinand Praeger who was later to write a book about the composer. Little was known about the composer in that country as his notorious anti-Semitic polemics, including the infamous "Jewry in Music," had not yet been translated. A piano reduction of the march from *Tannhäuser* – the notion of that inadequate medium for music of that majesty boggles the mind – had become known in England, and Londoners had heard the real thing played by their most prestigious orchestra. J.W. Davison, the music correspondent of *The Times*, had struggled with the daring of the new music and exclaimed, "such queer stuff that criticism would be thrown away upon it…so much fuss about nothing, such a pompous and empty commonplace has seldom been heard."[26]

Establishing himself amongst the expatriate Germans Wagner soon lost his initial enthusiasm for the place and told Liszt "I live here like a damned soul in hell." His grasp of English social manners was miniscule and he arrived at violinist Prosper Sainton's house at 9:00 A.M. in full evening tails![27] He refused to pay the usual courtesy calls on the critics let alone present the gifts – so-called "puffs preliminary" and "puffs direct" – to ensure favorable reviews. Although excerpts from his works were not well received – Davison called them "wild, senseless dabbling" – his conducting of the traditional symphonies was praised as "invariably intellectual and frequently beautiful."

---

23. Gal, *Richard Wagner*, 55.
24. Radcliffe, *Mendelssohn*, 115.
25. Christiansen, "Kultur Clash," A1.
26. Ibid.
27. Ibid.

Fortunately the poverty of his English spared him the former comments though he wrote to Otto Wesendonck – of whom (especially his lovely wife Mathilde) more in a moment – and said he found it impossible to "imagine anything more repugnant than the genuine Englishman."[28] He went on to elaborate on their penchant for the trough rather than the aesthetic delights of his own music. "Without exception they are all like sheep, and the Englishman's practical intelligence is about as reliable as a sheep's instinct for finding its food in the open fields; of course, it finds its food, but the whole of the beautiful fields and the blue sky above might as well not exist, such are its organs of perception."[29] So, who said his venom was exclusively directed at the Jews?

Queen Victoria and Prince Albert graced his concert on June 11 and Wagner described them in a letter to Minna: "she is not fat, but very small and not at all pretty with, I am sorry to say, a rather red nose but there is something uncommonly friendly and confiding about her – and although she is by no means imposing, she is nevertheless a delightful and kind person." The queen admired Wagner's satin trousers and her majesty requested the composer to send them to the palace so that they could be copied for Prince Albert. Less acceptable was her suggestion that his works be translated into Italian and given at the Italian Opera – Prince Albert commented to Wagner's delight that the libretti were "totally unsuited" to this treatment and that "Italian singers would have absolutely no idea how to sing them."

Wagner had a most awkward meeting with Meyerbeer, who had come over to conduct his latest opera *L'Etoile du Nord*. The two composers stared at each other in silence and their host George Hogarth was "greatly astonished," as Wagner put it, as he felt they must be acquainted. Hogarth had an additional reason to be remembered by posterity; he was Charles Dickens's father-in-law and fulfilled the posts of secretary of the Philharmonic Society and music critic of the *Illustrated London News* and the *Daily News*. Wagner urged him to ask Meyerbeer if he was acquainted with Wagner and when they met later in the evening Hogarth said that the former had spoken of Wagner "in terms of the warmest appreciation." Wagner then suggested Hogarth read certain reports in the Paris *Gazette*

---

28. Ibid.
29. Ibid.

Musicale in which Meyerbeer spoke in less charitable terms. Hogarth shook his head, puzzled as to "how two such great composers could meet in so strange a manner." If only he knew. Meyerbeer's diary recorded the meeting as follows: "Met also Richard Wagner. We greeted each other coldly without speaking."[30]

Wagner was a less than honorable man in many respects but he would never flatter or bribe the critics. The English critic Davison was used to being courted and snuffboxes, diamond pins and cuff links came his way from composers, including Berlioz and Meyerbeer. Sycophancy was second nature to the last mentioned, who wrote to Davison at that time "expressing deep gratitude for his admirable article" on a performance of one of his operas, which went much further than splendid journalism; it constituted what the French composer called a "second creation." Meyerbeer carried on, "you would double my obligation to you if you kindly accept the accompanying little souvenir, continue your valued friendship for me and remember me to the charming Madame Davison."[31]

Wagner also suffered the ultimate indignity of being at the receiving end of a decision of the House of Lords that deprived foreign composers of copyright in any work that had not been written for or in England. When he arrived he was greeted with a pirated version of the great Tannhäuser March, which had been produced in piano version and then orchestrated by a local hack musician![32] He also incensed the Mendelssohn clique who found every sort of excuse to criticize his music or his lifestyle. Not only had his music earned the displeasure of the rival faction, but also his uncanny ability to memorize whole works. The final straw was the accusation that no conductor worthy of his salt should conduct Beethoven's symphonies by heart![33] But then they were dealing with a special sort of genius and a foe of limitless energy. Wagner made no money on the tour to speak of – less than £40 – and vowed that the expensiveness of the place rendered the experience one he would never repeat. But he returned twenty-two years later and to a very different reception.[34]

He struggled on and put the galling English adventure behind him.

---

30. Newman, *Life of Richard Wagner*, vol. 2, 458.
31. Ibid., 467.
32. Ibid., 474.
33. Ibid., 461.
34. Ibid.

By 1857 he had progressed on the new journey to such an extent that *Das Rheingold*, *The Valkyries*, and two acts of *Siegfried* had seen the light of day. The greatest musical genius of all time was in full stride. His reading habits now took in the work of the philosopher Arthur Schopenhauer and he was submerged in the dark world of yearning, so well portrayed in the depressing message of metaphysical pessimism. On the positive side the philosopher had been a pioneer in the power of the libido. It should not be forgotten that Freud himself regarded Schopenhauer as a precursor of his own theories; as he said, "Arthur Schopenhauer, the philosopher, showed mankind the extent to which their activities are determined by sexual impulses – in the ordinary sense of the word."[35]

The outcome of Wagner's indulgences in the pessimistic sexual underworld of Schopenhauer on the physical side was an affair with Mathilde Wesendonck and on the artistic side was *Tristan und Isolde* (1857–59), the hymn to love, which portrayed another adulterous relationship. So impressed was the philosopher with the libretto of the work that Schopenhauer maintained that Wagner was destined to be a poet and should give up composing music!

During the composition of what Hitler reckoned was Wagner's greatest work, Wagner met Otto and Mathilde Wesendonck. Otto was a very successful businessman and the artful sponger soon gained an interest not only in the seemingly bottomless pits of Wesendonck's pockets but the tender heart of his wife. Mathilde helped console Wagner in exile for the loss of his fatherland and the absence of his wife Minna. So much had he insinuated his way into the heart of the loving wife that he persuaded Otto to build him a cottage – the *Asyl* ("the Refuge") – on the property. While he was there he received tragic news from Dresden – the conductor of the city's orchestra and his erstwhile great friend and coconspirator in the 1848 revolution, August Röckel, was sentenced to death and was lucky to have the sentence commuted to fourteen years of imprisonment.

Although her talents have never been reckoned as more than those of a dilettante, Mathilde wrote a number of poems, which Wagner set to music and these settings became studies for his opera *Tristan und Isolde*. The theme of the opera – the yearning for a woman who belongs to another – was appropriate and the relationship between the two ripened into

---

35. Freud, *On Sexuality*, 43.

a deep passion. Although Wagner claimed that Mathilde was his soul mate and that they explored a spiritual world, the evidence – particularly that provided by the passionate score – seems to point to sexual intercourse having taken place. Apart from the subliminal text of racism in the operas, after a series of fascinating explorations, musicologists were to find proof of infidelity hidden in the music.

Apart from the penetrating message of the subconscious through the music, the physical score of *Tristan*, and indeed, the first act of *The Valkyries*, is full of cryptic code letters. "G.s.M" means *Gesegnet sei Mathilde*, that is, "Blessed be Mathilde," and other letters when decoded reveal more. When Siegmund and Sieglinde gaze lovingly at each other he writes, "were it not for thee, beloved" and adds later, "I love you infinitely." Ironically enough, Sigmund Freud was to portray music as the sublimation of unfulfilled sexual desire. It would seem in this case that the desire was anything but unfulfilled.

In *Tristan* an alleged friend of the hero by the name of Melot betrays him to King Marke, the betrothed of Isolde. His own hand betrayed Wagner – he sent a copy of act 1 of *Tristan* with a passionate letter to Mathilde hidden in the leaves of the score. Minna, who had long since suspected that the passion in the score was being duplicated in the home of the Wesendoncks, intercepted the letter and flew into a fury. The composer tried to explain that it was all a total misunderstanding. Minna, according to Wagner, totally misconstrued his purely friendly relations with Mathilde, whose only interest in him was her solicitude for his peace of mind and well-being.

The letter has survived and excerpts reveal the passion the two enjoyed. Wagner occupied a separate part of the *Asyl* from his wife Minna, since they were not on particularly good terms at the time, and this apparently left him free for visits from his benefactor Otto Wesendonck's wife. "The day before yesterday at noon an angel came up to me who blessed and nurtured me…[He speaks of the torture he feels at not being able to see her because of a visitor she has received that evening.] In the morning I was rational again, and from the depth of my heart could pray to my angel: and this prayer is Love. Love! Deepest soul's joy in this love, the source of my redemption! Thus my whole day was a struggle between melancholy and longing for you…"

Into this maelstrom of emotional conflict arrived Hans von Bülow

*The conductor and musician Hans von Bülow, Gregor-Dellin, page 85.
Nationalarchiv der Richard Wagner-Stiftung/Richard Wagner Gedenkstätte, Bayreuth.*

and his young wife Cosima, destined to be Wagner's next spouse.[36] Cosima came from illustrious parents. Her father was Franz Liszt and her mother was the Countess Marie d'Agoult, who wrote under the pseudonym Daniel Stern. Marie's position in Parisian society in the 1840s had earned respect from every quarter. In 1827 she contracted a marriage of convenience with Colonel Charles d'Agoult, twenty years her senior. She had early shown strength of will and enthusiasm for justice and freedom, and her marriage disappointed her expectations. Meeting Franz Liszt, she decided in 1834 to run away with him. Their relationship lasted till 1839, when Liszt felt that his musical career prevented a settled life. Their separation became permanent in 1844.

Returning to Paris in 1839, Marie began her career as a writer and in 1846 published a largely autobiographical novel, *Nélida*. She was a close

---

36. Marek, *Cosima Wagner*, 33.

friend of George Sand, whose views on morals, politics and society she shared and in whose house she had lived for a time with Liszt. She also became the leader of a salon where the ideas which culminated in the Revolution of 1848 were discussed by the outstanding writers, thinkers and musicians of the day.[37] Three years after Liszt's separation from Marie he fell in love with Princess Carolyne Sayn-Wittgenstein, wife of a Russian prince. They apparently expressed both extreme religiosity and passion by making love under a ten-foot cross, suspended over their vast double bed![38]

Cosima was one of three daughters born to the hectic liaison between Liszt and Marie. According to Peter Cornelius, a close friend of Liszt, "Bülow's marriage to Cosima was a sacrifice of friendship he made to his master, Liszt, to give a brilliant and honourable name to the natural child and, hence, profound reassurance to the father."[39] While visiting the Wagners Cosima determined to end her life and asked her friend Karl Ritter to kill her. He was also the victim of an unhappy marriage and planned to commit suicide with her.[40] Nothing came of their plans. Cosima was to write to her daughter in later years, "how it came that we got married I still do not know."[41]

The von Bülows arrived to stay with the Wagners as the Wesendonck affair reached its zenith and soon thereafter Richard left for Venice and Minna for Dresden. Writing to his sister Klara, Wagner abandoned the mendacity that characterized his utterances to his wife and described the nature of his feelings. "For six long years it was the love of that young woman that kept me going."[42] After composing part of *Meistersinger* he wrote to Mathilde and explained what she meant to him in the context of the wonderful main character of the opera, Hans Sachs. "Keep hold of your emotions when it comes to Sachs, or you will fall in love with him…*One*

---

37. Her own writings included *Lettres républicaines* (1848); *Histoire de la révolution de 1848* (1850–53); a play, *Jeanne d'Arc* (1857); a dialogue, *Dante et Goethe* (1866); and *Mes Souvenirs 1806–1833* (1877), supplemented by *Mémoires, 1833–1854* (1927), interesting for the light they throw on the social, literary and musical circles of her time.
38. Marek, *Cosima Wagner*, 11.
39. Wagner, Nike, *The Wagners*, 186.
40. Richard Wagner Museum brochure, "About Richard Wagner," item 23l.
41. Ibid.
42. Gal, *Richard Wagner*, 61.

simply must have experienced paradise to get to the true heart of such a matter."[43]

His wife had been acutely aware of the "paradise" he had been enjoying and wrote to a friend where she described him acerbically as "a pocket edition of a man, this folio of vanity, heartlessness, and egoism." With deep emotion Minna informed her friend that the relationship with Mathilde had broken up a marriage of twenty-two years. "As regards forbearance with men, I am likewise enlightened and have already overlooked a good many things, like other women. I have besides gone on being blind a good six years. It is simply impossible, for the sake of Richard's honour, to remain here since her husband – I don't know how – has also learned of the relation."

Though Mathilde was clearly an intelligent woman Wagner seldom sought intellectuality from the persons he slept with, except perhaps Jessie Laussot, with whom he had relished the exchange of ideas.[44] In any event, his subsequent dealings with Mathilde included his shock that she used hair dye.[45] Wagner later saw her at Bad Ems in June 1877 with her daughter Myrrha. Mathilde declined to attend the premiere of *Tristan* in 1865 as the biographer Robert Gutman surmised "how painful it would be for Mathilde and her circle to observe the secrets of her Zurich garden unfolding on the stage."[46]

Wagner continued writing to Mathilde from Venice where he recorded how she had "dedicated herself to death that he might live." In his diary he reminisced about taking the poem of Tristan to Mathilde and what happened. "You led me to the chair by the sofa, threw your arms around my neck and cried: 'Now I wish for nothing more!'...A sweet creature, demure and coy, plunged into a whirlpool of pain and suffering to make this wonderful moment possible and to say to me; 'I love you.'"[47] There were long periods of loneliness and despair but he regretted the separation from Mathilde, not Minna, and consoled himself with the thought "that it is still granted to me to die in your arms." The "highly susceptible, intense, voracious sensuality" of which Wagner had once written had been at work,

---

43. Ibid., 70.
44. Gutman, *Richard Wagner*, 167.
45. Ibid., 241.
46. Ibid., 349.
47. Taylor, *Richard Wagner*, 214.

Two reputed friends and lovers of Richard Wagner – Jessie Laussot and Mathilde Wesendonck. Prawy, page 192.

but bourgeois society's demand that a wife stay faithful to her husband had put an end to his inspiration.

While George Bernard Shaw was to speak of *Tristan und Isolde* as "an astonishingly intense and faithful translation into music of the emotions which accompany the union of a pair of lovers," a professor of philosophy in Prague, Christian von Ehrenfels, inventor of gestalt psychology, found that Wagner was the "most powerful eroticism yet produced on Mother Earth."[48] Musicologists claim that final proof that Wagner and Mathilde had sexual relations lies in the score of *Tristan und Isolde* where two orgasms are identified. According to Ehrenfels it is possible to point to the bars in the second act of *Tristan* "in which the orgiastic ejaculations of that night twice burst forth and detumesce."[49] So who said opera was boring?

To some at least Wagner's story was no less than an allusion to his deeply held passion.[50] The story of the star-crossed lovers, who defy social convention and make love despite Isolde being betrothed to King Marke, was mirrored in the life of the composer and his lover. In a letter to Mathilde he explained how the creative process worked. "For once you are going to

---

48. Vetter, "Wagner in the History of Psychology," 57.
49. Ibid.
50. Franklin, *Life of Mahler*, 58.

hear a dream, a dream that I have made sound…I dreamt all of this: never could my poor head have invented such a thing purposefully."

We do not know much about her responses as the letters have been lost or destroyed. Hermann Levi, the Jewish conductor, who will feature prominently in our tale, was in possession of a poem written by Mathilde, which some biographers suggest indicates her innocence.

> *I have often wanted to ask you*
> *For the highest moment*
> *But an inexplicable fear*
> *A shudder held back the word.*[51]

That Wagner's life always followed his art is a viewpoint challenged by some but affirmed by Gutman.[52] Again it will be fascinating to read what later biographers would say about this affair. Trevor-Roper records that eighty years later, buried in his snow-covered headquarters in Rastenburg, East Prussia on January 24, 1942, Hitler would comment that "*Tristan* is Wagner's masterpiece and we owe [the creation of that work] to what the love Mathilde Wesendonck inspired in him."[53]

Not that there would be universal acclamation when it finally reached the stage. When it was first produced in Munich one critic called it "the clever concoction of a diseased imagination."[54] Others praised the score and posterity ranks it with the greatest masterpieces ever written. The great German writer Thomas Mann, who was later to flee Hitler's Germany after writing an article about Wagner, was unstinting in his praise of the opera. "The *Tristan* score is a miracle. It is the work of a completely unique eruption of talent and genius, a work that is both deeply serious and beguiling, the work of a magician as spiritual as he was drunk with intellect."[55]

Rumors of the Wesendonck affair spread and even the benign Otto was enraged. Wagner completed *Tristan* in Venice and Lucerne. While there he received a letter from Hans von Bülow that was to have a rich irony, given that Wagner was to steal von Bülow's wife and marry her him-

---

51. Richard Wagner Museum brochure, "About Richard Wagner," item 15l.
52. Gutman, *Richard Wagner*, 70.
53. Trevor-Roper, *Hitler's Table Talk*, 240–41.
54. Richard Wagner Museum brochure, "About Richard Wagner," item 21u.
55. Ibid., item 15l.

self – "My wife [Cosima] is again very charming – I wish you could get to know her as she really is…but she always fears that you would consider her childish and much too insignificant to be able to love and understand you. And yet she is one of the few who are capable of that."[56] His music had been enriched by his new experiments with leading motives in *Das Rheingold* and *The Valkyries* and he had developed greater psychological complexity – the great tapestry was growing stitch by stitch.

In February 1858 an event of great significance for the future of the composer took place. At a performance of *Lohengrin* in Munich, amongst the gilded throng of operagoers, was Baroness Meilhaus, the governess of the young Crown Prince Ludwig of Bavaria. After the performance she told the wide-eyed prince the story of the swan knight, and his romantic soul was kindled with a new fire. The legend the prince had heard from his youngest days was now linked to the music of Richard Wagner and some eight years later the new king was to remember that evening with particular reverence.[57]

Ever the wanderer, in 1859 Wagner returned to Paris, where, the following year, productions of a revised version of *Tannhäuser* were a disaster. The claqueurs had a field day and opera suffered. His old campaign against the king of the Paris Opera Giacomo Meyerbeer was to count against him in the end. He was reaping the whirlwind of the anti-Semitic seeds sown years before. There was some sanity in the French capital and the fair-minded recognized the worth of the work. The French poet Baudelaire was outraged and exclaimed, "what will Europe think of us, and what will they say in Germany about Paris? This handful of ruffians gives us all a bad reputation."[58]

The wet and murky climate of a winter in Venice did his health no good and the police hounded him for a while. His requests for amnesty were refused from time to time – in 1857 and thereafter. But eventually his political sins were forgiven and in 1861 an amnesty allowed him to return to Germany. Vienna was the city where he heard *Lohengrin* for the first time and he stayed in that city for twelve months or so trying to produce *Tristan*. During this period Wagner commenced the composition of his

---

56. Ibid., item 16.
57. Taylor, *Richard Wagner*, 217.
58. Richard Wagner Museum brochure, "About Richard Wagner," item 17l.

only comedy-opera *Die Meistersinger von Nürnberg*. That masterpiece harped back in some ways to the old opera and choruses and "arias" made an appearance albeit in a new guise.

His old friend Liszt acknowledged his appreciation of the merit of Wagner's work in a most unusual place – his last will and testament – in September 1860. "In contemporary art there is a name already glorious and destined to become more so – that of Richard Wagner. His genius has been a torch to me; I have followed it, and my friendship for Wagner has preserved the character of a noble passion."[59]

---

59. Newman, *Life of Richard Wagner*, vol. 2, 528.

Chapter six
A Royal Patron

Short stays in Biebrich and Vienna saw Wagner trying to persuade Mathilde Maier and Friederike Meyer to provide the home comforts that Minna no longer could. The first mentioned was the twenty-nine-year-old daughter of a notary and wrote a letter to Wagner saying, "when I first saw you, the deeply sorrowful strain in your character made an indelible impression on me." She was a trifle too virtuous for Wagner and he appointed a servant called Marie who was more accommodating to his real needs. He wrote to her after being away for a short visit calling her his "best sweetheart" and requesting her to "…perfume the study nicely: buy the best bottles of scent so as to give it a nice odour. Ach Gott! How delighted I will be to rest again with you there. (I hope the rose-coloured pants are ready?)" That preoccupation with clothes and scent was to follow him all his days.

His request to her is quite unequivocal: "…you must be pretty and charming; I deserve to have a thoroughly good time once more…I will give you all sorts of presents my sweetheart…I leave it to you to decide whether you meet me at the station. Perhaps it will be nicer if you meet me first in the house, in the warm rooms…many kisses to my sweetheart."[1]

Man cannot live on bread alone. Friederike Meyer was an actress who accompanied Wagner to Vienna and helped to comfort him while he was

---

1. Hurn and Root, *The Truth about Wagner*, 203.

there. In a letter written at about that time he told his old friend Dr Pusinelli that he has become "conscious through sufficient and strangely flattering experiences up to the present time, that soulful feminine natures cling to me easily to the point of wildest adoration, and through this become capable of the most extreme surrender."[2]

Lest one presume that Wagner hated all Jews a correction has to be made. While in Vienna he befriended two Jews: Heinrich Porges, a writer on musical subjects from Prague, and Karl Tausig, a gifted pianist, who both helped to arrange concerts at which excerpts from his operas were played.

The financial woes continued and he sponged, spent the borrowed moneys extravagantly and was then locked up in misery. He longed for the light. As he said: "I have excitable nerves; I must have beauty, brilliance, light. The world ought to give me what I need. I cannot live in a wretched organist's post like your Meister Bach. Is it an unheard of demand if I hold that the little luxury I like is my due? – I, who am procuring enjoyment to the world and to thousands."[3]

While he had endured many troughs in the helter-skelter journey through life, this period was the worst for the composer. On January 3, 1863 he wrote a letter threatening suicide: "On May 22 I shall be fifty years old. I will go on struggling until then. If, however, by that time my constant failures have not been counterbalanced by a decisive success, I shall disappear from the world and no one shall hear any more of me." But that auspicious day came and went and the composer lived on. As a matter of fact that Christmas Wagner overwhelmed his friends with expensive gifts.[4]

Thomas Mann was to comment half a century later so poignantly about this phase of Wagner's life. "It is shameful and extremely degrading to have to fight for life in this way and to go begging, when one does not mean life at all, but its higher purpose, which lies above and beyond it: Art, Creation, for which one must fight to have peace of mind."[5]

On Good Friday in 1864 Wagner stood before a shop window in Munich and looked, deeply moved, at a portrait of the newly crowned King Ludwig II of Bavaria. The eighteen-year-old looked the picture of

---

2. Newman, *Life of Richard Wagner*, vol. 1, 200.
3. Newman, *Life of Richard Wagner*, vol. 2, 408.
4. Richard Wagner Museum brochure, "About Richard Wagner," item 19l.
5. Ibid.

young health and affluence. How different their circumstances were! With sarcastic irony Wagner composed his own epitaph which began: "Here lies Wagner who became nothing…"

A few days later he was with his friends the Willes at Mariafeld where he wrote a letter, of deep prophetic significance, to Peter Cornelius, a fellow composer, whose opera *The Barber of Baghdad* still holds the stage today. "A light must appear, someone must come who will energetically help me…a genuinely helpful miracle must happen to me or everything is lost."[6]

In the preface to the Ring poem Wagner had thrown bread on the water and written that the project of producing his sixteen-hour, four-evening music drama could never be realized without royal assistance. "Will this prince be found?" he asked somewhat rhetorically. Both requests were to be answered. From Mariafeld he fled further to avoid imprisonment for debt. His financial penury was to be resolved when he was traced to a dingy hotel room in Stuttgart. He was informed that Herr Pfistermeister, secretary to the King of Bavaria, wished to see him. Wagner, fearing that his creditors had finally caught up with him – they had used countless ingenious stratagems to serve court processes on him on previous occasions – sent down word that he was out and commenced hurriedly packing. Frantically he searched for a rear exit to facilitate his escape.

Pfistermeister boldly knocked on the door, strode in and on seeing the discomfort on Wagner's face, informed him that he had already unavailingly sought the composer at Penzing and Mariafeld. Pfistermeister had been instructed by the King of Bavaria His Majesty King Ludwig II to give Wagner a ring and photograph of his majesty. Wagner stood open-mouthed and for once words failed him. Pfistermeister requested him to proceed to Munich to see the king who desired that the composer live under his protection. "With tears of the most heavenly emotion" Wagner thanked the king for saving him and his art.

The financial savior had been found and Wagner hurried to Munich to meet his royal benefactor. King Ludwig II was born in Nymphenburg Castle outside Munich in the early hours of August 25, 1845 – the eldest son of King Maximillian II and Queen Marie. His father was indifferent to his upbringing and he was subjected to constant beatings as a child but there were consolations. Amid the misery of the severe discipline he remembered

---

6. Ibid.

Wagner's financial sponsor and disciple, the gay King Ludwig II of Bavaria. Gregor-Dellin, page 125. Ludwig-II-Museum, München.

with particular fondness the summer holidays the family spent at the Royal Castle Hohenschwangau, which his father had restored between 1832 and 1836 in a romantic medieval style.[7]

Ludwig was a fanatical admirer of Wagner's art from his youngest years and had looked with wondering eyes at the wonderful paintings in Hohenschwangau Castle of the swan knight from *Lohengrin*.[8] The early performance of that opera his governess had told him about instilled in his mind a reverence for Wagner and he quickly took up the theoretical works. He learned the words of the operas by heart and even as a boy he would sign his correspondence with a cross and a swan.[9] He bought a copy of *Tristan* and read the text of the *Ring*, laying emphasis on the new preface that contained the dream of the festival Wagner wished to establish to properly perform his works.[10] His enthusiasm was to turn to fanaticism when he saw the opera at the Munich Royal Opera on February 2, 1861. The king was to support him for the rest of his life. The largesse commenced with 4,000 guilders from the king's privy purse to deal with his outstanding debts and a country villa near the king's residence at the Starnberger See.[11] Later Wagner was given an unlimited budget but that was not enough for the composer – he even overspent that. He prevailed on Bechstein, the manufacturer of pianos, to provide him with one of his instruments free of charge. That family was also to nurture and cosset the young Adolf Hitler in the 1920s when he was entering the political fray.

Installed in luxury Wagner journeyed on a daily basis to see the king and plan how to introduce the new operas to the Bavarian public. Among those to attend and help with the great endeavors were the tenor Schnorr von Carolsfeld, who was to make a dramatic appearance at the premiere of *Tristan*, Hans von Bülow, whose wife Cosima had met Wagner in Switzerland, and Karl Klindworth. The last mentioned was to adopt an English orphan, Winifred Williams, who was to play a crucial role in entertaining and supporting Adolf Hitler in the dark days that lay ahead. Winifred was later to marry Wagner's only son Siegfried and to have a relationship with Hitler that was of such a strange nature that it had the

---

7. See Yan, "King Ludwig II of Bavaria: His Life and Art."
8. Richard Wagner Museum brochure, "About Richard Wagner," item 20u.
9. Newman, *Life of Richard Wagner*, vol. 3, 212.
10. Taylor, *Richard Wagner*, 270.
11. Ibid., 267.

Richard Wagner and his second wife Cosima, daughter of Liszt and former wife of Hans von Bülow. Gregor-Dellin, page 161. Nationalarchiv der Richard Wagner-Stiftung/Richard Wagner Gedenkstätte, Bayreuth.

Allied psychologists reaching for their lexicons of perversion. On the same day that Wagner's financial circumstances changed so dramatically his old enemy Meyerbeer died. The French composer instructed those who buried him to tie bells on his fingers because he feared being buried alive. Perhaps he feared being buried alive by Wagner, but the bells never rang for him – they tolled for Wagner.

After many delays – Wagner himself admitted that the work was so powerful it would drive people crazy and could only be rescued by poor performances! – *Tristan* was first performed in the Court Theatre, Munich on June 10, 1865. Ludwig, a man of shyness that reached pathological proportions, sat in his box during the performance and wept constantly. Perhaps the anticipation had been too much – in the days preceding the performance he wrote to Wagner, "My heart's rapture gives me no peace… nearer and nearer draws the happy day – Tristan will arise! We must break through the barriers of custom, shatter the laws of the base world. The ideal must come to life! We shall march forward conscious of victory. My loved one, I shall never forsake you! Oh, *Tristan*, *Tristan* will come to me! The dreams of my boyhood and youth will be made real…"[12]

Richard Wagner was now a wealthy man but he needed company especially to help him with the cold nights. When Wagner visited Cosima and Hans von Bülow in Berlin in November 1863 he recorded in his autobiography that he and Cosima acknowledged sobbing and weeping that they henceforth belonged one to the other alone. This sentence was later to be deleted when Cosima was performing her second role as editress of his life story. No doubt for Wagner his new relationship with Cosima was to be a matter of great consolation for the future but Minna was to end her days in poverty and abject misery. This anguish was compounded by the fact that her husband was now a wealthy man sharing his bed with his most devoted disciple's wife.

Wagner invited the von Bülows to Villa Pellet on Lake Starnberg to stay. Cosima von Bülow arrived a week earlier than her husband, and the die was cast. What had been a wild passion now cemented into a permanent relationship. Although the composer and his new love used every measure possible to conceal their love, it was clearly impossible to keep it away from the scandal mongers of Bavaria. The scandal of Cosima's affair with Wagner had the tongues wagging in Munich. Every form of satire and innuendo was used to inform the public of what was going on. One of Mozart's greatest operas *Cosi fan tutte* ("All [women] Do It") has a risqué plot involving two soldiers who seduce each other's fiancés to prove that no woman can be eternally faithful. The Munich press thereafter referred to her as *Cosima fan tutte*![13]

The partnership with the Royal disciple prospered and ripened, to the chagrin of the politicians who saw danger to themselves. In November 1865 Wagner was to spend time with the king at the castle of Hohenschwangau,

---
12. Yan, "King Ludwig II of Bavaria: His Life and Art."
13. Marek, *Cosima Wagner*, 131.

The eternal triangle: Wagner, Cosima and Hans von Bülow. The reference is to Greek mythology where Paris, son of King Priam of Troy, abducted Helen, wife of King Menelaus. This was the cause of the Trojan War. Barth et al., illustration 149. B. Schott's Söhne, Mainz.

writing poems to each other and planning the artistic future of the kingdom. He arranged that the oboe players of the first infantry regiment played the morning call from *Lohengrin* from towers of the castle. The king spared no expense in producing spectacles to celebrate the new creative partnership. A marvelous fireworks display took place on November 21 with a huge ingeniously built swan, towing Lohengrin's boat.[14] Both were magically illuminated with electricity and musicians were brought from Munich to provide the appropriate music.[15] As Wagner's needs made further depredations on the treasury necessary the officials tried to thwart his plans by making the "loan" of 40,000 guilders unavailable – except in

---

14. See Petzet and Hojer, "Neuschwanstein Castle," 7–8.
15. Newman, *Life of Richard Wagner,* vol. 3, 485.

coin. Undaunted, Cosima hired cabs and carried the largesse back to the new house at Briennerstrasse in large bags.[16]

Munich was shocked by the affair and word reached the king that his royal composer was misbehaving. The politicians saw their chance to end what was perceived as a dangerous liaison and smelling blood they quickly moved in for the kill. Because of Wagner's relationship with Cosima and the embarrassment suffered by Ludwig, on December 6, 1865 Wagner was banned from Munich and sent again into exile in Switzerland.[17] It was not an easy decision for the king to make but, apart from the ostentatious adultery, Wagner had also been meddling in politics and made a lot of enemies. The king was devastated and on January 2, 1866 he expressed a desire to commit suicide or abdicate because he had been pressurized by politicians to ban his friend. Writing to Wagner he showed that his reverence had not diminished when he said: "I cannot describe how I love you…I kneel in adoration at your bust. I shed tears."[18]

The machinations of the politicians and the moral dilemmas of the bourgeois Müncheners did not affect the devotion of the young monarch. In June 1868 the king planned a new castle to be called Neuschwanstein, as homage to the genius of Wagner. He wrote an emotional letter to the composer telling him what he intended to create. "I intend to rebuild the old ruined castle of Hohenschwangau…a worthy temple to our godly friend, who has bestowed upon mankind unique salvation and true blessing…it will remind you of the Tannhäuser and Lohengrin sagas…"[19] And so began the wonderful building program that was to make the royal castles of Bavaria the envy of every other monarch in Europe.

In Neuschwanstein Wagner is portrayed in virtually every room and in another wonderful architectural creation – the converted hunting lodge at Linderhof – a grotto modeled on the Blue Grotto depicts the Venusberg in Wagner's opera *Tannhäuser*. When investigating the real nature of Wagner's sexual proclivities, psychologists were later to examine with some exactitude the original name of that opera. Wagner claimed to have originally called it *The Venusberg* (The Mound of Venus) but the puritans had warned him that offence would be taken.

---

16. Taylor, *Richard Wagner*, 294.
17. Marek, *Cosima Wagner*, 79.
18. Richard Wagner Museum brochure, "About Richard Wagner," item 22.
19. Petzet and Hojer, "Neuschwanstein Castle," 4.

Some believed the king's adoration for the composer was evidence of an unbalanced mind. The love for Wagner took extraordinary forms and servants spoke to the commission, investigating his mental state, about his dressing up as Lohengrin and making strange journeys in the middle of the night.[20] Such was the infatuation that absorbed the king – some said fetishism played a role – that when Ludwig's possessions were sorted out after his tragic death by drowning, a Lohengrin costume was discovered.

The great composer was deeply distressed by his banishment and needed time to ponder. Before settling down in Switzerland Wagner embarked on a long journey to determine his future. He had reached Marseilles in his quest for answers to his problems when he received news that his wife Minna had died on January 25, 1866. The love between them had long ceased and if the truth be told it was a merciful release for him from a matrimonial burden. He asked his friend Dr Anton Pusinelli to arrange the funeral for his "poor, unhappy wife" because he was too far away to make the trip to Dresden and was too ill to return – in reality, he had an infected finger.[21]

After seeking out various possible residences his exile was enjoyed at Triebschen near Lucerne in Switzerland. The multi-storied house was situated on a promontory at a charming spot near the lake and nestling in the shadow of Mount Pilatus. Not that the king's largesse dried up or that his idolatry waned. Wagner enjoyed the financial security but there were features of the king's behavior that bothered him. He said on one occasion that he regarded the king's love as a "veritable crown of thorns" but this did little to deter the awe and hero worship from him. The king even carried out a secret visit to Wagner and despite his disguise became an easy prey to the press. Writing to Cosima the king said: "Let us take a solemn vow to do all it is in human power…to banish care from him, to take every grief upon ourselves…to love him with all the strength that God has put into the human soul! Oh he is godlike, godlike! My mission is to live for him, to suffer for him, if that be necessary for his full salvation."[22]

Wagner continued composing the monumental tetralogy and borrowed some of his own music from a quartet he was composing at Starnberg,

---

20. See Yan, "King Ludwig II of Bavaria: His Life and Art."
21. Marek, *Cosima Wagner*, 80.
22. Ibid., 75.

where the relationship had been cemented with Cosima, for inclusion in the wonderful duet at the conclusion of *Siegfried*. The rapturous soaring melodies of the hero Siegfried and his newly found love, Brünnhilde – his aunt – are reckoned by musicologists to differ from the other music of the *Ring* in their passion and intensity. Wagner's "highly susceptible, intense, voracious sensuality" was being "flattered" by the great love and passion of Cosima Liszt (von Bülow) and he was "accomplish[ing] the agonising labour of calling a non-existent world into being."

The composer once said that had he not been an artist he wanted to be a saint.[23] That he fell very far short of that goal is self-evident; the question remains, however, whether he would ever have produced his works of great genius without the stimulation of women – the bliss of a new love, albeit an adulterous and illicit one, was calling forth the greatest works of his long and distinguished career. All these circumstances raised a lot of moral questions that may be less important in modern times but certainly exercised the excitable dispositions of the newspapermen of that age. Are artists entitled to extra license in order for them to enter the nonexistent world and bring forth great beauty? And what if when they trespass on the wrong side of sexual morality, they also enter the crass mire of racism? The manifest dangers that are created when they develop political ideologies are magnified by the idolatry they command – having entered that nonexistent world and produced the wondrous fruits, what if future generations so venerate them that they execute the racism?

Many important writers and analysts have tried to answer these vexed questions. Ernest Jones in the preface to his book on Sigmund Freud expresses the view that different standards should be applied and that "it is generally agreed that great men by their very eminence forfeit the privilege granted to lesser mortals of having two lives, a public and a private one; often what they have withheld from the world proves to be of equal value to what they have proffered."[24] The bosoms of geniuses often harbor great vices and prejudices – having set standards of musical and poetical excellence the general public expect the same high standards in questions of morality.

A strange contradiction would seem to arise in the process of creation –

---

23. See Cooke, Deryck, "The Symbolism of *Parsifal*," notes to Philips recording, 13.
24. Jones, *Life and Work of Sigmund Freud*, 25.

the artist appears obliged to throw away the fetters of ordinary bourgeois morality in order to bring forth his vision of the truth. A poem of W.B. Yeats makes the point with blinding simplicity when he tells us that "a man must choose perfection of the life or of the work."[25] That the composer had many shortcomings has become manifest and we should not be surprised when that of hypocrisy joins what is a most impressive list – Wagner was outraged that Munich society reported that Frau von Bülow and he had became lovers. His defense was an insult to the intelligence of the press and an outrage to his friends. He naïvely maintained that Frau von Bülow helped with secretarial work and nothing else. Cosima was more transparent and her physical appearance soon revealed that she had no stomach for the deception. Not so naïve as to maintain that "immaculate conception" had repeated itself again – not that a godlike status was out of the question for him – his plea was refuted when the innocent relationship yielded living proof of his mendacity: a daughter Isolde and after her two more children, Eva and Siegfried.

Although Wagner's private life was to be a rich vein of information for the gutter press and their more exalted cousins in the broadsheets of Munich, this did nothing to impede his artistic growth and Wagner's second exile of six years produced music of incomparable beauty. His motto for living was, after all, that he did not want to die until he had lived. The balm and comfort of a family home – not to mention the sexual satisfaction of an adoring and passionate woman – was the ideal environment for his creative powers to reach their fullest maturity.

Cosima described the composition of *Meistersinger* in poetic terms and referred to the disastrous stirrings of nationalism the work would subsequently evoke. "It is like a softly glowing musical radiance…One does not know whether one is listening to light or seeing sound. As the curtain falls…the whole of old Nürnberg is astir amid the pealing of bells, it is as though the old houses themselves were moving off in solemn procession. I think that on hearing this, the heart of every German must leap with prideful joy and consciousness of his heritage."[26]

Her words were prophetic. Nürnberg was to become the center of German pride – later xenophobia and anti-Semitism during the Nazi annual

---

25. Ibid., 12.
26. Marek, *Cosima Wagner*, 91.

rallies in the thirties – and finally the venue for Allied judicial vengeance, after the Second World War. *Meistersinger* was performed in Munich on June 21, 1868 and during the premier performance, Ludwig invited Wagner to sit at his side, a cause for more social opprobrium – to many Müncheners this was a further scandal and a gross breach of etiquette.[27]

The estranged husband of Cosima, Hans von Bülow, was distraught and devastated by Wagner's behavior. He must have remembered the reverence he showed to the composer from the earliest days and yet he had been betrayed in the vilest manner. In a letter to his friend Julius Stern shortly after getting married he eulogized the effect Wagner had on him. "For the last fortnight my wife and I have been staying with Wagner, and I can think of nothing more calculated to bring me a sense of blessing and refreshment than to be with this glorious, unique man, whom one must venerate like a god…I cannot talk to you about the Nibelungen…all resources of expression of admiration fail me…Nothing like it, nothing approaching it, has ever been produced in any art, in any tongue, anywhere, at any time."[28]

But the gods have feet (or was it some other protuberance?) of clay. It was Nietzsche who was later to claim that von Bülow had been crushed by a fallen idol – Wagner crushed him and stole his wife. In his grief and chagrin he clung to all he could grab and insisted that Isolde was a von Bülow and undoubtedly his child. For a long time she signed her name as such and in later years inherited part of his fortune but the fact of her paternity was to have a most unfortunate sequel forty years or more later. By that time she was so to dislike life in Bayreuth that she left to live in Rome until she was persuaded to return. When she married Franz Beidler, Cosima insisted she receive the same yearly stipend as Eva and Siegfried of ten thousand marks. This seemed adequate proof that Cosima acknowledged that she was indeed Wagner's child. The greed and avarice displayed in *The Ring of the Nibelungs* was to repeat itself in the family history. When the copyright on Wagner's works expired Isolde demanded of Cosima that she be declared Wagner's child so that she could share Wagner's fortune estimated at five million marks.

This presented a most intriguing dilemma to Cosima who had always maintained that Isolde was the fruit of her great love for Wagner. The rules

---

27. See Yan, "King Ludwig II of Bavaria: His Life and Art."
28. Newman, *Life of Richard Wagner*, vol. 2, 529.

of primogeniture were a further consideration – Isolde was older than Siegfried and her claim might prove commercially embarrassing. Cosima resisted the demand and stated that Isolde was the child of von Bülow. She asked her daughter not to force her to reveal to public scrutiny her "most intimate life." What she feared was that she would be forced to reveal the *ménage a trois* that had enacted itself at Starnberg, as she tiptoed from one bedroom to another. She was also concerned that a rival to Siegfried – in the form of Isolde's husband, a noted musician and successful conductor, Franz Beidler – would arise to run the festival.[29]

Isolde was adamant and refused a number of bribes and decided to "proceed with a lawsuit which would besmirch the name of Wagner ineradicably" as Cosima described the action.[30] The courtroom was packed as the curious sensation-seekers bent their ears to hear every titillating detail. What would the composer's widow say in evidence? Would she betray her husband Hans von Bülow in the witness box and admit to an adulterous affair, which would have the effect of having to divide the patrimony further?

It was a moment of deep emotional significance when the tall and regal Cosima entered the courtroom to take the witness stand. Pausing to wipe her tears with a beautiful lace handkerchief she testified that between June 12 and October 12, 1864 she had not been her husband's intimate exclusively. It became clear that she preferred to be regarded as unfaithful than to lose the aura surrounding one who had been the companion to such a great composer. And yet no one has ever doubted her great love for Wagner.

The paternity case was to provide further shocking evidence. A housekeeper employed in that year confirmed that Cosima had slept with Wagner but that she had also shared von Bülow's bedroom. The scandal sheets of Bavaria recorded every moment of the sordid testimony and when the court adjourned to make its decision no one knew which way the judgment would proceed. The ruling pleased no one. The court determined that Isolde had failed to establish that her father was Richard Wagner.

The evidence of the housekeeper only established that Cosima had tiptoed between two bedrooms and not what had happened between the

---

29. Wagner, Nike, *The Wagners*, 8.
30. Marek, *Cosima Wagner*, 237.

sumptuous sheets supplied by the largesse of the king. What finally decided the issue was the age-old wisdom of the law. The protection of children, specifically their legitimacy, had led to the establishment of a legal presumption that the husband was the father of the child. Thus Cosima's husband Hans von Bülow was declared to be the father of Isolde.[31]

Apart from her domestic chores and role as the carrier of future Wagners, Cosima was also a cultured musician and writer. In addition she was not unaware that she was living with a man whom posterity would want to know about. She started a diary, which recorded virtually every meal and every hiccup of the great man, from that date until his death in 1883. She explained why she was writing the account in an entry on March 21, 1873 and modestly recorded that "Carlyle writes how little we know of great men, how shadowy they appear to posterity…for that reason I write down everything he says…and yet I feel the attempt is unsuccessful…but perhaps it is better than nothing and so I continue my bungling."[32]

Embargoed from publication for many years, the eventual publication of the daily account was to shock and enrage the public. The diary reeked of anti-Semitism – every fourth page or so has something derogatory or snide to say about the Jews.[33] That Wagner was the source of this allows of little doubt – not that Cosima lagged far behind in her views. This was somewhat surprising given her upbringing; the Hungarian born Franz Liszt, Cosima's father, was a warm and tolerant human being to whom the notion of hating a religion or race was totally alien.

He is reported to have said to Cosima and her sister that because they were quite pretty and had some talent this did not give them the right to enjoy any attention from the world. "The one and only thing that will give you this right is if you give everyone you encounter the necessary *respect for their individuality, without distinction of person, or country or rank.*" Although Cosima claimed that she had passed on the message of respect to her children there was too much of the racism mixed with the benign portion to have left any real mark on them.[34] A form of xenophobia crept into the family ideology, which stigmatized outsiders as enemies and those

---

31. Ibid.
32. Ibid., 128.
33. Ibid., 104.
34. Wagner, Nike, *The Wagners*, 171–72.

who did not belong to the host of admirers – in what great granddaughter Nike Wagner calls the "primal broth" – as heathen.[35]

The needs of posterity were so important to Wagner that he made sure no important event in his life was left undiscovered. He was supremely confident he would be a famous man but he was also very keen that the generations that came after would find a man who answered to the grandeur of his works. Subduing all humility, which was in pretty short supply in his case, he started an autobiography in 1835 in *The Red Book* in which he noted down the main events in his life. From this red book he transferred the information to a brown book, which became the source for his autobiography *My Life*. Other writings of importance in this regard included his *Autobiographical Sketch* of 1843 and his *Communication to My Friends* of 1851.[36]

In July 1864 Wagner began dictating his autobiography to Cosima and he strove to repossess any of his letters that were at odds with the lies he planned to tell the king. He did not shrink from discussing his own influence nor did modesty or understatement cloud his judgment. A diary entry of September 1865 stated: "I am the most German of beings; I am the German spirit. Consider the incomparable magic of my works."[37]

Wagner had not made the effort to attend his wife Minna's funeral but he was soon at great pains to recover his correspondence with her. He went so far as to demand back his letters to Minna from her sister Natalie – actually her daughter, as we know she was raped as a teenager – on Nov 27, 1868.[38] But opposed to the Wagner hagiographer camp was lined up Mary Burrell, an enterprising Englishwoman, who was determined to find the truth.[39] She visited Natalie at the poorhouse in Leisnig and bartered successfully for the correspondence. Natalie was in no position to resist the offer of money and had also been denied any fruits from the royal windfall of the composer. Her situation was deplorable and reeked of poverty – her sole accommodation consisted of a room situated next door to one in which corpses of the old people were stored prior to burial. Of the letters to his first wife Minna, one hundred twenty-eight eventually found their

---

35. Ibid., 172.
36. Köhler, *Wagner's Hitler*, 206, 254.
37. Waite, *The Psychopathic God*, 104.
38. Burk, *Letters of Richard Wagner: The Burrell Collection*, 576.
39. Gutman, *Richard Wagner*, 373.

way to Burrell and posterity. They were spared the fate of the blue pencil or, worse still, the incinerator, that befell other correspondence relating to the life and work of the composer.

In certain of his correspondence Wagner revealed a refreshing candor that is at odds with his later duplicity. He wrote in describing the failure of his elopement with Jessie, "if this love be for me, then it could only content me if it worked my ruin as well." When writing his autobiography he had not yet completely mastered the mendacity necessary to ensure that the expurgated version of his life satisfied all his critics, including his new love Cosima von Bülow. Wagner had *My Life* printed by a man by the name of Bonfantini in Basel.[40] Fifteen copies were all that Wagner allowed to be made but the printer had some inkling that an extra copy might be a good investment.[41] He was right. On October 1, 1892, Mary Burrell purchased the extra copy from Thekla Bonfantini Stuckert, as his remarried widow called herself, and possession of this in independent hands was to have a dampening effect on those bent on falsifying the composer's story. As Newman was to relate, Wagner admitted too much in his first draft and his widow and her confederates wished he had not gone into the witness box in his own defense at all.

Cosima has been justifiably criticized for her role as a falsifier and for ousting Minna as Wagner's life companion. Let it be said, however, that she did so at great personal cost and no one denies that she was impelled by a grand passion for Wagner. Some of her suffering and passion for the man is revealed in a very frank entry of March 15, 1869 when Cosima wrote in her diary: "I will gladly suffer everything, only to stand by his side. They can besmirch me even unto a far-off posterity, if only I am permitted to help him, to take him by the hand and to say to him: I follow you unto death."[42]

Cosima is often portrayed as a cold, unfeeling princess with complete indifference to her husband's feelings. This is not completely true. She tried to communicate her own sense of his loss on June 15, 1869 when she wrote to Hans and said: "your only wrong was to marry me. I can honestly say that in the seven months of our separation the only worry, the only

---

40. Wagner's letter to Bonfantini re discretion of *Mein Leben*. See Burk, *Letters of Richard Wagner*, 578.
41. Subsequently published as *Mein Leben*, 2 vol. (1870–81).
42. Marek, *Cosima Wagner*, 100.

sorrow I have felt is the thought of you…I could not make you happy…" There was a fatalism about her love for Richard Wagner that meant that she could never leave him. She concluded her letter by trying to express this as honestly as she was able. "All the same, I would never have left you had I not encountered that being to whom my own attached itself so completely that detachment has become impossible for me."[43]

The same unfortunately could not be said for Hans. Von Bülow was so overwhelmed by the loss that he contemplated taking his own life. As Wagner's best interpreter and conductor the circumstances were hardly ideal for cooperation. He recognized the genius in Wagner and humbly accepted that his wife had deserted him for a better man. In a letter to Cosima's half sister on September 15, 1869 he expressed his grave disappointment with the composer. He said that he was seriously considering suicide but that he would abstain from that thought if he saw some loyalty from his twenty-year friendship with Wagner – so "sublime in his works as incomparably abject in his actions."[44]

As Friedrich Nietzsche is to assume such importance in the telling of this tale it is necessary to detail something of his life. He first met Wagner in October 1868 at the house of Wagner's sister Ottilie and her husband Hermann Brockhaus. Six months previously he had heard the prelude to *Tristan* and had responded with unrestrained ardor. "I cannot control my emotions sufficiently to judge this music coolly and critically. Every nerve in my body trembles. Not for a long time have I experienced such a lasting feeling of bliss and rapture."[45]

Nietzsche was very poor at that stage of his life – he was a student of philology – but felt he had to have a new suit made up by a tailor to meet Wagner.[46] He had heard rumors of the composer's own mode of dress and felt he had to be decently turned out if he was to make any sort of impression. The great composer's dress was certainly interesting on the evening he met the young student[47] – he was wearing a blue jacket with red braid and a

---

43. Ibid., 52.
44. Ibid., 66.
45. Taylor, *Richard Wagner*, 313.
46. The account of Nietzsche's meeting can be found in Gutman, *Richard Wagner*, 445. The tale of the new suit is contained in Fischer-Diskau, *Wagner and Nietzsche*, 12. See also Newman, *Life of Richard Wagner*, vol 4, 145.
47. Wagner did visit the Brockhaus family in Leipzig in October 1868.

yellow cap, trimmed with a green fringe. There was something of the effete dandy in Wagner; his sense of dress recalls the style of the young Werther, hero of the book by Goethe, which had so defined the fashion of the time. Lest we imagine that the mode of dress was reserved for private occasions, Wagner appeared at an audition of *Tannhäuser* in similar dress but this attire would only do for his rendition – on the piano, singing all the parts and acting them out himself – of the first part of the opera. He vanished before the startled eyes of the impresario Carvalho to reappear at the piano in a yellow coat with blue braid and a red cap with yellow edging.[48]

By the time Wagner met Nietzsche he was famous for his mature operas *Tannhäuser, Lohengrin* and *Tristan und Isolde*, and *Die Meistersinger von Nürnberg* had premiered in Munich recently. At the premiere it will be recalled the king had breached all etiquette by having Wagner sit in the royal box and acknowledge the thunderous applause from there. The critics were not all unanimous in their appreciation of the work. Hanslick called it a "symptom of illness" and warned that the other Wagner operas induced "unhealthy over-stimulation" and "oppressive fatigue."[49] Possibly he had heard that Wagner's hatred for his biting sarcasm had resulted in the principle scoundrel in the opera, subsequently renamed Beckmesser, bearing the appellation of Hans Lick. Wagner apparently subsequently thought better of this and renamed his rogue Beckmesser. The press was also divided in its views of the comedy drama. The *Signale* called it a "mountain of foolishness and triviality."

Sir Arthur Sullivan, composer of the Savoy Operas in conjunction with William Gilbert, was caught by Hermann Klein, music critic of the *Sunday Times*, listening to the opera, score in hand. Sullivan smiled wryly and confessed: "You see, I am taking a lesson. Well, why, not? This is not only Wagner's masterpiece, but the greatest comic opera ever written."[50] The English ability to recognize great art was not replicated in the case of the *Yorkshire Post* which announced a concert program with selections from the *Meistersingers of Wurthemburg!*[51] Ever the acute observer, Nietzsche praised its "grandiose, ancient art" and the "artist's own revealed pleasure in his art, which he is at no pains to conceal" but soon recognized the work

---

48. Gutman, *Richard Wagner*, 40 note 2.
49. Conrad, "He's Tricky, That Dicky."
50. Jacobs, *Arthur Sullivan: A Victorian Musician*, 338.
51. Ibid., 344.

The friend and later foe of the composer, the philosopher and writer Friedrich Nietszche. Wagners Welten, page 198. Münchner Stadtmuseum/Fotomuseum. Nachlass Verlag Hanfstaengl.

for what it prophesied. "Here is Germanism in its best and worst sense: a Teutonic showcase of variety and excess, of overbearing might and glutted symbolism…a mark of the German Spirit, this combination of youthfulness and age, of brittle decline ever ready for the upswing to a richer future."[52] The "brittle decline" commenced in 1889 with the birth of a maniac who was to promise a "richer future" to those of German origin at the expense of those Wagner had identified as society's worst enemies. The Arab academic Edward Said believed that "in *Meistersinger*…Wagner is trying to create a new Germany, given the fragmented state of the country."[53]

Nietzsche was at that time a brilliant young student of classical philology at Leipzig University with distinct musical talents. In later life he was placed in a lunatic asylum where he penned a confessional, *My Sister and I*, that recorded intimate details of his sexual exploits from his tender years to his maturity.[54] Some of these are significant when the lives of our

---

52. Harding, *Magic Fire*, 294.
53. Guzelimian, *Parallels and Paradoxes: Daniel Barenboim and Edward W. Said*, 40.
54. Wallace et al., *The Intimate Sex Lives of Famous People*, from 330.

two protagonists are considered. His sister Elizabeth was later to marry a proto-Nazi and anti-Semite who founded a colony on those lines in South America. When Elizabeth met Hitler in 1932 she spoke for many when she said her brother had left her with the impression of being a religious figure and not a politician.[55] Unfortunately the religion was based on the gospel according to Richard Wagner.

Nietzsche's dramatic account of his private life was smuggled out of the sanatorium by a sympathetic nurse and only saw the light of day in 1951 after years of suppression by his own hagiographers. The last mentioned continue to downplay the veracity of this account and cite his mental state at the time. The wealth of detail makes for convincing reading and there seems little reason or motive for falsification.

Reckoned by many to have been one of the greatest geniuses of all time, his life was plagued by unhappy relationships. His death from syphilis was but one indication that he did finally succumb to the temptations of the flesh. His account begins in his pre-puberty years and contains the sort of detail few would invent. On the traumatic night that Nietzsche's brother died his sister crept into his bed and played with his genitals "as if they were special toys of hers." In the language that came to enthral the world of literature he described the sensation. "She haunted the world of my senses with those marvelous fingers of hers, driving me to a premature and hopeless awakening – so that for a whole spasm of my life I was unable to think of beauty or pleasure except in terms of her eyes and her damnably wonderful fingers. So refurbishing my life that in place of the strange goddess who visits the imagination of every normal adolescent I could only look forward to headaches and a sister."[56]

From those early beginnings he moves on to his experiences as an adolescent. In his book he tells of his first love affair with a thirty-year-old countess who seduced him at fifteen years and used him "to quench the flame of her uterine passion." She goaded the blushing teenager until he took up a whip and flogged her, which had the effect of arousing her beyond endurance. One night she sneaked into the school dormitory he occupied disguised as a man and beat him with a blunt instrument. As he was about to lose consciousness she became visibly sexually excited and made love

---

55. Spotts, *Hitler and the Power of Aesthetics*, 49.
56. Ibid., 333.

to him. He felt humiliated as she insisted on riding him and urging him to greater heights.

The sexual mores of the day meant that sitting astride a male was a deviation enjoyed only by the most adventurous. This led the great philosopher to formulate a rule of human nature that was to have a dramatic effect on Adolf Hitler. "Cruelty does not quiet down a woman, but on the contrary intensifies it to a fever pitch."[57] His aphorism in *Also Sprach Zarathustra* concerning the method of treating a woman was also interesting in the present context. "You go to a woman; do not forget your whip." The chosen weapon in the masochistic amours was also to feature prominently in the perversions of the twentieth-century tyrant who galvanized the Germans into a war with catastrophic consequences. Of special interest is his use of the whip when demonstrating his manliness to a whole range of women, including his fateful relationship with his niece Geli Raubal, and more significantly with Winifred Wagner, the great composer's daughter-in-law.

When he was sixteen Nietzsche formed a society called Germania with two other students and they scraped together sufficient money to buy von Bülow's arrangement of *Tristan und Isolde*. He spent many happy hours hammering it out on the piano and was an amateur composer. At the time Nietzsche met Wagner he was working on his monumental *Ring of the Nibelungs*.

Wagner was to have a tremendous influence on the young man. Nietzsche's first book written in 1872 was entitled *The Birth of Tragedy from the Spirit of Music*. In that seminal work he argued that Greek tragedy arose out of the fusion of what he termed Apollonian and Dionysian elements – the former representing measure, restraint, harmony, and the latter representing unbridled passion – and that Socratic rationalism and optimism spelled the death of Greek tragedy. The final ten sections of the book are a rhapsody about the rebirth of tragedy from the spirit of Wagner's music. The passion and lack of self-restraint exhibited by the Greek god Dionysus, especially in his relationship with Ariadne, was to have an interesting sequel in Nietzsche's own life, notably when he began to lose full control of his mental faculties. Speaking after Wagner's death, in the classical metaphors that would only be understood by a select few,

---

57. Ibid.

he declared his great (though unrequited) passion for Cosima, alluding to her as his Ariadne.

Nietzsche attended every concert at which Wagner's music was played and wrote about the music with fulsomeness seldom equaled. "As the Orpheus of all our secret misery, Wagner was the greatest of them all. His music came from the realm of suffering and tormented souls. No one can hold a candle to him in the colours of late autumn, the ineffably poignant happiness of an ultimate and transient betrayal. He knows a sound for those secret and sinister midnights of the soul."[58]

Wagner's artistic growth as noted by Nietzsche had been heavily influenced by the pessimism of Schopenhauer and the notion of a pantheistic Will, which was an unconscious, supernatural and eternal force. Many reckon that this cosmic imperative insinuated its way into the great masterpiece *Tristan und Isolde* in which the protagonists project themselves as impelled by forces beyond their control. As Wagner wrote, "nothing really happens but what has issued from this will, a headlong blind impulse."[59] As will become apparent from his later writings Wagner's political views were to posit a "Führer" (a leader) who would arise in Germany and lead the country to greatness. This "Führer" would cleanse the nation of the Jews and would embody this will and act on the "headlong blind impulse."

There were a number of political consequences to this new philosophy that Wagner now so wholeheartedly embraced. Acceptance of this Führer meant rejection of democracy, which in Germany was for Wagner what he called a "purely translated Franco-Judaico-German form found only in the press."[60] Building on the work of Schopenhauer, as discussed by Wagner, Nietzsche accepted the difference between the world as we see it (phenomena) and the world as it actually was (noumena). In the transference of the ideology the composer had a unique role to perform. Music was unlike all other arts as it was not a copy of the world as we see it but a direct copy of the will itself. As such music provided a direct communication of what the composer wanted.

Much of Wagnerian music examined the ancient myths of the Nordic peoples that were then directly transferred to the psyche of the listener.

---

58. Nietzsche used the words "Orpheus of our secret misery." See Gutman, *Richard Wagner*, 18–19.
59. Viereck, *Metapolitics*, 104.
60. Ibid.

The myths in *The Ring of the Nibelungs* posited the racial superiority of the gods (Wotan, Fricka, Thor and Donner) and the Volsung race descended from Wotan's dalliances – over the Jewish stereotypes – the Nibelungs, particularly Alberich and Mime. The last Nibelung Hagen was to stab the Aryan superman and *Wunderkind* Siegfried in the back. It was Otto Weininger who described Siegfried as "the most un-Jewish thing imaginable" in his sensational book *Sex and Character*.[61] The stories in the music dramas would be interpreted, hopefully for Wagner, to indicate who would constitute the *Herrenvolk* (master race). There were still limitations on this conventional form of communication – this verbal (non-musical) process was subject to interpretation and misunderstanding.

On the other hand where the myth was portraying a subliminal racial superiority the music would be implanting the stereotypes *directly* on the mind. The possibility of misunderstanding and misinterpretation was completely eradicated. More importantly the normal defense mechanisms – including rationality, prior experience and learning – available to the hearers would be bypassed or neutralized as the ideology settled permanently into the receiver's subconscious.

No psychologist seeking to find out how programming commenced need look any further than this explanation. Forty years later in his book on art Sigmund Freud found that artistic creativity belonged in the realm of the unconscious and that it was similar to dreaming, its predominant concern being wish-fulfillment – what has been called "the symbolic realisation of repressed desires."[62] Was there any possibility that Wagner's deepest wishes – initially directed at his own personal vendetta against Meyerbeer, but later assuming a more generalized racism – would implant themselves on a man with the desire and opportunity to implement them?

Nietzsche commenced his relationship with Wagner as a sycophantic acolyte aping every gesture and repeating every bon mot or aphorism that fell from the table. This included the rampant anti-Semitism which permeated so much of the Wagner genre. When the philosopher commenced his campaign under the command of his general he hesitated little to mention the enemy by name and pointed directly at the sins of the Jews. Cosima was quick to warn Nietzsche of the folly of this in a letter of February 6,

---

61. Weiner, *Richard Wagner and the Anti-Semitic Imagination*, 62.
62. Vetter, "Wagner in the History of Psychology," 53.

1870. Of interest in this advice is the maternal attitude taken by the writer, given the later emotional relationship that Nietzsche was to nurture for the older woman. "I have a request to make of you, a request as from mother to son. Do not stir up a hornet's nest. Do you follow my meaning? Do not refer to the Jews by name especially not en passant. Later, yes – if you are prepared to take up the fearful struggle. But not yet."[63]

Wagner's works, according to Nietzsche, were models for a future society, and he proclaimed "the rebirth of German mythology" and "if we are looking for a leader to take us back to the land we abandoned long ago" he was alive and well and living in Bayreuth, where the spirit of the old Germany would be reawakened. He spoke of the agony suffered by the Germans "during their long years of degradation in distant lands, oppressed by a race of heinous dwarfs. Let this be understood." The philosopher went on to provide the solution, which was a resounding affirmation of the views of the composer: "the dragon will be slain, the wicked dwarfs destroyed and Brunnhilde awakened."[64] The subtext was clear and if you were confused the music would speak directly to your heart and explain who the dwarfs were. The dwarfs were the proto-Jewish subtypes Alberich, his brother Mime and the murderous Hagen in Wagner's mighty tetralogy and his greatest artistic and musical legacy *The Ring of the Nibelungs*.

The earliest political writings had constantly referred to the Jews as bankers and moneylenders who pillaged the fortunes of good honest Germans. In one of his final racist essays, "Know Thyself," Wagner refers to Alberich's ring, the symbol of the greatest power on earth, as a "stock portfolio."[65] Marc Weiner sums up this dichotomy as follows: "*Siegfried* thus constitutes a metaphor for the salvation of Germany's future, a salvation based upon racial exclusion available to the fatherland if only it were to 'know itself' and to stay within its corporeally recognizable borders, while Hagen's body is a physiological-metaphorical warning to a Germany that refuses to recognize the biological dimension of the purported Jewish threat."[66]

The next six years saw successful Munich productions of all of Wagner's new music dramas, including the first performances of *Tristan*

---

63. Köhler, *Wagner's Hitler*, 112.
64. Ibid., 108.
65. Weiner, *Richard Wagner and the Anti-Semitic Imagination*, 144.
66. Ibid., 310.

(1865), *Meistersinger* (1868), *Das Rheingold* (1869) and *The Valkyries* (1870). Although Cosima had cautioned Nietzsche against speaking plainly, the composer was either unaware of or uninterested in her advice and was not so subtle. He soon let the king know his views on race. The king, who sponsored the performances, was told by Wagner that since the Thirty Years War the German princes had lost touch with the German people and spirit. A fateful development, according to the composer, was taking place – "that strange phenomenon of the penetration of German culture and the German psyche by the most alien of influences – that of the Jews." Later he was to return to the theme of his sinister article on "Jewry in Music" when he told the king that "the essence of the German spirit, its profound musical emotions, is presented to the people today in a form distorted by the Jews."[67]

That von Bülow was the conductor of the first two music dramas was an added irony, given the musical beds played out when the threesome enjoyed the holiday at Starnberg, with the lithesome Cosima slipping from the bed of her husband to that of her grand passion. Gradually the conductor was becoming accustomed to the fact that the composer had stolen his wife and he adopted a philosophical resignation to a fate he could do nothing about. New honors were poured on him for his contribution to the musical culture of the country and it became clear that he finally regained his humor. When the authorities again recognized his services von Bülow refused the laurel wreath presented to him, saying "I am not a vegetarian!"[68] Not so the composer who was soon to give up all meat for reasons which were as quaint as they were unconvincing. At last the long struggle with Hans was over; Cosima was divorced in 1870 and married to Wagner in the same year.

In 1869 Wagner had resumed work on the Ring tetralogy and agreed with the king that it should be first performed in Munich. Honor in romantic matters was clearly absent with the composer and in commercial matters he was to prove no different. Wagner broke the agreement on the basis of an argument, without legal or moral foundation; that such a massive work needed a new type of theatre. He spent much time with Cosima searching out a site that would satisfy all the criteria.

---

67. Köhler, *Wagner's Hitler*, 255–56.
68. Marek, *Cosima Wagner*, 24–5.

Finally Bayreuth, home of the philosopher Jean Paul, who had predicted his coming, was chosen and Wagner toured Germany, conducting concerts to raise funds to finance the venture. The years of travel were wearying and taking their toll on the man. His heart was not strong and at times he had a grey look about him. Death was at work in his chest. Wagner was in need of a home to settle down permanently and wrote to the king in 1871 telling him as much. "I need to know at long last where I belong, where my permanent residence is and where I can care for my family like a bourgeois. I have had to sacrifice many years of my life to the savage workings of chance, I cannot call any property my own and I live in the world like a refugee…I have to live in a place where I can feel assured of finding an appropriate sphere of activity. This must be in the heart of Germany."[69]

On April 19, 1871 Wagner inspected Bayreuth and he had such terrible chills and fever Cosima feared for his life. She wondered if fate was warning them against living there. The doctor who was called could not believe who his patient was. "Well the strange things that can happen to one! Who could have prophesied that this very night I was going to make the acquaintance of Richard Wagner? You are the Richard Wagner, the very special Richard Wagner?" Wagner smiled, amused. "You mean the one who has written pretty things? Yes, I am he."[70]

Bayreuth lay conveniently situated in Bavaria, east-central Germany, on the Roter Main River between the Fichtelgebirge and the Franconian Jura, northeast of Nüremberg. The site originally chosen for the theatre was "an attractive meadowland site" with wild roses and hawthorn, with tall ash avenues at the rear in the margravial court garden. A long avenue of chestnut trees was especially appealing to the nature-lover in Wagner and he imagined orchards and vegetable gardens on either side of it.[71] There was an additional reason why Wagner felt a pressing need to start a cultural event that would represent what was best in Germany. The festival itself was founded as a bulwark against the political emancipation of the Jews that occurred in 1869.[72] That same year saw the reissue of his essay "Judaism in Music" and the equivocal call for the destruction or assimilation of the Jews at the conclusion of that pernicious document was replaced with

---

69. Wagner, Nike, *The Wagners*, 168.
70. Marek, *Cosima Wagner*, 142.
71. Wagner, Nike, *The Wagners*, 173.
72. Köhler, *Wagner's Hitler*, 142.

the more emphatic call "for the forcible ejection of the corrupting foreign element."[73]

The city of Bayreuth has a long history; it developed around a castle of the counts of Andechs-Meran and occupied a strategic position at the intersection of several trade routes. In 1603 the city became the residence of the margraves, who actively patronized the arts and were responsible for many fine Baroque buildings. The reign of the margrave Friedrich and his wife, Wilhelmina, the sister of Friedrich the Great, was a particularly rich period (1735–63). The New Palace, the old opera house, and parts of the Hermitage date from that era. Bayreuth was ceded to Prussia in 1791 and passed to Bavaria in 1810. Apart from the prestige given to the town by Wagner, the composer Franz Liszt and the philosopher Jean Paul are also buried in Bayreuth.

In 1872 the foundation stone was laid for the Festspielhaus and Wagner commented in his speech on the nearness of the mental asylum, with his customary caustic humor. "I confess I did not realize that the air in Bayreuth is so fresh that it can restore the mentally sick, and that patients who have gone out of their minds can be healed here by wise physicians."[74] Little did the world at large realize the madness that his philosophies would unleash when Adolf Hitler, enraptured by the music, took up the racist refrain in his polemical writings with their sinister subliminal codes.

In the summer of 1873 the composer Anton Bruckner arrived with a request that Wagner allow him to dedicate one of his symphonies to him. After careful studies of the scores Wagner chose the third. The occasion was a convivial one; Wagner had urged Bruckner to consume flagon after flagon of the heady Bayreuth beer. Bruckner had just left from a water cure at Karlsbad and being unused to liquor could not remember the next day which symphony had been decided on. Wagner's old friend Gustave Kietz who had also had his share of the libations seemed to remember some reference to D minor and a prominent trumpet theme but, in his intoxicated state, thought they had been talking about Beethoven's Ninth Symphony. The mere mention of the key by Kietz reassured Bruckner and he made the dedication of the third symphony to Wagner – and he was

---

73. Weiner, *Richard Wagner and the Anti-Semitic Imagination*, 240.
74. Taylor, *Richard Wagner*, 336.

fortified in his final decision as that symphony commences with a solo on the trumpet.[75]

In 1874 Wagner moved into a house which he called Wahnfried ("Peace from Illusion"). The festival was to establish Wagner's dramatic vision that the study of history leads ultimately to prehistory and mythology, the realm of absolute truths. The real world consisted for him in gods, giants, Nibelungs, dwarfs, magic potions and heroes who knew no fear. He wanted to use myth to reunite modern man with the passion from which rationalism, the industrial process and capitalism had separated him. He hoped to combine music, theatre, design and lighting to establish the primeval mood of myth.

Apart from new ideas about music and theatre there were to be changes in architecture as well. To house his music drama, Wagner designed a unique theatre, the Festspielhaus, where a number of innovations were featured. No longer would opera lovers sit behind one another stretching their necks to see the stage. The seating was now fan-shaped as good lateral sight lines were essential for the enjoyment of performances on a proscenium stage. Wagner did away with the box seats, from which the aristocracy had watched each other instead of the stage for hundreds of years. He had the orchestra lowered into a pit called the "mystic gulf," from which the subconscious message, via a hidden source of all-enveloping sound, insinuated itself into the ears of the listener. The man Egon Friedell dubbed "the greatest theatre genius of all time" was at work.[76]

The theatre remains to this day one of the finest in the world as far as acoustics are concerned – the reverberation time, the period it takes for sound to die, is perfect for his characteristically heavy orchestration and, timed at the optimal length of 1.55 seconds, makes it still the perfect venue for playing the music of Richard Wagner.[77] Daniel Barenboim maintained that Wagner "had a great understanding of, or intuition for (or perhaps a combination of the two), acoustics. He was the first person to have that, I think, except perhaps Berlioz, and in a certain way Liszt, although Liszt was more limited to the piano. By acoustics I mean the presence of sound

---

75. Newman, *Life of Richard Wagner*, vol. 4, 402.
76. Richard Wagner Museum brochure, "About Richard Wagner."
77. Spotts, *Bayreuth*, 8.

in a room, the concept of time and space. Wagner really developed that concept musically."[78]

If you could handle the hard seats at Bayreuth – for many years the bane of all listeners' lives – you might be forgiven for believing that no other theatre in the world gave such a faithful reproduction of an artist's ideals. In recent years the seating has been refurbished somewhat and the wooden seats have been covered with what the overoptimistic habitué might, with some exaggeration, call a cushion. Wagnerian music drama is not for the fainthearted. Only the stout of heart deserve the lengthy doses of ideology the composer devised. The formal dress is compulsory and during the intervals of an hour at least the audience stroll through the lovely grounds sipping champagne and supping. Taking place as it does in the middle of summer the theatre can be very hot, especially the orchestra pit. Edward Said was shocked to see Daniel Barenboim in T-shirt and shorts, and the members of the orchestra in similar clothing, amidst the evening dress of the theatergoers.[79]

Wagner's life had never been healthier – apart from the spasm gnawing away at his chest, and his finances, which were chaotic, as the king did not pay for Bayreuth. In fact, as rumor had it, his royal sponsor was gradually losing his mind. The servants whispered tales that circulated through the palace and thence to the political corridors. In 1873 he ordered dinner for twelve guests, entered, greeted the empty chairs and then proceeded to dine alone. Other incidents concerned his family and the politicians. He would enter a room by a door and only leave by the window.[80]

Although much of what he did was idiosyncratic to say the least, there is much controversy about the king's "madness" and, indeed, most of it emanates from the political machinations of his ministers. His sponsorship of Wagner and his castles were providing a drain on the state's resources. The fact that the ministers were required to attend the lengthy music dramas was the least of their worries. The whole of the opera *Tosca*, *La Bohème* and many of the masterpieces of the Italian oeuvre last a shorter time than the first act of *Parsifal*. That act, lasting as it does a little less than

---

78. Guzelimian, *Parallels and Paradoxes: Daniel Barenboim and Edward W. Said*, 80.
79. Ibid., 89.
80. Marek, *Cosima Wagner*, 151.

two hours, taxes not only the patience of the hearers but the endurance of their bladders.

That Ludwig was homosexual is clearly established and was a cause of concern in those times – especially to politicians bent on limiting his power and influence. The literature on his life makes mention of his love affairs with attractive young army officers. Many a handsome young officer was appointed Ludwig's aide-de-camp or valet to facilitate intimacy. Gifts were exchanged which included expensive gold rings, studded with Ludwig's initials in radiant diamonds.[81] The longest relationship was with his equerry, Richard Horning, who remained in the king's service for twenty years.

Ludwig kept a diary most of his adult life, in his personal secret code – a blend of German, French and occasionally Latin – and in it confessed to his "failing," in a poetical orgy of self-flagellation. "I lie in the sign of the Cross…in the sign of the sun…and of the moon (orient! rebirth through Oberon's magic horn). May I and my ideals be accused if I should fall once more. Thank God this cannot happen again, for God's holy will and the King's august word shall protect me. Only spiritual love is allowed; sensual love is accursed! I call down a solemn anathema upon it…"[82]

His frailty and determination not to indulge in sexual practices is touchingly portrayed time and again in his secret confessional. "Not again in January, nor in February! The important thing is as far as is *possible* to get out of the habit of it – with God and the king's help!" The self-imposed punishment was severe and he constantly remonstrated with himself. "No more pointless cold baths…" was the poignant entry for January 11, 1870. That Richard Horning became a temptation, too difficult to resist after wine and intoxicants, became clear from the entry of June 29, 1871. "Solemn oath taken before the picture of the Great King; 'To abstain from every kind of stimulation for 3 months.' Forbidden to approach closer than 1½ paces."

Always a fanatical admirer of the French King Louis XIV, he recorded what happened on the anniversary of Louis's death, January 21, 1872 when Ludwig committed "symbolic-allegoric final *sin*, redeemed by the expiatory death." The adulation of Louis XIV, "the Sun King," was largely on account of the fact that he had built the incomparable pleasure palace at Versailles. Never a homosexual, he had been described by Voltaire as a person who

---

81. See Yan, "King Ludwig II of Bavaria: His Life and Art."
82. Ibid.

"liked the ladies and it was reciprocal" and conducted his court as a never-ending party. He had six children by his queen Marie Therésé of Austria but was somewhat shocked when one was black. Anyone with any knowledge of biology would have been mystified by her explanation as to how it all occurred. An African prince had given a black dwarf to the queen as a gift and he became part of the royal household, much like a family pet. The queen claimed that during her pregnancy the dwarf had frightened her and caused the baby to be born black.[83]

Ludwig's self-condemnation continued – in another revealing entry in the diary he referred to another "falling," which was expiated by a more chaste embrace, as "that catastrophe on the fifteenth of this month, cleansed from all impurity, a pure cup of Richard's [Horning] love and friendship…pure and holy kiss…just *one*." But the flesh was weak and the strict morality of the time imposed horrible strictures on his love. Ludwig and Richard Horning constantly promised themselves and each other that they would repent of their "sin." They even signed an oath: "Let it be sworn on our friendship, no further fall before 3 June…" What happened on that day is not recorded.

The length of his relationship with Horning and the venue of their discovery of each other were also recorded in the secret diary. Ludwig noted on March 6, 1872, "in exactly 2 months it will be 5 years since that blessed 6th day of May when we first came to know each other, never to part until death. Written in the Indian Pavilion…" That Ludwig and Horning could not hold out till the June 3 deadline is clear from an entry of February 13, 1873. "Never again as on 12 May 1872 and likewise as little as possible…Even kissing must be avoided."

The entry "never to part until death" was a trifle optimistic it transpires, from further notes in the diary. That Richard was not the only object of the king's desire is apparent from other entries – as is the king's *modus operandi* when pursuing his quarry, and the subsequent hunt. "On 21 March spoke to Freiherr von Varicourt for the first time. On the 23rd appointed him aide-de-camp…3 April with Varicourt to the Residenz Theatre: *The Pompadour's Fan* and the private audience, then supper with him in the Winter Garden 7–1 o'clock…Beyond any possible doubt our friendship will endure. After the Easter festival supper again with him till 2:00 am. On the

---

83. Wallace et al., *The Intimate Sex Lives of Famous People*, 276.

Richard Wagner in his prime. Gregor-Dellin, page 147. Nationalarchiv der Richard Wagner-Stiftung/Richard Wagner Gedenkstätte, Bayreuth.

15th with Varicourt in the Kiosk, then a ride along the shore by moonlight till 3:45 AM…1873." How long Varicourt lasted is not stated but later in the same month another lover has appeared on the scene. "On 27 April with Leonhard the wig-maker to the Residenz Theatre…8 days at Berg."[84]

The tragedy of a form of love that the times would not accept ended in horror and death. The politicians and press swooped like vultures on the susceptible idealistic young king and devoured him to the entrails. Of greater interest to us, not that it was of no concern to them – for the thought of killing two birds, the king and Wagner with one stone, was almost too much to resist – was the relationship between the fifty-year-old composer and the eighteen-year-old monarch.

In 1989 the Technics Company ran a newspaper advertisement for a new stereo system. It showed a picture of a wild and insane-looking Richard Wagner staring madly at the reader and the advertisement then stated "to

---

84. Ibid.

Wagner loved silk and soft materials to such an extent that he was rumored to have a clothing fetish. Barth et al., 227. Der Floh, Vienna, June 24, 1877, Historisches Museum, der Stadt, Vienna.

hear what he intended, a hi-fi system has to be perfectly composed…" The gist of the message was that only the Technics system produced the sound that matched the genius of the composer. The advertisement then went on to pronounce that Wagner "founded a revolutionary movement, married Liszt's daughter and had an affair with King Ludwig II."[85] The truth is not as simple as that but much has been written about Wagner's sexual preferences.

What admits of little doubt is that Ludwig's own sexual peccadilloes were to "infect" the reputation of his musical god. In 1877 the noted Viennese journalist Daniel Spitzer published sixteen letters Wagner wrote to a Viennese seamstress which contained orders for countless satin dressing

---

85. Vetter, "Wagner in the History of Psychology," 58.

gowns and bedspreads, also satin fabrics, silk ribbons and rose garlands; one order, apart from other items, included 435 yards of satin.

These revelations concerning the composer, when added to his close friendship to Ludwig, persuaded Magnus Hirschfeld – a leading campaigner for homosexuals – to readjust the charge leveled by Cesare Lombroso that Wagner was a "sexual psychopath" to that of an allegation that their relationship was "homo-erotically tinged."

The charge amused Wagner and had there been a trial of his sexual morals he would have been able to call of string of witnesses to establish his preference for the female sex – Minna, Mathilde Wesendonck, Jessie Laussot, Mathilde Maier, Friederike Meyer, Cosima and a number of rather juvenile witnesses – the products of his relationship with Cosima, including Siegfried, Isolde and Eva. Not that such a probability would have satisfied those who peddle these kinds of rumors, who later modified their charges to the more encompassing allegations of "bisexuality." There is a document in Wagner's own hand dated 1873 in which he addresses the question of homosexuality. "There is one thing about the Greeks that we shall never be able to understand, a thing that separates them utterly from us: their love – pederasty."[86] At the beginning of the next century H. Fuchs continued the allegation of homosexuality in his book *Richard Wagner and Homosexuality*, and Heinrich Pudor, a former director of the Dresden Conservatory, pointed to the essential bisexual nature of the musician and concluded that the predilection for satin indicated that he was homosexual.[87]

Just before the First World War the sexologist Alfred Kind in a monumentally erudite work *Gynaeocracy in the History of Humankind* – the title alone bespeaks him immediately as a politically correct and gender sensitive author – returned to this topic and after mentioning the orders for satin referred to a series of charges which had not hitherto seen the light of day. Kind said that "homosexual circles have claimed [Wagner] as their own and he has, at the very least, been dubbed a fetishist…in its day [the press] blurted out these secrets from an artist's boudoir. Since then many value judgments have been passed: sybaritic, homosexual, dermatite [inflammation of the skin], fetishistic, transvestite, feminine streak." It

---

86. Newman, *Life of Richard Wagner*, vol. 3, 237.
87. Vetter, "Wagner in the History of Psychology," 52–53.

was Lord Byron who referred to the Lords of Lacedaemon as true soldiers, but the English were sybarites in the sense of people devoted to luxury or pleasure, effeminate voluptuaries and sensualists.

Having catalogued the moral offences Kind then pronounced none of them accurate, but proposed an interesting topic for his colleagues' next conference. "Much to the dismay of the diagnosticians, none of these assessments is wholly true…A competition should be set up for the next psychiatric congress: Wagner's illness."[88] Perhaps the most quaint diagnosis was that of Robert Greenblatt, professor emeritus of endocrinology at an American medical school who wrote about *Richard Wagner: The Voluptuary Genius* and said Wagner "suffered from hemorrhoids, and there will be some who say he *deserved them*."[89]

Wagner's relationship with the king had the tongues wagging in Bavaria – not that it was a matter of great concern to either of them – as Oscar Wilde said, "the one thing worse than being spoken about is not being spoken about." Nicknamed Lolotte by the press and the savage newshounds baying for his blood Wagner had to face comparison with the legendary dancer and courtesan. The allusion was to Lola Montez, the Irish-born daughter of a Spanish mother and British father – later the mistress of Ludwig's uncle King Louis I of Bavaria and a temptress who slept her way through the aristocracy of Europe. So successfully did the erotic actress and dancer insinuate her way into his favors that the king of Bavaria made her Countess of Landsfeld, but her unpopularity led to his abdication in favor of his son Maximilian II, King Ludwig II's father.[90]

So incestuous had the sexual antics of the courts become that Lola counted amongst her amours Franz Liszt, who had a brief fling with her in 1843, but found her so sexually demanding that he devoted no time to his music. Described by one reporter in poetic terms Lola clearly had a hold on the attention of the red-blooded males who frequented the courts of Europe. Plagued by a succession of illnesses including the dreaded sexually transmitted variety, her beauty seemed to emerge unimpaired. "Her skin was white, her wavy hair like the tendrils of woodbine, her eyes tameless and wild, her mouth like a budding pomegranate. Add to that a dashing

---

88. Ibid., 54.
89. Ibid., 58.
90. Wallace et al., *The Intimate Sex Lives of Famous People*, 316.

figure, charming feet, and perfect grace." That unbeatable combination of qualities clearly was what attracted the virtuoso and rue but her insatiable sexual appetite was too much for Liszt. Shaking his patrician locks and sneaking quietly down the back steps the great composer left her sleeping in a Paris hotel room, paid the manager for "the furniture she will break when she discovers my absence," and fled to the Riviera.[91]

Despite the rancor of false accusation – the nickname of Lolotte really stung the king and the composer, for her relationship with Louis I had resulted in his political demise – Wagner's fame went from strength to strength. The *Ring* was eventually produced in great triumph in the new Festspielhaus at Bayreuth on August 13, 14, 16 and 17, 1876. Counts and countesses by the score trekked to the small town, and musicians including Anton Bruckner, Edvard Grieg, Peter Tchaikovsky, Saint-Saens and Liszt, as well as managers and conductors from every German opera house and sixty music critics, crammed into trains to be present. Wagner's greatest enemy, the music critic Hanslick, whom he had parodied in the figure of Beckmesser in *Meistersinger*, recovered his favor with the Bayreuth clan – perhaps in fear of being pilloried in the next opera – and called the festival "one of the most remarkable events in the entire history of art." Grieg compared it to the work of Michelangelo and called it "a true giant in the history of art" and the critic Wilhelm Mohr compared Wagner to "two masters of all masters, Shakespeare and Beethoven."[92]

Tchaikovsky was less complimentary. At the end of the Ring cycle he told his brother in a letter that he felt that he had been finally let out of prison: "how many thousand times finer is the ballet of Sylvia [by Delibes]."[93] He carried on saying that "before, music strove to delight people – now they are tormented and exhausted."[94]

Mention has to be made of one particularly important visitor: Dom Pedro II, the emperor of Brazil. He was a fan of Wagner's who had tried to persuade him in 1857 to take a company to South America and conduct his operas in Rio de Janiero. Ever on the scent for funds, Wagner had sent him expensively bound piano scores of some of his operas hoping for tangible results – to no avail. He heard little more from the potentate until the first

---

91. Ibid., 317.
92. Spotts, *Bayreuth*, 71.
93. Evans, *Tchaikovsky*, 36.
94. Poznansky, *Tchaikovsky*, 181.

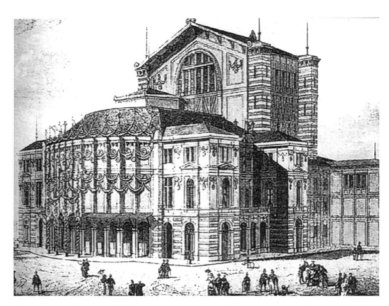

The Bayreuth Festspielhaus. Spotts, Bayreuth, page 42. Nationalarchiv der Richard Wagner-Stiftung/Richard Wagner Gedenkstätte, Bayreuth.

festival when His Eminence arrived, completely unannounced, and took up residence in the town. His status might have never been discovered had he not signed the occupation column of the hotel register with one word – "Emperor."[95]

The dislocation in the transport system and the demands on accommodation had some strange repercussions for another famous personality – in fact the German ideologue plaguing the ruling classes of Europe. Karl Marx was traveling from London to Karlsbad in mid-August and could not get a bed in Nürnberg, as every one was taken. He wrote to his sponsor and great friend Friedrich Engels denouncing the great composer and calling him "the Bayreuth Fool's Festival of State Musician, Wagner." He had clearly read some of the music dramas and was aware of the myths upon which they were based. He would have been interested to read George Bernard Shaw's analysis of the work as a socialist allegory and the consequences that flowed from the refusal of Wotan to pay the giants their dues for building Valhalla.

Marx told his daughter that the extended Wagner family was every

---

95. Newman, *Life of Richard Wagner*, vol. 4, 520.

bit as queer as the Nibelungs and merited its own tetralogy. Anyone following the bitter squabbling amongst the descendants will see how true his comment was.[96] To this day the blood relatives of the great man rattle sabers and joust rhapsodically in the press about their rightful claims to the patrimony that is Bayreuth. The books of great grandchildren Nike and Gottfried Wagner chronicle these unseemly wranglings for anyone seeking respite from the other form of entertainment that has captured the hearts of the people – contemporary soap operas.

Wagner was not totally satisfied with the first festival and would tell Cosima from time to time about how he could improve it. Referring to the final scene from *The Valkyries*, reckoned by many to have been the finest he ever penned, he said, "I will change that some day when I produce the work in heaven, at the right of God, and the old gent and I are watching it together."[97] The décor never matched up to the majesty of the music: he would tell people to close their eyes and imagine what was going on. The papier-mâché rocks, chain mail and horned Valkyrie helmets distracted the audience and stood incongruously next to the endless flow of melody. "Fantasy in chains" was Nietzsche's pithy comment.[98] It was only when Appia analyzed this aspect and proposed symbolical representation on the stage – a comment taken up without proper acknowledgement by Wagner's grandson Wieland eighty years later, that the drama began to match the music.

Ludwig attended the first festival on condition he was seen by none – the paranoid shyness was riding high – and was overawed by the majesty of the works. The king wrote to Wagner, comparing him this time to Prometheus. "Words are too inadequate for me to begin to express my enthusiasm and deepest thanks. You are a god-man, the true artist by God's grace who has brought the sacred fire from heaven to earth to cleanse, sanctify and redeem it! …Never before have I been transported into such a state of inebriation, such unprecedented sanctity, so filled with such an unprecedented sense of joy."[99] When Bismarck opposed a State contribution to the Bayreuth fund Wagner said of him, "Bismarck is certainly a great

---

96. Spotts, *Bayreuth*, 67.
97. Ibid., 70.
98. Ibid., 75.
99. Ibid., 68.

politician but not a great man, for he has no comprehension of Bayreuth." The world of Wagner was a small one and was dominated by one man.

That gloomy wet and cold Bayreuth was to be the home for Wagner, who spent the rest of his days there, apart from journeys in 1877 to London and to Italy to escape the rain. He flirted with Buddhism and its "larger view of the world" but never regained his belief if he ever had one. Those who believe that his final opera *Parsifal* represents his spiritual growth should look more closely at the subtext and listen to the music. "The midnights of the soul" was the phrase Nietzsche coined for that delicious, intoxicating kaleidoscope of sound that represents at one moment the pinnacle of Western music and then, subliminally, the clearest exhortation to racial cleansing that music can ever utter.

Cosima, on the other hand, had abandoned Catholicism for his sake and embraced Lutheran Protestantism – a malleable concoction that condoned adultery and espoused rampant anti-Semitism – and continued with her religion. Luther had views on Jews that she could live with. Of all the faults that could be placed at the door of the composer, a lack of humor was not one of these. On one occasion seeing Cosima, elegantly dressed for church, with the cleanly washed and neatly dressed children in tow, Wagner said to her: "Give my best to your Saviour, though from the very beginning He has created an awful lot of confusion."

For him Christianity had dangerous antecedents. "The Christian dogma leans on the Jewish religion and that is its misfortune" was his reason for not rising early enough to attend church. The services were tainted by their ancient roots and even the buildings did not escape censure. When visiting the Sistine Chapel Cosima records in her diary, "Richard finds the Jewish element predominant...fanaticism, mourning, hate."[100]

Roman Catholicism provoked his wrath more frequently than any other Christian denomination. He regarded the writing of religious music as a waste of time and was vastly amused when Liszt became an Abbè. When they met it was smooth sailing while the Hungarian listened and the German spoke. The father and son-in-law got on famously when Wagner was playing his latest opera on the great grand piano at Wahnfried. But if Liszt tried to play some of his latest compositions Wagner fumed telling Cosima that her father had insisted on playing him "his latest Ave Maria."

---

100. Marek, *Cosima Wagner*, 122.

When Cosima reproached him and reminded Wagner of Liszt's great contribution to music – "Didn't you say recently that he had inaugurated a new epoch in art?" – his retort was cutting in the extreme. Wagner replied, in a reference not only to music, but also to the Hungarian composer's reputation, in matters of the heart, for having wandering hands, "yes, in fingering."[101] Liszt must have told Wagner about Lola Montez or perhaps the rumormongers of Bayreuth trumpeted it abroad.

Others told a different story of Wagner's admiration for the aged Hungarian composer. Count Apponyi visited Bayreuth and was present one evening when the discussion turned to Beethoven's late sonatas, with a focus on the *Hammerklavier*. Liszt extolled the virtues of the fine adagio in F sharp minor and to prove a point strode into the music room, which was large enough to reach to the roof of the double-storied house. Wagner had retired to bed by that time. When the wizard of the keyboard had filled the listener's ears with the mysticism of the late works, a most extraordinary event occurred. "Suddenly from the gallery, on the first floor, there came a tremendous uproar, and Richard Wagner in his nightshirt came thundering, rather than running, down the stairs. His bedroom led on to the inner gallery, and he had apparently crept out in silence on hearing the first notes and remained there without giving a sign of his presence. He flung his arms around Liszt's neck and, sobbing with emotion, thanked him in broken phrases for the wonderful gift he had received."[102]

The Wagners escaped the wet and cold Bayreuth to raise funds in London to try to keep the festival solvent. Still smarting from his previous visit he was gratified to hear that *The Flying Dutchman* had been produced – but his glee was quickly transformed to wrath when he heard that it had been produced in Italian, as Queen Victoria had suggested twenty-two years previously. His reputation as a racist had successfully crossed the English Channel, as had his own assessment of himself as persecuted. "We cannot forget [*The Daily Telegraph* wrote on May 9] who turned upon the operatic composers of his own time with a fury which even now men wonder at; who ransacked the capacious German language for its strongest

---

101. Ibid., 125.
102. Beckett, *Liszt*, 136.

terms of contempt and scorn…and charged a whole race [the Jews] with conspiring to ruin him…"[103]

In London the Wagners met the royal family and a number of dignitaries including the great English novelist George Eliot (the male appellation adopted by Mary Ann Evans) who, according to Cosima, "makes a noble and pleasant impression." Cosima had read *Silas Marner* and *The Mill on the Floss* with much admiration. Perhaps Cosima empathized with a woman, such as her mother Marie, who had been forced to adopt a man's name to succeed in the world of writing.

Little is recorded of the exchange and Cosima would have wanted to discuss literature but the authoress was quick to take up the sword rather than its traditional literary rival. Eliot was aware of the anti-Semitism, spewed out by the doyens of Bayreuth. Eliot was more than usually direct when she said to her: "I hear your husband does not like Jews. My husband is a Jew." History has not recorded the Wagners' response to this direct challenge.[104] Not that they would have worried, so certain were they in the justness of their cause. Later Eliot was to comment: "she is a genius. He is an epicier (literally a grocer and figuratively a small minded mean person)!"[105] No doubt she was not attractive enough to have tempted the aged Wagner. Henry James described her as "magnificently ugly – deliciously hideous," a comment only exceeded by his sister who described her as "a fungus of pendulous shape."[106]

Cosima accompanied Eliot to the concerts where excerpts were played of Wagner's works. So moved was the novelist during the scene in *The Valkyries* where Brünnhilde announces to Siegmund that he is destined to die, that she sobbed quietly into her handkerchief – unless it was the prospect of spending an evening with such virulent anti-Semites. Eliot's partner George Henry Lewes was an eminent philosopher and had written a *Life of Goethe* which was hailed as a masterpiece. Lewes could not divorce his own adulterous wife as he had accepted her four children by an extramarital union as his own. Never married, Eliot and Lewes "eloped" to

---

103. Christiansen, "Kultur Clash," A9.
104. Marek, *Cosima Wagner*, 178–79.
105. Taylor, *Richard Wagner*, 383.
106. Wallace et al., *The Intimate Sex Lives of Famous People*, 146.

Germany in 1854, when Eliot was thirty-five, and on returning to Britain lived in a happy union until 1878 when he died.[107]

After meeting the monarch, Queen Victoria recorded in her journal that she met "the great composer Wagner, about whom the people of Germany are really a little mad." She had seen him with her "dearest Albert" in 1855. She recorded that "he has grown old and stout, and has a clever but not pleasing countenance."[108] Her meeting was something of a surprise given that *The Times* of May 12 had called *Tristan und Isolde* a glorification of adulterous love "scarcely to be tolerated on the boards of an English theatre."[109] The next day's edition of the same paper showed that Wagner had started to appeal to the fashionable young. "Bad form not to be well up in Wagnerism, don't you think?" Davison the music critic, who had previously been seduced by the bribes of Meyerbeer, attributes these words in the newspaper to "a swell in our hearing." The pretty girls' response to the question by the young "dandies" was also memorable: "Oh yes! I don't know what they mean, but they're awfully sublime, I understand."

The pianist and pedagogue Edward Dannreuther records the response of his friend Eddie Hamilton: "the great last act of Walküre was overwhelming…Hamilton went to sleep once or twice…but I think on the whole he appreciated it." Wagner dropped into a performance in Italian of *Tannhäuser* ("the worst I have ever seen for ensemble") and when the march in the second act struck up Wagner led his friend Dannreuther to a German restaurant in the Strand where the composer poured forth comic anecdotes before returning to the theatre.

Dannreuther was fortunate that he did not have to listen to his political diatribes on that evening. On another occasion over a chop and a pint of Bass's Ale Dannreuther later wrote that "he began to pour out story after story…about German Jews told in their own jargon." That these racist ravings were overheard is clear from Dannreuther's further account. "A young foreigner, a painter apparently, had taken his seat at a table opposite, and was quietly watching and listening. Soon his face began to twitch – I could see that he was making efforts to look serene. But the twitches increased – and when one of the stories came to the final point, he snatched up his hat

---

107. Marek, *Cosima Wagner*, 179.
108. Ibid.
109. Christiansen, "Kultur Clash," A9.

and vanished."[110] If the insane political rhetoric prevailed on this second visit his music was well received and it was clear that some, at least, of the music critics were beginning to understand what he was trying to achieve. *The Musical Standard* of June 16 described his tour as a "singular triumph for the man who has boldly braved a generation of adverse criticism."

Oscar Wilde had praised Wagner's music, as it was loud enough to permit him to regale his friends unnoticed with his countless witticisms. The music was also to have a profound effect on his most famous fiction hero Dorian Gray, who was described as having heard *Tannhäuser* at Covent Garden. The profligate, whose picture decayed while he stayed young, recognized the prelude to that opera as a confessional commentary on the lugubrious "tragedy of his own soul." Gray repents of his debauchery and desires nothing more than the absolution Wagner had lavished on all his sinners, but no redemptive female volunteers – Senta or Elizabeth are obvious candidates for this mission – rescued the depraved Dorian.[111]

Possibly the greatest character in Wagner's operas is Wotan the mythological god, who is married to Fricka. He assumed many guises including that of a wolf, which was to be so appealing to Adolf Hitler, and the Wanderer. While masquerading as these other persons Wotan sired Valkyries and Volsungs, who subsequently marry or couple so contagiously that a reading of the genealogy of the *Ring* becomes a vast incestuous riddle. At its simplest the twins Siegmund and Sieglinde, children of Wotan, couple vigorously at the end of *The Valkyries* and sire Siegfried, who marries Brünnhilde, also a daughter of Wotan, by Erda the earth goddess.

But matters are not as simple as that. In the early 1910s an anonymous writer in a Berlin theatre journal tried to sum up the relationships. "Siegfried is the son of his uncle and the nephew of his mother. He is his own cousin, as the nephew and son of his aunt. He is the nephew of his wife, and therefore his own uncle and his own nephew by marriage. He is nephew and uncle in one. He is the son-in-law of his grandfather Wotan, the brother-in-law of his aunt, who is at the same time his mother. Siegmund is the father-in-law of his sister Brunnhilde and the brother-in-law of his son. He is the husband of his sister and the father-in-law of

---

110. Ibid.
111. See Conrad, "He's Tricky, That Dicky."

the woman whose father is the father-in-law of his son. Brunnhilde is the daughter-in-law..."[112] Phew!

Much of Wagner's work was autobiographical and, while Cosima was to fill a void, he still had a need to wander. This was, of course, to stimulate the creativity in him. Judith Gautier swam into his orbit and in 1876 there had been an emotional episode at her lodgings in Bayreuth, when an exhausted Wagner had fallen on her breast and sobbed his heart out. No doubt once her susceptibilities had been overcome she joined a long list of those who had enjoyed Wagner's favors. The next year he wrote to her to remind her about his love. He called what must have been temporary infatuation or – at best, an elevated form of lust – "the most exquisite intoxication, the highest pride of my life, the last gift of the gods, whose will it was that I should not break down under the delusive glory of the Nibelungen performances."[113] Two years before this the great psychoanalyst Carl Jung was born and he had something to say about the phenomenon of Nazism to follow in the next century. He also coined a maxim on marital fidelity that would have had Wagner applauding. "The prerequisite for a good marriage is the license to be unfaithful."[114]

The affair with Judith Gautier lasted a year and during the time Wagner wrote to her, he also took advantage of her home in Paris, ordering satins, velvets and strong perfumes, to help him compose the wonderful intoxicating harmonies of his last masterpiece *Parsifal*.[115] And like all males he showed off his physical prowess by climbing trees to show her his virility.[116] Years later Hitler would tell his female admirers that he could stand for hours maintaining the Nazi salute – never tiring. Freud would have understood that gesture. At that time the great psychoanalyst was twenty years old, having been born in Moravia and moved to Vienna at the age of four years.

Freud was to note the process he called sublimation in artists of great talent. "This enables excessively strong excitations arising from particular sources of sexuality to find an outlet and use in other fields, so that a not inconsiderable increase in psychical efficiency results from a disposition

---
112. Wagner, Nike, *The Wagners*, 58.
113. Marek, *Cosima Wagner*, 169.
114. Wallace, *The Intimate Sex Lives of Famous People*, 247.
115. Marek, *Cosima Wagner*, 169.
116. Waite, *The Psychopathic God*, 106.

which in itself is perilous."[117] The fields he is talking about clearly include the artists of this world as he goes on to mention the source of artistic endeavor. "Here we have *one of the origins of artistic activity*; and, according to the completeness or incompleteness of the sublimation, a characterological analysis of a highly gifted individual, and *in particular of one with an artistic disposition, may reveal a mixture, in every proportion, of efficiency, perversion and neurosis*."

Wagner visited the city that was to symbolize his notion of German culture – Nürnberg – in 1877 with his family. It was not far from Bayreuth and was the first city to convert to Lutheranism. Another advantage recommended the place to the family; it had successfully kept Jews out until the middle of the nineteenth century.[118] After their arrival they had perpetrated the ultimate sin for Wagner; a synagogue was built in a Moorish style on the river Pegnitz and consecrated in 1874. Cosima recorded in her diary that Wagner's good mood was disturbed by the sight of the building in the Hans-Sachs-Platz. The square had been named after the benign shoemaker and hero of his opera *Die Meistersinger von Nürnberg* but that quality eluded the composer who found the synagogue "insultingly gaudy and vulgar."

Wagner had earlier donated the proceedings from a performance of the opera to the erection of a statue of Hans Sachs as he was very displeased by the decision to build the synagogue, which had been erected in the "most explicitly Oriental style."[119] Adolf Hitler was later to use the city as the venue for all his Nazi Party annual gatherings, the anti-Semitic laws were promulgated there and it was to lend its name to the trials of war criminals after the Second World War. The synagogue was one of the first targets of applied Bayreuth ideology. During that same year, 1877, the family Wagner traveled through Lucerne, Siegfried's birthplace. Cosima noted in her diary, "the place is overgrown and decayed, inhabited by French Jews" and Richard agreed and added the comment "as it always was."[120]

The children were growing up and Cosima looked for a tutor for Siegfried who turned ten in 1879. She was looking for particular qualities in

---

117. Freud, *On Sexuality*, 163.
118. Köhler, *Wagner's Hitler*, 253.
119. Ibid.
120. Pachl, *Siegfried Wagner*, 39.

the man entrusted with the cultural future of Germany. The one described by Wagner as having a "sword in his eye." After searching far and wide she found the ideal candidate and he was predictably enough "devoutly Christian, completely un-Jewish."[121]

---

121. Marek, *Cosima Wagner*, 182.

Chapter seven
Ideological Lunacy

The tragedy of the life of Richard Wagner was his forays into the world of politics and ideology. In music and theatre, apart from the subliminally sinister messages, his work was that of a genius. The will that drove him to achieve the impossible in the theatre and festival at Bayreuth urged him on to solve the world's political problems. He learned little from his interventions in Bavarian politics when he bent the ear of the young king with his ideas.

That he achieved a godlike status as musician inclined others to find his every utterance a divine revelation. Nor was he very astute in disabusing their minds of the sycophancy. Mention has been made of his early struggles with Meyerbeer and his venomous essays. With old age came not wisdom but a rabid lunatic fanaticism. Those who would deny this madness point to individual Jews whom he befriended such as Porges and Tausig. Later he was to tolerate Hermann Levi, the conductor of his first *Parsifal*. Much of this alleged affection and toleration was opportunism and betrayed no detraction from a visceral anti-Semitism. He was not much admired by the German government who prosecuted a certain Count Harry Arnim for saying in a political article that "next to Wagner, Bismarck is the greatest man living today." Such a comment was an insult to Bismarck because, so

Joseph Arthur de Gobineau – the diplomat and race biologist who influenced Wagner's views on the Jews. Gregor-Dellin, page 203. Nationalarchiv der Richard Wagner-Stiftung/Richard Wagner Gedenkstätte, Bayreuth.

it was stated, "Richard Wagner is universally regarded as a man suffering from megalomania."[1]

At Bayreuth he was to hold court and then pontificate – he would pronounce his answers with an aura of papal infallibility. One visitor in particular fascinated Wagner and shared his theories of race – the mysterious Count Joseph Arthur de Gobineau whom he had met in Rome in 1876. Not that the count's ideas were new when he arrived at Bayreuth on one of those typical rain-washed November evenings, when the Wagners were wishing themselves in Italy. Wagner had read the count's contribution to biological determinism – translated by Adrian Collins – the *Essay on the Inequality of the Human Races*.[2] Wagner first met him at a soiree by Italian artists in which they played some of the beautiful songs by Sgambati. In contrast to the massive polyphony produced by the Wagner orchestra with its minimum of a hundred and twenty players, on that occasion a mandolin band was playing. The composer later read and enjoyed the count's political theories and his stories *Nouvelles Asiatiques* on Asian themes.

---

1. Newman, *Life of Richard Wagner*, vol. 4, 570.
2. Newman, *Life of Richard Wagner*, vol. 1, 257, 261. See also W.M. McGovern, *From Luther to Hitler* (New York: Houghton Mifflin Company, 1941), 505.

In 1881 Gobineau was Wagner's guest at Wahnfried for a month, accompanying him to the Berlin season of the *Ring*. As a political thinker Gobineau became the spokesman for pronounced aristocratic conservatism and he denounced democracy, revolution from below and everything that he contemptuously called the "community spirit."

The pseudo aristocrat had divided mankind into three races – Negro, Chinese and European – and ordered them in a bio-cultural totem pole of proficiency. In intellect the Europeans were the highest, the Negro the lowest and the Chinese occupied the middle zone, having a monopoly on mediocrity; they were practical and law-abiding but incapable of producing great leaders or geniuses.[3] The stereotypes propagated by him were capable of further subdivision and the Aryans were rich in reason, energy, resourcefulness and creativity. The blacks excelled in music: a circumstance that Wagner found somewhat upsetting, given his views on the decadence of Jewish art. But Gobineau comforted him with the role of cultural all rounder for his preferred race. "The Aryan German is a powerful creature…everything he thinks, says and does is thus of major importance."[4]

Gobineau further expounded his views on the Semites, who were the black sheep of the white European stock and were a mixture of white and black races. He predicted that if a way were not found to develop the Aryans, the human race would soon come to an end after its fourteen-thousand-year history. Gobineau had taken up the views of Darwin concerning the survival of the fittest, which meant of course the German race. He did not much care for Darwin's thesis that mankind was descended from monkeys and advocated the contrary; he suggested that the species was headed in that direction!

Gobineau had led an interesting life and had been the French ambassador to Sweden. Despite his quaint and bizarre racial theories Gobineau was much sought after by the fairer sex and a scandal linked him with Countess La Tour, the wife of the Italian ambassador in Stockholm. An artist with a *joie de vivre*, she painted his portrait. Apart from his amatory adventures Gobineau was a fund of information – he once spent a whole evening telling Wagner the virtues of learning Persian; the next night was

---

3. Shirer, *Rise and Fall of the Third Reich*, 136.
4. Ibid.

reading excerpts from his *Amadis* and his theories of language, including the Swedish verb from which the English "I am" derives.

That was but a fraction of the knowledge the quixotic theorist was to impart. The two then turned their attention to the Irish, whom Gobineau reckoned were the laziest inhabitants of the earth and incapable of working. Wagner agreed but then embarked on a long dissertation as to their tragic oppression at the hands of the "bloody" English aristocracy. As the small hours yawned openly and the dawn prepared to take over their shift, Gobineau turned his fertile mind to an exegesis of the church. The fiery race aesthete stigmatized them as purveyors of false hope and blamed the gospels for the churches interceding on behalf of the poor. The Irish, it seemed, were so damned and inferior they ought also to be denied the solace of religion.

They shared the same ideological idiocy and Gobineau was one of the few people who could make Wagner laugh. After they had been staying at the Hotel du Nord in Berlin Wagner especially remembered him coming to a performance of his opera *Die Walküre* (*The Valkyries*) in a hat borrowed from Paul von Joukowsky. More appealing was Gobineau's analysis of the subliminal messages to be found in the music; the Ring cycle conveyed "the ideal expression of all his ideas of race…on extinction and survival."[5]

Wagner recognized that he had written operas that conformed with the mad geo-biologist's views. In Cosima's diary entry of October 17, 1882, she reported on a performance one evening of the third act of *Siegfried* played by Herr Rubinstein which pleased her and the great composer. "That is Gobineau music," Richard says as he comes in, "that is race. Where else will you find two such beings looking at each other! Here is just forest and rocks and water and nothing rotten in it."[6] Wagner later presented Gobineau with a complete set of his writings, with an inscription extolling the bond between the Saxons and the Normans.

Their brief and intensive exchanges meant elevation to the pantheon of gods for the race apologist. Wagner decided that Gobineau was his only contemporary and that in future he would read only the utterings of the Trinity – Gobineau, Schopenhauer and his own writings. Nothing else was worthwhile. Gobineau kept in touch with Wagner and often wrote

---

5. Köhler, *Wagner's Hitler*, 63.
6. See Solomon, "Wagner and Hitler."

long polemical tracts that fascinated the composer and were read out to all and sundry at Bayreuth. So great was Gobineau's kinship for Wagner that he determined to settle down in Bayreuth on his retirement but fate intervened and he died of heart failure in Turin.

Another famous visitor to what was to become a Mecca of European culture was Renoir, the French impressionist painter, who wanted to paint Wagner's picture. Initially, when the servant announced his presence, Wagner did not catch the name properly and thought it was Victor Noir, a French journalist shot dead in 1870 by Prince Pierre Napoleon Bonaparte. "I heard muffled steps approaching across the thick carpets. It was the Master, in his velvet gown with wide sleeves faced with black satin. He is very handsome and kind and shook my hand, invited me to sit down, and we launched into a bizarre conversation half in German and half in French." That was how the painter remembered the visit.[7]

Wagner also explained his theories of race and especially his aversion to the German Jews to the painter, who did not seem very impressed.[8] Some of that disillusionment was to influence the portrait. Renoir initially made a sketch of the head and shoulders of the famous composer in Palermo and later completed it in full color. Renoir was part of the Impressionist school and his work was characterized by brightness and light. His lack of appreciation of the domestic political views did not show and he certainly amused Wagner with his many grimaces as he worked. The result was a very curious blend of blue and pink that made the composer look like the embryo of an angel, an oyster swallowed by an epicure.

Gobineau liked the picture and he saw genius in the face. Wagner recognized how perceptive Renoir was about Michelangelo and the Renaissance. Although Wagner saw himself as "the plenipotentiary of downfall," he was certain that if his ideas were to strike root all these great men would be listened to as teachers and would not, as it were, have lived in vain. The portrait did not impress the composer who thought it made him look like a Methodist minister.

Parsifal was his last work and for many it was the highlight of his achievements. His last labor of love commenced in 1877 and after a long gestation was produced at Bayreuth in 1882. Once again Wagner mined the

---

7. Taylor, *Richard Wagner*, 396–97.
8. Gutman, *Richard Wagner*, 584.

rich vein of myth that had been his forte. This time he explored the fate of the Holy Grail, the goblet in which Jesus served wine to the disciples at the Last Supper. The legends upon which Wagner based his prose drama told how this vessel, together with the spear used to pierce Christ's side on the cross, were kept by the Knights of the Holy Grail, a chivalrous order that performed good deeds, rescued damsels in distress and bore the moral authority in the area.

Into the mediaeval tale of *Parsifal* Wagner ingeniously wove the legend of the Wandering Jew, the sources of which have been mentioned. Wagner transformed the Wandering Jew Ahasuerus into a Jewess, Kundry, who traveled through the ages, making atonement for the fact that she laughed at Jesus on the cross.[9] "If you knew the curse which afflicts me, asleep and awake, in death and life, pain and laughter, newly steeled to new affliction, endlessly through this existence. I saw Him and mocked" is the way Wagner expresses it in the text of the opera. Gurnemanz explains that she is "perhaps reincarnated to expiate some sin from an earlier life." That she regards Parsifal as the Second Christ is clear from the text as she explains that "through eternities I have waited for you, the savior so late in coming whom I dared revile."

Already in 1865 Wagner was noting in his Brown Book this vital change in the legend.[10] In the opening scene of act 2 Klingsor calls Kundry "Herodias…She-Lucifer…[and the] Rose of Hades." At the time of the opera – set as far as can be made out by the laconic comments in the script in the Middle Ages in Spain – Kundry has been enslaved by the Semitic necromancer Klingsor and bound by magical spells to carry out his wishes. As Klingsor's aim was world power hers was the task to seduce the leader of the grail knights Amfortas and steal the symbol of earthly might.

In the myth upon which the prose drama was based, Amfortas was seduced and while distracted left the Holy Spear unattended. The spear was a talisman and source of power when the Knights of the Grail fought "holy" wars. During the ensuing battle – the sexual encounter had blinded him to the approach of Klingsor's soldiers – Amfortas is wounded, appropriately enough to any disciple of Freud, in the testicles, and the wound refuses to heal. Klingsor steals the symbol of power – the Holy Spear – and

---

9. Rose, *Wagner: Race and Revolution*, 37.
10. Köhler, *Wagner's Hitler*, 221.

he guards it in his heathen castle. Only an innocent fool will rescue the weapon and return it to the brotherhood and enable them to continue their good works.

The sensitive viewer will be relieved to learn that Wagner amended the text of the myth – to be specific the location of the sword thrust – and placed the wound in the abdomen. In an imitation of the Last Supper and the modern act of Eucharist or communion, the Knights of the Grail are given bread, which transforms itself to provide "body's strength and power to toil to the end required by the Savior."[11] The wine served to the Knights of the Grail – again the reference to communion is inescapable – is transformed into "blood…to fight with holy courage."[12]

The task of rescuing the spear and returning it to the Knights of the Grail falls to Parsifal, who has to fight his way past all the soldiers protecting Klingsor in his castle, which Wagner places in Arabic Spain. A bevy of flower maidens are the next foe, and each attempts to win his favor and deter him from his mission. Only when Parsifal refuses the blandishment and attempted seduction of Kundry does he become worthy of winning back the spear. The blatant Christian nature of the drama and the Jewish character of Klingsor are established beyond all doubt when Parsifal holds up the sword as a cross to thwart his adversary. Klingsor is defeated and his castle destroyed with a mighty crash in the brass.[13]

At the end of the opera, in a scene lifted bodily from St John's gospel, Kundry anoints Parsifal's feet with rare perfume, dries them with her hair and then dies. That end has been widely interpreted to mean the end of Jewry.[14] Parsifal and Christianity survive.[15] A white dove descends and hovers over Parsifal's head; much as its avian predecessor-in-title obliged the Savior from Galilee.[16] Wagner's stage directions could not be plainer: "a beam of light; the Grail glows at its brightest. From the dome a white dove descends and hovers over Parsifal's head – Kundry slowly sinks lifeless to the ground in front of Parsifal, her eyes uplifted to him. Amfortas kneels in

---

11. Waite, *The Psychopathic God*, 111.
12. Ibid.
13. Gutman, *Richard Wagner*, 584.
14. Waite, *The Psychopathic God*, 111.
15. On the significance of Parsifal holding up the cross see Gutman, *Richard Wagner*, 600, as this represents a thwarting of Klingsor the Jew.
16. Waite, *The Psychopathic God*, 111–12.

Karl Hill as the magician and necromancer Klingsor at the premiere production of Parsifal in 1882. The dress and use of a beard was a further illustration of Wagner's idea of Klingsor as a prototype of a Jew. See Weiner, page 248. Nationalarchiv der Richard Wagner-Stiftung/Richard Wagner Gedenkstätte, Bayreuth.

homage to Parsifal, who waves the Grail in blessing over the worshipping brotherhood of knights."

Marc Weiner sums up his interpretation of the message of Parsifal: "when [Parsifal] holds up aloft the holy spear over the newly bleeding Grail…the evil of the foreign (both as Jew and as woman-as-temptress) is banished from the world through the demise of Klingsor and the death of Kundry and is subsumed within the holy office of those who firmly stand on the higher moral ground of the sexually and racially pure."[17] The theatergoer may be tempted to conclude that the allusion to Jesus is deliberate but Ernest Newman warns against regarding Parsifal as Christ. He cites as authority the fact that Wagner often cautioned against the idea, for a reason that again illustrates his caustic wit. "The idea of making Christ a tenor…phew!!" was the composer's response.[18]

Paul Rose in his seminal study of anti-Semitism in Wagner summed up what Parsifal meant to him:

---

17. Weiner, *Richard Wagner and the Anti-Semitic Imagination*, 306.
18. Newman, *Life of Richard Wagner*, vol. 4, 761.

Wagner intended *Parsifal* to be a profound religious parable about how the whole essence of European humanity had been poisoned by alien, inhuman, Jewish values. It is an allegory of the Judaization of Christianity and of Germany – and of purifying redemption. In place of theological purity, the secularized religion of *Parsifal* preached the new doctrine of racial purity, which was reflected in the moral and indeed religious purity of Parsifal himself. In Wagner's mind, this redeeming purity was infringed by Jews, just as devils and witches infringed the purity of traditional Christianity. In this scheme, it is axiomatic that compassion and redemption have no application to the inexorably damned Judaized Klingsor and hence the Jews."[19]

The spear that pierced Christ's side is sometimes referred to as the Spear of Destiny and it was housed in a museum in Vienna where Wagner and Nietzsche inspected it on a special visit for that very purpose.[20] It was to be a special object of veneration for the young Adolf Hitler in his dismal days in Vienna and when he annexed Austria in 1938 he made a visit again at the dead of night. The knowledge of the origins was well known to the power-hungry Führer who stole it and took it back to Nürnberg. He must have also been aware of the other legend linked to it; that whoever decoded its secrets would have control of the world for good or evil.[21]

Scarcely two years before Wagner commenced his composition of the last masterpiece in 1877 the fifteen-year-old Gustav Mahler had a most revealing dream. He must have been mindful of the legend of the Wandering Jew that Wagner ingeniously interpolated into *The Flying Dutchman* and *Parsifal*. Mahler, who suffered the great tragedy of the loss of his brother Ernst, a year younger than he, when he was scarcely fifteen years of age, made mention of it in later life. He recalled how he, his mother and Ernst had been standing at the window of their first-floor sitting room when their mother had suddenly exclaimed "God what's happening?" as the sky filled with sulfurous mist as if some apocalypse were imminent.

Mahler then found himself in the marketplace and through this infernal vapor he glimpsed the fearful figure of the Eternal Jew, his large overcoat

---

19. Rose, *Wagner: Race and Revolution*, 166.
20. Ravenscroft, *Spear of Destiny*, 34.
21. Icke, *…and the truth shall set you free*, 231.

billowing behind him in the gale, as if he were a hunchback. His staff was held clutched in his hand and had an innovation from the details of the legend; it was topped with a gold cross, and he pursued the teenage Mahler, endeavoring to hand over the staff to him. Mahler awoke with a cry and interpreted the dream as follows: the staff symbolized endless wandering and the fate of the Eternal Jew he linked to his lifelong desire – in answer to a question posed by a relative – to be a martyr.[22]

Mahler was the subject of intense anti-Semitism and later converted to Christianity to become conductor of the Vienna Opera House. That seems to be the fairest interpretation of the cross on top of the staff in his dream. In a letter to a friend four years later Mahler describes a scene in a church: "the clouds become denser, and then suddenly, as in Raphael's painting of the Madonna, a little angel's head peers out from among these clouds, and below it stands Ahasuerus in all his sufferings, longing to ascend to him, to enter into the presence of all that means bliss and redemption, but the angel floats away on high, laughing, and vanishes, and Ahasuerus gazes after him in immeasurable grief, then takes up his staff and resumes his wanderings, tearless, eternal, immortal."

It should not be forgotten that the very Ahasuerus he was dreaming about was the selfsame character pilloried by Wagner and the personification of Jewry. Mahler continued with his dream. "O earth, my beloved earth, when, ah when will you give refuge to him who is forsaken, receiving him back into your womb? Behold! Mankind has cast him out, and he flees from its cold and heartless bosom, he flees to you, to you alone! O take him in eternal, all embracing mother, give a resting-place to him who is without friends and without rest!"[23] Had he suddenly acquired prophetic powers and was this a foretaste of the fate that Adolf Hitler had in store for the Jews some fifty years later?

Mahler came close to speaking to Wagner in Vienna in 1877, when the latter was there to conduct *Tannhäuser* and *Lohengrin*. Mahler had joined the Wagner society with Hugo Wolf and they shared lodgings. The reason for their eventual ejection was certainly not one justified by the law. They played excerpts of *Götterdämmerung* and sang the parts so loud that the landlady finally evicted them. Mahler and Wagner met for a brief moment

---

22. Franklin, *Life of Mahler*, 22–23.
23. Ibid., 46–47.

The Jewish musician and controversial conductor of Wagner's music – Hermann Levi. Gregor-Dellin, page 207. Nationalarchiv der Richard Wagner-Stiftung/Richard Wagner Gedenkstätte, Bayreuth.

when the sixty-four-year-old Wagner struggled to put on his overcoat – the seventeen-year-old Mahler fought valiantly with his shyness and desire to help but timidity overcame him and he held back, a reticence he was to regret all his life.[24]

Although Wagner denied the links to Christianity, which are manifest from the text of his last opera, he paradoxically decreed that *Parsifal* was so sacred that no Jewish conductor should have any part in its production. In 1881 Wagner wrote to Ludwig and said: "I regard the Jewish race as the born enemy of pure humanity and everything that is noble in it; it is certain that we Germans will go under before them, and perhaps I am the last German who knows how to stand up as an art-loving man against the Judaism that is already getting control of everything."[25]

Wagner's decision not to permit a Jew to have anything to do with the conducting of his operas caused problems for him in the figure of Hermann Levi. He first came into contact with Levi when the latter conducted *Meistersinger* in Karlsruhe with great success. Wagner reckoned his Jewishness was marginally pardonable because, as he told Cosima he accepted the surname "Levi" and did not change it to Lowe, Lewy, etc.,

---

24. Ibid., 34.
25. Poliakov, *History of Anti-Semitism from Voltaire to Wagner*, 447.

as many Israelites had done.[26] Levi wrote to Wagner asking advice about conducting his operas and Wagner replied, praising his conducting of *Meistersinger*. "I need not assure you how beneficent it is for me to be able to greet a conductor of true talent in a German opera house!"[27]

The real dilemma lay with *Parsifal* with all its pseudo religious ceremonies. Wagner's first solution was to persuade Levi to convert to Christianity though how that would improve his conducting was a mystery to everyone. It was the unkindest cut of all.[28] Levi declined. Wagner had also not reckoned on royal intervention and was somewhat chastened when the king insisted that Levi should handle the baton. In fact the king added the corollary that this was a condition of him placing the court orchestra at Wagner's disposal for Bayreuth.[29]

Wagner had seriously misunderstood where the king stood on the issue of anti-Semitism and the king showed considerable courage in facing up to his god. The king wrote a letter and said that he found "nothing more objectionable, nothing more distasteful" than the composer's hatred for the Jews. The king was aware that the Jews had showed great toleration in trying to understand the composer's bizarre views. He placed on record his astonishment "that the Jews you find so repulsive, dear friend, still, against all the odds, retain their unshakeable attachment to you."[30]

For once the king took on the role of moral mentor to the composer. "All men are basically brothers, in spite of their denominational differences," was the salutary lesson the gay and dilettante king was to impart to his hero.[31] No doubt for Wagner this was the final and irrefutable proof of the king's madness. In his last letter to Wagner in November 1882 he was still calling him "the divine light which, I trust, may yet shine for a long, long time, a sun to refresh and quicken the world with its celestial rays."[32]

Wagner was intransigent and answered the king by accusing him of having no daily contact with Jews. He said for him Jews were only "an idea, for us they are an experience," even though a lot of people who had lent

---

26. Marek, *Cosima Wagner*, 136–37.
27. Ibid., 137.
28. See ibid., 190, quoting Ernest Newman.
29. Köhler, *Wagner's Hitler*, 107.
30. Ibid.
31. Ibid., 318.
32. Taylor, *Richard Wagner*, 412.

money and support to the composer all his life fell into that category.[33] But eventually Wagner agreed to Levi conducting his beloved *Parsifal*. Hardly had Levi been back at Wahnfried two days when an anonymous letter arrived begging Wagner not to allow a Jew to conduct the work and begging him to "preserve its purity." A codicil to the letter was as unkind as it was untrue. It accused Levi of having sex with Cosima.[34] Wagner rather untactfully showed the letter to Levi, who fled Bayreuth in total disgust.

Although it was a close race, Wagner's love for excellence in the production of his own works won over his anti-Semitism, by a very short head. He agonized over a final decision but ended up begging Levi to return to conduct his sacred festival opera. The obsequious letter sent by Wagner is reckoned by some to contain a prophecy that the music and subliminal message of *Parsifal* would so intoxicate the Jewish conductor that he would convert to Christianity. "Lose nothing of your faith…*perhaps you will experience a great change in your life*…you are my *Parsifal* conductor," wrote Wagner. As always Levi swallowed his pride and returned to Bayreuth to be welcomed with a great concession at lunch with the Wagners – Jewish wine![35]

One of the most ardent admirers of the music attended the first performances of *Parsifal*. Houston Stewart Chamberlain has described in almost religious terms his introduction to Wagner. Prior to meeting the composer Chamberlain said his life was aimless and limited by his inadequacies. When he came to Bayreuth he became part of a greater whole of cosmic significance and found a measure to judge the world; he met the sun of his life who was and always would be Richard Wagner.[36] Here was the man the Spanish painter Roger de Egusquiza, who saw him in his last days, described to Chamberlain as a genius and other men as porcelain puppets stuffed with straw. After a thirty-hour journey from Switzerland Chamberlain arrived in Bayreuth on July 23, 1882, and managed to secure a seat in the same restaurant where the composer would dine after a performance of *Parsifal*.[37]

Chamberlain describes with scarcely disguised awe how Wagner

---

33. Marek, *Cosima Wagner*, 190.
34. Ibid.
35. Ibid., 191.
36. Chamberlain, *Lebenswege Meines Denkens*, 159.
37. Ibid., 236.

arrived for the meal and says his heart stopped beating. The ramrod stiff posture, reminding him of a young Goethe, the transfigured visage, the proud and invincible gait all were the physical characteristics of the man he knew was a god. He even uses a capital letter to describe Him. Parts of the composer reminded him of Bismarck, especially the calmness and unshakeable stature, which he compared to a rock in the angry breakers. Yet he lacked the melancholy in Bismarck's eyes, those of Wagner being bright and penetrating, and his physique was powerful like a ship, cutting through the angry elements to reach the safe haven of the port.

The great composer arrived on the arm of a lady and Chamberlain almost fell into a stupor holding onto a rail to control himself. "With him everything was alive from head to toe…his whole conduct showed a superiority of spirit and an energy of will that I have never seen in any person before," was the way he described his first impressions.[38] When Wagner addressed the diners his speech was so moving that two Frenchmen who understood nary a word were reduced to tears. He reminded the persons present that after the first festival in 1876 he had said, "now it is up to you to follow what I have done and then we will have art." He was stung by criticism by those who reckoned he saw no merit in the music of his predecessors. He now preferred to remain silent. "Out of this silence I have created *Parsifal*." The young man saw in his sharp and well chiseled features a wonderful grace and an indescribable goodness. What a tragedy it was, Chamberlain said, that the world had taught Wagner silence when he had so much to say which it needed to hear.[39] Although Chamberlain came within a few meters of greatness his natural shyness robbed him of all resolve and he never spoke to the god he had begun to worship. He did however no doubt vow that he would learn all he could about Wagner and tell the world that his voice was one to be obeyed. His writings including his biography of the composer were to be the foundations of the racial and political policies of the small Austrian corporal who visited him in his sick bed some forty-one years later.

After his years in the galleys Wagner was deeply concerned lest his young family suffer the same financial privations he had to endure. As copyright, as we know it today, did not exist, he therefore decreed in his

---

38. Ibid., 237.
39. Ibid., 238.

will that *Parsifal* should never be performed outside Bayreuth; it was to be a legacy to be enjoyed by his descendants. Unfortunately for him and his family his will was only binding in Germany. The only courts that could protect his property in the operas were German ones whose jurisdiction did not extend beyond the borders of that country. The Americans boldly ignored it and performances took place in the United States. Thereafter the work became regularly performed throughout the world.

Wagner's views as pontificated from Wahnfried had a limited circulation and he was persuaded – without much effort it has to be said – that a genius such as the Master of Bayreuth needed a much wider audience. To this end Wagner founded a newspaper, the *Bayreuther Blätter*, in 1878, which was to run for sixty years and, apart from parochial chitchat and operatic happenings, became the mouthpiece for his most dismal anti-Semitic utterings.[40] Apart from articles in this newspaper he published other essays and occasional pieces all combined in volume ten of his collected works and entitled *Regeneration Writings*.

An analysis of these polemical works is of crucial importance in understanding why Adolf Hitler was to find the wellspring of all his ambitions and ideas in the Wagnerian ideology. In the first place the composer was to articulate before anyone else the concept of the Führer. Wagner called for a leader who would rescue Germany and inherent in his music lay the secret of the future leader who had to be a Wagnerian. "My baton will become the sceptre of the future," he was heard to say in 1880.[41]

The Führer concept, which was to have such prominence in the next century in Germany, originated in the thinking of Wagner, who suggested that the great leader was not an ordinary mortal, but a demigod.[42] The wonderful thing about the German race was its unique gift for producing "the quite special German *great man*."[43] As an individual the leader was, Wagner explained, a mere atomistic mortal and as the personification of the German *Volk* (people), he shared its divinity.

Wagner explained in *The Wibelungen* an essay he read to his friend Eduard Devrient in 1848 that "The Germans are the custodians of the oldest royal lineage in the world. *It derives from a Son of God known to*

---
40. Köhler, *Wagner's Hitler*, 109.
41. Waite, 99.
42. Viereck, *Metapolitics*, 110–14.
43. Newman, *Life of Richard Wagner*, vol. 4, 601.

his immediate kinsfolk as Siegfried but to the other peoples of the world as Christ."[44] The linking of Siegfried with Christ is significant as it establishes that the enemy of Siegfried must be the Antichrist. In the Ring cycle the enemies of Siegfried are the Nibelungs, widely believed by commentators to represent the Jews.

So warped did the thinking of the Bayreuth Master become that he did not believe that Jesus was a Jew but was the son of Pantherus, a Greek soldier in the Roman army.[45] Christ's blood was of a special kind which was only found in one other person namely Parsifal.[46] That idea was also later rejected in favor of a new pantheon of pagan gods. Wagner resurrected the ancient god Wotan, whom he had depicted so vividly in *The Ring of the Nibelungs.* Wotan, who would have none of the humanist and loving features of Christ, became the symbol of the vengeance to be wreaked on the Jews. Wagner said that "in Christ we recognize Wotan again and as Christ died, was mourned, and avenged so we still avenge Christ on the Jews of today."[47]

Instead of the word Führer Wagner often expressed this concept by a number of other terms: hero, folk king and Barbarossa. Wagner called the medieval Kaiser Friedrich Barbarossa the mystic spiritual reincarnation of Siegfried.[48] The Kaiser was drowned on a crusade in 1190 and was first mentioned in Wagner's essay on *The Wibelungen.* The essay revealed "his great enthusiasm for the concept of world domination as found in early legends and sagas, with the figure of the Emperor Barbarossa arising in all his power and splendour as the mightiest embodiment of that concept."[49]

When this Siegfried-Barbarossa returned, said Wagner, the destruction of Satan would be effected because at his side "will hang the sword that once slew the dragon." Wagner concludes with the fervent prayer that was to have such an impact on the Austrian corporal sixty years later. "When, O great Friedrich, wilt thou return, thou noble Siegfried, and slay the dragon that is tormenting mankind."[50] The dragon referred to, apart from

---

44. Köhler, *Wagner's Hitler*, 281–82.
45. Gutman, *Richard Wagner*, 594.
46. Waite, *The Psychopathic God*, 109.
47. Poliakov, *History of Anti-Semitism from Voltaire to Wagner*, 435.
48. Viereck, *Metapolitics*, 111.
49. Köhler, *Wagner's Hitler*, 281.
50. Ibid.

the physical manifestation of Fafner in the Ring cycle, is clearly intended to be the Jews, whose commercial greed and quest for world domination, in Wagner's warped reasoning, deserves to be slain.

The precise location where Barbarossa was lying in wait for his mission was to be of the greatest significance to Adolf Hitler forty years later. The site where the sleeping Barbarossa was to reawaken and resume his rule over Germany was Berchtesgaden. The author James Bryce in his book on *The Holy Roman Empire* says that "In Berchtesgaden…among its limestone crags, in a spot scarcely accessible to human foot, the peasants of the valley point out to the traveler, the black mouth of a cavern and tell him that within Barbarossa lies in an enchanted sleep waiting to descend with his crusaders and bring back to Germany the golden age."[51]

According to Wagner, Barbarossa-Siegfried would return some day to save his German people in time of deepest need. The time of deepest need would be when the Antichrist had arrived. Reference to the Antichrist would have a loud resonance to nineteenth- and early twentieth-century Europeans. While there is some controversy as to the precise personality referred to as the Antichrist, the predominant view is that set out in the tenth century by Adso of Montier-en-Der. He laid down the catalog of action to be taken against the Antichrist, whom he described as a Jew of the tribe of Dan – and this remained authoritative throughout the Middle Ages.[52] Old sources revealed that the emperor Barbarossa would massacre the Jews in this new crusade.

Barbarossa was one of seven Hohenstauffens of Swabia – his grandson Friedrich II another, who had the sort of qualities that Wagner loved as did Hitler thereafter. Cruelty in battle, chivalry, courage and limitless energy were qualities he had in abundance and used when he tried to reestablish the Roman Empire, succeeding in unseating the Pope and driving him into exile. After suffering a number of military reverses he was forced to kneel at the pontiff's feet as a ploy to reconquer Italy. In his hands, significantly enough, he held the sacred spear, which he was clutching when he died crossing a stream in Sicily.[53]

So enraptured was Hitler with his affinity to the great emperor in

---

51. Viereck, *Metapolitics*, 111.
52. Cohn, *Pursuit of the Millennium*, 78.
53. Ravenscroft, *Spear of Destiny*, 17.

matters ideological that he ordered his troops to fight a bloody rearguard action in Italy with tremendous loss of life to assist engineers to remove a memorial stone to the man. With immense care the soldiers loaded the epitaph onto a military transport and sent it back to Germany under armed guard. He was a guardian spirit of the greatness of Germany and with his talisman the great spear, had to be protected from the depredations of the Allied soldiers and the Jews.[54]

Even the composer's subconscious was anti-Semitic. Wagner once had a dream that he told Cosima about in 1878 in which he was standing in a crowd between two abysses. One man cried out "only a ruler of genius can help us" and a bridge appeared that spanned the abyss, crossed by the leader. The next year he explained that the Jews' excessive influence on German life was the abyss and "who is there to save us from it?"[55] Adolf Hitler answered the rhetorical question.

The third stage of his Führer concept Wagner evolved in his 1881 essay "Heroism" where conveniently for Hitler the man of providence was no longer called a king, nor was he contemporary, like Ludwig, nor of the past, like Barbarossa. He was the divine hero. "We must now seek the hero of the future who turns against the ruin of his race."[56] An important change in the Führer mission, urged upon the Saxon and Bavarian kings, was made when Wagner added the holy duty to achieve redemption of Germany's lost Aryan purity.[57]

For Wagner legend was truer than history and the Franks were the royalty of all races in ancient times.[58] In his last writings including *Heroism and Christendom* he said:

> We cannot withhold our acknowledgment that the human family consists of irredeemably disparate races, whereof the noble could rule the ignoble, yet never raise them to their level by commixture, but simply sink to theirs. Indeed this one relation might suffice to explain our fall…Whilst yellow races have viewed themselves as sprung from monkeys, the white traced back their origin to gods, and deemed

---

54. Ibid., 18.
55. Köhler, *Wagner's Hitler*, 224.
56. Viereck, *Metapolitics*, 142.
57. Ibid., 114.
58. Gutman, *Richard Wagner*, 601.

themselves marked out for rulership. It has been made quite clear that we should have no History of Man at all, had there been no movements, creations, and achievements of the white man…Incomparably fewer in number than the lower races, the ruin of the white races may be referred to their having been obliged to mix with them; whereby, as remarked already, they suffered more from the loss of their purity than the others could gain by the ennobling of their blood…Nowhere in history do the root qualities of the Aryan race show forth more plainly than in the contact of the last pure-bred Germanic branches with the falling Roman world…

It was a weighty feature of the Christian Church that none but sound and healthy persons were admitted to the vow of total world renunciation; any bodily defect, not to say mutilation, unfitted them. Manifestly, this vow was to be regarded as issuing from the most heroic of all possible resolves, and he who sees in it a "cowardly self-surrender" – as someone recently suggested, may bravely exult in his own self-retention, but had best not meddle any further with things that don't concern him…

It certainly may be right to charge this purblind dullness of our public spirit to the vitiation of our blood – not only by departure from the natural food of man, but above all by the tainting of the hero-blood of the noblest races with that of former cannibals now trained to be the business agents of Society.[59]

Stigmatizing the Jews as parasites, the second number of his Bayreuth newspaper moved on to the familiar themes touched on in "Jewry in Music" and called them the "demons of decadence" and warned against the evils of miscegenation.[60] Intermarriage or intercourse between Aryans and Jews would lead to the blood of the former being polluted and defiled.

In the essay "Heroism" he returned to this theme and warned that although inferior races might be raised by Aryan impregnation the resulting improvement they enjoyed was paltry compared to the catastrophic decline the admixture of their blood worked upon their masters. Sickening images that would help found the ideology of racial hygiene emerged in this mad

---

59. Solomon, "Wagner and Hitler."
60. Ibid., 110.

diatribe. "The power of the Jew is inherent in his blood even mixing does not harm it; man or woman, if he marries into races most foreign of his own, he will always produce a Jew."[61]

Cosima's diary is a further source of Wagner's thinking in this regard. In 1879 Wagner was discussing the sudden rise in anti-Semitism in Germany and Cosima wrote, "we are amused by the thought that his essay on 'Music and the Jews' really does seem to mark the beginning of the struggle."[62] What the end of the struggle was to be, only emerged later on.

In 1882 Wagner returned to the theme that the Jews were making no contribution to music and culture in Germany, a theme that had arisen many years previously in his unseemly and rabid attacks on Giacomo Meyerbeer. The culture of the Jews was that of commerce and he therefore stigmatized them as the "plastic demon of mankind's decadence" and referred to the fact that "the invention of money – worse of paper money – was a diabolical plot of the Jews."

Back were the sentiments of the 1848 speech he made to the Fatherland Society when, in a strange mixture of anti-Semitism (directed at Mendelssohn and Meyerbeer) and socialism he advocated the end of the "evil, nocturnal, demonic concept of money…with all its despicable train of public and secret usurers, paper swindling, interest and bank speculations" (clearly a Jewish pursuit) because deliverance from these evils would bring about "the emancipation of the pure doctrine of Christ."[63] The notion of financial avarice of the Jews was an ever present one and nowhere more clear than in his essay "What Is German?" – where he queried "this invasion of German essence by an utterly alien element…It everywhere appears to be the duty of the Jew to show the nations of Europe where haply there may be a profit they have overlooked…upon the hindered and dwindling prosperity of the nation the Jewish banker feeds his enormous wealth."[64]

The modern commercial world, dominated by Jewish business and bankers, had ousted the old quaint German culture, represented by the master craftsmen, the artisans employed in their trade guilds and represented by the benign shoemaker Hans Sachs in *Meistersinger*. This in itself

---

61. Poliakov, *History of Anti-Semitism from Voltaire to Wagner*, 448.
62. Köhler, *Wagner's Hitler*, 119.
63. Richard Wagner Museum brochure, "About Richard Wagner," item 12u.
64. Weiner, *Richard Wagner and the Anti-Semitic Imagination*, 55.

was a disaster and the composer was determined to do something about it. Wagner wrote that the fact that "mankind is nearing its end is not by any means impossible…if our culture is collapsing, there is no harm in that; but if it collapses through the Jews, that's a disgrace."[65] Germans, after all, had a monopoly on determining what true culture was. "The German has the exclusive right to be called 'musician'" was the hubristic comment of the composer.[66]

The next illogical step in the tortuous argument was that it was an inherent characteristic of the Jewish culture to fight those whose culture was different. Wagner's 1881 paper "Know Thyself" stated that "It is an inevitable outcome of Jewish culture that in the last analysis the Jews always find themselves facing the need to wage war."[67] Cosima noted in her diary that Wagner described the Jews as "calculating beasts of prey," a similar metaphor to that which dominates the essay.[68]

From the "need to wage war" to protect their culture the composer moved irresistibly on to the next step in the path of Jewish tyranny – the conquest of the world. Cosima's diary recorded a discussion she had with him after he had read her the article. "Whether the Jews can ever be redeemed is the question which, in connection with it, occupies our thoughts – their nature condemns them to the world's reality. They have profaned Christianity, that is to say, adapted it to this world, and from our art, which can only be a refuge from prevailing conditions, they also expect world conquest."[69]

The next step was one he was to articulate in the broadest possible terms but it has to be evaluated in the context of Jews bent on destroying proper German culture and seeking to achieve world conquest. Clearly drastic measures were required to challenge or thwart such a campaign. Wagner went on to say that only when his countrymen awakened and ceased party bickering, would there be no more Jews, a "great solution" he foresaw as uniquely within the reach of the Germans, if they could conquer false shame and not shrink from ultimate knowledge.[70] "It is easier for us

---

65. Poliakov, *Richard Wagner and the Anti-Semitic Imagination*, 442.
66. Kater, *The Twisted Muse*, 131.
67. Köhler, *Wagner's Hitler*, 273.
68. Weiner, *Richard Wagner and the Anti-Semitic Imagination*, 344.
69. Skelton, *Cosima Wagner's Diaries*, 416.
70. Gutman, *Richard Wagner*, 602, 603.

Germans to achieve this grand solution to the problem of ridding the world of the Jews than for any other nation."[71]

It is difficult to avoid the conclusion that the composer was calling for the "final solution" – proposed and executed less than sixty years later – the annihilation of Jews in a literal rather than a figurative sense. In Frederic Spotts's memorable phrase, "here lay serpent's eggs that, generations later, hatched to release ideological monsters."[72] The drastic nature of his solution is supported by his response to an incident in the theatre. He attended a production of Lessing's play *Nathan the Wise*, which preached religious toleration. During the performance there was a line in which it was stated that Jesus was a Jew; a Jew in the audience responded enthusiastically to this fact and shouted "bravo." Cosima admired the German humanity of the play and had read it to the children but Wagner found it to be totally lacking in profundity. He commented afterwards that if he ever had his way all Jews would be burned at a performance of *Nathan the Wise*.

The vicious nature of the man is illustrated by another tragic example. When a terrible fire occurred in Vienna's Ringtheater on December 8, 1881, hundreds of people lost their lives and there was a widespread humanitarian response to the crisis. Amongst the dead was a large contingent of Jewish theatergoers. The daily recorder of the events of the life of the composer, Cosima noted his cold and indifferent response in her diary – "that 416 Israelites perished in the conflagration does not increase Richard's sympathy for the tragedy."[73]

It is not without significance that Wagner had placed political economist Eugen Dühring in a leadership role in the *Bayreuther Blätter* in 1879. In his work "The Jewish Question as Race Pestilence" written in 1881, he defined his race theories and declared that the "northern peoples had the duty to annihilate the parasitic races in the same way that people annihilate poisonous snakes and wild beasts of prey."[74]

At an emotional level the Wagnerian ideology was devoid of all logic. Rationalism was jettisoned in favor of emotion and instinct. Pity, empathy and humanitarianism were gone. In their stead were the qualities that dictators love in their troops. Wagner's art and weird genius was aimed not at the

---

71. Köhler, *Wagner's Hitler*, 110.
72. Spotts, *Bayreuth*, 77.
73. Marek, *Cosima Wagner*, 191.
74. Prawy, *Richard Wagner: Leben und Werk*, 48.

critical understanding but at the pent up emotions of the subconscious. He said: "I pour young life through all your veins. Life is law unto itself…we must be brave enough to deny our intellect."[75] In a sense a dulling of the reasoning faculties was the only way to ensure that the monstrous implications of his master plan were carried out.

With the historical imperative as a backdrop and ideological principles in place the parameters were now in place for Wagner and his greatest disciple. A Führer would awaken from his sleep and cleanse Germany of its race problem. Liberal democracy was undesirable because it advocated peace and concord between nations. Wagner proclaimed the salutary effect of war – and with it a veiled prophesy that only a state of general unrest and dislocation, in which the ordinary law was suspended, would permit the "great solution" to be implemented. "History proves that man is a beast of prey, developing through constant progress. The beast of prey conquers countries, founds great realms by the subjugation of other subjugators, forms states and organizes civilizations, in order to enjoy his booty in peace…attack and defense, suffering and struggle, victory and defeat, domination and servitude, all sealed with blood; this is the entire history of the human race…"[76] The Jewish culture bent on world domination would be subjugated in the great cleansing program of the Führer.

As Köhler puts it: "a political precept, born of envy, resentment and dramatic necessity, became raised to the status of dogma, and the next generation of Wagnerians, who called themselves 'Knights of the Grail,' inclined less and less to metaphysical circumlocution and openly preached the radical solution proposed by Wagner in his so-called 'regeneration writings.'"[77]

Much of this thinking was to be shared with Nietzsche as we will see anon. Nietzsche, himself an amateur musician, spent many happy hours exchanging views with Wagner, and was commissioned to perform domestic tasks as mundane as buying presents for the children or as important as securing the first impression of Wagner's autobiography *Mein Leben*.[78]

---

75. Rose, *Wagner: Race and Revolution*, 51.
76. Waite, *The Psychopathic God*, 112–13.
77. Köhler, *Wagner's Hitler*, 108.
78. Nietzsche also surveyed the vast and dangerous domain he had traveled with Wagner and his letter to his sister about his alliance with an anti-Semitic boss. See Fischer-Dieskau, *Wagner and Nietzsche*, 146.

Later even his most ardent disciple was to part ways with the master. He was to say, "I hate Wagner, but I cannot stand any other music."[79] Nietzsche would have agreed with the Alsatian writer Edouard Schure, who met Wagner in Munich at the time of the *Tristan* performance and was also his guest in Triebschen and Bayreuth. Schure identified the compositional and dramatic genius but also saw the great evil in his ideology. "Looking at him one could see in his face two persons; from the front a Faust, in profile a Mephistopheles. The fullness of that protean nature was dazzling – incandescent, willful… extravagant in every respect, and yet wonderfully in balance because of his all-embracing intellect… The frankness with which he bared his inner nature the qualities and defects which he unveiled unashamedly was of magical attraction to some, repellent to others."[80]

A great chasm came between Wagner and Nietzsche and the real reason was not known. Rumor had it that Wagner said something deeply hurtful of Nietzsche – that he indulged in masturbation – and the philosopher had come to hear of it. A cold shower was the proffered remedy. Recent studies have revealed the letter Wagner wrote to Dr. Eisner on October 23, 1877 in which he states that "in my attempts to assess N.'s condition, I have been thinking for some time of identical and very similar experiences which I recall having had with certain young men of great intellectual ability. I saw them being destroyed by similar symptoms, and discovered only too clearly that these symptoms were the result of masturbation."[81]

As anyone growing up in the fifties and sixties in a rough boarding school environment will attest, one of the dangers of masturbation alluded to by puritanical schoolmasters and anxious mothers was blindness. Wagner goes on to establish such a point in his letter. "It is only to confirm the great likelihood that I am right that I mention the striking experience I had whereby one of the young friends whom I mentioned, a poet who died in Leipzig many years ago, became totally blind when he was N.'s age…"

Medical men as enlightened as Sigmund Freud misdiagnosed the effects of masturbation and in a letter to his collaborator Wilhelm Fliess in 1893 the great psychologist and psychiatrist stated that "neurasthenia [atonic nervous debility] in males is acquired at puberty and becomes

---

79. Taylor, *Richard Wagner*, 426.
80. Gal, *Richard Wagner*, 126.
81. Weiner, *Richard Wagner and the Anti-Semitic Imagination*, 338.

manifest in the patient's twenties. Its source is masturbation..."[82] There is extensive literature on the grave dangers and the titles alone emphasize the seriousness of the practice (see also Deslandes, *A Treatise on the Diseases produced by Onanism, Masturbation, Self-pollution, and other Excesses*). The eminent English physician Henry Maudsley wrote in his work *Physiology and Pathology of Mind* that the onanist's state was one of "extreme perversion of feeling and corresponding derangement of thought, in the earlier stages, and later by failure of intelligence, nocturnal hallucinations, and suicidal or homicidal propensities."[83]

For Wagner, who was reading Darwin's *The Descent of Man*, published in 1871, masturbation provided a perfect example of Darwin's theory of "reversion" in terms of which a "long lost structure is called back into existence." The Greeks were victims of this when they descended from an "enervated and corrupt state" to one of "extreme sensuality."[84]

As always, the great humorist and writer Mark Twain, who later visited the Bayreuth festival, came to the rescue in a little known paper, "Some Thoughts on the Science of Onanism," read to a private club in Paris in 1879. He hilariously lampooned and pilloried the notion that masturbation seriously damaged the body and the mind. "The signs of excessive indulgence in this destructive past-time are easily detectable. They are these; a disposition to eat, to drink, to smoke, to meet together convivially, to laugh, to joke, and tell indelicate stories – and, mainly a yearning to paint pictures."[85]

Given the serious nature of the consequences of the practice it is not difficult to understand why Nietzsche felt so offended by the crass indictment of his personal life. A perusal of his book *My Sister and I* seems to bear out Wagner's challenge. In that work Nietzsche talked about his days at university: "I did a great deal of maturing in Leipzig, a vast amount of masturbating, and not nearly as much whoring as I should have."[86] The philosopher had noted the change in Wagner from atheist to disciple weeping at the foot of the cross. If there was any doubt as to the hidden meaning of the last music drama Wagner made no bones about explaining it to the philosopher. *Parsifal* represented the purification and the redemption of the

---

82. Ibid., 330.
83. Ibid., 333.
84. Ibid., 343.
85. Ibid., 395.
86. Wallace et al., *The Intimate Sex Lives of Famous People*, 331.

How a Leipzig Jew slowly became Richard Wagner. Published in *Der Floh*, Vienna

Wagner was frequently depicted as the Jew from Leipzig, the city of his birth. Gottfried Wagner, The Wagner Legacy, page 96. From Der Floh, Vienna.

A further caricature of Wagner as a Jew by K. Klic from Humoristische Blatter, Vienna, 1873. From Eduard Fuchs and Ernest Kreowski, Richard Wagner in der Karikatur, Berlin: B. Behr's Verlag, 1907. Also reproduced in Weiner, page 9.

Jews through their destruction. By this stage Nietzsche had grown weary of Wagner's anti-Semitism and was preparing for a break.

That Wagner represented his views as the pinnacle of Romanticism also meant little to him. The philosopher was of the view that Goethe was right in his answer to the question "what is the danger which hovers over all romantics?" His answer was, "Suffocation by chewing moral and religious absurdities over and over again." Nietzsche regarded *Parsifal* as a religious absurdity but found the music deeply moving. Finally the phi-

Despite his anti-Semitism Wagner was regarded as a Jew and is depicted here with other Jews in Der Floh, a Viennese publication. Wagners Welten, page 235.

losopher identified the moral absurdity of the race views – but it was in all probability too late. The die had been cast, the music had been written, the master plan printed in the "regeneration writings," the countless issues of the Bayreuth newspaper, and the sinister subliminal messages awaited a receptive and powerful psychopath who would have the desire and opportunity to carry them out.

Nietzsche pondered on the anti-Semitism of a man whose background was not itself free from connection with Jewishness. As everyone realized Wagner had grown up in Brühl, the Leipzig Jewish Quarter. As mentioned earlier his first girlfriend and school chum was Jewish. He was taunted as a child as a Jew-boy and later the critics called him the Rabbi of Bayreuth.[87] Those more anti-Semitic than Wagner – a quaint notion in retrospect – delighted in publishing cartoons of him with so-called Semitic physical features. That great irony was compounded when certain newspapers called his music "Jewish."[88]

In 1881 the philosopher saw Wagner in Sorrento for the last time.[89] Nietzsche's views had initially embraced anti-Semitism but he soon saw

---

87. Viennese humorists were fond of calling him the Rabbi of Bayreuth. See Poliakov, *Richard Wagner and the Anti-Semitic Imagination*, 429.
88. Viereck, *Metapolitics*, 96.
89. Fischer-Dieskau, *Wagner and Nietzsche*, 153.

the folly in them. Not so his sister who presented a huge problem for the philosopher, especially in her choice of husband and his religious views. One should not forget the sexual molestation he suffered at her hands in his early years. A few years after the meeting with Wagner, Nietzsche's sister and her anti-Semitic husband Forster left Germany to found Nueva Germania in Paraguay, a colony based on the racist principles of Wagner.

In his last days Wagner was in Italy for the warmth where he saw lots of visitors and when staying in Venice he saw Hermann Levi for a week. At times it seemed that all had been forgotten and they spoke about the music and the performances. Despite Levi's presence the racist in Wagner could not be suppressed and he sounded off several times in his own intemperate way about the Jews and their evil influence. One is reminded of the words of Shylock to Antonio in *The Merchant of Venice*: "For suffering is the badge of all our tribe. You call me misbeliever, cut-throat, dog, and spit upon my Jewish gaberdene…"[90] Not surprisingly Levi became deeply depressed and conversation became difficult. Little did Levi know that the day after he departed the composer would have a fatal heart attack. As they parted Wagner kissed him and appeared to be deeply moved. The composer let it be known how he hated himself for talking about Jews in Levi's presence and it was clear to all that it was causing him to fall into a state of great melancholy.[91] Levi had translated Mozart's *Il Nozze di Figaro* into German, and the fact that he was a Jew, coupled with the further alarming aspect that the original librettist Lorenzo da Ponte was also of that religion, meant that the Nazis were not prepared to produce it fifty years later.[92]

Richard Wagner died of heart failure in Venice at the height of his fame, and was buried in the grounds of Wahnfried. Ludwig was totally bereft – he ranted and raged and broke furniture. "Wagner's body belongs to me…this artist whom the whole world now mourns – it was I who first understood him, I who saved him for the world."[93] As an example of the awe in which the composer was held the *Dresdener Anzeiger* reported his death as follows: "A heavy and altogether unexpected bereavement has befallen musicians of every race, country and degree. We learned by telegraph from Venice that the greatest of contemporary composers Richard Wagner,

---

90. Shakespeare, *Complete Oxford Shakespeare*, vol. 2, 607.
91. Marek, *Cosima Wagner*, 205.
92. Kater, *The Twisted Muse*, 86.
93. Taylor, *Richard Wagner*, 417–18.

the second husband of Cosima Lizst died there at four o'clock of yesterday afternoon, the 13th February 1883. He occupied a loftier station than King or Kaiser, Pope or President. No monarch was ever more enthusiastically served than has been Richard Wagner. Infallibility embodied in a Roman Pontiff has never been more implicitly believed in by the most orthodox Catholic than has been in the person of the Bayreuth prophet."[94]

Gustav Mahler was enduring a short appointment in the east-Moravian town of Olmütz when he learned of the death of his idol. A friend and habitué of some of his hangouts, Jacques Manheit, tells of finding Mahler "running demented, weeping loudly, through the streets." His friend assumed that Mahler's aged father had died but it was the demise of the Master of Bayreuth that had emotionally crippled the man.[95] Mahler was to see *Parsifal* for the first time in July of that year and he described it as the "greatest, most painful thing…I should have it with me in all its sanctity for the rest of my life."[96]

The relationship between Jews and Wagner was to have the most tragic consequences for one young Jewish fan. A newspaper columnist in Israel by the name of Neuman wrote of this man who wrote to Wagner and in his letter said he had to commit suicide in order to kill the Jew who lived within himself. True to his word after hearing of his death he committed suicide on the grave of his fatal idol.[97] Verdi who had been born in the same year as Wagner described him as a "great personality, who would leave a powerful impression on the history of art." He then crossed out the word "powerful" and inserted the words "the most powerful."[98] Nietzsche was staying in Rapallo in Italy busy with *Also sprach Zarathustra* when he was told by his friend Franz Overbeck that Wagner was dead. Nietzsche is reported to have said to Overbeck: "Although Wagner was by far the most complete man I have ever known, and although in this respect I have felt a deep sense of deprivation over the last six years, there was a kind of

---

94. The *Dresdener Anzeiger* of February 14, 1883 is quoted in the television program on Wagner produced by London Trust Cultural Productions Limited in association with Hungarofilm and Magyar Television Budapest.
95. Franklin, *Life of Mahler*, 54, 55 and 208.
96. Ibid., 55.
97. Sheffi, *Ring of Myths*, 96–97.
98. Taylor, *Richard Wagner*, 418.

destructive grievance between us, and the situation could have become terrible if he had lived longer."

By contrast the father of Richard Strauss and principal horn player in the Munich orchestra had hated Wagner and the music of the future. On the day after Wagner's death Levi asked the orchestra to stand as a mark of respect to the departed genius. All rose and bowed their heads sadly save only the principal horn player.[99] No one worshipped a hero more passionately – no one grieved more deeply at the decay of a god than Nietzsche. He heard the prelude to *Parsifal* in Monte Carlo in January 1887 and wrote to a friend, "speaking from a purely aesthetic point of view has Wagner ever written anything better?" He referred to the "extraordinary sublimity of feeling…the penetration of vision that cuts through the soul like a knife…" and then posed the question, "has any painter ever depicted a look of love as Wagner has done in the final accents of the prelude?"[100]

No one analyzed his faults more accurately. When Nietzsche had time to consider the whole picture and understand what the composer stood for he thrust his knife deeply into the corpse that the obsequious embalmers had caused to smell so sweet. In the 1887 essay "Die Unschuld des Werdens" he said the following about the Bayreuth Master: "German youth honors in Wagner a dictator…in the name of the 'chosen people' the Germans! Wagner belongs to the demagogues of art, knowing how to play upon the instincts of the masses and thereby knowing how to win over the instincts of such youths as crave power."

The sickly philosopher predicted the effect Wagner would have on future German generations – the appeal to the Aryan race and to the instincts of the masses. He went on to say, "Wagner was something complete; he was complete corruption; Wagner was the courage, the will, the conviction of corruption…He was not a man but a disease…Wagner became an oracle from the other world." For Nietzsche the heady broth dished up in the regeneration writings was a message from the underworld.

The notion that Wagner was a disease was not new. In 1872 the Munich psychiatrist Theodor Puschmann, who published a text *Richard Wagner: A Psychiatric Study*, which was popular enough to warrant a second edition, concluded that the composer was clinically insane and suffered from

---

99. Newman, *Life of Richard Wagner*, vol. 3, 378.
100. Ibid., 709.

"chronic megalomania, paranoia, ambiguous ideas and moral derangement."[101] Little did he know how well his diagnosis would fit the man who was to carry out the bizarre ideas of the Bayreuth Master.

Like a soothsayer staring fixedly into the unfolding twentieth century Nietzsche called down anathema on his countrymen who followed the cult of Bayreuth. "I like not the agitators dressed up as heroes, like Siegfried, the anti-Semites who excite the blockhead elements of the populace. The invariable success of intellectual charlatanism in present day Germany hangs together with the desolation of the German mind… whose cause I look for in a too exclusive diet of papers, politics, beer, and Wagnerian music…not forgetting the condition precedent of this diet; the national vanity, Germany, Germany above everything. I worshipped Wagner and now I have been crushed by the fallen idol. Richard Wagner is leading us to ruin…"

The oracle had spoken but would anybody listen? One final matter was to shock the Wagner disciples and set them wondering about the times he spent with the family in Bayreuth and in exile in Switzerland. In 1889 when the philosopher was only forty-five years old he collapsed in tears on a street in Turin, after flinging his arms around a horse, savagely whipped by its owner.[102] He was not so mad as not to understand the difference between cruelty and masochism. After this incident he sent Cosima a note in which he likened himself to Dionysus – the Greek god of license and indulgence, always juxtaposed to Apollo, the god of order and law – and said "Ariadne, I love you." When brought to the asylum he told the doctors, "My wife, Cosima Wagner, has brought me here."[103]

Nietzsche spent the last eleven years of his life in total mental darkness, first in a Basel asylum, then in Naumburg under his mother's care and, after her death in 1897, in Weimar in his sister's care. While in her care he must have thought of his long relationship with the Russian girl, Lou Andreas-Salomé, and the ménage a trois he shared with her and Paul Rée. That strange threesome, called the "Trinity" to poke fun at the God Nietzsche had pronounced dead, broke up because his sister Elizabeth had a distorted jealousy for her. Having once referred to Lou as "the most intelligent of

---

101. Spotts, *Bayreuth*, 67.
102. Wallace et al., *The Intimate Sex Lives of Famous People*, 331.
103. Ibid.

women" he then referred to her as that "scraggy dirty she-monkey with her false breasts." But he never stopped loving her – he was driven mad by his loss of Lou and he recognized this. "Having been separated from the love of my life (Lou), the love that made me human, I made my desperate plunge into the fires of madness."

Lou had studied with and was to become the confidante of Freud and to count amongst her friends Turgeniev, Tolstoy, Strindberg, Rodin, Rainer Rilke and Arthur Schnitzler. Some held that her greatest achievement was to attach herself to the greatest men of the nineteenth and twentieth centuries – Nietzsche and Freud.[104] She wrote a seminal paper on anal eroticism, and showed how the history of the first prohibition which a child comes across – the prohibition against getting pleasure from anal activity and its products – has a decisive effect on a child's whole development.[105] Little did she know how appropriate her analysis was to the greatest tyrant of the twentieth century. Nietzsche died in 1900 of syphilis in the Weimar Sanatorium. The supreme irony of it all was that Nietzsche had himself reported many years earlier that too much exposure to Wagner's music would lead to mental decay and that young pilgrims to Bayreuth had been lured into dementia.[106]

Wagner's patron King Ludwig II went progressively madder and was declared certifiable in 1886 and found his death that same year while boating with his hated doctor whom he took with him to the watery depths of Lake Starnberg.[107] The king had to perish as he was not able, in his own pessimistic view, to successfully carry out the vocation of a monarch within a constitutional monarchy. He had dreamed of a utopia and the cruel machinations of realpolitik in the Germany of the last two decades of the nineteenth century consumed him.

The king had written to Wagner to try to express his worldview and the purpose of his architectural projects and musical endeavors – in an "ideal, monarchical, poetical solitude" he had tried to create an art in harmony with his personal view of the universe.[108] After Ludwig II drowned

---

104. Jones, *Life and Work of Sigmund Freud*, 428.
105. Freud, *On Sexuality*, 104.
106. See Conrad, "He's Tricky, That Dicky."
107. Gal, *Richard Wagner*, 104.
108. Petzet and Hojer, "Neuschwanstein Castle," 18–19.

it transpired that Wagner had dreamed thirteen years before that he would be shot by a wicked scoundrel as had been the case with Louis Philippe.[109]

Paul Verlaine, the great French writer, whose bohemian lifestyle and bisexual love affairs caused scandals in a country synonymous with such callings, called him the "only true king of the century."[110] Little did the king, whose patronage – more than any other mortal – made Wagner's work possible, know that when he penned a love letter to a male servant in his household the document would become the keepsake and favorite possession of Adolf Hitler.

The reality of his madness has been the subject of much writing and Newman and other experts reckon he was framed as such by the politicians. Newman says that the evidence would not hold up in an English court and comments on the fact that more than one of the famous "psychiatrists" attributed his madness to the "narcotic" influence of Wagner's music on the "cerebral nerves."[111]

---

109. Pachl, *Siegfried Wagner*, 73–74.
110. Petzet and Hojer, "Neuschwanstein Castle," 19.
111. Newman, *Life of Richard Wagner*, vol. 3, 565.

Chapter eight
The Hagiographers

The first biography of Wagner by Carl Friedrich Glasenapp was published in 1876 and was subsequently translated into English by Ashton Ellis.[1] Houston Stewart Chamberlain, a mad and quixotic Englishman, was the next to take up the pen to record the life of the composer. He will feature prominently in the march of ideology from the composer to the dictator and it is necessary to investigate something of the background of a man destined to have an enormous influence on the next half-century.

He was born on September 9, 1855, the son of an admiral and the nephew of Sir Neville Bowles Chamberlain. As a child Chamberlain explained his euphoria when he heard Wagner's music. The significance of the various motifs in the music was not lost on him. He was taught to play the piano from an early age and he learned to play the "sword" motif on the village organ, having been taught that it was expressive of "Wotan's sudden urge to see a hero conquer the world."[2] Little did he know as his young fingers raced across the faded ivory keys of the instrument, how close he was to come to the Wagner family and a "hero" who attempted to enslave the universe.

---

1. See also the official German and English biographies by C.F. Glasenapp, *Das Leben Richard Wagners*, 6 vol. (Leipzig: Breitkopf and Härtel, 1894–1911); and W.A. Ellis, *Life of Richard Wagner*, 6 vol. (London: Kegan Paul, 1900–08).
2. Köhler, *Wagner's Hitler*, 120.

The Englishman and later fervent German nationalist Houston Stewart Chamberlain as a young man. He was to write a hagiographic biography of Wagner and help transmit his crass anti-Semitism to Adolf Hitler. Wolf Siegfried Wagner, page 41. Richard Wagner Archiv, Bayreuth.

When he was fifteen years of age he was taught by Otto Kuntze, the most Prussian of that particular breed, who filled his receptive mind with tales of bravery and daring in the annals of military conquest.[3] Prevented by ill health from entering the army, after going to school at Cheltenham and in Paris, he studied natural science at Geneva and in Vienna from 1879 to 1884. He also avidly read the works of German musicians and poets Beethoven, Schiller, Goethe and Richard Wagner, whom he came to venerate like a god. A woman, ten years his senior and also highly-strung and neurotic, Anna Horst, claimed his heart and he married her in 1885.[4]

In 1879 Chamberlain became a subscriber to the Bayreuth festival and offered his services to the Wagnerian newspaper, the racist *Bayreuther Blätter*.[5] He soon jettisoned his English culture and heritage and became a great admirer of the German people and saw them as the future of mankind.[6] Chamberlain visited Bayreuth and saw *Parsifal* in its premiere year, 1882, and met Cosima for the first time in 1888 in Dresden. With uncanny

---

3. Shirer, *Rise and Fall of the Third Reich*, 138.
4. Ibid.
5. Köhler, *Wagner's Hitler*, 121.
6. "Houston Stewart Chamberlain," in *Encyclopaedia Brittanica*, vol. 5. (William Benton, 1970), 246.

insight Cosima saw in the Englishman an ideological pen more adept and true than that of her own son Siegfried.[7]

His meeting with Wagner a year before he died in 1883 was to generate a discipleship, equal if not superior to the Pauline conversion on the road to Damascus. "The greatest moment in my life" was how he expressed the experience to Cosima and he was to entreat her to allow him to write on the great man's music, his life and his ideas. Not a religious man, he worshipped a trinity of poets that encompassed Homer, Shakespeare and Wagner – but there was no doubt in the mind of the tall, balding and fanatical Englishman that the greatest of the three was the composer from Bayreuth.[8]

He was not only wedded to the composer but he was also a fervent admirer of the festival and the ideological Mecca that had been established in the small Bavarian town. When Chamberlain first met Cosima in 1888 he told her he was not only a Wagnerian but also a "Bayreuthian." By that she understood that he was a supporter of the family and the festival. Clearly he saw the Wagner heritage as worthy of support and encouragement. Cosima called him a "proud and original personality of great value. We talked continuously for five hours and neither of us got tired." A voluminous correspondence ensued between the aged widow and the Englishman for twenty years that filled a book of 695 pages.[9]

The year 1888 was a difficult year for a number of reasons, one being the proposal that the festival and Wagner's private home be nationalized. An article in the *Berliner Tageblatt* made much of the fact that the composer had been insulated in the town and cut off from society by a clique, bent on ensuring a closeted and elitist management style. The author suggested that the German princes should make the festival into a national monument open to all irrespective of social rank or relationship with the family.[10] From the point of view of the family their future was tied up in the festival and they were much relieved when little came of the suggestion. Seventeen years later the suggestion was repeated; this time Wagner's legacy was compared with that of Friedrich Schiller and the point was emphasized that these were national treasures.

---

7. Pachl, *Siegfried Wagner*, 80.
8. Waite, *The Psychopathic God*, 113.
9. Marek, *Cosima Wagner*, 261.
10. Sheffi, *The Ring of Myths*, 28.

The impression created by Cosima after the death of Wagner in Venice was that of a grieving widow who had sat for twenty-four hours, shunning all food, with his head cradled in her arms. She perpetuated publicly the image of a woman deprived of her great love, who would never again want any sort of relationship. After the meeting with Chamberlain there must have been considerable feeling between them – the thirty-year-old man wrote to the still attractive fifty-year-old, "if only I could tell you everything that is in my heart! But I cannot. Yet at least we both have eyes." Her reply was no less effusive. "It is so long since I received such sympathy that at the beginning my heart felt unsure. But now it shines into my soul like a ray of sunlight, bringing me joy and happiness."[11]

The letters continued and the passion seeped out from the old-fashioned and stilted metaphors of that sentimental age. Cosima described visiting a palm garden and being overcome by "passionate melancholy while the scent of the silent palms had formed a union in my aching heart with the languishing sounds of distant music." What was the hidden text of the "union" alluded to in the imagery? What may remain a mystery to the reader of the yellowed pages a hundred years later was clearly interpreted by the adoring Englishman. The description of the palms, he replied to the Bayreuth widow – who wore nothing but black to remind everyone of her great loss – had "caused my heartstrings to quiver."[12] Cosima had been a vibrant and passionate woman until the death of the composer. While there is little evidence of any physical relationship, apart from odd comments in her letters, it seems improbable that a life force such as hers had ceased or that her wellspring of physical needs had dried up.

Chamberlain lived in Dresden for four years and then came to Vienna in 1889, the year of Hitler's birth, and stayed for twenty years.[13] His first book, published in France in 1892, was an analysis of an early masterpiece of Wagner, *Notes sur Lohengrin*; other books on Wagner included *Das Drama Richard Wagner* and a biography emphasizing the Teutonic element in Wagner's thought. It became clear that Cosima saw in Chamberlain the sort of personality who would respond to her notions of true biography. Mention has been made of Wagner's early attempts at recording his

---

11. Köhler, *Wagner's Hitler*, 122.
12. Ibid.
13. Shirer, *Rise and Fall of the Third Reich*, 138.

life – in 1835 *The Red Book* which was transferred to a brown book – and his *Autobiographical Sketch* of 1843 and *A Communication to My Friends* of 1851, which became the source for his autobiography *My Life*.[14]

One would have thought that the widow would have immediately made these sources available to any writer bent on recording Wagner's life. They were after all the *ipse dixit* of the composer himself. The strange feature of the matter was that Chamberlain wrote his biography of Wagner in 1896 and was not allowed to see *My Life* before that. It was after all the account that Wagner had wanted the world to see and written at the specific request of King Ludwig. That the composer had gilded the lily was clear to everyone especially his erstwhile friend Friedrich Nietzsche. "What has hitherto circulated as Wagner's Life is *fable convenue*, if not worse. I confess my mistrust of every point attested to only by Wagner himself. He did not have pride enough for any truth about himself…"[15] The only acceptable reason for withholding the materials was that Cosima believed that Wagner's own writings revealed too much.

Not always a well man, Chamberlain was "troubled by demons" and yet he was driven to explore many fields including biology, botany, fine arts, philosophy, music and history. Returning from Italy in 1896 one particularly determined demon, assuming the shape of a malign muse, pestered him until he stopped off at a small inn in Gardone. Shutting out the world and eating a spare diet, he worked frantically until he had coalesced his theories of biology and history.

Emerging pale and distracted, with a menacing glint in his eye, he was clutching the manuscript in which he propounded his worldview – a tangled skein, describing the races of the world and their contribution to culture.[16] One of the phantoms that troubled him the most was the ancient Hebrew prophet Phineas who had originally forged the spear that came to symbolize hegemony and power. That selfsame spear was used to pierce Christ's side, became central in Wagner's opera *Parsifal* as a symbol of power, and became a talisman to Adolf Hitler after his first sighting of it in the museum in Vienna.

As Konrad Heiden put it in his brilliant biography of Adolf Hitler, *Der*

---

14. Köhler, *Wagner's Hitler*, 206, 254.
15. Vetter, "Wagner in the History of Psychology," 52.
16. Ibid.

Führer: "Chamberlain had learned from the great masters of world domination, from the Jewish prophets Ezekiel, Ezra and Nehemiah, who created as he says, by order of the Persian King, the race-conscious Jewish people. To penetrate other nations, to devour them from within by superior intellect, bred in the course of generations, to make themselves the dominant intelligence in foreign nations, and thus to make the world Jewish – this, according to Chamberlain, is the aim of the Jewish Race."[17]

And in those unlikely circumstances there came into being a triumvirate of megalomaniacs: Gobineau, Wagner and Chamberlain, steeped in pseudoscience, who were to provide the heady diet of an eight-year-old boy with piercing blue eyes, performing at that stage somewhat indifferently at junior school – apart from some ability to sketch profiles of his friends.

In his biography of Wagner, Chamberlain deals with the composer as an anti-Semite and quotes "Jewry in Music" where Wagner explained that his purpose was "to explain the unconscious feeling which in the people takes the form of a deep-rooted antipathy to the Jewish nature, to express therefore in plain language something really existing." Chamberlain goes on to explain how this "really existing thing" was to be removed in the writings of the composer. What Chamberlain refers to as "the baneful yawning abyss" is to be bridged over by Wagner's theory of "the regeneration of the human race." Further quotes from Wagner are given which advise the Jews to "bear your share undauntedly in this work of redemption, gaining new birth by self-immolation; we shall then be one and undivided! But remember that there can only be release from the curse, which rests upon you: the release of Ahasuerus – destruction."

Chamberlain then examines what Wagner means by destruction and finds that it is evident from an earlier sentence: "to become men in common with us is, for the Jews, primarily the same thing as to cease to be Jews."[18] Fortunately the more extreme "great solution" of the later writings is not referred to. For this reason there are those who maintain that all Chamberlain understood Wagner to be requiring of the Jews was to abandon their religion. This interpretation, however, takes little account of the idea that Jews should seek "self-immolation" and places a very benign meaning to the notion of "destruction." "Conversion" would have been so easy to say

---

17. Ravenscroft, *Spear of Destiny*, 119.
18. Wagner, Gottfried, *Twilight of the Wagners*, 68.

if that was the true intention. Writing to Chamberlain in December 1899, during the Anglo-Boer War, Cosima regretted that so many men on both sides had to die "just for the Jew Rhodes." In fact he was not Jewish but when she directed her venom at her enemies the worst stigma was to be labeled Jewish. She even suggested Nietzsche was of Slav origin which his sister refuted vehemently saying he was from noble Polish ancestry.[19]

Bruckmann, a firm that was later to support Hitler in his early endeavors, printed the book on Wagner by Chamberlain. Chamberlain's adulation of the composer is apparent throughout the book and at times he equates the Maestro from Bayreuth with the Savior from Galilee. The author described Wagner's thought as being like holy writ; he spoke of him as one raised from the dead, "a man who had lived and suffered on earth and whose name should be cherished in our hearts as in a holy shrine…a savior in the mould of Jesus Christ."[20] In a quaint reversal of roles Wagner is described as having been tormented by Jews, according to Chamberlain, and spent his last days sad and lonely in Bayreuth.[21]

It was clear that the heartstrings of the tall Englishman continued to quiver as far as Cosima was concerned. Chamberlain was effusive in his adulation of her and anyone with doubts as to the future of the Bayreuth festival and her role as heir apparent was worrying unnecessarily. He wrote that "the immediate rise in the standard of the festival was due first and foremost to the circumstance that from now on an intelligence [Cosima] was shaping and ordering it, which reflected the will of the artistic creator as no other in the world."[22] Not so reverent was the great humanitarian, musician and missionary Albert Schweitzer, who saw her in 1904 and spoke of the fact that "her manner of receiving people was lacking in simplicity and naturalness…she liked them to approach her with the reverence due to a princess."

Schweitzer records that members of the Bayreuth orchestra told him that they were "not unanimous in their opinion that it was a real advantage to have a woman of such an imperious will as Madame Cosima directing the performances."[23] He revised his opinion somewhat and concluded that

---

19. Newman, *Life of Richard Wagner*, vol. 3, 285, note 13.
20. Köhler, *Wagner's Hitler*, 21.
21. Ibid., 22.
22. Skelton, *Wagner at Bayreuth*, 72–73.
23. Ibid., 74.

she was a woman with a "delicate and vital soul" but that she was "haunted by the idea that the master's enemies remained active and formidable."[24] Doubtless Cosima continued to believe such enemies to be the Jews whom her husband had always believed were out to conquer the world and destroy Teutonic culture.

Walther Siegfried tells a wonderful story of how Cosima was able to make sure that her will prevailed whatever the circumstances. The soprano who played Elizabeth in *Tannhäuser* had learned from her teacher that when entering the hall of song in the second act the hands should be outstretched to welcome the guests. Cosima thought that in the medieval times more modesty was required and that she should keep her hands by her side. The soprano hatched a plot with her teacher; she would appear to obey the princess of Bayreuth at all rehearsals but on the night she would do it her way. The teacher was so certain of her decision she threatened to wring her neck if she obeyed Cosima. Come the night the soprano did not raise her arms and kept them modestly at her side. Furious, her teacher called for an explanation; Cosima has sewn the soprano's sleeves to her side![25]

Any doubts as to the reasons for Chamberlain's literary coyness were dispelled when he sent a very revealing letter to the "princess of Bayreuth." On January 13, 1905 Chamberlain wrote to Cosima as follows: "after my book [Wagner] was published in 1896 you invited me to come to Bayreuth and to peruse the unpublished autobiography. That was the finest possible proof of your confidence in me and your benevolence toward me… yet with the stubbornness which you have known in me and which you, if you do not approve of it, at least excuse as a characteristic trait of my personality, *I refused to glance at anything which was not common knowledge.*"

Chamberlain was not prepared to repeat any revelations inadvertently made by the composer. If Wagner in a fit of pardonable veracity were to let slip some detail, which showed him up as a scoundrel or philanderer, then the family would see to it that it was covered up. Chamberlain was comfortable in his role as hagiographer. The importance of truth, and the assistance contemporary letters and documents provided in that great quest, also did not appeal to him.

He continues in the letter to emphasize this point: "I believe that we

---

24. Ibid.
25. Newman, *Life of Richard Wagner*, vol. 3, 290.

suffer these days by an exaggerated search for documents. *A great man ought to be judged by his works – and with few documents, the fewer, the better.* Up to now I have not read the autobiography. And though I know the iron safe in the small salon in Wahnfried where you keep the manuscripts and letters of the Meister, though I was present on one occasion, when you opened the safe to search for something, nevertheless I have never, not once, looked at any letter preserved there..."

Chamberlain's first wife became progressively more neurotic and later mentally and physically ill, with the result that he divorced her in 1905. That same year he settled in Bayreuth. While Cosima remained out of reach for him, not so her daughter, and some three years later he married as his second wife Eva Wagner.[26] His writings on Wagner were to be devoured by Adolf Hitler as were his other books including the seminal *Foundations of the Nineteenth Century*. When the young National Socialist politician met Chamberlain in 1923, a wasting muscular disease had crippled the old man. Not so Hitler, who was on the point of challenging the political authorities in Germany and preparing to assume the mantle of the heir apparent of Richard Wagner.

Other hagiographers were as frugal with the truth as Chamberlain and included the dilettante Ferdinand Praeger, who lived from 1815 to 1891. The last mentioned, like Wagner, was born in Leipzig, and had no personal acquaintance with the composer till he spent a night in his house in London in 1855, on his arrival to conduct the concerts of the Royal Philharmonic Society. Praeger had settled in London as a composer and thespian in 1834.

Wagner's contact with him was through the father of a coconspirator of his in the 1848 revolts – August Röckel, the Dresden conductor who was sentenced to death for his treason. In 1892 Praeger's book of reminiscences was published – *Wagner as I Knew Him* – allegedly full of false claims subsequently exposed, ironically enough, given their own propensities for manipulation, by Ashton Ellis and Chamberlain.

Little would have become known of the real Wagner but for the efforts of a remarkable English woman. Mary Burrell was the wife of the Honorable Willoughby Burrell and the daughter of Sir John Banks KCB, a prominent physicist of Trinity College Dublin. Over a long period she made

---

26. Shirer, *Rise and Fall of the Third Reich*, 138.

pilgrimages to the Wagnerian cathedrals to hear the wonderful music in Bayreuth, Munich and Berlin. She thought the music constituted the most overwhelmingly passionate and plaintive sounds ever produced and she determined to write a biography of the man who produced them.

She had idealism, lots of it, a quaint British passion for the truth and bags of guts. She had devoured all existing accounts of the life of Wagner and she could never equate the passion of the music with the cardboard character she read about in the hagiographies. Although she died a relatively young woman in 1898, by that time she had tracked down 840 items, mostly letters relating to Wagner's life.[27] Not all Mrs. Burrell found was of great assistance – she came into possession of the diary from Wahnfried in 1875 of Susanne Weinert and described it as a "ludicrous journal of an idiot governess."[28] Her own account of Wagner's early life was the first attempt at authentic and honest biography and the limited large format book is to be found in the British Museum. The publication of it stemmed the tide of falsification that had threatened to overwhelm an unsuspecting public.

Fortunately we now have a number of reasonably accurate accounts of the composer's life and none more impressive than the immensely erudite Ernest Newman, whose book *The Life of Richard Wagner*, in four volumes written between 1933 and 1947, remains the classic account. There are other impressive biographies as well – Ronald Taylor emphasizes the historical background of his life[29] and Robert W. Gutman's biography,[30] though regarded by some as largely hostile, is probably the best single-volume account. Those in search of primary materials would do well to consult the numerous compilations of his letters and other original sources including the diaries of Cosima.[31]

George Bernard Shaw[32] has much of value to say about the social, political and economic ideas behind the *Ring* and the psychological zealot

---

27. See Burk, *Letters of Richard Wagner: The Burrell Collection*, 1–4 and see introduction to Curtis Institute of Music Richard Wagner Collection brochure by Ann Viles, 1978, 9–11. In the brochure a portrait of Mary Burrell is at p. 139 and the notes are on p. 163.
28. Gutman, *Richard Wagner*, 12.
29. Taylor, *Richard Wagner: His Life, Art and Thought*.
30. Gutman, *Richard Wagner: The Man, His Mind and His Music*.
31. See for example Skelton, *Cosima Wagner's Diaries*.
32. Shaw, George Bernard, *The Perfect Wagnerite*, 4th ed. (New York: Brentano, 1911, reprinted 1967).

will find something to put him to sleep in the Jungian interpretation of the same work by Robert Donington.[33] If the reader wants to understand the technical details of the wonderful music, the best analytical introduction to Wagner's music dramas is that of Ernest Newman,[34] though others, notably Stein and Lorenz, have gone into greater detail. These analyses are not for the fainthearted and require a sound knowledge of German.[35]

The standard of biography attained by Newman, Gutman and others is incredibly high and anyone intent upon finding out all the details of a great composer should immerse themselves in one of those. I intend dealing fairly briefly with the contributions to the knowledge of Wagner's life, or more accurately the lack thereof, by the hagiographers. An important question remains to be considered. If accurate biography is now available what is the point of investigating what crank writers wrote where their only motive was to hide those aspects of the life of Wagner that did not measure up to his music? The only legitimate reason for an endeavor such as this – apart from a morbid interest in the duplicity and the exposure thereof – lies in understanding the sort of biography that existed when Adolf Hitler was voraciously consuming all that Wagner wrote, and all that had been written about Wagner.

What matters in a book such as this is not so much what the modern reader need be satisfied with. What is more important in my enquiry is the sort of man Hitler came to adulate. Of importance is the material that was available to him when his mind was fomenting the bizarre thoughts that turned the civilized world upside down. What the reader needs to know is what ideology went through his mind in his formative years? What vision of Wagner did he rely on when his depraved sexual practices revealed that his was a madness that might contemplate fulfilling a task the composer had been unable to undertake?

There are large areas where Cosima and her sycophantic biographers

---

33. Donington, Robert, *Wagner's Ring and Its Symbols*, 2nd ed. (New York: St Martin's, 1963).
34. Newman, Ernest, *The Wagner Operas* (New York: Knopf, 1949); republished with the title *Wagner Nights*.
35. A detailed study of Wagner's development as a musical dramatist is Jack M. Stein's *Richard Wagner and the Synthesis of the Arts* (Detroit: Wayne State, 1960). A.O. Lorenz, *Das Geheimnis der Form bei Richard Wagner*, 4 vol. (Berlin, Hesse, 1924–33), provides an exhaustive bar-by-bar analysis of the musical construction of his major works.

mutilated the truth or left it out completely. It is not necessary to deal with all the instances but a few examples will suffice. There was large-scale destruction in that the letters to Wagner by his close associate and fellow composer Peter Cornelius were burned.[36] Cosima destroyed many of Nietzsche's letters, though drafts of some of them have survived in his papers.[37] According to Eva all Cosima's letters to Wagner were destroyed in 1909 and the composer's letters addressed to her were incinerated in 1930.[38]

Of interest to the reader are the details of the life of Richard Wagner expunged or altered by the hagiographers. The first issue of factual falsification relates to the identity of Wagner's father. If one purchases a modern English translation of *My Life* one will read that the father of Richard was Friedrich Wagner. Glasenapp, under the influence of Cosima, confirmed the paternity of Friedrich, who was married to Wagner's mother Johanna. We have the gravest doubts that this was the case. Glasenapp explained that Ludwig Geyer married Wagner's mother Johanna some *two years* after the death of Friedrich Wagner. We now know that he married Johanna some *nine months* after Friedrich's death, the earliest time allowed in Saxon law.

Mrs. Burrell had read the version of Glasenapp concerning Wagner's birth and could not believe what it described. The production of the private edition of *My Life* was given to Bonfantini of Basel and Burrell managed to get a copy from Bonfantini's widow in 1892.[39] She could not accept that Wagner was the author of the later expurgated version of the autobiography, which she described as a "miserable book." The find was to reveal much about a number of issues including the paternity of Richard Wagner. Mention has been made of the facts that have emerged concerning the probability that Geyer was his father. Wagner probably believed Geyer was Jewish but subsequent research has showed otherwise.

Mention has been made that on the cover of the private edition Wagner had ordered that a vulture be embossed. The word for vulture in German is *geier* and Wagner believed that his real father was Ludwig Geyer. When the first copy arrived he was deeply offended, as the cover had em-

---

36. Marek, *Cosima Wagner*, 68.
37. Ibid.
38. Ibid., 47–48.
39. Gutman, *Richard Wagner: The Man, His Mind and His Music*, 320.

bossed on it what looked more like an eagle. Friedrich Nietzsche who had befriended the family was sent to have it changed into a vulture. Nietzsche was worried that vultures lived on carrion and that Sigmund Freud had given an account of the Egyptian myth of the vulture representing the son without a father.[40]

The hagiographers suppressed another side to Wagner – his personal and important contribution to the uprising in Dresden in 1848. Had Wagner taken part in an attempt to overthrow law and order in Saxony? Was Wagner a revolutionary? He denied it and claimed that he was a mere spectator. The truth emerged from his earlier letters to Theodor Uhlig, a friend of Wagner's in those heady days of excitement. Uhlig was the first violinist in the Court orchestra there and helped with the piano score of *Lohengrin* and attempted to stage *The Flying Dutchman* and *Tannhäuser*. Uhlig loved Wagner like a brother and they shared the same political and musical ideas. Uhlig, incidentally, was the poet in Zurich who rated a mention in Wagner's letter to Nietzsche's doctor as having gone blind from masturbation.[41] After Wagner fled from Dresden Uhlig visited him in Switzerland. Uhlig was not to live long thereafter – they went on a walking tour in the William Tell country and he died of consumption scarcely a year and a half later.

Cosima published the letters of Uhlig in 1888, with an English translation two years later, with numerous deletions, including all mention of Wagner's revolutionary character.[42] Glasenapp suppressed part of a poem written by Wagner including the verses where he commended the Viennese "heroes" for "having drawn the sword" and he exhorted the Saxon people to follow suit. Newman in his indefatigable manner tracked down the original poem and revealed the truth.[43]

Mary Burrell visited Uhlig's daughter Elsa, named after the heroine of *Lohengrin* and her brother Siegfried, as she was worried that an expurgated version of Uhlig's letters had been published. Elsa had dared to publish three letters in the *Allgemeine Musikzeitung* and there was a flurry in the Wahnfried dovecot – Cosima was now worried that more letters would

---

40. On the Freudian theory of the vulture see Poliakov, *History of Anti-Semitism from Voltaire to Wagner*, 171.
41. Weiner, *Richard Wagner and the Anti-Semitic Imagination*, 341.
42. Burk, *Letters of Richard Wagner: The Burrell Collection*, 607.
43. Newman, *Life of Richard Wagner*, vol. 2, 8.

be discovered. Elsa then received thinly veiled threats from Eva, Cosima's daughter and later wife of Chamberlain. "Do not divulge anything further of the letters which are in your possession." Elsa refused to assist in the cover-up of letters sent to her father, which she had inherited and were her property. Elsa sent a defiant reply saying that they could go to hell. Further rumblings were heard from Wahnfried. "Since Mama's request to you, worthy Fräulein, as presented by me not to publish the letters has had your answer that no consideration would prevent you from publishing them, Mama has had no recourse but to take legal steps."

Nothing came of the threats and, indeed, no legal foundation existed for an action to repossess what was her property. Elsa's courage paid off and though she sat on the letters for eleven years, she eventually sold them to a dealer in memorabilia, Richard Bertling in Dresden. Mrs. Burrell lost no time in retrieving the letters from Bertling and they revealed a Wagner who was a far cry from the conservative racist of later times. Mention has been made of Wagner the socialist and economic reformer whose political tracts had helped galvanize the people of Dresden to armed rebellion. He had also distributed arms and hand grenades to the militia and orchestrated the burning of the palace to signal the start of the revolution. That he narrowly escaped the death penalty was due in no small part to the celerity of his departure. His great friend and musician August Röckel was initially sentenced to death but his sentence was commuted and he served fourteen years.

Mrs. Burrell then checked what Wagner had said in his autobiography against the letters she found with Natalie and the other sources. She was to find a yawning chasm between the great pretense and the sordid truth. The documents seemed to tell a different story as has been set out earlier in this book. Cosima had falsified and deleted material to such an extent that only twenty-three of ninety-three letters to Uhlig published in her book of 1888 escaped unscathed from her insatiably censorious blue pencil.[44]

The philandering of Wagner was another area that engaged the attention of the literary censors and the blue pencil ripped through the account of the affairs with Jessie Laussot, Mathilde Wesendonck and the genesis of the romance with Cosima. Chamberlain, true to form, spent some considerable time and effort gilding the lily and covering up the loud and worri-

---

44. Marek, *Cosima Wagner*, 212.

some rumors of infidelities. Concerning Jessie Laussot, the beautiful lady friend Wagner acquired in Bordeaux, he wrote, "*A lady personally unknown to Wagner* Madame Laussot, the wife of the French merchant, possessed the means of rendering him more substantial assistance. She was English born, Miss Taylor, and during her long stay in Dresden she had acquired an enthusiastic admiration for Wagner's works…"[45]

Ferdinand Praeger took a different tack on the incident: "At Bordeaux an episode occurred similar to one which happened later at Zurich (the Wesendonck affair) about which the press of the day made a good deal of unnecessary commotion and ungenerous comment. I mention the incident to show the man as he was. The opposition have not spared his failings, and over the Zurich incident were hypercritically censorious. The Bordeaux story I am alluding to is that the wife of a friend, Mrs. H having followed Wagner to the south, called on him at his hotel and throwing herself at his feet, passionately told of her affection. *Wagner's action in the matter was to telegraph to the husband to come and take his wife home.* On telling me the story, Wagner jocosely remarked that poor Beethoven, so full of love, never had his affection returned and lived and died, so it is said, a hermit."[46]

Wagner, it will be recalled, chastised Jessie on the basis that she was not sufficiently mature to elope with him! Glasenapp makes no mention of the Jessie Laussot incident though he must have known about it. Mathilde Wesendonck, whose name is also linked romantically with Wagner, wrote to Ashton Ellis and made mention of the Bordeaux incident. Her loyalty is so touching and she has an interesting take on the question of biographical veracity as well. She told Ellis that "The Episode" of Bordeaux has been related by the Meister himself, and is to be found in the Edition of "Hinterlassene Schriften." May we not be content with what He tells us about it? *Need we know more?*

Also deleted by the Bayreuth falsifiers was a passage in the correspondence between Wagner and Mathilde in which he tells of the pact between Cosima and Karl Ritter to commit suicide some time in August 1858 as a result of their unhappy marriages. Ritter was a homosexual and he also

---

45. Newman, *Wagner as Man and Artist*, 54.
46. On Jessie Laussot there is interesting material on what Wagner told Praeger about her in Newman, *Wagner as Man and Artist*, 77. See also Hurn and Root, *The Truth about Wagner*, 114.

featured in Wagner's letter to Nietzsche's doctor as one who suffered from the depredations of onanism.[47]

Mrs. Burrell wanted to know more and she was not seeking to blacken the composer's name, but merely to tell the unvarnished truth. Cosima again threatened litigation to prevent publication but the indomitable Mrs. Burrell eventually obtained the letters.[48] The truth of Wagner's passionate affair with Jessie Laussot as it finally emerged from the correspondence was somewhat different and has been set out above.[49]

Apart from Cosima and her allies, who excised compromising passages from Wagner's letters to Mathilde,[50] Mathilde also entered the lists in suppressing the truth. Her husband Otto had financed Wagner on the security of his works, which incidentally were also securing a host of separate debts to other friends. In the letter Mathilde wrote to Ashton Ellis, quoted above, she also accused him of "darkening the Meister's Memory to Mankind, by making 'gossip' on the intimacy of his private life." It was very difficult at that time to admit to sharing a love, even to a great man.

In those days "gossip" was probably rated higher on the scale of social delinquencies than today, but no doubt, even in those Victorian times curiosity thrived and, after all, biographical veracity is an immemorial virtue. The outraged Mathilde continues in her letter to supply a reason why great artists should deserve literary protection against the truth. "Did he not bequeath to us his unequalled, unrivalled and everlasting works? And is this holy Testament not above all Doubt and Calumny?"

There is no love like that of a true and fanatical disciple – his writings, which often stretched the truth in directions it is not wont to go – are referred to by Mathilde as a "holy Testament." Mathilde finally reaches her own defense and explains that "...*The tie that bound him to Mathilde Wesendonck, whom he called his Muse, was of so high, pure, noble and ideal a Nature* that alas it will only be valued of those that, in their own noble chest, find the same elevation and selflessness of Mind..."

---

47. Newman, *Life of Richard Wagner*, vol. 3, 297, and Weiner, *Richard Wagner and the Anti-Semitic Imagination*, 341.
48. Burk, *Letters of Richard Wagner: The Burrell Collection*, 608.
49. That Wagner planned a flight to Greece is clear from Gutman, *Richard Wagner*, 82. The meeting with Jessie Laussot is described by Gutman (p. 168) as is the subsequent development and crisis (pp. 198–202).
50. Marek, *Cosima Wagner*, 68.

There were limits to what could be achieved by the falsifiers and hagiographers once Mary Burrell had bought up so many letters available to the public. The publication of Burrell's partial biography in 1898 indicated to Cosima that she was in possession of the original private copy of *My Life* and this stayed her editorial hand.

There was one final matter in which Cosima had a personal interest in suppressing the truth of what had taken place – her own relationship with the composer. We know that when Wagner visited Cosima and Hans von Bülow in Berlin in November 1863 he (Wagner) recorded the fact that "with tears and sobs we sealed our confession to belong to each other alone."[51] Wagner specifically insisted that this be included in his autobiography. But there were a number of important implications. Cosima's adulterous relationship with Wagner caused considerable pain and anguish to his first wife Minna. Secondly Cosima was anxious to establish that the genesis of their relationship took place some years later when she had finally parted from her husband Hans. The notion that she tiptoed between the two bedrooms at Starnberg was a cause of great embarrassment to a person who cast herself in the mould of a princess. Cosima took out her blue pen and struck out the words recording this incident in the first edition of *My Life*.[52]

Unfortunately for Cosima Wagner and a matter of significance for those interested in the truth, Mary Burrell had purchased a copy of the original manuscript from Mrs Tekla Bonfantini and comparisons are odious. This was a crucial deletion because it established the intensity of the relationship; in fact it was the first time they made love, as the subsequent diaries of Cosima reveal, and she did not want to be thought to be responsible for the breakup of her marriage.[53] Wagner emerges as a man who has some respect for the truth but what exacerbated the situation was that he had promised to visit his wife Minna at that time. The Catholic upbringing and later Lutheran conservatism clearly left a deep imprint on the Bayreuth widow. Although her diaries often reveal a candor that is deeply moving – together with a distressing racism – her literary efforts as an editor of her husband's biographies revealed a sort of petit bourgeois morality that sat uncomfortably in the sordid narrative of the life of the composer.

---

51. Newman, *Life of Richard Wagner*, vol. 3, 303.
52. Marek, *Cosima Wagner*, 45.
53. Gutman, *Richard Wagner*, 320–21.

Chapter nine
The Widow Spider

After Wagner died Cosima decreed that nothing was to be changed in the house and at the theatre either internally or externally.[1] At the time of his death she cut off her hair and sat with the body for some twenty-four hours and for days she refused food and sleep. But the iron will was not dead. Within a week she had determined to carry on with the festival for that year.[2] She also had herself and Siegfried declared the legal heirs to the vast patrimony.

Her decision not to change the productions was not to please everyone. One of the great stage reformers Adolfe Appia saw the 1886 *Tristan* and was astounded by the conservatism of the production. "A living thing is being presented in an atmosphere without life."[3] He wrote a critical review and suggested a setting with symbolism rather than verisimilitude. "A few ropes of typical rigging" would suggest the first act on board ship – but Cosima would have nothing of it. She told Chamberlain that she looked at his proposals searching for something of value "unfortunately in vain…Appia appears not to know that in 1876 the *Ring* was performed here and consequently there is nothing more to be discovered with regard to staging and setting."[4]

---

1. Wagner, Nike, *The Wagners*, 175.
2. Spotts, *Bayreuth*, 90–91.
3. Ibid., 106.
4. Ibid., 107.

After the death of Ludwig that same year Cosima was informed that the *Ring* and *Parsifal* now belonged to the new Prince Regent and the Munich opera. The successful banker Adolf von Gross, who had assisted Cosima from the time of the death of the composer, countered this by producing a waiver of rights in favor of the Wagners signed by the late king. Count von Crailsheim the Minister of the Household in the Bavarian government then quoted the madness of Ludwig as a reason why the waiver was invalid and for a while Bayreuth was stymied. Von Gross, however, was not only stolid but also inventive. If the madness of the king invalidated the waiver in favor of the Wagners of the rights of the two operas then von Crailsheim's appointment as a minister was tainted by the same ailment and must also be illegal. The ploy worked and the Bavarian government retired in disorder.[5]

Cosima continued producing the festivals thereafter but still struggled to find the necessary funds to ensure productions of a uniformly high standard. It had always been assumed that the festival would be restricted to the great man's works. To that end she made a decision that was to be breached in the most interesting circumstances in 1945: she decreed that only Wagner's works would be produced there.[6] As for the short-term interests of Bayreuth Cosima decided that the festival for that year would continue and she employed Emil Scaria, the legendary bass, as the artistic director, while Julius Kniese controlled the rehearsals.[7] The last-mentioned slotted into the appropriated ideological role established by the composer. He attacked Levi and tried to dismiss him as the conductor, for reasons that remained undisclosed but had nothing to do with his abilities as a conductor. It was not difficult to guess the real motives behind the venom. In his memoirs Kniese betrayed his anti-Semitism when he said that Levi "pretended to be hurt but he knew perfectly well and admitted that it had less to do with him personally than with him and his race's tragic destiny."[8]

In an ironic repetition of the dilemma faced by her husband, Cosima needed Levi because of his ability and she had to repress her deep-seated anti-Jewish feelings to continue employing him. Her letters to Prince Hohenlohe-Langenberg, published in 1938, betrayed anti-Semitism of the

---

5. Ibid., 101.
6. Ibid., 90.
7. Ibid.
8. Ibid., 92.

A placard commemorating 25 years of work by Hermann Levi, caricaturing him as a Jew. Wagners Welten, page 219. Münchner Stadtmuseum/Graphiksammlung.

worst order and Ernest Newman commented that "any Nazi" could have written them. "The 'Jew' leit-motive, combined with that of 'Regeneration through Bayreuth,' runs through these letters with the persistency of the 'gold' motive in the *Ring*: the only difference is that Cosima repeats her leit-motives a thousand times without the slightest variation." That was how Newman assessed her correspondence.[9]

In the end Cosima was desperate and determined that art had to triumph over ideology despite the strong camp lined up against her employment of the conductor. She decided to call the bluff of those wanting him removed. Revealing a cunning that was to characterize her stewardship of the festival, she compiled a memo to the effect that "conductor Levi is morally unworthy and artistically unqualified to conduct *Parsifal*." The memo was circulated amongst all the interested parties and Cosima watched with great interest which way the dice would fall. The ploy worked and the racists skulked off into their burrows; no one signed it – Levi survived and Kniese was fired.[10]

The need for funds continued and she even looked in a most unlikely source for assistance. In 1884 she wrote to Glasenapp and in all probability had in mind the Jewish bankers that her husband had attacked so viciously.

---

9. Ibid.
10. Ibid.

"Forty millions, that's what I need to give the Germans the Festivals. Perhaps one of these good days a good soul will give them to me, a Jew who wants to atone for the evil of his race."[11] Her relationship with her father Franz Liszt had seen stormy waters, especially during the period of her relationship with Wagner, but his invitation to the 1876 inaugural Ring cycle had done much to repair the damage. After a life that had spanned the entire century, crammed full of physical passion and religious zeal, Franz Liszt died on July 31, 1886 and was buried in Bayreuth.[12] To the end he remained a humanitarian who deplored the anti-Semitism of his son-in-law and daughter.

That same year Felix Weingartner was employed as a musical assistant and he attended a dinner at Wahnfried where he was amazed at the manner in which Levi conducted himself. Servile and self-effacing to a degree that Weingartner found degrading, he taxed the conductor on his attitude. "It is easy enough for you in that house, Aryan that you are."[13] Once again Shakespeare said it so much better than we mere mortals when he had Shylock comment: "I am a Jew. Hath not a Jew eyes? Hath not a Jew hands, organs, dimensions, senses, affections, passions; fed with the same food, hurt with the same weapons, subject to the same diseases, healed by the same means, warmed and cooled by the same winter and summer as a Christian is? If you prick us do we not bleed? If you tickle us do we not laugh? If you poison us do we not die?"[14]

Weingartner was a straight shooter but he did little to remedy that fault. He deplored the fact that Cosima employed a bunch of sycophants and no men "who with the frankness of conviction, with the bluntness of the love of truth would have enlightened her when she made mistakes, would have held her back from countless errors in casting and staging."[15]

The education of the children was undertaken by Cosima herself and religion played a most important part in that endeavor.[16] The main focus of attention was the male heir Siegfried and much was expected of a son with Wagner, Liszt and D'Agoult blood. His upbringing was, however, a

---

11. Marek, *Cosima Wagner*, 211.
12. Ibid., 187.
13. Spotts, *Bayreuth*, 98.
14. Shakespeare, *Complete Oxford Shakespeare*, 615.
15. Richard Wagner Museum brochure, "About Richard Wagner," items 36–40.
16. Ibid., 183.

disaster and his playmates – selected by a censorious mother, who dressed him in old-fashioned tailored suits – found much of what he did the subject of great mirth.[17] The family music cognoscenti looked for signs of genius and the precocious lad did not disappoint them, initially at any rate. A private tutor taught Siegfried the rudiments of education and to his immense satisfaction – he found the home education stifling and oppressive – when he reached puberty, he was liberated into the local grammar school in Bayreuth.[18]

After leaving the grammar school his musical education was placed in the hands of Engelbert Humperdinck,[19] who had assisted with the first production of *Parsifal* at the feet of the Master. Humperdinck was almost credited with having written a few bars of that wonderful score. In the first act the scene shifts from the woodland to the Grail temple and, in what has become termed as the "transformation scene," a moving backdrop suggests the journey. The scenic innovation – modeled on a production in Paris – moved too slowly and more music was requested from the exhausted composer. Wagner jocularly claimed that he was now requested to compose three more meters of music. In the event he was disinclined to engage in such a menial task and Humperdinck was asked to compose a few more bars to cater for it. Finally it was not necessary – as the backdrop was geared up to fit into the existing music.

Humperdinck, whose name was to be shamelessly taken by a modern British singer, was a very considerable composer in his own right. His opera *Hansel and Gretel* is one of the great masterpieces of the art and holds the stage throughout the world, particularly at Christmas. His then was the task to make sure the chip was of the same quality as the block. The portends had to be good: a father, one of the greatest artistic geniuses of all time; a grandfather, reckoned a great pianist and composer; and a grandmother, author of literature of considerable quality.

But biology is no slave to expectation and Siegfried grew up a mild and conciliatory man, lacking in many of the qualities of his distinguished ancestors. He felt the unwholesome pressure of expectation on him and resisted for a while. The Jewish critic, friend and biographer of Siegfried

---

17. Ibid.
18. Ibid.
19. Ibid.

Wagner, Ludwig Karpath, related the father's attitude to his son's career. He did not concern himself that Siegfried did not necessarily choose the career of a musician and also approved of that of an architect. His untimely death Siegfried maintained meant that the question was never explored more fully.[20] His brief flirtation with architecture did not last and he undertook a tour of world discovery. Siegfried met the homosexual Clement Harris and it seems clear that a relationship developed. A contemporary photo shows Siegfried in a travesty role as a prima ballerina.[21]

Clement Harris visited Bayreuth in 1891 and was accepted as part of the family. He described Cosima as a woman of great fascination and made himself useful with English correspondence and spent time entertaining his own countrymen. In the cathedral preacher Adolf Stocker the young Harris acknowledged with great shock the greatest anti-Semite of his time and he confided a sinister note to his diary that Stocker and Prince Hohenlohe spoke very animatedly about the role of Jews in the future of Germany.[22]

The call of the blood and the warm bosom of his family in Bayreuth were, however, too strong and Siegfried's character was to be influenced by his mother and the other strong women of Wahnfried.

In 1889 Siegfried betrayed the inherited anti-Semitism when he saw the opera *Patrie* composed by Palladilke and wrote and described it to his sister Blandine as "a miserably contrived Jewish opera" and even took the legendary Sarah Bernhardt to task. He compared her interpretation of Joan of Arc as similar to the Virgin Mary. Wagner's hatred of the French and the mother tongue of Cosima was finding its way into his otherwise carefree disposition. "Everything that Paris has to offer is stinking muck."[23] Siegfried told his sister that "Jewry had suffocated every German cell and the French Semitic world put on the stage the most pathetic products." All this he compared unfavorably to the crowning glory of Bayreuth with its shiny and sensitive soul.[24]

Having decided on a musical career – or more correctly, accepting the twin pressures of heredity and family, Siegfried settled down in 1892 to devote himself to his own compositions and producing those of his father,

---

20. Pachl, *Siegfried Wagner*, 83.
21. Ibid., 89–90.
22. Ibid., 105.
23. Ibid., 85.
24. Ibid., 88.

tasks that presented many challenges.[25] Contemporary composers were to comment on what his cultural and physical inheritance held out for him. Not quite as simple as "taking over the draper's shop," as Claude Debussy had observed, but there was every hope that he would be equal to the task.[26] Writers at the time described Siegfried as an elegant, if somewhat effete, dresser with his favorite being a tasteful cream suit with a brown belt across the midriff, reminiscent of Prussian Junkers and equestrians.[27]

The climate of Bayreuth had already nurtured the philosopher Jean Paul who predicted the coming of a man – Richard Wagner – who would write the libretto and music for great operas. As has been shown the art of prophecy was passed on to the great composer who set out his blueprint for the new Germany and its leader. Wagner's widow Cosima continued in the same vein in 1892 when she repeated that the people were waiting for a "Führer" who would realize that his people were being "sucked dry by the Jews."[28] In that same year she added a new cottage for the gardener and one for Siegfried to compose in.[29] Her prescience was to take on a more concrete form as that very building was to house Adolf Hitler when he made his annual pilgrimages to the festival forty years later.

That Cosima meant the Führer to rule as a dictator was always clear, as her views on democracy were very strong. In fact in this regard she inherited or aped the excesses of her late husband and his powerful use of metaphor was to be her chosen vehicle for invective. "Universal suffrage is like an ulcer on the body of the nation, full of foul-smelling pus. Where shall we find a surgeon with the courage to perform the operation that is needed," Cosima said in a letter to a friend in January 1901.[30]

Cosima was awaiting the savior to cleanse Germany of Jews but she was not keen that such a fact be widely known. In the same way Nietzsche had been cautioned against speaking directly on the subject she also counseled veiled language and innuendo in passing on the message. She feared a reaction from the public at large and that the festival would be affected. In 1894 Hans von Wolzogen, the editor of the *Bayreuther Blätter*, told the

---

25. Wagner, Nike, *The Wagners*, 196.
26. Ibid.
27. Ibid.
28. Köhler, *Wagner's Hitler*, 142.
29. Wagner, Nike, *The Wagners*, 175.
30. Köhler, *Wagner's Hitler*, 113.

Wagner used as a prophet in the anti-Semitism campaign of later German nationalists. The words quoted are drawn from his polemical writings, "Golden Words." "The Jew is the concrete demon of the decline of humanity. We did not mind the fact that the Jews erected a Jerusalemic [Semitic] Empire but regret that Mr. Rothschild was too clever by far in making himself the King of the Jews as he would prefer to be the Jew of the Kings [i.e., a money lender to the leaders of society]. Very subtly the creditor of the kings has become the leader of the believers in requesting the emancipation and equalization of the Jews. We cannot but find the request of this leader naïve because we are compelled to fight for our emancipation from the Jews. We cannot imagine Jews performing the role of hero or lover as their unfeeling portrayal is unsuited and ridiculous." Wagners Welten, page 232. Marcel Prawy, "Nun sei bedankt..." München 1982.

racist agitator Ludwig Schemann, who traveled the country organizing anti-Semitic rallies, that it was not in their interests "at this early stage, when we are only just embarking on our campaign, to make the broader public aware of exactly what we have in mind. We do not want the Jews and their friends to get wind of our plans and resort to counter-measures."[31]

Gustav Mahler realized just how powerful the anti-Semitic lobby was as he wrote in 1894 from Hamburg to his friend Fritz Lohr about his difficulty finding a decent post. "The situation in the world being what it now is,

---

31. Ibid., 116.

the fact that I am Jewish prevents my getting on in any court theatre…neither Vienna, nor Berlin, nor Dresden, nor Munich is open to me."[32]

The anti-Semitic ideology was to pose special problems for the next forty years in the quest for artists of great ability. Music was an art form dominated by Jews and their contribution had been immense. Cosima was searching for new singers for the new production of the *Ring* and she needed vocalists who were receptive to the Bayreuth spirit. The great soprano Lilli Lehmann maintained that "all roads may lead to Rome but to the Bayreuth of today there is but one – the road of slavish subjection."[33] Although Cosima was indifferent to their country of origin she was not careless about their religious persuasion. Whereas Wagner had said, "we have a German Reich of the Jewish nation," she added the cultural refinement, "now we want a German theatre of all nationals except for the 'chosen people.'"[34]

The greatest successor to Wagner, Richard Strauss, whose operas have a magic that paralleled that of the Bayreuth master, inherited his race views. In 1889 he had acted as a musical assistant at Bayreuth and rehearsal conductor in 1891. If he had taken the trouble that year to go through the lists of visitors to the festival he would have found the name of Mark Twain who had famously called Wagner's music better than it sounded. Twain was to write up his visit to Bayreuth in his witty and sardonic manner and he was appalled by the censure of any person coughing, sneezing or making the slightest noise in the *sanctus sanctorum* of German art. "You seem to sit with the dead in the gloom of a tomb," he said.[35]

Strauss joined the "great hunt" against the Jews as Wagner had described it to Liszt, forty years before, and he wrote to Cosima urging her to get rid of the Jew Hermann Levi. In an outburst, out of character for this bluff and genial Bavarian, who was later to refuse the Nazis the use of his house to billet soldiers, he harped back to the problems Wagner had with Levi conducting his sacred work. "Yes the Jews have come a long way with us…Is it really too much when I say from the bottom of my heart 'too bad'?

---

32. Franklin, *Life of Mahler*, 93.
33. Spotts, *Bayreuth*, 114.
34. Ibid.
35. Ibid., 26.

So is poor *Parsifal* never to be let out of the Jewish torture chamber; why must the poor work suffer from the 'services' of Levi?"[36]

Fifty years later the question would be transposed; Jews were to be placed in torture (gas) chambers because of a madman's interpretation of his spiritual mentor's political program including the subliminal text of *Parsifal*. However for once the fates were lined up against the racists and Strauss was not able to take up the baton because of illness. Thereafter he fell out of favor with the widow of Siegfried – the controversial Winifred, whose relationship with Hitler was to cause such a stir – until he replaced Toscanini on the podium, forty years later, when Adolf Hitler had angered the Italian maestro with his treatment of Jewish musicians.

Richard Strauss was to share an adulation for the music of Wagner that almost bordered on idolatry and there is more than a hint that his craftsmanship owes much to his creative mentor. He referred to himself as Richard III – Wagner was Richard I – and there could be no real successor. One solace from his early debacle at Bayreuth was his decision to marry his fiancée of the time Pauline de Ahna, who had sung at the festival. He had a dim view of the small town and its maneuverings and told her Bayreuth was a "pigsty of pigsties."[37]

In the summer of 1889 *Die Meistersinger von Nürnberg* appeared for the first time at the festival. Hans Richter was to conduct and he proposed that a popular Jewish singer from Hamburg be hired. Cosima opposed this vehemently and said, "I have reservations about a Jewish appearance in *Meistersinger* and it should be kept clear of any Israelite contamination." She must have been recalling the antipathy Wagner had to the Jewish critic Eduard Hanslick who was the stereotype of Hans Beckmesser the clerk in the opera. Wagner had in fact originally called the Beckmesser character Hans Lick to make the connection impossible to miss, but ultimately changed the name to Beckmesser because even he had to admit this was going too far.[38]

The saddest note in what is a disgraceful melody of racist intrigue was to be struck by the exit of that old warhorse Hermann Levi, who had stuck to Wagner through thick and thin and conducted the first *Parsifal*.

---

36. Ibid., 115.
37. Ibid.
38. Pachl, *Siegfried Wagner*, 82.

He retired for "health reasons" and wrote to Cosima setting out his reasons for going. At last he had a chance to put his side of the case. "I believe that everything centres on one point: I am a Jew and in and around Wahnfried it has become a dogma that a Jew appears a certain way, thinks and acts in a certain way and above all that a Jew is incapable of selfless devotion to anything; as a result everything I do and say is judged from this point of view and therefore everything I do and say is considered indecent or at least alien."[39]

He died in 1900 and Cosima could not even respect the dead sufficiently to forget his race. "Though he could not get away from his extraction, and numerous failings of his race showed themselves markedly in him, yet he distinguished himself by his great fidelity to Bayreuth, and I confess that the Jewish element in him often amused more than it irritated me, because it showed itself with such diverting openness."[40]

Cosima's productions were to earn the censure of many distinguished critics. George Bernard Shaw, that great Wagnerian, who described music as "the brandy of the damned,"[41] had visited the festival in 1896 – the first of five visits – and was highly critical, saying, "the singing is sometimes bearable, sometimes dreadful. Among the singers are some who are nothing but living beer barrels. The costumes of the women are prudish and foolish."[42] One wonders why he kept on returning. The answer, however, was the magic of the place – "those who go to Bayreuth never repent of it," he wrote. He was impressed by the fact that electricity was used for the first time, replacing the dangerous and outmoded gas.

The riding Valkyries were represented by schoolboys on wooden horses earning extra pocket money for the long summer holidays. Shaw's favorite way to enjoy the *Ring* was to sit in the back of the house and "listen without looking." For Richard Strauss and many others the role of the orchestra outranked that of the singers.[43] The latter is alleged to have urged the huge forces involved in a Wagner opera to greater volume. "Louder, louder, I can still hear the voices," he cried.

Shaw would have seen the Swedish star Ellen Gulbranson, a large

---

39. Ibid.
40. Newman, *Life of Richard Wagner*, vol. 3, 286.
41. Conrad, "He's Tricky, That Dicky."
42. Richard Wagner Museum brochure, "About Richard Wagner," items 36–40.
43. Spotts, *Bayreuth*, 19.

woman who was to make the part of Brünnhilde hers for eighteen years. Others remembered her for her wonderful singing and horsemanship, which had something to do with the fact that she was a farmer, when she was not singing.[44] At the end of *Götterdämmerung* when the script required her to ride into the flames en route to Valhalla, she controlled her horse Grane with great skill. Cosima was not impressed by this aspect of her versatility, which reminded her of Therese Vogl's "circus tricks" on the horse.[45] Albert Schweitzer was a regular at Bayreuth before he left for Lambarene and praised the "splendidly simple production of the *Ring* in 1896…and the *Parsifal* of the eighties."[46]

Although Wagner had written to the king in 1881 bemoaning the fact that one day his Siegfried might be forced to be a soldier and "fall a victim to some stupid bullet in one of the wretched wars brought on us by Prussian politics," he was not looking in the mirror as he should have. Saint-Saens had attended the first festival and was a great admirer for some time. He wrote four years later that "what German music brings us is not solely music but also German ideas, the German soul." It had been different, reasoned the French composer, when the German soul was that of Goethe and Schiller but Sachs's address to the Nürnbergers in the final scene of *Meistersinger* is "the cry of pan-Germanism and war on the Latin races."[47]

Sir Arthur Sullivan succumbed to Wagner in 1897 and attended the festival. Other English composers had already made the acquaintance – Parry had been to the first festival in 1876, and again in 1882, Stanford in 1876 and 1883, Delius, Elgar and Granville Bantock had paid visits as had Ethel Smyth. The last mentioned was there with Sullivan and reported that "the entire world is Wagnerian now, and Bayreuth is the world's fair." Perhaps Sullivan recognized the true characters hidden behind the caricatures as he said, "it is difficult to know how Wagner could have got up any enthusiasm or interest in such a lying, thieving, blackguardly set of low creatures as all the characters in his opera prove themselves to be." He was not terribly impressed. "What a curious mixture of sublimity and absolute puerile drivel are all these Wagner operas. Sometimes the story and action would disgrace even a Surrey pantomime…I have got to hate a leitmotif!

---

44. Skelton, *Wagner at Bayreuth*, 101.
45. Ibid.
46. Skelton, *Wagner at Bayreuth*, 163.
47. Newman, *Life of Richard Wagner*, vol. 4, 600.

Each opera has about a dozen phrases, which are repeated over and over again in different rhythms and shapes until one wearies of them."[48]

The political milieu of the small town could not be completely hidden and visitors to the festival noted the links between the composer's works and the developing ideologies. In 1899 a very young Thomas Beecham visited Bayreuth and saw *Parsifal* under the baton of Franz Fischer, the *Ring* with Siegfried Wagner and *Meistersinger* with Hans Richter on the podium.[49] Sir Thomas described his visit as a pilgrimage to "some shrine such as that of Thomas à Becket in the Middle Ages" with singing, playing and stage production below expectation. He also observed the bookshops full of books linking the music dramas with philosophy, politics, science and hygiene including vegetarianism, the last-mentioned a by-product of the subliminal programming of *Parsifal*.[50]

Friedrich Nietzsche wrote one of the books that was enjoying particular popularity at the time. The philosopher predicted that future generations, concerned to preserve the Wagnerian spirit, would raise their voices to "shock and frighten us...as though the voice of some evil spirit, hitherto hidden from sight, suddenly made itself heard."[51]

Sir Thomas would have been sure to pick up the book or another in which Nietzsche painted the image of the free spirit who would embody *The Will to Power* in frighteningly prophetic words. He might not have appreciated coupling his fellow countrymen with cattle and women but he would have appreciated the menace in the prediction:

> The man who has become free spurns the contemptible sort of well being dreamed of by shopkeepers, Christians, cows, women, Englishmen and other democrats. *The free man is a warrior...life itself is essentially appropriation, injury, overpowering of the strange and weaker, suppression...I greet all the signs that a more manly, warlike age is coming, which will, above all, bring valor again into honor! One cannot fail to see at the core of all these noble races the animal of prey, the splendid blond beast prowling about avidly in search of spoil and victory. We have Napoleon, who wanted one Europe, and this as mistress of*

---

48. Jacobs, *Arthur Sullivan; A Victorian Musician*, 377.
49. Skelton, *Wagner at Bayreuth*, 217.
50. Marek, *Cosima Wagner*, 229.
51. Ibid.

the earth, to thank that a couple of warlike centuries can now follow, which all coming centuries will look back on with awe and envy as at a piece of perfection…[52]

The animal of prey was born in 1889 and he set about his task of fulfilling the prophecy.

---

52. Nietzsche's words are quoted from Lomas, "A Nietzsche of Sweetness and Light," 29.

Chapter ten
Nearly Schickelgruber

If the predictions of Jean Paul in Bayreuth were the source of the prophecy that a man would be born who would write libretto and music for the perfect opera or music drama, then the Old Testament was the place to find the oracle that spoke of the influence of Adolf Hitler. Isaiah the Hebrew prophet spoke nearly three thousand years before about a maniac. "Is this the man that made the earth quake to such a degree that kingdoms trembled? Who made the world into a wilderness and destroyed the cities thereof…?"

Hitler was born at half past six in the evening on April 20, 1889 at Gasthof zum Pommer, Vorstadt nr 219, Braunau am Inn in Austria.[1] Hitler's father, Alois (born 1837), was illegitimate and for a time bore his mother's name, Schickelgruber, but by 1876 he had established his claim to the surname Hitler. Adolf never used any other name, and the name Schickelgruber was revived only by his political opponents in Germany and Austria in the 1930s. It was indeed fortunate for Hitler that his father changed his name from Schickelgruber to Hitler. "Heil Schickelgruber" would not have had the same resonance.

His father was a man of bad temper, a heavy smoker, who enjoyed a few drinks after work rather than the comfort of his own hearth. His great

---

1. Kershaw, *Hitler 1936–1945: Nemesis*, 10.

passion was keeping bees and he kept smallholdings on which he tended his hives with great care.[2]

Both Hitler and Wagner suspected that they were partly Jewish and yet became rabidly anti-Semitic. Much has been written about Hitler's alleged grandfather Frankenberger, a Jew from Graz in Austria, and therefore that Hitler himself was a quarter Jewish. Denials that Frankenberger was his grandfather on his paternal side were usually met with the fact that his grandfather Frankenberger paid maintenance to his grandmother for fourteen years. Why would he do that, one might ask, if he was not responsible for the birth of Hitler's father? It was also peculiar as pointed out by Walter Langer that Alois Hitler, a customs official in Braunau, should choose a Jew named Prinz, of Vienna, to act as Adolf's godfather unless he felt some kinship with the Jews himself.[3]

Hitler spent most of his childhood in the neighborhood of Linz, the capital of Upper Austria, after his father's retirement from the Habsburg customs service. As a child he appeared to be frightened by females and when his mother wanted him to get up in the morning she would merely suggest to his sister that he be given a kiss and that had the desired effect of galvanizing him into action.[4] There are suggestions in *Mein Kampf* that Hitler may have been the witness of parental violence and sexual intercourse which affected his attitude to a normal relationship.

As Freud himself explained, "the libido changes over to an inverted sexual object (homosexuality) after a distressing experience with a normal one."[5] A psychoanalyst has concluded that Adolf saw or rather "fantasized that he saw – his drunken father rape his dear mother"[6] – that image was transferred to the gory notion of the desecration of the nation by the Jews. Hitler was to frequently use the same violent metaphor in his speeches and writings, invoking the phrases "by what wiles the soul of the German has been raped" and "our German pacifists will pass over in silence the most bloody rape of the nation."[7]

He seems to have painted such a picture in his own writings. As he said

---

2. Ibid., 11.
3. Langer, OSS *Psychological Report on Adolf Hitler*, 96.
4. Waite, *The Psychopathic God*, 51.
5. Freud, *On Sexuality*, 48.
6. See Waite's afterword in Langer, *The Mind of Adolf Hitler*, 162, 227.
7. See Langer, OSS *Psychological Report on Adolf Hitler*, 169.

in *Mein Kampf*, "when the parents fight almost daily, their brutality leaves nothing to the imagination; then the results of such visual education must slowly but inevitably become apparent to the little one."[8] After the war his younger sister Paula was to describe family life in the Hitler household and she was clearly not unaware of the savage nature of her father's treatment of her brother and the love he received from his mother. She was "a very soft and tender person, the compensatory element between the almost too harsh father and the very lively children who were perhaps somewhat difficult to train. If there were ever quarrels or differences of opinion between my parents, it was always on account of the children. It was especially my brother Adolf who challenged my father to extreme harshness and who got his sound thrashing every day…How often on the other hand did my mother caress him and try to obtain with her kindness what the father could not succeed [in obtaining] with harshness."[9]

As Freud so eloquently pointed out there are grave dangers when a small child is exposed to experiences and incidents such as the above. The child frequently misinterprets what is going on about him and builds his personality on false constructs – the recipe for the disturbed and deviant personality.[10] Freud was to be quite explicit about the effects on the child "if children at this early age witness sexual intercourse between adults – for which an opportunity is provided by the conviction of grown-up people that small children cannot understand anything sexual – they inevitably regard the sexual act as a sort of ill-treatment or act of subjugation; they view it, that is, in a sadistic sense." This can cause sexual deviations in later life including sadism. "Psychoanalysis also shows us that an impression of this kind in early childhood contributes a great deal towards a predisposition to a subsequent sadistic displacement of the sexual aim."[11] While current psychological theory may diverge from Freud's views, it is difficult to argue against this assessment of Hitler's later development.

Who can guess the deep significance the sight of his parents having intercourse had on the youngster? "In Hitler's case this early experience was almost certainly the discovery of his parents in intercourse and his interpretation of this as a brutal assault in which he was powerless. He refused

---

8. Ibid., 143.
9. Kershaw, *Hitler 1936–1945: Nemesis*, 12–13.
10. Langer, oss *Psychological Report on Adolf Hitler*, 142.
11. Freud, *On Sexuality*, 115.

to believe what his eyes told him, and the experience left him speechless."[12] This was the conclusion reached by Walter Langer, an American psychiatrist, after reviewing the evidence of Hitler's early childhood.

Freud's work suggests another possible problem area in Hitler's childhood when he points out that since the publication of Jean Jacques Rousseau's *Confessions*, corporal punishment on the buttocks "is one of the erotogenic roots of the passive instinct of cruelty (masochism)." The great psychoanalyst concluded that corporal punishment "should not be inflicted upon children whose libido is likely to be forced into collateral channels by the later demands of cultural education."[13] While it may strain the twenty-first-century intellect to suggest that Hitler's erotic association with his father's spankings was the cause of his later behavior, it is once again difficult to argue against Freud's assessment of a libido gone awry, and the disastrous psychological results.

Adolf commenced his schooling on May 1, 1895 near Lambach and appeared to make good progress for two years. In November 1898 the family moved to Leonding in the Linz area, where Hitler engaged in all the sorts of games boys play including cops and robbers, in which he was regarded as a leading light.[14] Little evidence exists in his early life to suggest the development of his sexual perversions in the future. There is one account of an incident in Leonding when a young Hitler and his playmates, including Stefan Wasner, captured a young billy goat in a pasture. They wedged a piece of wood into its mouth and Adolf urinated into it. Unfortunately the piece of wood became dislodged and the animal closed its jaws on his penis. He screamed out in great pain. That incident can be excused as a youthful prank but it had a tragic sequel.

During the Second World War his youthful friend Wasner used to amuse his friends with stories of his time with Hitler including the goat incident. When the officers got to hear of the story Wasner was court-martialled and defended by a legal officer with the pen name of D. Gustrow who wrote an account of the trial. Despite intensive interrogation Wasner stuck to his story that the goat had bitten Hitler's penis and he was found guilty. Clearly a story such as his damaged the image the Führer wanted

---

12. Langer, OSS *Psychological Report on Adolf Hitler*, 156.
13. Freud, *On Sexuality*, 111.
14. Kershaw, *Hitler 1936–1945: Nemesis*, 14–15.

A caricature of one of Hitler's professors done by him when he was eleven years old. One interpretation is that the learned professor is masturbating, whereas a close examination shows that he is eating from a bag of nuts or ice-cream. But what would Freud have made of the position of the bag and the suspicious shape? Bundesarchiv, Berlin. From Redlich, page 220.

the public to venerate. A psychiatric expert witness was called on his behalf but despite this he had to pay the ultimate penalty – he was executed.[15]

Freud was to deal with this form of cruelty in his works on sexuality. "Children who distinguish themselves by special cruelty towards animals and playmates usually give rise to just suspicion of an intense and precocious sexual activity arising from the erotogenic zones…"[16] There are grave dangers in the link between sex and cruelty that can affect the rest of the adult life. Freud continues by pointing out that "the absence of the barrier of pity brings with it the danger that the connection between the cruel and erotogenic instincts, thus established in childhood, may prove unbreakable in later life."[17]

Adolf enrolled at the Realschule for his secondary schooling on September 17, 1900 and began quarreling with his father as he wanted to be an artist and his father wanted him to obtain a position in the civil service. A neighbor of the Hitler family in Urfahr, a suburb of Linz where the family lived, records that when the postmaster asked Adolf one day

---

15. Redlich, *Hitler: Diagnosis of a Destructive Prophet*, 18.
16. Freud, *On Sexuality*, 111.
17. Ibid.

what he wanted to do for a living and whether he wouldn't like to join the post office, he replied that it was his intention to become a "great artist."[18] Herr Keplinger, who was a schoolmate of Hitler's there recalls him calling another boy "Du Saujud" ("You filthy Jew!"). The boy was somewhat taken aback as he knew nothing of his Jewish ancestry at the time and only discovered it for himself many years later.[19] From such small beginnings the seeds sprouted.

Just before the beginning of the Second World War Carl Burckhardt, League of Nations Commissioner for Danzig, met Hitler and commented on his dual personality, "the first being that of the rather gentle artist and the second that of the homicidal maniac."[20] He would make valiant attempts to achieve the first aim and when it was thwarted by what he perceived to be a conspiracy of Jews he would embark on the latter.

In his twelfth year he was nearly expelled from school for a "sexual indiscretion" that the family doctor Dr. Bloch recalled having been told by one of the teachers related to a little girl.[21] These two early incidents provide slender evidence of the disturbed mental state that was to manifest itself in the later perversions.

Adolf's father Alois Hitler died in 1903 but left an adequate pension and savings to support his wife and children. Adolf received a secondary education and, although he had a poor record at school and failed to secure the usual certificate, did not leave until he was sixteen in 1905. Another story put out by Hitler himself was that he got drunk for the only time in his life on Heuriger wine and after defecation wiped himself with his school certificate, which he had intended proudly showing to his mother. Years later he was still embarrassed by the incident.[22]

---

18. Kershaw, *Hitler 1936–1945: Nemesis*, 2.
19. Cornish, *The Jew of Linz*, 10.
20. Spotts, *Hitler and the Power of Aesthetics*, xiii.
21. Langer, OSS *Psychological Report on Adolf Hitler*, 114.
22. Waite, *The Psychopathic God*, 149.

Chapter eleven
Opera Lover and Aspirant Composer

We know much of Hitler's youth and his adulation of the music and political writings of Wagner from the reminiscences of his young friend August Kubizek[1] who wrote a full account of his times with Hitler.[2] Hitler used to attend all the operas at the theatre in Linz. He could only afford a ticket for standing room and he therefore went to the promenade from which one could get the best view. Moreover it was central and the acoustics were very good. Just above the promenade was the royal box, which was supported by two wooden columns. These columns were very popular with the standing room spectators as they had an undisturbed view of the stage and a spectator could prop up his tired body against them.[3]

Of course to obtain a position against one of the columns you had to be there early and there was a mad scramble for the best position. Sometime around All Saints' Day in 1904 – Ian Kershaw points out that it was in fact

---

1. Gutman, *Richard Wagner*, 596, describes the use Hitler made of Wagner's writings. The story of Wieland the Smith is also set out in Gutman, 196–97.
2. The relationship between Hitler and Kubizek is summarized in Cross, *Adolf Hitler*, 44–45. Kubizek himself wrote a full account of his times with Hitler. See Kubizek, *Young Hitler*.
3. Kubizek, *Young Hitler*, 5.

1905[4] – Hitler met Kubizek there. They fought for a position on the right-hand column and Hitler won. They got chatting and afterwards went back to Adolf's home at 31 Humboldtstrasse.

The two became firm friends. One disadvantage of standing room in the promenade was that it was the haunt of the claque. This odious man was usually hired by a singer to pull together a bunch of philistines to applaud the singer concerned. Sometimes they applauded at the wrong time and Adolf remembered punching one man who kept shouting "Bravo" in the middle of the overture to *Tannhäuser*. Outside the man was waiting for Hitler with a policeman. Hitler spoke out in his own defense and defended himself so brilliantly that the policeman let him go. Afterwards he caught up with the claqeuer and punched him again for good measure.[5]

Hitler shared all his ideas with Kubizek, especially regarding opera and architecture. His reconstruction of Linz began with Wildberg Castle where he planned a return to medieval life with artisans and workmen plying their trades in the guilds. "An island where the centuries stood still" was the way he described it. The workmen would dress in the medieval fashion and there would be a Master Singer School as was so deftly portrayed in Wagner's great opera *Die Meistersinger von Nürnberg*. Tourists could visit and pay a toll, which would help with the upkeep of the place.[6]

Also planned by the young Hitler was the demolition of the Kaiser-Franz-Josef-Warte in the *Jägermayerwald*, which would be replaced with a wonderful monument, including in the Hall of Fame, busts of all the famous men who had served Upper Austria. His blue eyes glinting with excitement he described how the whole edifice would be crowned by an enormous statue of Wagner's hero Siegfried triumphantly holding aloft his sword Nothung. This sword had been forged anew from the splinters of Siegfried's dead father's weapon and symbolized a resurgence of the German national spirit.[7]

In Hitler's view, however, the metaphors derived from the gigantic operatic spectacles of the composer were not all positive. The betrayal of the German people by their political leaders and the influence of foreigners, especially Jews who dominated the commercial life of Austria, was a

---

4. Kershaw, *Hitler 1936–1945: Nemesis*, 21.
5. Kubizek, *Young Hitler*, 139.
6. Ibid., 56.
7. Ibid., 57.

sore point. Also festering in the brain of the young dreamer was the fate of Siegfried, who was stabbed in the back by the Nibelung Hagen during the penultimate scene of Wagner's opera *Götterdämmerung*.

Kubizek's account of his life with the young Hitler was replete with accounts of their fanatical visits to the opera. In May 1906 Hitler went to Vienna for the first time and stayed for two weeks. Overwhelmed by the mighty majesty of the opera he sat spellbound in the Burgtheater at performances of *Tristan und Isolde* and *The Flying Dutchman*. In a letter to Kubizek he described his raptures. "When the mighty waves of sound flooded through the room and the whine of the wind gave way before the fearful rush of billows of music, one feels sublimity."

The production of *Tristan* was that of Alfred Roller and the young Hitler was so impressed with the set for act 2 that he made a sketch of it.[8] The production starred Erik Schmedes and Anna von Mildenburg and discarded the naturalism of earlier times for partly theatrical symbolical space, with lighting, color and structural designs predominating. In the first act Isolde's heavily curtained orange-yellow tent was placed in the foreground and the Viennese audience was astonished by the illusion of the ship sailing away, lit from behind by a green light, subtly introduced from unseen hatches in the wings. Act 2 was stunning with gold stars set in a violet sky that gradually changed with the mood to a cold grey before the blood red dawn with the denouement.[9]

When he returned to Vienna in 1908 he was offered an opportunity he would have been foolish to refuse. A friend of his mother's had actually met the legendary Roller and he was offered a position painting backdrops for the Vienna Opera. The work would combine his great love for Wagner and opera and his zest to paint. A letter was written on his behalf to the legendary set designer who agreed to see the unknown talent. Hitler, armed with Roller's positive reply and a sample of his best art, took off for the opera house. Courage deserted him and three attempts were insufficient. On the first occasion he made it to the front door, a few minutes later he edged up to the grand staircase and finally he approached Roller's office.

---

8. Spotts, *Bayreuth*, 184.
9. Franklin, *Life of Mahler*, 148.

An assistant asked him his business and he fled, abashed by the enormity of the occasion.[10]

His reticence was never explained and his failure in this regard was a great disappointment to his mother.[11] Years later in 1934 in Bayreuth he was to persuade Winifred Wagner, wife of Siegfried, to allow Roller to design a new production of *Parsifal*.[12] There were violent protests after the first performance of that production – not directed, let it be said, at the excesses of the Third Reich, but against the new settings – the conservatives calling for the return of the old.[13]

There followed two idle years in Linz for the young Hitler, when he indulged in grandiose dreams of becoming an artist without taking any steps to prepare for earning his living. His mother was overindulgent to her willful son, and when he decided he might enjoy playing the piano she bought him a Heitzmann grand. In addition she drained the meager family resources even more when she sent him to an expensive teacher, Josef Prevatsky-Wendt, who recorded Hitler's disinterest, particularly in the finger exercises, which have been the bane of every piano pupil since time immemorial.

Four months was all he could handle of the piano and decided that his talents lay in art, which he then studied under Professor Grober in the Blütenstrasse in Schwabing.[14] Even after his mother's death in 1908 he continued to draw a small allowance to maintain himself in Vienna. "I have never seen anyone so prostrate with grief,"[15] wrote Dr. Bloch, a Jew whom Hitler never ceased to praise for his care of his mother, even after he had become chancellor.[16] He even sent two of his hand-painted postcards to show his appreciation for the work he had done to help her.[17]

In that same year, in the city that heard the waltz for the first time, a Jewish psychologist was analyzing the work of artists that helped to explain the passage of ideology from the composer to the politician; Sigmund

---

10. Spotts, *Hitler and the Power of Aesthetics*, 223.
11. Waite, *The Psychopathic God*, 393.
12. Ibid.
13. Richard Wagner Museum brochure, "About Richard Wager."
14. Waite, *The Psychopathic God*, 175.
15. Kershaw, *Hitler 1936–1945: Nemesis*, 24.
16. Köhler, *Wagner's Hitler*, 69.
17. Waite, *The Psychopathic God*, 40.

Freud published his seminal work *Creative Writers and Day-Dreaming*. In a quirk of fate Hitler was to formulate his demonic political views in the very city where streets away – Freud lived at 19 Berggasse – was the very man who would understand the sort of personality that was to dominate the landscape and cause more than fifty-five million deaths. In later years (1928) Freud was to confess that he had little specialized knowledge of musical composition and his views on the creators thereof amounted to heresy to the disciples of Bayreuth. He maintained that he was "completely unmusical" and "barely capable of enjoying a few pretty tunes by Mozart, I find even Wagner foreign to my nature…"

In his book he found that artistic creativity belonged in the realm of the unconscious and that it was similar to dreaming, its predominant concern being wish-fulfillment – what has been called "the symbolic realization of repressed desires."[18] Regression of oral, anal and phallic desires in the different stages of infantile psychosexual development gave life to the work of art, which was vicariously enjoyed by the audience.[19] Was there consequently reason to believe that Wagner's repressed desires to avenge himself on the Jews vicariously insinuated their way into the subconscious of the young opera addict, who sat entranced by the magic intoxication of the music, while the world waited unknowingly for the horror he would unleash?

While the music and the subliminal text worked its way into the dark recesses of the psyche, Kubizek joined Hitler in Vienna in about February 1908 and they shared a room at Stumpfergasse 9, which was in an unfashionable area near the West Railway Station, through which they had arrived from Linz. Hitler began a lifestyle that was to characterize most of his adulthood – he stayed up late at night and slept late every morning, long after Kubizek had departed for the music academy. On many evenings with Kubizek in tow, he indulged his passion for opera, especially the lush harmonies and prophetic myths that made up the music dramas of Richard Wagner. He would live for days just on bread and milk in order to afford the cheapest standing room at the opera.

The great Gustav Mahler was conducting during that period, including the legendary Roller production of Tristan, but according to Kubizek

---

18. Vetter, "Wagner in the History of Psychology," 53.
19. Ibid.

Mahler's Jewishness made no difference to Hitler's enthusiasm and later when he stayed in a hostel he counted a number of Jews as his friends.[20] If Hitler did not mind Mahler's conducting he would have been aware of the anti-Semitic voices in Vienna who suggested that his elaborate gestures when directing the orchestra from the podium were more appropriate for making love.[21] Despite this the Jews were very enthusiastic about the German culture and the music of Richard Wagner. Vienna was a cosmopolitan city with a reputation as a cultural city of music, art and theatre that matched Paris, London and Berlin.[22]

Hitler would have been interested to know that Cosima had opposed Mahler's application to become the director of the Vienna Opera on the grounds of his race alone.[23] So keen had Mahler been to obtain the post that he underwent conversion to Roman Catholicism in 1897 at the "Kleine Michaelskirche" in Hamburg.[24] Years later Mahler would articulate what thousands must have felt – that he had felt himself "thrice homeless…as a native of Bohemia in Austria, as an Austrian among Germans and as a Jew in all the world. Everywhere an intruder, never welcomed."[25] He must have been thinking of the dream he had as a fifteen-year-old boy in 1875 when he encountered the Wandering Jew with a gold topped cross.

There were other examples of relationships with Semites that illustrate that Hitler's hatred for the race had not yet taken hold of him. He had no problems visiting Dr. Rudolf Jahoda, a Jewish amateur musician, with Kubizek and he took a particular interest in his library.[26] The two inseparable friends saw *Lohengrin* ten times in seven months, plus *Meistersinger* and *Tristan* numerous times over. The first-mentioned opera was for years the favorite of the young man and he loved the patriotism – "for German land a German sword!" In other respects he admired the hero and this adulation was to be of particular importance in trying to penetrate the secrets of his

---

20. Köhler, *Wagner's Hitler*, 69.
21. Franklin, *Life of Mahler*, 112.
22. Hamann, *Hitler's Vienna*, 328.
23. Marek, *Cosima Wagner*, 254.
24. Franklin, *Life of Mahler*, 92.
25. Ibid., 82.
26. Köhler, *Wagner's Hitler*, 69.

bizarre sexual practices – Lohengrin could not tarry in the bedchamber with the lovely Elsa because he had a higher mission in life.[27]

Trevor-Roper has written a book in which are recorded Hitler's table conversations during the war from 1941–44 when he often spoke of his love for Wagner. "I was so poor, during the Viennese period of my life that I had to restrict myself to seeing only the finest spectacles. Thus I heard *Tristan* thirty or forty times and always from the best companies."[28] During those days Hitler would rather spend money on opera than on food, which meant that he could, in most instances, only afford seats at the Peoples Opera, not the Court Opera.

According to Kubizek Hitler preferred second-class Wagner at the subsidiary Peoples Opera to first-class Verdi at the main Court Opera – of Verdi's works only *Aida* attracted him. On their return from the opera house Hitler, overcome by the music, would walk up and down the little one-room apartment and ramble on for hours. Kubizek was not expected to contribute anything to the discussion but just to agree to the strongly held views of his fanatical friend. If he dared to drop off to sleep, Hitler did not hesitate to wake him. A mobile Reich's Orchestra that would bring music to the farthest reaches of the new empire – Wagner's music of course – was the next musical project that entertained the small shabby youth with the wispy moustache.[29]

At one point Hitler decided to write an opera based on the play of *Wieland the Smith* on which Wagner had worked. The mise-en-scène was reminiscent of Wagner at his best.[30] The first scene was set on the Wolf Lake with a background of the pale ice of the glaciers, the bare dark rocks and the flaming volcanoes, the savage elements that made up the passionate destiny of the protagonists. Wieland and his brothers Egil and Slaghid are depicted fishing on the lake when three Valkyries in the form of clouds visit them. One of the practical difficulties Hitler and Kubizek wrestled with was to effect flight for the rotund operatic Valkyries, who also wore heavy coats of mail and helmets. Being a blacksmith Wieland assumes the

---

27. Waite, *The Psychopathic God*, 101.
28. Trevor-Roper, *Hitler's Table Talk*, 333.
29. Waite, *The Psychopathic God*, 194.
30. Kubizek, *Young Hitler*, 146.

duty of forging such wings, including a pair to soar away with at the end of opera.[31]

There was action aplenty in the opera as Wieland kills his sons out of vengeance, rapes his daughter and drinks out of skulls carved from his offspring. The themes were the familiar heady diet inherited from the Master of Bayreuth and included avarice and power – in the person of King Nidur – and redemption.[32] First and foremost in the scenes that fascinated the young novice composer was the macabre scene when Wieland meets Bodvild after she has murdered her brothers. With rich overtones of Hagen summoning the Gibichung retainers, the ending features Wieland, Egil and Slaghid marrying the three Valkyries, as mighty horns cleave the air, summoning the vassals to the wedding feast at the Wolf Lake.

In some respects the novice creator exceeded his famous progenitor. Not for him the impressive forces of the modern orchestra – and Wagner harnessed some one hundred twenty players at times, including a new instrument, the Wagner tuba – the opera would be played on the original instruments rattles, drums, bone-flutes and luren, the last mentioned being two-meter-long brass instruments, curved like horns. The singers would sing in the manner of the Skalds who were accompanied by ancient harps. In a further innovation that would fascinate the musicologists the notes would be reproduced in rich colors in the score and replicated in the mise-en-scène.

Hitler composed the prelude, which consisted of the main themes of the opera. As he composed tunes he would rush off to Kubizek at any time of day or night for him to write them down and insert appropriate harmonies.[33] The multitalented fanatic would then employ his artistic talents to draw charcoal sketches of costumes and settings. Almost as quickly as the urge had come upon him to compose and create the work, it left him – and he became inevitably a bitter and disappointed young man. He had aimed too high and his musical resources were inadequate to cope with the task. Realization came later that the artist side in him had been exhausted by his earlier work. What remained was his sacred mission. Kubizek was clearly an acute observer and quickly recognized the idolatry in his young friend.

---

31. Ibid., 152.
32. Ibid., 149.
33. Ibid., 148.

He said that Hitler looked for much more than a model and an example in Wagner – he literally appropriated Wagner's personality as if he wanted to make it an integral part of his individuality. "Sometimes he would quote by heart from a letter or passage from Wagner or recite from one of his essays…Wagner's world became far more real to him than the real world itself."[34]

During their days in Linz in 1909 Kubizek relates how Hitler succumbed to the music of Richard Wagner and often went to the opera night after night. "The charged emotionality of its music seemed to have served him as a means for self-hypnosis, which he found in its slush air of bourgeois luxury, the necessary ingredients for escapist fantasy."

Kubizek was not alone in his views of the effect that Wagner had on a young Hitler. Another youthful buddy of Hitler, Reinhold Hanisch remembered him saying that "Wagner was a fighter and [his operas] were the best divine service."[35] The effect the music had on Hitler has been supported by the work of Jerome Sehulster who – seventy years later (1980) – analyzed Wagner's work from the point of view of the listener. The music, he maintains, induces a "trancelike state" as a result of the "constant, regular pulse, gradual transitions and the omnipresence of the past in the shape of leitmotifs, as well as a harmonic writing that never comes to rest."

Nietzsche called him the "master of hypnotic effects" and Bertolt Brecht spoke of "Wagner's theatre of intoxication" and his work as a drug that dulled all social criticism.[36] Science seems to bear out what these distinguished writers have expounded. Experiments have even been conducted at the end of the twentieth century to measure the degree of excitement felt by the listener during the playing of Wagner's music – in this case the *Meistersinger* prelude – by use of a Vehrs lever.[37]

Apart from the all-encompassing awe with which Hitler approached the composer, Kubizek recalled one specific occasion that was to have momentous significance for the world. Hitler reacted strongly to a performance of Wagner's opera *Rienzi*. On a night that was to have memorable and sinister premonitions he wore a black overcoat and a dark hat was pulled down over his face. It was a cold and unpleasant November

---

34. Köhler, *Wagner's Hitler*, 83.
35. Viereck, *Metapolitics*, 133.
36. Vetter, "Wagner in the History of Psychology," page 67–68.
37. Ibid., 54.

evening with a hint of snow in the air; the evening started badly as he was irritated with Kubizek who was late.[38] To secure a position against the columns under the promenade would be difficult for the two young men, racing through the already dark streets. Throughout the performance the two listened spellbound – Hitler allowed no discussion, even during the intermissions. Once the curtain fell and the last handclaps faded into the ornate ceiling of the opera house the two tore themselves from their pillar and walked dazed into the street.

Although they usually spoke about the opera immediately afterwards Hitler felt a sense of destiny and when Kubizek attempted to converse he quickly shut him up. Hitler beckoned to his friend and they started walking through the deserted streets. A cold damp mist hung over the city and they made their way up the Freinberg in solitude and darkness. Hitler felt great emotion and clasped both of Kubizek's hands in his. Words tumbled from his lips and he excitedly described how he saw in *Rienzi* a visionary model for all his ambitions. Gone were the artist, painter, opera composer and architect – his political mission had been revealed to him.

There, with Linz lying in darkness below them, Hitler began to speak and as Kubizek recalled, "Words burst from him like a backed-up flood breaking through crumbling dams. In grandiose compelling images he sketched for me his future and that of his people."[39] He commented on the sort of hero Rienzi was and it is easy to see why he appealed to Hitler. As a student of twenty years he was sent by the government of Rome to Pope Clement VI in Avignon to plead the case of the Roman popular party, which had just gained ascendancy. The Pope appointed him notary of the Roman civic treasury, and Rienzi returned to Rome in 1344. He began to plot a revolution that would return the city to the glory of ancient Rome. He summoned the people to a parliament on the Capitoline Hill and announced a series of edicts against the nobles and, to the acclaim of the multitude, he assumed dictatorial powers.

A few days later he took the ancient title of tribune. After declaring reforms of the tax, judicial and political structure of Rome, Rienzi conceived the grandiose idea of reestablishing Rome as the capital of a "sacred Italy," an Italian brotherhood whose mission would be to spread peace and

---

38. Kubizek, *Young Hitler*, 64.
39. Ibid., 65.

justice to the world. The Roman nobles, led by the Orsini and Colonna families, rose against Rienzi, and he was eventually captured and burnt. In the opera he saved his sister when the patrician Orsini was trying to abduct her. Hitler saw a direct link between the corruption of the patricians in Rienzi and the leaders in Germany.

He recognized the need in Germany for a hero, a leader and messianic redeemer of the people. Rienzi had used terror to slaughter his opponents and Hitler prophesied that he would mobilize the masses in similar fashion to lead the country to greatness. Although Rienzi had failed Hitler would triumph, as he understood where the Italian leader had erred. Hitler recognized that the people turned against Rienzi and burned him to death – that was the way to die, mused the young man with distant city lights glinting in his eyes. For Hitler the notion of fire was a holy baptism and he was mindful that in Wagner's opera *The Valkyries* the leader of the gods Wotan surrounds his favorite daughter Brünnhilde with fire in a magic sleep for disobeying him. If she were to be taken by a man – she exclaims in the opera – it would have to be a great hero who had no fear of the fire. Siegfried, the Aryan superman, breaks through the fire and claims her love. After the Semitic Hagen stabs Siegfried in the back he is burnt on a magnificent funeral pyre – fire then was the baptizer and the great cleanser.

The man who would restore Germany's greatness had a premonition he would be burned and around him great flames would leap into the sky – little did he realize the cause would be the menacing Russian flamethrowers and incendiaries. As the morning cocks saluted the dawn the two young men stumbled home in a dazed silence. When these friends met again thirty years later in 1939 in Bayreuth Hitler remarked that "it all began at that hour."[40]

Apart from the childish prank with the goat in Leonding there was little hint of the serious sexual deviations Hitler was to manifest in his mature years. In fact he shared the sort of infatuation and disappointment any teenager might expect. There was a girl that Hitler admired by the name of Stephanie – a bourgeois girl who lived in Linz. She was two years older than Hitler when he first set eyes on her. At that time Hitler was all of sixteen years, painfully shy and awkward in his threadbare clothes. Kubizek and

---

40. Ibid., 66.

Hitler often saw her with her mother during their long walks through the city. For four years he dreamt about that wonderful girl. If she smiled at him the day was good and beautiful and well ordered.[41] If she failed to see him or turned her gaze aside he was crushed and ready to destroy himself and the whole world.

When he was in Vienna and saw Lucie Weidt as Elsa in *Lohengrin* the highest praise he could think of for her was that she reminded him of Stephanie. He and Kubizek often mused over which part she would best play in the operas[42] and whether she had the necessary voice and musical talent. Hitler was overwhelmed with excitement when he found out from a cellist who knew Stephanie's brother that she did have a good voice.[43]

Hitler wrote countless poems about her in his little black notebook, including the rather affected *Hymn to the Beloved*. Paraphrased the verses described how Stephanie, a high-born damsel, in a dark-blue, flowing velvet gown, went riding on a white steed over the flowering meadows, her loose hair falling in golden waves about her shoulders. Above her the clear spring sky radiated the blue from her wondrous eyes and everything was pure, radiant joy. He felt the fervent ecstasy as he recited his verses to Kubizek and Stephanie filled his thoughts so completely that everything that Hitler ever said or planned for the future was centered on her. With his growing estrangement at home Stephanie gained more and more influence over him. Hitler never spoke to her during those four painful, wonderful years and yet in his head they had a thousand conversations.[44] He knew that once he met her all would be clear and understood, without a word having to be spoken. Whatever the subject that occupied his mind at any given moment Hitler knew that Stephanie would know his ideas exactly and she would share them enthusiastically. When Hitler told Kubizek about the synchronicity of their thought patterns his friend expressed skepticism, which made Hitler furious. When the love-smitten young dreamer learned that she had men friends, mostly military officers, he rationalized her behavior as a diversion to conceal her tempestuous feelings for him. Despite his intense feelings for her the reader will be relieved to learn that, according to Kubizek, Hitler

---

41. Ibid., 40.
42. Ibid.
43. Waite, *The Psychopathic God*, 179.
44. Kubizek, *Young Hitler*, 41.

did not masturbate but he flew into terrible rages about the officers and dreamed up the most painful punishments for them.[45]

He designed a house in renaissance style in which he and Stephanie were going to live. When Hitler left for Vienna he wrote her a letter telling her he was going away to become a great success. She must wait for his return and then they would be married. That she did not wait is well known, as Hitler discovered she married an army officer who was killed in the war.

There were other women in his life of course – Mimi Reiter, Geli Raubal, Renate Müller, Winifred Wagner and Eva Braun – and yet, his sexual relations with them were to manifest perversions that had psychoanalysts exploring the depths of depravity. There is more than a hint that the relationship with Kubizek was either homosexual or homoerotic. When female students visited Kubizek, Hitler flew into a frenzy of jealousy. Kubizek maintained that, apart from the idealistic love for Stephanie, women held absolutely no sexual attraction for Hitler. "It was understandable, therefore, that Adolf did not engage in love affairs or flirtations, and that he always rejected the coquettish advances of girls or women. Women and girls took an interest in him in Linz as well as Vienna, but he always evaded their endeavours."[46]

One incident showed the extent of Hitler's problem. While investigating a possible room to let, the landlady, showing him and Kubizek around, allowed her silk dressing gown to fall open, revealing nothing but a pair of knickers. Hitler fled in terror and on other occasions Kubizek mentioned Hitler's horror at the idea of sexual intercourse with a woman.[47]

Hitler isolated the year after his mother died in 1908 as the year he became a violent anti-Semite and a rambling letter in the Gestapo archives confirms this fact. He later told British Prime Minister Neville Chamberlain that his racial views commenced in his nineteenth year, which would have meant his calculations were accurate.[48] One incident stands out as an indication of his desire to understand the Jewish religion and its ceremonies. Hitler took Kubizek to a synagogue where a wedding was taking place. He urged his companion to keep his hat on and they watched as the ceremony

---

45. Ibid.
46. Machtan, *Hidden Hitler*, 41–42.
47. Kershaw, *Hitler 1936–1945: Nemesis*, 45.
48. Waite, *The Psychopathic God*, 187.

proceeded, with alternate chants and a sermon in Hebrew.[49] Kubizek was convinced that Hitler was serious in trying to understand the problems he had with Judaism but it now appears that he was merely confirming what he had already decided on. A day or so later he came bursting into Kubizek's room and announced, "Hey! Today I became a member of the anti-Semitic Union and I enrolled you too."[50]

His ambition to become an art student was unsuccessful on the two occasions he applied to the Academy of Fine Arts in Vienna. On the first day he was required to draw a picture to represent "The expulsion from Paradise" and the next day "An episode of the Great Flood."[51] He slaved away at the task and emerged confident that he had passed but his optimism was misplaced – he failed. "Test drawing unsatisfactory. Few heads," was the verdict of the examiners.[52] He was humiliated by his rejection as being "totally unsuited" for a career as a painter.[53] "I was so convinced that I would be successful that when I received my rejection, it struck me as a bolt from the blue."[54] Of course the growth of his anti-Semitism meant that the Jews were blamed for everything. His mother's death was their fault and his rejection by the academy also. Years later he was to tell his friends that he had found out that four out of the seven members of the art jury were Jews. He then sat down and wrote a letter to the director of the academy to express his dissatisfaction with the result – the letter concluded with a sinister threat "For this the Jews will pay."[55]

For some years Hitler lived a lonely and isolated life, earning a precarious livelihood by painting postcards and advertisements and drifting from one municipal lodging house to another. Ironically enough given his racial views, at one stage he was forced to stay in a hostel for the homeless in the Meidling district set up by the generous donations of the Jewish Epstein family and he probably sampled the free food in Erdbergstrasse at

---

49. Kubizek, *Young Hitler*, 187.
50. Waite, *The Psychopathic God*, 188.
51. Langer, OSS *Psychological Report on Adolf Hitler*, 180.
52. Kershaw, *Hitler 1936–1945: Nemesis*, 24.
53. Köhler, *Wagner's Hitler*, 52.
54. Kershaw, *Hitler 1936–1945: Nemesis*, 2.
55. Waite, *The Psychopathic God*, 190.

Hitler was an amateur artist and became fanatical about architecture. Old buildings had a particular fascination for him and he drew this sketch of Charles Church, Vienna. From Spotts, Hitler and the Power of Aesthetics, page 234–5.

the Warming House, also the recipient of donations from a Jewish patron, Baron Moritz Königswarder.[56]

While in the Männerheim (men's hostel) he studied the 1848 revolts, and particularly the role his heroes Richard Wagner and Gottfried Semper had played.[57] The composer was his mentor in matters of war as well as race.

His art continued in the form of copies of watercolors of his own work or others. These were later sold to art dealers and picture framers in the Jewish quarter. Reinhold Hanisch, who assisted him by selling the paintings, wrote reminiscences of this period of Hitler's life and made a significant observation. "Hitler at that time looked very Jewish, so that I often joked with him that he must have Jewish blood, since such a large beard rarely grows on a Christian's chin. Also he had big feet, as a desert wanderer must

---

56. Ibid., 195.
57. Hamann, *Hitler's Vienna*, 111.

have."[58] Years later Nazi Party archivists hunted down the works and were distressed to find many of them in the hands of Jews.[59]

Hitler's fascination for Richard Wagner continued and he drew elaborate and imaginative set designs and portraits of the main characters from the operas. Under one sketch he drew in 1912 of *Young Siegfried* he appended a comment that showed the development of his political ideology "Wagner's work showed me for the first time what is the myth of blood."[60] The blood for the young painter consisted of nothing more than the establishment of pure strains and the eradication of the impure – the Jews, who had become an obsession with him.

Hitler already showed traits that characterized his later life: an inability to establish ordinary human relationships; intolerance and hatred both of the established bourgeois world and of non-German peoples, especially the Jews; a tendency toward passionate, denunciatory outbursts; a readiness to live in a world of fantasy and so to escape his poverty and failure. The hints of sexual deviations began to creep into the documents of the time. There is evidence from a man referred to as Jahn by Walter Langer who said that "he had information from a Viennese official that on the police record Hitler was listed as a sexual pervert, but it gave no details of the offences."[61] The police records were to provide a most compelling account of the young man's proclivities.

---

58. Langer, *The Mind of Adolf Hitler*, 119.
59. Ibid.
60. Spotts, *Bayreuth*, 141.
61. Langer, *The Mind of Adolf Hitler*, 120.

Chapter twelve
Soldier and Anti-Semite

In 1913 Hitler moved to Munich, in Bavaria, where his bohemian existence stuttered on. Temporarily recalled to Austria to be examined for military service in February 1914, he was rejected as unfit; but when World War 1 broke out he volunteered for the German army and joined the 16th Bavarian Reserve Infantry Regiment. His enthusiasm for the struggle was echoed from a musical and ideological quarter he would have welcomed. While decent Germans deplored the fact that their country was immersed in a bloody struggle Cosima Wagner wrote a letter from Bayreuth that same year in which she said that "war seems to suit us Germans more than peace."[1] Her contribution to the history of culture had not gone unnoticed; the University of Berlin awarded her an honorary degree in 1910.[2]

Other academics were to plunder the rich vein of aggression in Wagner's polemical writings to try to understand his worldview. Jewish historian Richard Sternfeld commented in his book on *Richard Wagner and the Holy German War* that the First World War was a predestined step, foreseen and predicted in Wagner's operas to facilitate the domination of the world by the Germans.[3]

---

1. Spotts, *Bayreuth*, 155.
2. Wagner, Nike, *The Wagners*, 169.
3. Spotts, *Bayreuth*, 155–56.

Other books of the time related the influence Wagner had on the geopolitics of the region. A popular book published under the title *The Consummation of the Aryan Mystery in Bayreuth* by Leopold von Shröder in 1914 recorded the links between the composer and the new racial order. Von Shröder said that "thanks to the Master, Bayreuth had been made the ideal centre for all Aryan peoples…a hallowed spot where the miracles of the Holy Grail are revealed, where the dragon is slain by the sword of the pure, fearless hero, and where the radiant thought of salvation shines out like a beacon across the dark chasm of primeval thoughts."[4]

Hitler's role in the First World War as a dispatch rider is surrounded by great controversy. It seems clear that he was twice wounded and he greeted the war with enthusiasm, as a great relief from the frustration and aimlessness of his civilian life. The comradeship, discipline and participation in conflict were intensely satisfying to Hitler and he was confirmed in his belief in authoritarianism, inequality and the heroic virtues of war.

While most soldiers carried Bibles or cheap paperbacks, a piano reduction of the opera *Tristan* was his constant companion, "long stretches of which I knew by heart." He told a friend: "so familiar was I with the music that I could hum or whistle all the most important sections in all three acts, often scene by scene, such as only someone can do who knows the work inside out. At every bar I could picture what was happening on the stage."[5] Not that he was the only soldier to have felt the influence of Wagner in the military sphere. The generals used characters in the operas to describe their operations and defensive positions, including the Siegfried and Hunding lines and Operation Valkyrie.[6] At other times he claimed to have carried the five-volume collected works of Schopenhauer on him throughout the war. His must have been the heaviest knapsack in the First World War![7]

History records that Hitler earned the Iron Cross, presented to him without demur by a Jew,[8] second and first class and a number of other medals including the Military Merit Cross, a regimental citation for outstanding gallantry, and the Service Medal. The heroic acts that justified the award of the medals are shrouded in mystery and there was no mention of the Iron

---

4. Köhler, *Wagner's Hitler*, 118.
5. Ibid., 55.
6. Spotts, *Bayreuth*, 156.
7. Spotts, *Hitler and the Power of Aesthetics*, 11.
8. Köhler, *Wagner's Hitler*, 69.

Cross (first class) in the history of the regiment. The facts differ from time to time. One moment he was credited with capturing twelve Frenchmen, including an officer, single-handedly, but in subsequent accounts – from sympathetic sources, the Nazi propaganda agencies – different numbers of soldiers are credited to him. Two newspapers differ on the date that the daring capture was carried out, the one mentioning August 4 and the other October 4, 1918.[9]

Not everyone admired his exploits and his commanding officer declared, "never will I make this madman a corporal," so he stayed a private throughout the war.[10] One night during the war he had a terrible dream that he was buried alive and from that moment he determined that he should not be buried but opted for cremation. That would be appropriate, as his comments in Linz to Kubizek with regard to the fate of Rienzi had revealed. Brave men, such as Siegfried, died on immense funeral pyres with circles of mourning Valkyries waiting to take them to Valhalla, the heaven for fallen heroes. After his dream he leaped up and left the foxhole; moments later a shell landed where he had been sleeping. This reinforced his feeling of predestination.

He showed no interest in women and did not share the soldiers' rough talk and jokes with sexual innuendoes.[11] Hermann Rauschning maintains that a high Nazi official informed him that he had seen Hitler's military record and that he had been found guilty of pederastic practices with an officer and that this was the reason he had never been promoted. The particular charge referred to by Rauschning involved posing in the nude for a homosexual officer named Lammers, who was described as a Berlin artist in civilian life. Hitler was alleged to have gone to bed with him thereafter.[12] The same source maintains that while in Munich, shortly before the war, he was found guilty of a violation of paragraph 175 of the criminal code that dealt with pederasty.[13] Rauschning also claimed to have spoken to two boys who had claimed to be Hitler's homosexual partners.[14] In later life he

---

9. Langer, *The Mind of Adolf Hitler*, 123.
10. Köhler, *Wagner's Hitler*, 77.
11. Redlich, *Hitler: Diagnosis of a Destructive Prophet*, 38.
12. Machtan, *Hidden Hitler*, 100.
13. Langer, *The Mind of Adolf Hitler*, 124.
14. Ibid., 173.

Hitler's sex life was a mystery to the people of Germany. Many suspected he preferred men to women and in this cartoon he is caricatured as gay and effeminate. See Machtan, page 246–7. Drawing by the famous Munich caricaturist Thomas Theodor Heine for the leftist intellectual magazine, Tage-Buch from 1930.

derived sexual pleasure in looking at other men's bodies and his personal bodyguard was composed entirely of homosexuals.[15]

Rauschning's account has been corroborated from other sources. There is proof of his homosexuality in the account of fellow dispatch rider Hans Mend who described incidents in the war. Mend maintained that Private Ernst Schmidt was his special pal and that Hitler "never looked at a woman." Mend described some of the incidents. "In 1915 we were billeted in the Le Fèbre brewery at Fournes. We slept in the hay. Hitler was bedded down at night with 'Schmidl,' his male whore. We heard a rustling in the hay. Then someone switched on his electric flashlight and growled, "'Take a look at those two nancy boys,' I myself took no further interest in the matter."[16]

After the conquest of France at the end of June 1940 Hitler was joined by Schmidt and Max Amann for a reminiscence tour of their experiences in

---

15. Ibid., 174.
16. Machtan, *Hidden Hitler*, 68.

Hitler was a private in the First World War and earned a controversial Iron Cross. He is pictured here with his two wartime pals Ernst Schmidt (left) and Anton Bachmann (center), with their English terrier Foxl. See Hitler and Geli by Hayman, page 116.

Flanders.[17] Schmidt appears to have been a brave man and had the "reputation for coming through the heaviest bombardments unscathed."[18]

Mend also made mention of what happened when Hitler and the others had baths: "they all ran around naked [and] Hitler did all kinds of things to them and went around with them in the night." Finally they had enough and visited their wrath on the future dictator in the most humbling manner. "In the billet [Mend] and other men had smeared Hitler's prick with boot polish while he was asleep."[19] Freud was to explain how an external influence led to a "fixation of their inversion (homosexuality)…such influences are exclusive relations with persons of their own sex, comradeship in war…"[20] Lothar Machtan describes in some detail in his book *The Hidden Hitler* the problems Mend encountered when he tried to blackmail Hitler,

---

17. Kershaw, *Hitler 1936–1945: Nemesis*, 299.
18. Lewis, *The Man Who Invented Hitler*, 116.
19. Machtan, *Hidden Hitler*, 87.
20. Freud, *On Sexuality*, 50.

once he became the German leader. Nevertheless, one of King Ludwig II's love letters to a manservant of his was reckoned to be one of Hitler's most prized possessions.[21]

The clemency of one English soldier in the First World War changed the course of world history. In September 1918 Private Henry Tandey had Hitler in his sights but decided not to kill him. "I took aim but couldn't shoot a wounded man so I let him go," was how he later explained his actions. When Neville Chamberlain visited Hitler in Berchtesgaden in 1938 he saw a painting of Tandey carrying a wounded comrade to a first aid station. Hitler pointed out Tandey and said: "That's the man who nearly shot me. That man came so near to killing me that I thought I should never see Germany again. Providence saved me from such devilishly accurate fire as those English boys were aiming at us." He asked Chamberlain to convey his gratitude to Tandey.[22]

Ironically, Hitler fell prey to one of the hazards of the fighting arena and was a victim of poison gas, from which he nearly went blind. Physical healing did not bring relief, however, and his blindness persisted in a psychosomatic state. He spent sleepless nights walking up and down the wards telling all who would listen to him that the setbacks in the war were caused by the treachery of the Jews and Marxists. What was needed, he told the listeners, was a heroic leader in the Wagnerian muld.[23] The doctor who treated him, Dr. Edmund Forster, knew of the fifteenth-century shepherd who became known as the drummer because of the drumbeat of his oratory. The drummer knew how to exploit the problems of the oppressed and claimed to be sent by God to lead his people out of darkness into light. His fame became so great that he provoked mass hysteria wherever he went. The princes of the region feared his influence, dragged him before an ecclesiastical court and he was burnt at the stake. As he was about to die he predicted that when Germany was at its direst need another would arise who would lead the nation to glory by representing the ordinary German's needs.[24]

Dr. Forster played on Hitler's belief that he was the reincarnation of the drummer and persuaded him that God would restore his sight by a

---

21. Waite, *The Psychopathic God*, 235.
22. Lewis, *The Man Who Invented Hitler*, 118–19.
23. Ibid., 236.
24. Ibid., 237.

miracle. The treatment worked and the psychosomatic blindness was cured. Hitler became more entrenched in his belief that he was the savior sent to deliver Germany. He joked in *Mein Kampf,* "Holding down under poison gas 12–15,000 heads of the Hebrew corrupters of the people would have made the First World War worthwhile." Clearly the anti-Semitism was well established in his mind. He was still hospitalized when the war ended.

Discharged from the hospital in the confusion that followed the German defeat, Hitler determined to take up political work in order to destroy a peace settlement that he found unacceptable. He stuck with his pal Ernst Schmidt and they performed guard duty at a small prisoner of war camp on the Austrian border in order to escape the chaos and confusion in Munich.[25] As an army political agent he joined the tiny German Workers' Party in Munich in September 1919 but remained with his regiment until April 1920.

Asked by Captain Karl Mayr of his regiment to draw up a document as to what view the Social Democrat government should show to the "Jewish threat to the nation," Hitler wrote an essay in September 1919 in which he said, despite his instinctive dislike for Jews, one had to move beyond mere feelings and realize that the most striking consistent characteristic of the Jews was their urge to make money and gain power. "They prostrate themselves before kings and princes and at the same time suck out their blood like vampires." He went on to propose solutions. "Our ultimate goal must be the removal of the Jews." He proposed that "only when there is no corner in which they can find refuge, no hope of survival in the future, will their fate be sealed…[Which could only be achieved] by total commitment on the part of patriotically minded men with a gift for leadership and a sense of unqualified responsibility."[26]

Police reports from Ettstrasse in Munich after the war paint a sordid picture of the "war hero," for the police records contain many references to Hitler's unsavory sexual activities during the postwar period. One sworn affidavit filed in the police records read as follows: "I, Michael, eighteen years old, met a man of youngish appearance who invited me to have a meal with him and – in return for payment – to spend the night with him. Having been unemployed for months, and because my mother and brothers

---

25. Ibid., 180.
26. Köhler, *Wagner's Hitler,* 146.

were also suffering from hunger, I accompanied the gentleman to his home. In the morning I left."[27]

"Joseph," who was also solicited in the same manner and for the same purposes made a further sworn statement. "Because I told him that I had been a keen soldier when I was younger and would have liked to become a noncommissioned officer, he spoke to me for hours about a new German army and urged me to engage in propaganda among my comrades on behalf of a new military formation founded by himself…I spent the night with him…"

"Franz" spoke of a man with an Austrian dialect who "proceeded to explain the need for the reunification of Germany and Austria. He asked if I would be willing to devote myself to that end. He then wanted to get me some books and periodicals on the subject, which was why we went to his home. And since it was already late and the streetcars had stopped running, he invited me to stay the night with him, and I accepted…the gentleman's name is Adolf Hitler; he wore a pale gabardine overcoat, and one of his distinctive features is a lock of hair that kept flopping onto his forehead."[28]

The details of Hitler's private life are only relevant in the context of his later campaign against close lieutenants, who were homosexual, and to try to understand what sort of personality would carry out the barbaric acts that characterized his later life. The perverted manner in which Hitler treated his "girlfriends" and lovers also becomes easier to understand if his sexual proclivities are explored. Klaus, the highly-strung son of Thomas Mann, was later to repudiate any links of the media between homosexuality and fascism. In an article, "The Left and Vice," he argued vehemently against making this linkage merely on the basis of the fact that "there are reputed to be many members of National Socialist organizations who love young men rather than women…Sharing one's erotic disposition with a few bandits does not make one a bandit oneself."[29]

Klaus later wrote an autobiography in which he described meeting Hitler at a café in Munich in the 1920s and the impression he made on him. "Without doubt, he looked like a man with whom I wasn't person-

---

27. Machtan, *Hidden Hitler*, 136.
28. Ibid.
29. Ibid., 260.

ally acquainted, but whose picture I had often seen. Who could it be? Not Charlie Chaplin. Certainly not! Chaplin has the little moustache, but not the nose, the fleshy, and nasty – indeed obscene – nose, which had instantly struck me as the vilest and most characteristic feature of Hitler's physiognomy. Chaplin has charm, grace, wit, intensity – characteristics of which nothing could be detected in my lip-smacking, whipped-cream-guzzling neighbor."[30]

Finally Klaus identifies the person Hitler had reminded him of – Haarman, the boy murderer of Hanover. "Was he, the Austrian operetta habitué at the next table, as proficient as his North German Doppelgänger? That homosexual Bluebeard had succeeded in luring thirty to forty boys into his hospitable parlor, where he bit through their throats during the act of love and made tasty sausages out of their corpses."[31]

The police kept an eye on Hitler not only for his sexual prowling, but also for his increasingly strident political activity. Police reports of the early twenties describe his gifts of oratory as immense and "masterful" and note how when he had concluded he was invariably drowned by "tumultuous applause." According to Otto Strasser, who later fled to Canada, Hitler took lessons on speaking and mass psychology from a man named Hanussen, who also dabbled in astrology and fortune-telling.[32] A later biographer, Konrad Heiden, then a student, recorded the impression Hitler made on him. "Suddenly this man, who has been awkwardly standing around...begins to speak, filling the room with his voice, suppressing interruptions or contradictions by his domineering manner, spreading cold shivers among those present by the savagery of his declaration, lifting every subject of conversation into the light of history...the listener is filled with awe and feels that a new phenomenon had entered the room – this thundering demon was not there before; this is not the same timid man with the contracted shoulders. He is capable of this transformation in a personal interview and facing an audience of half a million."[33]

In 1920 he was put in charge of the party's propaganda and left the army to devote his time to building up the Nazi Party. The country was in economic chaos with resentment at the loss of the war and abject

---

30. Ibid., 261.
31. Ibid., 262.
32. Langer, *The Mind of Adolf Hitler*, 32.
33. Waite, *The Psychopathic God*, 208.

misery caused by the humiliating peace terms. Bavaria, where Hitler lived throughout the 1920s, was the center of the potential rebellion and dislike of the republican government in Berlin. In March 1920 a coup d'état by the army established a strong right-wing government and Munich became the gathering place for members of the Freikorps, comprising soldiers unwilling to return to civilian life, and for political plotters against the republic. Many of these joined the Nazi Party including Ernst Röhm, who recruited the "strong arm" squads used by Hitler to protect party meetings, to attack political opponents including Socialists and Communists, and to exploit violence for the impression of strength it gave.

On August 3, 1920 in a Munich beer cellar at the beginning of his political career, Hitler made a speech of crucial importance in explaining why he advocated anti-Semitism.[34] "So the race we label Aryan was the inspirer of all the later great cultures…We know that Egypt was raised to its cultural height by Aryan immigrants, similarly Persia and Greece. The immigrants were blond, blue-eyed Aryans, and we know that apart from these states no cultured states ever existed on earth…"

He went on to explain the contribution of Jews to art. "The Jew has never had his own art. Even his temples had to be built by foreigners, first by the Assyrians and in a later period by the Romans. He has left no art behind, nothing in the way of painting, no buildings, nothing."[35] The punishment for that was extreme. He explained that the death penalty was the only solution to the problem of the Jews. Healthy elements of a nation knew that criminals guilty of crimes against the nation, i.e., parasites on the national community, could not be tolerated, and under certain circumstances they must be punished only with death, since imprisonment lacks the quality of irrevocableness.

No other punishment would meet the needs, the man with the shiny blue eyes and lank forelock of hair across the forehead thundered. The heaviest bolt was not heavy enough, Hitler continued, and the securest prison was not secure enough that a few million could not in the end open it. Only one bolt could not be opened and that was death. The time for vacillation was over, he shouted, to cheers from the excited crowd. He said that they had, however, decided that they would not come with "ifs,

---

34. Gilbert, *The Holocaust: The Jewish Tragedy*, 24.
35. Spotts, *Hitler and the Power of Aesthetics*, 16–17.

ands, or buts," but when the matter came to a solution, it would be done thoroughly. By this he meant seizing the evil and exterminating it root and branch.[36]

The Nazi Party included anti-Semitism in its articles of faith and provided that "only our fellow countrymen can be citizens. Only those of German blood can be fellow countrymen, without regard to creed. Therefore no Jew can be a fellow countryman."[37] As was to be the pattern throughout his life, Hitler never liked to perform any deed, make a speech or write without quoting from scripture, which meant the gospel according to Richard Wagner. In his book *Mein Kampf* Hitler says of the first meeting of the Nazi party, "Out of its flames was bound to come the sword which was to regain the freedom of the German Siegfried."[38]

The defeat of the Germans in the First World War was blamed on the treacherous German Parliament which had stabbed the country in the back, much as Siegfried was stabbed by the Nibelung (Jewish) Hagen.[39] In the Ring cycle the greatest hero in the world, Siegfried, the man who did not know fear, had been smeared with a magic potion to protect him from any attack. The protection given to Siegfried did not encompass his back as he was reckoned to be so courageous he would always face the foe. It is not without significance that the Nazi Party was founded in Munich in the *Bratwurstglöckl*, whose modern equivalent would be a "gay bar." The large percentage of homosexual members made this inevitable and some of the rituals and symbols came from sodomite organizations and individuals, among them the "Sieg Heil" salutation, the twin lightning bolt "ss" symbol, and the inverted triangle used later to identify classes of prisoners in the concentration camps.[40]

The modern equivalents of the Siegfrieds of the operas were organized as strong-arm squads or thugs in 1921 under Röhm. A private party army, the SA (Sturmabteilung), came into being with such power that the Bavarian government appeared unable to prevent its breaches of law and Röhm's policy of intimidation. Conditions were thus favorable to the growth of the party but no one apart from Hitler had the initiative to take

---

36. Goldhagen, *Hitler's Willing Executioners*, 424–25.
37. Hilberg, *The Destruction of the European Jews*, 18.
38. Hitler, *Mein Kampf*, 309.
39. Spotts, *Bayreuth*, 156.
40. Stang, "Hitler and Homosexuality: Nazism is just one version of homosexuality."

full advantage of them. The party at that stage was small, largely ineffective and was committed to a program of nationalist and socialist principles, which he accepted on his own terms as a means to political power. His propaganda methods and his personal arrogance caused a ruffling of feathers with other members of the committee, but Hitler – ever the master of psychological manipulation – petulantly offered his resignation.

His power to organize publicity and to acquire funds were the key features of his hold on leadership and they soon capitulated. By July 1921 he had secured the position of president with unlimited powers and he set out to create a mass movement, whose spellbinding credo and ruthless discipline would be sufficient to bind its members in loyalty to him. Propaganda was conducted through the party newspaper, the *Völkischer Beobachter*, and through adroitly organized political meetings, where he developed his unique talent for demagoguery and mass leadership.

The sexual perversions hinted at with the goat incident at Leonding as a young boy, coupled with the war and Munich experiences, persisted. Ronald Hayman, in his book on the relationship between Hitler and Geli,[41] makes mention of the ten-mark promissory notes used as receipts when the Nazi newspaper *Völkischer Beobachter* floated a loan. On the note was a man unmistakably resembling Hitler; in his right hand was a sword dripping with blood, in his left he held a severed female head by the hair. The caption urged the lenders to acts of savagery, hitherto unknown in the banking trade – "Warriors of truth, behead the lie."[42] Freud was to comment on the disparagement of women that arose from the influence of the Oedipus complex, whom his researches showed were regarded as castrated. "In extreme cases this gives rise to an inhibition of their choice of object (identity of lover), and, if it is supported by organic factors, to exclusive homosexuality."[43]

While his virulent anti-Semitism was more than apparent in his speeches, 1922 was the year that Hitler commenced with his predictions of the demise of the Jews. Speaking to a friend he was suddenly seized by a great trembling and his body shook with emotion. He promised that when he came to power in Germany he would see to it that every Jew was killed.

---

41. Hayman, *Hitler and Geli*.
42. Ibid., 144.
43. Freud, *On Sexuality*, 376.

"As soon as I have the power, I shall have gallows after gallows erected, for example in Munich on the Marienplatz…Then the Jews will be hanged one after another, and they will stay hanging until they stink. They will stay hanging as long as hygienically possible. As soon as they are untied, then the next group will follow and that will continue until the last Jew in Munich is exterminated. Exactly the same procedure will be followed in other cities until Germany is cleansed of the last Jew!"[44]

Hitler and his henchmen began looking for victims to satiate their lust for blood. One of the first targets of their anti-Semitism was Walther Rathenau, the Jewish Foreign Minister who had negotiated a treaty with the Soviet Union. Rathenau had written in 1918 about his pre-war countrymen and the influence of Richard Wagner. "It is scarcely possible to exaggerate how deeply the last generation was spellbound by the influence of Richard Wagner, not so decisively by his music as by the gestures of his characters, by his ideas…There is always someone – Lohengrin, Walther, Siegfried, Wotan – who can do everything and knock down everything, who can release suffering virtue, punish vice and bring general salvation, striking an exaggerated pose, with the sound of fanfares and with lighting effects and staging."[45]

No doubt the new generation of Siegfrieds and Lohengrins, acting under the impulses of their black souls, spurred on by the mighty kaleidoscope of polyphonic sound, saw him as a vice to be punished and that his death would bring general salvation. On June 24, 1922 he was assassinated after a campaign in which thugs yelled "Knock off Walther Rathenau, the dirty God-damned Jewish sow." Following his murder Hitler expressed great pleasure and was sentenced to four weeks in prison. On his release he shouted, "The Jewish people stands against us as our deadly foe, and will so stand against us always, and for all time."[46]

The next year saw the start of the anti-Jewish newspaper *Der Stürmer* by Julius Streicher with the banner headline and slogan "The Jews Are Our Misfortune."[47] The decent members of society were aghast at the levels of racism that were permeating German society. But few spoke out. There were, however, isolated voices of sanity in a population still reeling from

---

44. Waite, *The Psychopathic God*, 363.
45. Spotts, *Bayreuth*, 130.
46. Gilbert, *The Holocaust: The Jewish Tragedy*, 25.
47. Ibid.

the ravages of a world war, trying to understand who their true foes were. Jean-Paul Sartre, the French philosopher and humanist, went on record as describing the Jew-hater as an inhuman, cold and indifferent coward and killer. "We are now in a position to understand the anti-Semite. He is a man who is afraid. Not of the Jews, to be sure, but of himself…He is a coward who does not want to admit his cowardice to himself; a murderer who represses and censures his tendency to murder without being able to hold it back…The existence of the Jew merely permits the anti-Semite to stifle his anxieties…The anti-Semite is a man who wishes to be a pitiless stone, a furious torrent, a devastating thunderbolt – anything except a man."[48]

---

48. Waite, *The Psychopathic God*, 362–64.

Chapter thirteen
Bayreuth Spectator

Siegfried Wagner took over the running of the Bayreuth festival in 1906, the year in which Cosima suffered several severe heart attacks while visiting her friend Prince Hohenlohe.[1] A further attack in 1910 saw her confined to her room where, dressed in a silver kimono and described as a "white apparition" – given the silver hair that still adorned her regal bearing – she awaited the grim reaper who would unite her with her Richard.

The insidious anti-Semitism spawned in the years that the Master reigned lived on and waxed stronger with the tide of German chauvinism. An article by Reinhold von Lichtenberg, a cultural historian, assessed the 1911 festival and found in the *Ring* and *Parsifal* "the love of nature and animals that is deeply rooted in the Teuton." There was a political message in the former work, namely the tragedy that arises from the avarice of the "non-Aryan" Alberich, the Nibelung.[2]

Siegfried wrote a number of works including fourteen operas, the most famous of which, *Der Bärenhäuter*, achieved 350 performances. His contemporaries were largely critical of his music and Richard Strauss called him a "classicist simpleton" while Karl Kraus was even more scathing:

---

1. Spotts, *Bayreuth*, 122.
2. Ibid., 135.

"such a fellow never inherits the talent, but always the nose."[3] However his conducting was widely praised and Hans Richter, who had learned the art at the feet of the Master, commented very favorably. "It is good that you have the score in your head and not your head in the score," he said.[4] Albert Schweitzer praised him as a "magnificent" producer and a "workmanlike and sensitive conductor."[5] His innovations on the stage are often unrecognized and yet he was responsible for modernizing staging, including the use of spotlights, a cyclorama and the projection of colors and images.[6]

Siegfried's sex life was complicated and he appeared to be mostly homosexual, a fact that his family was not aware of in the beginning. Degrees of sexual persuasion are always a difficult concept and understanding the personal life of Wagner's son and heir, one is reminded of the dream of Oscar Wilde to "eat the fruit of every tree in the garden." But to continue the dubious metaphor, doubt is cast on Siegfried's total commitment to any one variety, for by 1901 he had already fathered a son who later bore the name of Walter Aign by a Bayreuth pastor's wife. His illegitimate son was integrated seamlessly into the festival administration as a musical assistant between 1924 and 1931 and after a considerable gap, again in 1951 for six years.[7]

Cosima discovered the secret of his homosexuality when it became apparent that blackmailers were on his trail. The newshounds picked up the scent and the muck purveyor of the court of Kaiser Wilhelm II, Maximilian Harden, the editor of *Zukunft*, learned of the fact. Once that worthy smelled scandal he went to extraordinary lengths to gain whatever political and editorial mileage he could. He had been the ruin of Count Philipp von Eulenburg and action was necessary to stem the tide of scandal.[8] The family's financial adviser Adolf von Gross negotiated with the blackmailers and reluctantly had to settle their demands.[9]

What was more significant was that Harden was a Jew and staunch

---

3. Wagner, Nike, *The Wagners*, 197.
4. Richard Wagner Museum brochure, "About Richard Wagner," items 42–46.
5. Skelton, *Wagner at Bayreuth*, 106.
6. Richard Wagner Museum brochure, "About Richard Wagner," items 42–46.
7. Ibid., 202.
8. Ibid.
9. Ibid., 197.

nationalists described his activities as "Jewish muckraking."[10] Adolf Hitler was not impressed by the activities of the editor and this served to exacerbate his desire for vengeance. "Siegfried Wagner had been through a serious crisis when he found himself compromised by his homosexuality and was made to marry in a hurry," Hitler told Goebbels in 1942. Siegfried was terrified that this trait would be discovered and would jeopardize the festival.[11] But that sort of mudslinging had its own dangers: on July 3, 1922 Harden narrowly survived an attempted assassination with serious head injuries and was rendered an invalid. His quest to hunt down all homosexuals had made him many enemies, including Siegfried Wagner.[12]

Siegfried's sister Isolde had married and produced a male heir, who threatened the succession of Siegfried. Mention has been made of the lawsuit which resulted in Isolde failing to be declared a Wagner. To save the situation Siegfried, who had always stipulated that his future wife had to be "quite poor" and "without family," married a destitute English orphan, Winifred Williams, who had drawn loving pictures of him when she was at school.[13] She was born in England in 1897, the daughter of a father who was a bridge engineer – later theatre critic and novelist – and a mother who had Thespian aspirations.[14] Both died before her second birthday and Winifred was shunted around from orphanage to orphanage until she reached the age of ten. From that age she was brought up in the comfortable and friendly home of seventy-eight-year-old Wagner disciple and friend Karl Klindworth, a pianist, great admirer of Franz Liszt and the editor of a number of piano scores by the Bayreuth Master.[15] Klindworth was a committed anti-Semite and he planted those treacherous seeds in her mind even before he and Winifred (nicknamed Senta by Klindworth, after the heroine of *The Flying Dutchman*) had visited the festival in 1914.[16] He regarded opera as "always being under the destructive influence of the

---

10. Machtan, *Hidden Hitler*, 47.
11. Köhler, *Wagner's Hitler*, 195.
12. Hamann, *Winifred Wagner*, 62.
13. Wagner, Nike, *The Wagners*, 7.
14. Spotts, *Bayreuth*, 137.
15. Wagner, Nike, *The Wagners*, 154.
16. Ibid., 203.

Jews." He regarded Gustav Mahler, Bruno Walter, Leo Blech, Felix von Weingartner and Otto Klemperer as a "popular Jewish gang."[17]

During the lengthy intervals between acts Siegfried took Winifred for tea and a warm friendship developed.

The next year Siegfried was in Berlin conducting benefit concerts and he renewed the friendship. When she reached maturity, reckoned in those days as eighteen years, she moved into Wahnfried, where she brought a breath of fresh air into the death-laden atmosphere created by the aged Cosima, who ran the house like a mausoleum. To the delight of the moral custodians of Bayreuth his marriage gave his step a more invigorated spring but he was never to forsake his other sexual peccadilloes.[18]

Winifred's first Christmas at Wahnfried was to witness a reading of Hans von Wolzogen's fairy tale *Der Jude im Dorn*. This dealt with a courageous laborer and his battle with a rich Jew with a long grey beard. The story tells how the laborer outwits the Jew, locks him in a thorn-hedged enclosure and makes him dance by using his magic violin. "You have oppressed the workers enough; now you will not escape the thorn hedge." The tormented and exhausted Jew begged for mercy and gave the laborer a bag of gold, which stopped the torture. In court the servant was sentenced to death but the laborer managed to save himself by forcing the judge and hangman to dance with his magic violin. That ended the case and neither the laborer nor the Jew were hanged which made for a happy ending.[19] Read as it was under the Christmas tree during the war the fairy tale brought hope that the alleged war of survival against the Jews would end with the death of their adversaries.[20]

Klindworth died at the end of July 1916 and his death notice was headed with a swastika as a sign of nationalist sentiment.[21] With considerable trauma – he was born blue and almost dead – Wieland the first son was born in 1917 and Cosima celebrated the event by coming downstairs and playing a few bars on Wagner's piano which had been shut since his death. In a musical salute to heredity Siegfried composed a *Wahnfried Idyll*

---

17. Hamann, *Winifred Wagner*, 14.
18. Ibid.
19. Ibid., 41–42.
20. Ibid.
21. Ibid., 46.

Siegfried Wagner, son of the composer with his wife Winifred and their children. Wolf Siegfried Wagner, page 79.

for solo voice and piano, though cognoscenti reckon it falls far short of the *Siegfried Idyll* composed by his father at the time of his birth.[22]

Winifred took on the role of secretary and would write at Siegfried's dictation and later on her own initiative letters to Wagner societies in which he wittily and cuttingly parodied the "moderns," the Jews and the Reds.[23]

Children followed year by year and Friedelind, the second born, was followed by Wolfgang and finally Verena. Joy and tiny footsteps rang through the great halls of Wahnfried and there were memories of the home twenty years previously. Wieland attended school in Bayreuth and, except for a few years at university, spent his whole life there.[24] As a youngster

---

22. Wagner, Nike, *The Wagners*, 204.
23. Hamann, *Winifred Wagner*, 47.
24. Wagner, Nike, *The Wagners*, 147.

he was easily identified by the famous Wagner nose – a protuberance, reckoned to properly identify those infused with the sacred blood – but in his case, to the amusement of the townsfolk, it led him irresistibly to the sausage factory in the town.[25] His love for the frankfurters was his only discernable virtue at the time and as a child he was sullen and bad-tempered and bullied his younger brother Wolfgang unmercifully.[26]

Whereas Newfoundland dogs had been the first choice of the great composer – so much so that they earned their own burial sites in the garden – the choice of the next generation were schnauzers that chased the children around the large house and garden.[27] Theatre dominated their play and suits of armor, swords and drinking horns – props from many productions – provided the wherewithal to put on vast plays of the imagination. The puppet theatre donated by Judith Gautier to her aged lover Wagner also provided endless pleasure to the children, steeped in a tradition of make-believe.[28]

Although Siegfried had sired four lusty children his enthusiasm for the bedroom – or at least that occupied by his spouse – waned somewhat. Siegfried had a free hand in most things and traveled at will. His energetic wife looked after the correspondence and daily work at Wahnfried. In most instances she was loyal to him and discreet as to his homosexual dalliances. It seems she never told her children about this facet and she had learned toughness and resilience from her difficult upbringing. She was well aware that her husband was the son of the Master and therefore in a sense entitled to every freedom.[29]

What is clear is that later on Winifred's frustrations mounted and finally she was to exhibit a feature that was to characterize her later life – a total lack of discretion. She lamented to Goebbels that Siegfried was so listless and she wept because the son was not like his father.[30] In his diary the future propaganda minister noted, "she put her sorrows to me. Siegfried

---

25. Ibid.
26. Ibid., 150.
27. Ibid., 182.
28. Ibid.
29. Hamann, *Winifred Wagner*, 66.
30. Köhler, *Wagner's Hitler*, 196.

is so limp."[31] Clearly the Master's "universal eroticism", to repeat Thomas Mann's immortal phrase, had not extended to his son.[32]

The First World War was, according to Bayreuth, the work of the Jews who stabbed Germany in the back. They also caused the revolution in Russia and Siegfried maintained that they were the cause of the French Revolution and names like Robespierre and Marat were really pseudonyms for Rubinstein and Marx. Siegfried wrote to his old teacher Engelbert Humperdinck and said: "It is now all over for Germany for all time. Jehovah has led his people to victory and we have been enslaved."[33]

Hitler settled in Munich after the end of the First World War and for a while stayed with Winifred's guardian Edwin Bechstein, the great manufacturer of pianos. In fact the Bechstein family was the most important bond between Hitler and the Wagner family. They had financed Dietrich Eckart's German Nationalist newspaper *Auf Gut Deutsch*; the writer Eckart was a proud Wagnerian whose essay on *Parsifal* appeared in the 1911 festival brochure.[34] Eckart had brought Hitler to meet the Bechsteins saying that "this is the man, who will one day free Germany." His protégé was already filling a Munich stadium with five thousand cheering spectators and was heading a campaign to cancel the reparation payments.

Hitler's personal lifestyle left much to be desired and very subtly Frau Helene Bechstein helped him with his manners and the other social graces that a future political leader would require. The death of his mother had been a devastating blow and Helene became a substitute figure – he remembered with great fondness laying his head in her lap and letting her stroke his soft brown hair. The Bechsteins contributed to Nazi Party funds and introduced him to Berchtesgaden, the alpine mountain resort on the frontier with Austria. He fell in love with that place and determined to make a home there. The natural beauty of the mountain retreat had much to recommend it and it had a very special significance to every German. It was the place where the new Führer of Germany would awake from his magic sleep and lead Germany to greatness.

Frau Bechstein spoiled Hitler by taking him to the opera, giving him money and introducing him to all the influential people in Munich. His

---

31. Wagner, Nike, *The Wagners*, 207.
32. Ibid., 171.
33. Hamann, *Winifred Wagner*, 55–57.
34. Ibid., 73.

lifestyle was otherwise stereotypical and his breakfast invariably consisted of milk, rusks, peppermint or chamomile tea, an apple and cheese. Lunch consisted of vegetable soup and was taken in the mid afternoon.[35] He liked to go to an Italian restaurant – the *Osteria Bavaria* – in the Schellingstrasse in the Schwabing district. Drinking lemonade or his own brand of heavily sweetened tea he would while away the hours chatting to friends and bowing to the elegant ladies who often came especially to the place to see him.[36]

A tiny apartment above a chemist shop at 41 Thierschstrasse in Munich was his home from May 1920 to October 1929 and consisted of a main room of about nine by ten feet, with a few rugs on a dilapidated lino floor.[37] It was sparsely furnished with a small bookcase, a bed, a chair and table and a picture of his mother. Apart from the small Munich apartment he spent long periods in Berchtesgaden and stayed for some time at the Pension Moritz during June 1923. Frau Buchner, the six-foot stunning blonde wife of the innkeeper impressed him with her sexuality and he made desperate attempts to gain her attention. He strode around banging his leg with his whip, according to his good friend Dietrich Eckart, trying to impress her to no avail. The sexual experiences of Nietzsche must have seeped through the erudite prose and penetrated the saturnine recesses of a darkened soul. He then resorted to tales of his bravado and mentioned an occasion in Berlin when he witnessed the moral and ethical depravity of the Jews. "I nearly imagined myself to be Jesus Christ when He came to His Father's temple and found it taken over by the moneychangers." Banging his leg again with his whip to emphasize his story he continued, "I can well imagine how He felt when He seized a whip and scourged them out." Frau Buchner's indifference continued.[38]

Anti-Semitism ruled the Wahnfried household and Winifred quickly fell into the pattern. She wrote to a friend and made mention of her personal friend Arthur Dinter who had written a novel, *The Sins against the Blood*. She described him as a terribly original and fanatical anti-Semite whose main activities seemed to be to conduct lawsuits against rabbis and up to that stage he had lost none. In the same letter she made reference to

---

35. Waite, *The Psychopathic God*, 222.
36. Ibid., 95.
37. Ibid., 220.
38. Ibid., 240.

Wagner's famous essay on "Jewry in Music" published in 1850, which was the cornerstone of the Wagner family's views on race. It will be recalled that in 1879 Cosima recorded in her diary that one of the solutions favored by Wagner for the Jews was deportation. Cosima and Wagner laughed about that proposal and brought to mind that his essay had been the first salvo in the war against the Jews.[39]

When the singer Carl Clewing was married the Wagner family did not see fit to send him a message of congratulations. Winifred wrote a letter complaining about the students' organization he had belonged to and then the real nub that he had married a glaring Jewess. "Fie for shame, the devil!!!" was her disgust at the "mismatch."[40] A visitor explained why she had arrived twelve hours too late for a lunch at Wahnfried. This account illustrated graphically the lengths anti-Semites went to show their feelings. Originally she was on a fast train from Breslau when a Jewish family entered her coupè. She was so upset she disembarked and caught a slow train from Leipzig arriving at nine in the evening![41]

At the end of August 1923, after careful preparation by Hess, Hitler visited General Wille in Zurich in search of much needed party funds. Clara Wille noted in her diary "how extremely likeable he was" and that "his whole person trembles when he speaks. He speaks wonderfully."[42] When he spoke to the general he no doubt made mention of Wagner's great love Mathilde Wesendonck, as the general's mother Eliza was a great friend of hers. It was also politic for Hitler to portray himself as a knowledgeable Wagnerian to the skeptical military man. As Hitler was leaving he predicted, "in the spring we will strike," and the general warned him against violence. Hitler also said "the Jews must get out" to which the old man added "if you do that everything will go wrong."[43] On his return he took over leadership of the Kampfbunds and there was much speculation that a putsch (a coup d'état) would take place similar to that undertaken by Mussolini. Hitler dreamed of becoming Rienzi and leading his people against the red democracy in power.[44]

---

39. Hamann, *Winifred Wagner*, 60.
40. Ibid.
41. Ibid.
42. Ibid., 75.
43. Ibid., 76.
44. Ibid., 77.

Possibly the most auspicious day in the life of the young politician was the day Hitler met Siegfried and Winifred Wagner at Bayreuth. It was an interesting day on the monetary front as on September 28, 1923, one dollar was worth 142 million marks. Hitler staged a German day in Bayreuth and paid homage to Wagner and met the family.[45] It was a day of great excitement for the mad enthusiast for the great man's music. He could scarcely believe that he was in his house with Wagner's son. For several years after the war the family lived in the small bachelor house next to Wahnfried as they could not afford to heat the main house. There were no lawns and gardens and they grew cabbages and potatoes instead. Times were very difficult in Germany at that time. By the time Hitler visited they were back in the main house.

There were some facts that the family would not have told him. Hitler would not have been told that the Wagners had even approached the Jewish community of Bayreuth – and specifically Emil Holzinger – for funds. Siegfried told these families that the anti-Semitism of Richard Wagner was not to be taken seriously. They were fortunate enough to emigrate before the insincerity of those words was to be proved in the most disastrous manner possible.[46]

On the day Hitler arrived at Bayreuth he was thin with cheekbones sticking out of his pasty cheeks. Dressed in Bavarian leather breeches, short thick woolen socks, a red and blue checked shirt and a short blue jacket, he walked in with the reverence of one entering a shrine. Winifred was on hand to introduce him to the family. As he courteously shook hands with the Wagners he struggled to hold back the tears and said that Wagner was the greatest German who ever lived.[47] "I have read everything he ever wrote and I have the most intimate familiarity with Wagner's mental processes. At every stage of my life I come back to him."[48] In sixteen years' time speaking to his staff after taking over the rest of Czechoslovakia on March 15, 1939, he assumed the same mantle himself. "I will go down as the greatest German in history."[49]

---

45. For an account of the visit by Wagner's granddaughter Friedelind see *Heritage of Fire* by Friedelind Wagner and Page Cooper, 6–8.
46. Wagner, Gottfried, *Twilight of the Wagners*, 129.
47. Wagner and Cooper, *Heritage of Fire*, 7.
48. Waite, *The Psychopathic God*, 103.
49. Kershaw, *Hitler 1936–1945: Nemesis*, 155.

Lost for words for some time he reverently looked around the room where the great man worked. He gazed with wonder at the pictures illustrating the Ring cycle, donated by King Ludwig of Bavaria. The crystal opium pipe given to Cosima, the lovely shrine of Buddha, the collection of butterflies; each was examined with a measure of secular awe. At one stage Hitler stood frozen looking at the plate of the great composer's last photograph. He stopped at a chest of drawers and closed his eyes. Then slowly he opened the drawer and saw Wagner's reading glasses just where he had left them. When the Allies bombed Bayreuth twenty or so years later the same pair of glasses was to be rescued from the ruins of the building. He ran his fingers over the black Steck piano on which Wagner composed *Parsifal*. Wagner's wooden feet, which served as a model for his shoemaker, were picked up and handled like holy relics.[50] What sort of god was needed to fill the shoes of the Master of Bayreuth?

Many were not privy to the secrets kept upstairs. Somehow Winifred knew that the visitor was special – taking him by the hand she led him upstairs to the bedroom and showed him the couch on which Wagner died in Venice. At last he found the words to express his wonder and he told Frau Wagner that he intended to make the Bayreuth festival the cultural summit of artistic life in Germany.

She looked up at the young man whose eyes shone with fire and quietly told him of the financial problems that were being experienced. At that stage, the problems arose out of the consequences of the war but Hitler was to face this problem most acutely in the mid thirties when the festival became a Nazi showpiece. By that stage, Winifred was at the helm of a most controversial ship. Her brother-in-law Chamberlain had made sure that posterity judged the Master with the respect he deserved by writing the authentic biography. Hitler closed his eyes as he confirmed the lasting impression that book had on him and turned to Siegfried, the son whom Wagner had described as born with the sword in his eye.

Siegfried, initially at any rate, did not seem to share his wife's veneration for the young politician. He confirmed that the festival would feature *Parsifal*, the *Ring* and *Meistersinger*. The composer's only son told him that he was working with the renowned set designer Kranich and they had

---

50. Wagner, Nike, *The Wagners*, 179.

replaced the flat hand-painted canvas with three-dimensional scenery.[51] At the conclusion of the *Ring* the scenery would realistically represent the burning of Valhalla and the end of the world. The electric power still came from a disused locomotive, Siegfried told the young politician, but that was soon to be changed for a Trafo-station with four rows of switches and 144 levers to achieve unseen and magical lighting effects.[52]

Hitler thought of Parsifal and the fall of Klingsor's palace. He smiled indulgently as he imagined the feast of sounds in that magical score; what with the bells pealing and the orchestra interweaving motif after motif in a huge polyphonic mosaic. As he looked at the rooms his mind took in the journey of a young Parsifal from the enchanted forest to the great vaulted cupola of the Temple of the Holy Grail. He saw the agony of the wounded Amfortas whose wound would never heal. Again there was silence as the group moved through Wahnfried. Hitler looked at the six marble statues presented by King Ludwig of Bavaria representing Wagnerian heroes: Lohengrin, Siegfried, Tannhäuser, Tristan, Walter von Stolzing and Parsifal.

Siegfried Wagner coughed and sought an appropriate moment to introduce a sensitive topic. He was worried at the new attitude to race in the country, and troubled in his quest to obtain the best singers, given that many artists who sang at Bayreuth were Jewish. Hitler mumbled that some arrangement could be made. The topic was quickly changed and Winifred asked him how the party was developing. Hitler told them they were planning to seize power that year as Streseman's Jewish government had to fall – Hitler and his party had enough SA men to carry the day. Ludendorff, Hess and Göring were doing great work preparing the people for a government that understood the future of Germany. For a moment the humble disciple was gone and he raised his voice to announce that Munich was the key to Bavaria and from there the whole Reich would be at their mercy.[53]

Hitler regained his subservience when he was introduced to Chamberlain, who had married Richard Wagner's daughter Eva on December 27, 1908. It was not always clear whether this was a love match or a marriage

---

51. Wagner and Cooper, *Heritage of Fire*, 6–8.
52. Richard Wagner Museum brochure, items 47–51.
53. Wagner and Cooper, *Heritage of Fire*, 6–9.

of convenience to secure a foothold in the family. From his honeymoon Chamberlain wrote to Cosima that "we confessed to each other that, over and above a love between man and woman sanctified by marriage, we felt that our relationship had something brotherly and sisterly about it, so that we found it difficult to imagine that we had not always lived together."[54] The couple was given a house next to Wahnfried by Cosima as a wedding present and they moved in immediately.[55]

In a letter on January 1, 1912 to Kaiser Wilhelm II, Chamberlain said that the "exalted mother [Cosima], in the goodness of her heart, has given this union her blessing. I have the feeling that this marriage is bringing me closer to Your Majesty both in space and in spirit."[56] He described Wagner as the center and sun of his life and moved on to more familiar Wagnerian rhetoric. The composer's work struck at "the life-giving nerve of a reborn Germany, a Germany which had been freed from the crushing embrace of the Jews."[57] Cosima's anti-democratic sentiments have been mentioned and these were echoed by the sycophantic Chamberlain who recommended that the Kaiser call a meeting of all the political parties in the Reichstag "and blow the whole place sky-high with dynamite."[58] In the Kaiser he was to find a Wagner fan who was sufficiently enamored of the composer's music to have had his motor horn tuned to the Thunder motif from *Das Rheingold*. The tetralogy made people believe in his view that the Germans were the leaders of Europe and perhaps the world.[59]

Hitler had read and admired Chamberlain's work *Foundations of the Nineteenth Century*[60] and his autobiography *Pathways of My Thoughts* published in 1919. In addition Chamberlain had written books on Kant and Goethe. His love of his new Fatherland had not always stood him in good stead in his adopted country, especially during the First World War, when he was accused of being a British spy. Indignantly he demanded public vindication and then applied for German citizenship, which was not granted until the Kaiser intervened.

---

54. Marek, *Cosima Wagner*, 263.
55. Wagner, Nike, *The Wagners*, 193.
56. Ibid., 194.
57. Köhler, *Wagner's Hitler*, 114.
58. Ibid.
59. Marek, *Cosima Wagner*, 253
60. Wagner and Cooper, *Heritage of Fire*, 42.

Such a drastic act had infuriated his erstwhile countrymen and his fortune in England was confiscated. His relatives there called him a traitor. In 1915 he became subject to a creeping paralysis that was to rob him finally of all meaningful movement.[61] The First World War according to Chamberlain was a "diabolical attack, a calculated act of plunder and murder" and had taken place because "England has fallen into the hands of the Jews and the Americans…it is basically a struggle on the part of the Jews and their allies, the Americans, to rule the world."[62]

It was clear why he had fitted so seamlessly into life at Wahnfried and taken over the ideological mantle of the composer, without missing a beat. Chamberlain told the theologian Alfred von Harnack, "with all the strength at my command I hate the Jews and hate them and hate them." With a vehemence worthy of the stable he had joined he continued, "Their very existence is an offence against the divine laws of life," and they could only be "purged from an offence…they have committed without knowing it."[63] Salvation would not come from the aristocracy or the politicians for as Chamberlain said in 1916, after the onset of his withering disease, the bright new sword would come from "a man from the trenches…that is where our redeemer will come from."[64]

Despite this reservation his friends and admirers reached to the highest echelons of German society and the Kaiser attributed *The Foundations of the Nineteenth Century* to God and prescribed it in all the schools. Hitler accepted the Divine Authorship for an additional reason – Chamberlain had based his ideas on race on the rabid and poisonous regeneration writings of Richard Wagner.

In his book Chamberlain interpreted European history in a series of bold hypotheses as the history of the racial struggle. Heiden, the great biographer of Hitler, was no lover of the Nazis but he acknowledged that Chamberlain "was one of the most astonishing talents in the history of the German mind, a mine of knowledge and profound ideas."[65] Chamberlain advanced his theory that the human races were in reality as different from one another in character as were dogs such as the greyhound, bulldog,

---

61. Shirer, *Rise and Fall of the Third Reich*, 137–44.
62. Köhler, *Wagner's Hitler*, 130.
63. Ibid., 170.
64. Köhler, *Wagner's Hitler*, 132.
65. Shirer, *Rise and Fall of the Third Reich*, 139.

poodle, and Newfoundland dog – and of course the German shepherd dog, the true Aryan of dogs. "Once you have recognized the miracles selection can achieve, how a race horse or a dachshund or an 'exuberant' chrysanthemum is gradually bred by carefully eliminating all inferior elements, then you will also recognize the efficiency of the same phenomenon in the human race."[66] He referred to one of the most "beneficial laws of the Greeks, Romans, and Germans" in the achieving of this, namely, "the marooning of frail children" with the aim of strengthening the race. Chamberlain believed that the Aryan race and more particularly the Teutonic division of the Aryan race, had proved so superior to other races in essential qualities that all modern advances in art, science, philosophy, religion and politics could be traced to it.[67] "Just as a pearl can be grown through the medium of an artificial stimulant, so the German mind must guide the Aryan peoples to racial supremacy and world domination."[68]

He regarded the decline of the Roman Empire as the classical model of historical decadence resulting from contamination of bloodlines. Like declining Rome he posited the Dual Monarchy as being swamped by the admixture of oriental races and warned ominously that the "disease was advancing at a furious pace."[69] In both cases "not one specific nation, not just one people or one race" was causing disintegration, but "a motley agglomeration" of races.

This racial hodgepodge was the consequence of multiple mixings by people with "easy talents and also the peculiar beauty that the French call 'un charme troublant'…frequently characteristic of bastards. Nowadays this can daily be observed in cities where, as in Vienna, a wide variety of races meet. But at the same time one can also perceive the peculiar spinelessness, the low resistance, the lack of character, in short the moral degeneration of such people."

Chamberlain carried the parallel even further comparing the Teutons, thronging the gates of Rome, with the noble race of Prussians who had rightly been victorious in their clash with the racially chaotic Austro-Hungarian monarchy. His definitions were somewhat disappointing for those hoping for a blonde Siegfried model for the utopian Aryan – "whoever

---

66. Hamann, *Hitler's Vienna*, 203.
67. Kershaw, *Hitler 1936–1945: Nemesis*, 135.
68. Ravenscroft, *Spear of Destiny*, 116.
69. Fest, *Hitler*, 55 and following pages.

behaves as a Teuton is a Teuton, whatever his racial origin."[70] But the mood of this elitist individualist was far from cocky, and he was filled with anxiety and defensiveness. In recurrently pessimistic visions he saw the Teutons "on the brink of the racial abyss engaged in a mute life and death struggle." He was tormented by fantasies of bastardization. "It is still morning but again and again the powers of darkness stretch out their octopus arms to fasten their sucking cups on us in a hundred places and try to draw us back into the darkness."[71]

The Germanophile sounded a chord in the heart of Hitler with his elevation of the cultural ancestors of his people. "The Teuton is the soul of our culture…If we look around we see that the importance of each nation…is dependent upon the proportion of genuinely Teutonic blood in its population." Of the Teutons the Germans are the highest order and that gave them the right to be masters of the world. "God builds today upon the Germans alone. This is the knowledge, the certain truth, that has filled my soul for years."[72]

Though the trumpet call to German nationalism and the emergence of the *Herrenvolk* must have been crystal clear to every reader, some found that he had not gone far enough in propagating the message from Bayreuth. After Chamberlain had written his book Cosima wrote to him in May 1899 and said: "I wish to emphasize above all…your reasonable and convincing treatment of the racial question…I was astonished that you ascribe 'intellect' to the Jews. I would rather have thought 'cleverness.' They are anarchic (which Christianity is not)…I regret your chapters [*The Jews as Prophets* and *Christ a Jew?*] I do not find your proofs convincing."[73]

Not much is known about what transpired when the young Nazi politician met the aged and infirm "prophet." Writing to Hitler a week later on October 7 Chamberlain lauded him not as a precursor but as the savior himself. He had expected to meet a fanatic, he wrote, but now his instinct told him that Hitler was of a higher order; more creative and despite his palpable force of will, not a man of violence. The meeting, Chamberlain

---

70. Shirer, *Rise and Fall of the Third Reich*, 140.
71. Ibid.
72. Ibid., 141.
73. Marek, *Cosima Wagner*, 262.

Houston Stewart Chamberlain died after a long and painful illness. He is shown here as an old and sick man. Wagners Welten, page 237. Münchner Stadtmuseum/Fotomuseum, Nachlass Verlag, Hanfstaengl.

added, had set his soul at rest for, "The fact that in the hour of her greatest need Germany should produce a Hitler is a sign that she is yet alive."[74]

Winifred wrote a letter to the young politician which revealed some understanding of his racial program of future years. "For years we have been following with the greatest inner sympathy and approval the uplifting work of Adolf Hitler, this German man who, filled with ardent love for his fatherland, is sacrificing his life for his idea of a *purified*, united, national greater Germany, who has set himself the task of opening the eyes of the working class to the enemy within…" She also said she believed that he was "the coming man" and it was his task to draw the sword out of the German oak. This last reference was pregnant with meaning for the Wagnerian as it referred to Sigmund in *The Valkyries* drawing from the oak the sword with which he would fight for the (pure Aryan) Volsung race against their mortal enemies the Nibelungs (Jews).[75]

And Siegfried whom many regarded as incapable of racism wrote to a friend: "The times of the Spanish Inquisition have returned. Perjury and betrayal are sanctified, and Jew and Jesuit are working hand in glove to

---

74. Fest, *Hitler*, 180–81.
75. Hamann, *Winifred Wagner*, 91.

exterminate Germanness! But perhaps Satan has miscalculated this time. Should the German cause really succumb, then I'll believe in Jehovah, the god of revenge and hatred. My wife is fighting like a lioness for Hitler – first rate!"[76]

A pamphlet was issued three months later from Bayreuth lauding Hitler as a rare phenomenon whose courage matched Luther's and who also shared Bismarck's diplomacy, no "mere peddler of empty phrases" but a person who had "thought through the logic of his ideas and drew the conclusions without flinching."[77] Few would doubt the courage of Martin Luther but his views on Judaism have long been shrouded in mystery and conjecture. Four hundred years before Hitler, Luther had said of the Jews: "they hold us captive in our country. They let us work in the sweat of our noses, to earn money and property for them, while they sit behind the oven, lazy, let off gas, bake pears (an idiom for laziness), eat, drink, live softly and well from our wealth. They…mock us and spit on us, because we work and permit them to be lazy squires who own us and our realm."[78]

The German poet and writer Heinrich Heine, who had befriended Wagner in Paris, had called Luther "the most German man of our history" and written fulsome praise for the founder of the new church. "He was at the same time a visionary mystic and a practical man of action. His thoughts not only had wings; they had hands…The man who could curse like a fishwife could be tender as a young virgin. After spending a day working out rigorous scholastic distinctions, he took up his flute at night and lost himself in melody and reflection among the stars. Often he was as wild as the storm that uproots oaks, and then gentle as the zephyr that strokes the violets. He could become completely absorbed by spirituality…his was the motto, 'Who loves not wine, women, song – Remains a fool his whole life long…' In his character was combined in the most magnificent way, all the virtues and vices of the Germans."[79]

When cursing like a fishwife, as Erik Eriksen has recorded in his book on the young Luther, he found practical remedies for the devil and suggested one should "fart in his face" and addressed his own personal message to him. "Note this down; I have shit in my pants, and you can hang them

---

76. Wagner, Gottfried, *Twilight of the Wagners*, 70–71.
77. Köhler, *Wagner's Hitler*, 16.
78. Goldhagen, *Hitler's Willing Executioners*, 284.
79. Waite, *The Psychopathic God*, 248–49.

around your neck and wipe your mouth with it."[80] He advocated marriage for pastors and made arrangements to help nuns escape, one of whom, Katharina von Bora, became his wife. He believed women should stay at home: "the way they were created indicates this, for they have hips and a wide fundament to sit upon." He preferred bigamy to divorce and thought that if a married man needed another female companion he should rather take a mistress.[81] Luther's message to politicians and the attitude that they should adopt must have been of great comfort to those who peddle that infamous trade. "The princes of this world are gods, the common people are Satan…I would rather suffer a prince doing wrong than a people doing right."[82]

He wrote a venomous pamphlet *On the Jews and their Lies* and his program of 1543 was emphatic as to how Jews were to be treated. "*First*, to set fire to their synagogues or schools…*Second* I advise that their houses also be razed and destroyed…*Third*, I advise that all their prayer books and Talmudic writings, in which such adultery, lies, cursing and blasphemy are taught, be taken from them…*Fourth* I advise that their Rabbis be forbidden to teach henceforth on pain of loss of life and limb…*Fifth*, I advise that safe-conduct on the highways be abolished completely for the Jews. *Sixth*, I advise that…all cash and treasure of silver and gold be taken from them…*Seventh*…Let whosoever can, throw brimstone and pitch upon them. So much the better…and if this be not enough, let them be driven like mad dogs out of the land…"[83]

The program of action for Hitler could not be clearer. It was no accident that Hitler was reported to have said "side by side with Friedrich the Great stands Martin Luther as well as Richard Wagner."[84] Can it be an accident that Hitler chose Luther's birthday for the launching of the first full-scale attack on the Jews, *Kristallnacht*, November 9–10, 1938? History records that Friedrich the Great (1712 – 1786) was gay and his picture accompanied Hitler from his house to the military headquarters in the field and to his final redoubt in the depths of the Chancellery bunker. It is a pity he did not adopt the Prussian king's religious views. "All religions must

---

80. Ibid., 254.
81. Wallace et al., *Intimate Sex Lives of Famous People*, 282.
82. Ibid.
83. Waite, *The Psychopathic God*, 250.
84. Ibid., 248.

be tolerated…for in this country every man must get to heaven his own way" was a marginal note he made on a report by the Board of Religion on June 22, 1740.[85]

No one knows what Hitler and Chamberlain discussed when they met in Bayreuth. What can be gleaned from subsequent letters written by Chamberlain shows that it was that hardy old annual – the Aryan race and anti-Semitism – but now dressed up in a far more menacing garb. From this Hitler must have realized his own views had the official sanction of the cultural and political heir to Wagner – indeed a family member.

The oracle continued with his prophecies. On New Year's Day 1924 Chamberlain wrote an open letter to the newspaper saying that Hitler was "bequeathed by God" as the new leader "who loves his German *volk* with a fervent passion from which…his oft-deplored anti-Semitism flows."[86] He went on to say that "Hitler's greatest quality is courage, which he possesses in abundance. In this he reminds us of Luther…and to what do these two men owe their courage?…to their religious seriousness…[and it is inconceivable that Hitler] should share *our awareness of the lethal influence exerted by the Jews on the life of the German nation without taking the appropriate action*."[87] His conclusions are horrific. "Once the threat to the German race has been recognized, counter-measures must immediately be taken. Everyone knows this but no one dares say so – no one dares to act on the conclusions to which these thoughts lead. No one, that is, except Adolf Hitler." If Chamberlain's source was the turgid racist prose of Wagner, the avowed and recognizable basis of Hitler's racial doctrines was Chamberlain's *Foundations of the Nineteenth Century*.[88]

Hitler and his ragtag bunch of hooligans, which included Alfred Rosenberg, Rudolf Hess, Hermann Göring, and Julius Streicher, went ahead and tried to seize power in Munich but their attempted putsch, commencing in the Bürgerbräu beer cellar, failed. Siegfried and Winifred Wagner were by chance in a hotel opposite the Feldherrnhalle and saw the march and the shooting.[89] Earlier in the day workers had made fun of the march

---

85. Leonard, *Quotationary*, 294.
86. Köhler, *Wagner's Hitler*, 173.
87. Ibid., 174.
88. Hitler, *Mein Kampf*, 258, 544–45.
89. Wagner and Cooper, *Heritage of Fire*, 14.

Adolf Hitler worshipped Richard Wagner like a god. He regarded himself as Wagner's only real heir and successor and is depicted here as Siegfried, the Aryan hero of the four-part cycle of operas – The Ring of the Nibelung. Sketch by George Grosz, 1923. From Larry Solomon website.

and the SA with their firearms. "Has your mummy given you permission to play with such dangerous things here on the street?" one worker asked.[90]

The painter Georg Grosz gave graphic content to the links between Hitler and Siegfried with a famous painting of the politician marching along in the guise of Siegfried armed with a spear. The painter was a member of the Spartacist opposition and the movement was to prove a thorn in the side of the growing Nazi party.[91] Even Siegfried, often regarded as the least sympathetic of the Wagners to the Nazis, approved Hitler and wrote to a friend before the putsch, "Hitler is a splendid man, a genuine German. He will not fail us,"[92] but complained that his wife was always running off to meetings in her efforts to help Hitler.[93] They were going to travel to America to raise funds to reopen the festival and were in Munich on that fatal day November 9, 1923. They saw Hitler marching down the street with General Ludendorff at the head of a company of storm troopers dressed in ordinary khaki waterproof jackets.

Hitler was subsequently injured in the shoulder during the march but was lucky to be pulled down during the march by a fellow marcher named

---

90. Kershaw, *Hitler 1936–1945: Nemesis*, 210.
91. Sheffi, *Ring of Myths*, 32.
92. Köhler, *Wagner's Hitler*, 178.
93. Wagner, Nike, *The Wagners*, 161.

Erwin von Scheubner-Richter, who died and became one of the Nazis first martyrs. As Ian Kershaw put it, "Had the bullet which killed Erwin been a foot to the right, history would have taken a different course."[94] Walter Langer, an American psychiatrist who later analyzed Hitler, reported two other versions of the incident. "Some report that when the troops fired on them Hitler fell to the ground and crawled through an alley which carried him to safety while Ludendorff, Röhm and Göring marched ahead. Some claim that he stumbled, others that he was knocked down by his bodyguard, who was killed. The Nazi version is that he stopped to pick up a small child who had run out into the street and been knocked down! Years later they produced a child on the anniversary of the event to prove the story!"[95]

Göring was shot in the groin – shades of the wounded Amfortas of *Parsifal* fame – and fled to Innsbruck in Austria and Siegfried helped him to get to Venice. His wife Carin was also ill but Siegfried sorted out the bills. Five days after the attempted putsch anyone attempting to purchase an American dollar needed 837,900,000,000 marks.[96] There were problems in America when a rumor was spread that Siegfried had spent festival funds, donated by opera fans around the world, on the failed putsch. Winnie had raised money for the other Nazis who were jailed at the same time and this had landed her in trouble. The chief of police in Bayreuth had warned Winifred to stay away from the Nazi troublemakers.

After Hitler's arrest and incarceration in Landsberg prison Winifred brought him his favorite sweets and cakes and wrote an open letter to the press giving him her blessing. "For years we have been following with the deepest personal sympathy and approval the constructive work of Adolf Hitler, this German man who, filled with the most ardent love of his Fatherland, sacrifices his life for his ideal of a purified, united national Greater Germany, who has taken upon himself the dangerous task of opening the eyes of the working class to the internal enemy and the danger of Marxism and its consequences, who has managed as no one else to bring people together as brothers, who has learned how to overcome implacable class hatred and who has given thousands upon thousands of confused people the welcome hope and firm belief in a revived, worthy Fatherland."[97]

---

94. Kershaw, *Hitler 1936–1945: Nemesis*, 211.
95. Langer, OSS *Psychological Report on Adolf Hitler*, 230–31.
96. Hamann, *Winifred Wagner*, 92.
97. Spotts, *Bayreuth*, 141–42.

Of great interest was the account Winifred gave of her support of the Nazis to the Denazification Tribunal after the war, in which she managed to pass herself off as an unwilling bystander. Europe was full of "innocents" in the postwar years.

Hitler and nine others including Ludendorff were charged with treason on February 24, 1924. Two days later Ludendorff spoke in Bayreuth in support of the Nazi Party for the election. He agitated against reparations quoting Friedrich the Great, "only cowards submit to the yoke and drag their chains in capitulation and submit peacefully to the oppressor." Bearing in mind the venue he very naturally quoted Wagner to the effect that his audience were "heroic German people."[98] After the election Hitler wrote one of his longest letters to Siegfried and Winifred Wagner ascribing the election successes to their help, and explained how he was filled with pride and joy. The Bayreuth victory had been the result of the use of the spiritual sword forged by Wagner and Chamberlain.[99]

At his trial Hitler had the court and the gallery eating out of his hand. During the proceedings, which lasted all of twenty-four days, he crossexamined the witnesses brought forward by the authorities. During his defense he took the opportunity of making a lengthy address to the court mentioning his debt to Wagner. For maximum impact he rehearsed his speech until he knew it by heart. In later years Hitler's secretary was to say that he had great talent as an actor and could impersonate anybody.[100] Gone was the grubby revolutionary and in his place was the utopian patriot – working and fighting for a Germany free of Marxists and Jews.

All the newspapers carried news of his address and Hitler was mindful of its importance to his future political career. "In what small terms tiny minds think! I want you to come away from here with the clear understanding that I do not covet the post of a minister. I consider it unworthy of a great man to want to make his name go down in history by becoming a minister…What I had in mind from the very first day was a thousand times more important than becoming a minister. I wanted to become the destroyer of Marxism. I shall carry through this task, and when I do, the title of minister would be utterly ridiculous. *When I first stood at Wagner's*

---

98. Hamann, *Winifred Wagner*, 118.
99. Ibid., 119–20.
100. Köhler, *Wagner's Hitler*, 144.

grave, my heart overflowed with pride that here was a man who had forbidden his family to write on his stone, 'Here lies Privy-councillor, Music Director, his excellency Baron Richard von Wagner.' I was proud that this man and so many men in German history have been content to transmit their name to posterity, not their titles."[101]

After saying this he added something that signified the end of one role and the assumption of another. It also harked back to his time in the Pasewalk hospital and his cure from psychological blindness. "No longer did modesty dictate that I be the drummer. I wanted the top position and the rest was too petty." He impressed many with his eloquence but was found guilty of treason and sentenced to five years imprisonment. At the close of the trial his supporters thronged the public areas outside the courthouse yelling "Heil Hitler" and called repeatedly for him until the warders permitted him to appear and say a few words.[102]

He spent only nine months in Landsberg jail and while there he dictated *Mein Kampf* to his friend Rudolf Hess on writing materials sent by Winifred Wagner.[103] The prison authorities made things very comfortable for them and they were allowed visitors as often as they chose. A copy of Chamberlain's book on Wagner could be found on Hitler's bookshelf in prison.[104] On April 20, 1920 – his thirty-fifth birthday – military airplanes flew around making swoops and saluting the jailed leader and his cell resembled a candy store with sweetmeats of every description.[105] He told Hess that had he a greater talent for hypocrisy he would have entered the ministry. When he had ascended to the highest position in the ecclesiastical world he would have started a new Reformation and revolt within the institution.[106]

Naturally he made a point of taking along a portable phonograph and a set of recordings from the Wagner operas.[107] While he was dictating *Mein Kampf* he used to listen to excerpts of the operas including the Prelude to *Parsifal*, the Transformation and the Good Friday music. From

---

101. Fest, *Hitler*, 192.
102. Waite, *The Psychopathic God*, 214.
103. Wagner and Cooper, *Heritage of Fire*, 16–17.
104. Köhler, *Wagner's Hitler*, 123.
105. Waite, *The Psychopathic God*, 215.
106. Koch-Hillebrecht, *Homo Hitler*, 63.
107. See B. Lansing, "Adolf Hitler," *Life*, Sept 25, 1939.

the *Ring of the Nibelungs* he listened to Siegfried's funeral march and the Forest Murmurs music.[108] Attendance at the performance was obviously prohibited but if he could not get to the operas he was determined to have the music with him.

Again and again he played the records – the music and its subconscious message seeped slowly into his heart – the rhythms of a bygone age. The narcotic effects of the stirring passages made him aware of what his mission was – to make Germany great and pure. His long experience of the operas and the leading motifs associated with events in the dramas meant that ever after Hitler had the habit of humming Wagnerian music to himself during political conversations.[109]

The excess of sweetmeats provided by Winifred and others meant that he put on a lot of weight while in prison because he refused to participate in the games and exercise privileges. His explanation showed the extent of his egotistical self-image. "No. I keep away from them. It would be bad for discipline if I took part in physical training. A leader cannot afford to be beaten at games."[110]

Hitler's time was spent in planning the future and his ideas included little that cannot be traced to earlier writers such as Wagner, Gobineau and Chamberlain. Writing to Siegfried from prison to thank him for his help, as well as assistance for the party in the recent political campaign, he prophetically pronounced that Bayreuth was "on the line of march to Berlin" and indeed it was the place on his ideological journey where "first the Master and then Chamberlain forged the spiritual sword with which we fight today."[111]

In his monumental account of the period Shirer quotes Hitler as saying "whoever wants to understand National Socialism must know Wagner."[112] Of principal importance in *Mein Kampf*, of course, was the question of race. He regarded inequality between races and individuals as part of an unchangeable natural order and the Aryan race was very naturally, given his sources, seen as the sole creative element of mankind. The natural unit of mankind was the *Volk*, of which the German was the greatest. The *Volk*

---

108. Viereck, *Metapolitics*, 136.
109. Ibid.
110. Waite, *The Psychopathic God*, 215.
111. Spotts, *Bayreuth*, 142.
112. Shirer, *Rise and Fall of the Third Reich*, 133.

was to be served by the state and this mission had eluded the decadent Weimar Republic.

There was a thinly veiled reference to the man of destiny lying asleep in the "limestone crags" of the Obersalzberg, as Wagner had predicted, after pontificating about Barbarossa, in the insane excesses of his regeneration writings. The unity of the *Volk* found its incarnation in the Führer, endowed with absolute authority. The title of Führer was thought to have emanated from the opera *Lohengrin* where the line appears "Zum Führer sei er euch ernannt!" – Accept him as your leader.[113] Below the Führer the movement was recruited from the best elements of the *Volk*. The greatest enemy of Nazism was Marxism, which for him embraced Social Democracy as well as Communism, and internationalism and class conflict. Behind Marxism he saw the greatest enemy of all – the Jew.

The passages in *Mein Kampf* should have warned any reader that a fanatic was bent on wreaking vengeance for previous slights. He stigmatized money-lending and usury as an evil which was monopolized by the Jews. Again the sources were clearly Wagnerian, who had addressed these very topics in his early essay *The Wibelungs* of 1848 and come back to it in his political dotage. The scourge of usury was now linked to prostitution and the management of the world's oldest profession was in Semitic hands. "I did vacillate for a long time over the Jewish question. Then I made the acquaintance of a Jewish pimp. When I saw the Jew for the first time in this role of an ice-cold, shameless efficient manager of this disgraceful and vicious commerce amongst the dregs of the city, a chill ran up my spine. Then everything exploded inside me, I no longer shrank from discussion of the Jewish question. On the contrary, I actively sought it out."[114]

After the First World War he had became a voracious reader and read books from the libraries and spoke to all manner of people. He was determined to find out what the Jew was doing to his city and country. *Mein Kampf* was the product of his investigations. There were many who immediately linked the title with Wagner's autobiography *Mein Leben* (My Life). Other parts of the book confirmed Hitler's obsession with the Jews and his solution should have warned any reader that their total destruction was planned. "Today it is not princes and princes' mistresses who haggle

---

113. Spotts, *Bayreuth*, 141.
114. Hitler, *Mein Kampf*, 61.

and bargain over state borders; it is the inexorable Jew who struggles for his domination over the nations. *No nation can remove this hand from its throat except by the sword.* Only the assembled and concentrated might of a national passion rearing up in its strength will be able to defy the international enslavement of peoples. Such a process is and remains a bloody one."

The perverted sexuality, of which some examples have been cited – and who knew what further obscenities lurked in the dark recesses of his twisted soul – was linked to the anti-Semitism as emerges from another passage from *Mein Kampf*: "Was there any form of filth or profligacy, particularly in cultural life, without at least one Jew involved in it? If you cut even cautiously into such an abscess, you found, like a maggot in a rotting body, often dazzled by the sudden light – a kike…The relations of the Jews to prostitution and, even more, to the white slave traffic, could be studied in Vienna as perhaps in no other city in Western Europe, with the possible exception of southern French ports."[115] Hitler had a paranoid fear of syphilis and hatred for prostitutes and devoted ten full pages in *Mein Kampf* to the topic.[116] Was this the reason he was to handle women in the strange way he did? Or was it the homosexuality that had manifested itself from time to time? When his war minister Blomberg married a woman thirty-five years his junior, with Hitler's consent, and he discovered that she had been registered as a prostitute by the Berlin police, Hitler is reported to have bathed seven times to remove the taint of his lips which had kissed the hand of the woman.[117]

The images of maggots in a rotten body refer directly back to Wagner's horrible metaphors in his attack in "Jewry in Music" on Jewish composers, chief among them Giacomo Meyerbeer. When Hitler dealt with his interpretation of the opera *Die Meistersinger von Nürnberg* he showed how much he had read. The story of the opera sketches the rivalry of Beckmesser (the proto-Jew), with (the Aryan) Walther for Eva, the daughter of Pogner, one of the established mastersingers of Nürnberg. Beckmesser was a town clerk and Hitler states that in the First World War in the army "almost every clerk was a Jew and almost every Jew a clerk." He returns

---

115. Redlich, *Hitler: Diagnosis of a Destructive Prophet*, 31.
116. Ibid., 32.
117. Kershaw, *Hitler 1936–1945: Nemesis*, 53.

to what Wagner and Schumann had been saying nearly a hundred years before. "What the Jews have produced in the field of art is either parody or plagiary."[118] Nietzsche was very perceptive when he called *Meistersinger* "a lance against civilization."[119]

While in prison Hitler was shown a cartoon of himself that had appeared in a magazine. It showed the young politician riding a stallion like Rienzi, victoriously entering the Brandenburg Gate. What would have doubled his pleasure was that the cartoon showed that at his side rode the emperor Barbarossa. Clearly the leader had awoken from his magic sleep and was accompanying the new savior of Germany in his role as Führer. Finally the prescient drawing showed that, beneath a fluttering swastika, a Teutonic warrior was killing a Jew. If a picture is better than a thousand words the artist had captured the link Hitler hoped the German people would make. The Führer predicted by Wagner to be sleeping at the Obersalzberg was returning to save the country and get rid of the Jews. Asked if the cartoon accurately portrayed his mission Hitler said "that can happen provided we remain firm." The artist Thomas Heine, a Jew, had a premonition of what was to come – not only in general terms but also with particular reference to his own personal safety – and fled in 1933.[120]

What Wagner had stated in his late writings when he called for a "great solution" to the Jews was a theme Hitler was to address without equivocation and circumlocution in *Mein Kampf*. "The Jews are fighting unremittingly for domination of the whole world. The only way to get rid of the hand that has us by the throat is by the sword. The only force that can stand up against this worldwide enslavement is the concerted resistance of a powerful national passion. This cannot happen without bloodletting…Can one in fact eliminate ideas with the sword?"[121] His answer to the question was that force alone would not be enough "unless it takes the form of the complete annihilation of all who hold that idea, down to the very last person and the removal of all traces of that idea."[122]

The heirs of his political mentor Wagner were to be called upon to put their seal of approval on his emphatic program for the extermination of

---

118. See Köhler, *Wagner's Hitler*, 261.
119. Viereck, *Metapolitics*, 98.
120. Köhler, *Wagner's Hitler*, 196.
121. Ibid., 207.
122. Ibid.

the Jewish race. Elsa Bruckmann, the wife of the publisher of *Mein Kampf*, says that the Chamberlains, husband and wife corrected the proofs and even the very old Cosima read parts of the book.[123] Their response has not been recorded but they altered not one jot or tittle of it. "The moving finger writes and having writ moves on…"

Prior to the putsch Hitler and General Erich Ludendorff took advantage of the prevailing lawlessness and opposition to the Weimar Republic to force the leaders of the Land government and the local Reichswehr commander to proclaim a national revolution. When released from Landsberg prison, however, they rescinded the proclamation. Hitler learned a valuable lesson from the putsch – that the movement must achieve power by legal means.

The Wagners went on a concert tour to America to find money for the festival and the Nazi Party and they successfully enlisted the aid of Henry Ford, a known anti-Semite. He published a book *The International Jew: the World's Foremost Problem* that incorporated a lot of material from the vicious forgery entitled the *Protocols of the Elders of Zion*. The last-mentioned work stands out in history as a gross distortion of the truth and was fabricated by the Russian Secret Police to help foment anti-Semitic pogroms.[124] Little is known of their success in soliciting funds from him but the probabilities favor that Ford would have dug deep into his pocket for them. So popular did the car manufacturer become with the Nazi regime that in 1938 Hitler honored Ford with a medal.[125] This was the highest honor a non-German could ever receive – the Grand Cross of the German Eagle. Ford's portrait hung behind Hitler's desk in his private study.[126]

Lest it be thought that the Wagners unevenly distributed their favors, they paid court to another dictator, whose machinations further south were coercing the peace-loving, musical Italians to see themselves as modern Caesars. They visited Mussolini on their return with Siegfried commenting on the similarities between his seizure of power and that of Rienzi.[127] The link with Hitler was to have a detrimental effect on the tour of America. Siegfried's concert tour of America raised only $8,000 and the fundraising

---

123. Köhler, *Wagner's Hitler*, 208.
124. Waite, *The Psychopathic God*, 119.
125. Wallace et al., *Intimate Sex Lives of Famous People*, 170.
126. Icke, *…and the truth shall set you free*, 104.
127. Köhler, *Wagner's Hitler*, 187.

was a failure because "since 1923 there existed a fast friendship between Wahnfried and the Fascist leader Hitler."[128]

During Hitler's absence in prison the Nazi Party disintegrated through internal dissension. Thanks to the efforts of the Wagner family ten thousand signatures were obtained to a petition asking for Hitler to be released. The governor of the prison wrote a very positive report on his most famous inmate, dated September 15, in which he mentioned, "[Hitler] is not drawn to the female sex. He meets women with whom he has contact on visits here with great politeness…"[129]

Posterity would be pleased to note that the governor described him as "a man of order and discipline, contented, modest, accommodating, quiet, reasonable, serious and without any abusiveness" who would be "no agitator against the government, no enemy of other parties with a nationalist leaning."[130] Apart from the writing paper and food parcels, Winifred sent Hitler "a touching sketch of the dear little ones." Siegfried's initial suspicions of the man had clearly evaporated as he wrote to a friend that Christmas saying that "we shall stay loyal to him even if it lands us in jail…[the defeat of Hitler's uprising has led] to the glorification of treachery and perjury, with Jew and Jesuit walking arm in arm in order to destroy the soul of the German people."[131]

Hitler was released on December 20 and Putzi Hanfstaengl arranged a celebration dinner in his new Munich home for the Nazi leader. The weather was icy and Hitler was wearing his ill-fitting blue serge suit but his indulgences in prison meant that it was tighter than usual. His first thoughts were not for the state of the party or the health or well-being of his guests; he asked for music and of course it had to be Wagner. He insisted that Putzi play the Liebestod from *Tristan und Isolde* on the piano immediately. After that Putzi played other favorite transcriptions from the operas and Hitler became less agitated – Cerberus had been pacified by the music of one Nietzsche called "the Orpheus of all our secret misery." Hitler then assumed the role of raconteur and mimic – he entertained the guests

---

128. Marek, *Cosima Wagner*, 271.
129. Kershaw, *Hitler 1936–1945: Nemesis*, 235.
130. Ibid.
131. Köhler, *Wagner's Hitler*, 185–86.

with imitations of all the weaponry used in the First World War, separately and then to their vast amusement and cheers, in unison.[132]

'Putzi' Hanfstaengl was another interesting personality to encroach on the inner circle; he was of German extraction but had spent five years at Harvard University in America. A bohemian life deserving of its own account, his private life was trenchantly described by a "lover" of his, Hanns Ewers, as "a maze of paths through a sexually pathological swamp." He made a marriage of convenience to Helene and returned to Munich in 1921 where he met Hitler after an introduction by the equally colorful Kurt Lüdecke. His rise was meteoric and as the *Münchener Post* wrote in 1923 "it was an open secret that Hitler listened to no one more readily than Ernst Hanfstaengl."[133]

Hanfstaengl told an American magazine how he got to know and serve Hitler for whom he had the greatest admiration. Hanfstaengl after describing his own life and how he accidentally became interested to attend a Hitler meeting tells of the typical beer hall gathering: "the audience was a nondescript crowd, men who were there out of sheer desperation. I regretted coming. I would have been happier working on my book." His literary efforts, incidentally never finished, were directed at a man who had helped Wagner out of his economic quagmire, Ludwig II of Bavaria.[134]

Drexler introduced Adolf Hitler and Hanfstaengl goes into raptures recalling the day. "He didn't look very impressive standing there in repose. That is, until you noticed his eyes. He had clear blue eyes and in them there was neither guile nor fear. There was honesty; there was sincerity; there was a hint of scorn." Hanfstaengl then went into an orgasmic rapture as the little man spoke. "Then he began to speak. More of a musician than anything else, I could only interpret his speech musically. He spoke mezzo voice, quietly, soothingly, at first. His hands never stopped moving and they fascinated me – as the hands of Fritz Kreisler had fascinated me. He had all of the effectiveness – but none of the tricks – of the trained orator."[135]

Hanfstaengl became an ardent disciple. "Within three minutes I felt the man's absolute sincerity and love for Germany. Within ten I had forgotten everything else but the words which that man was quietly dropping

---

132. Waite, *The Psychopathic God*, 215.
133. Machtan, *Hidden Hitler*, 129.
134. See Hanfstaengl, "My Leader."
135. Ibid.

into the consciousness of everyone present – words which burned all the more for their softness; words which lashed us as men who had failed in a great responsibility. Kreisler, you know, never comes to the end of his bow. He always leaves just the faint anticipation of a tone yet to come. Then suddenly those overtones are forgotten in a surge of dazzling, beautiful notes which march triumphantly toward a crescendo. Hitler was like that. He completely mesmerized that audience – without paralyzing it."

Hanfstaengl and his wife hid Hitler in their Uffing home for three nights before the police found out after the 1923 Munich Beer Hall Putsch. When Adolf Hitler walked into his home that Christmas Eve he was immediately at ease – Hanfstaengl clasped his hand warmly and gave him the greatest encouragement. "You will go on. Your party still lives. I have something for you – a good-luck talisman. It is an autograph of Friedrich the Great. He once sat beside a broken drum. He was once in the depths of despair after his defeat on the field of battle. But today Germany worships his memory and glory in his achievements." Hitler took the autograph of Friedrich. Years later the same picture was to adorn the walls of every redoubt Hitler occupied in the field.

It is not without significance that Friedrich was widely regarded as homosexual – he wrote to a curious nephew advising him to avoid "Greek pleasures" (sodomy, especially anal intercourse) because from "his personal experience" he could attest to the fact that it was "not pleasant."[136] The acerbic Voltaire, who often visited his court, recorded that Friedrich said that whereas King Solomon's harem of a thousand was not enough for him, "I have only one [Elizabeth Christine] and that is too much for me."[137] One of Hitler's most prized possessions was a letter of Friedrich the Great, given to him on his fiftieth birthday in 1939.[138] It was a fit companion to that of Ludwig II.

Ever the snob, Hanfstaengl found much in the little politician to sneer at. On Hitler's visits to the Hanfstaengl's house his awkward use of cutlery "betrayed his background," as the host was later to write. In other respects his description of various aspects of Hitler's personality was to be as accurate as any other. Putzi described Hitler as a "virtuoso on the keyboard

---

136. Wallace et al., *Intimate Sex Lives of Famous People*, 176.
137. Ibid.
138. Spotts, *Hitler and the Power of Aesthetics*, 102.

of the mass psyche" who shocked him when he put sugar in the vintage wine he gave him.[139] Although Hitler paid quaint Viennese style homage to Helene her feminine instincts revealed that he was no real threat to her "fidelity" – "he's an absolute neuter, not a man" was how she described his attentions.[140] She probably guessed that the awkward man was more interested in her "husband."

There is more than a hint that a sexual relationship developed and they spent nights together at Hitler's Thierschstrasse quarters. Putzi endeared himself by pounding out Wagner on the piano. Putzi later confessed to his son Egon – Hitler's godchild – that he found Hitler very attractive sexually and part of the attraction arose from the latter's speeches, which he described in a fascinating manner. "The whole fabric of leitmotifs, of musical embellishments, contrapuntal melodies and contrasts, was precisely reflected in the layout of his speeches; they were constructed like symphonies and culminated in an immense outburst like the sound of Wagnerian trombones."[141] The power of the man was compelling and in the thundering orations was situated a call to his libido – possibly an eargasm? It should not be forgotten that musicologists have identified two sexual orgasms in the score of *Tristan und Isolde*. Hanfstaengl recorded that Hitler knew *Meistersinger* "absolutely by heart and could whistle every note of it in a curious penetrating vibrato, but completely in tune."[142]

In the task of reconstruction after his release, Hitler faced a new and improbable enemy – currency reform and the Dawes Plan had achieved economic stability. Hitler's abortive coup attempt had immediate political consequences – he was forbidden to make speeches, first in Bavaria, then in many other German states until 1927. The lure of the Mecca of his career soon became too strong and he visited Bayreuth, where he became a regular visitor virtually until his death. He seldom came empty-handed – one of the first presents Hitler presented to Winifred was a gilt-edged copy of *Mein Kampf*, with an inscription that harked back to Wotan's alter ego in the Ring cycle – "From Wolf to Winnie."[143]

Hitler's incarceration had another consequence which caused him

---

139. Kershaw, *Hitler 1936–1945: Nemesis*, 187.
140. Ibid.
141. Machtan, *Hidden Hitler*, 131.
142. Toland, *Adolf Hitler*, 183.
143. Wagner, Gottfried, *Twilight of the Wagners*, 94.

great regret – it meant that he was not able to attend the first festival in Bayreuth in 1924, which became a refuge for members of the now banned Nazi Party. Wagner was described in the festival brochure as the "Führer of German Art," "a guide to National Socialism," a trailblazer of Nazism and the enemy of Americanism and Judaism.[144] In the same document an explanation was proffered as to what was to be done with the last-mentioned. Hans Grunsky, a friend of Chamberlain's, wrote that "an intense racial dislike" existed between the Nibelungs, who exercised "a pernicious influence on the rest of the world" and who he, unsurprisingly, equated to the Jews and Siegfried. With his review Grunsky carried an outrageous message of menace and violence. He told the theatergoers that there was a solution to the problem of the Nibelungs, "though we would be well advised not to explain in so many words what this solution involves."[145] It was a return to the innuendo of the early days of Cosima's advice to Nietzsche and her later campaign.

After the conclusion of the first opera, *Meistersinger*, three verses of *Deutschland über Alles* were sung and the liberal press and foreigners were horrified.[146] Siegfried responded immediately and forbade any connection with the Nazis and erected a sign forbidding singing after the operas.[147] It was a quote from Wagner's opera *Meistersinger* – "Art is what matters here." After the Second World War there was to be a repeat of the notice and a ban on political discussion, when theatergoers were questioning the role the Wagner family played in the events that unfolded in Nazi Germany. Despite his perceived weakness Siegfried could be resolute on occasion – he was also very firm with conductor Fritz Busch who raised questions about the singing and orchestral playing and was told to mind his own business.[148]

Money problems led to the German Bayreuth Festival Foundation being formed on June 21, 1921. Wagner societies led by Leipzig Wagnerian Richard Linneman wanted Jews excluded from their midst. The editor of the *Deutschen Zeitung* August Puringer advocated an Aryan paragraph for members of the festival foundation which had been the norm in many Wagner societies. The reaction from Jewish Wagnerians was one of justifi-

---

144. Spotts, *Bayreuth*, 142.
145. Köhler, *Wagner's Hitler*, 63.
146. Spotts, *Bayreuth*, 142.
147. Ibid.
148. Ibid., 18.

able outrage and Siegfried felt compelled to issue a statement via Puringer to gainsay them;

"We have amongst the Jews many true, honest and unselfish followers, who have given proof of their friendship in many different ways. We want to withdraw the notion that we have closed our doors to these people merely on the grounds of the fact that they are Jews. Is that humane? Is it Christian? Is it German? No!" It was certainly a big change but was it sincere and genuine? He went on to say: "On our festival hill we want to put forward a positive image not a negative one. It is a matter of complete indifference to us whether a person is Chinese, Negro, American, Indian or Jew." He included the sentiment that "the Germans could learn a lot about cooperation and mutual help from the Jews,"[149] and he finished off by saying that "If I was a Jew all my operas would have been performed in all theatres. As things now stand I have to wait even until I am dead." This has tended to leave the impression that anti-Semitism was not one of his faults.[150]

However it is clear that publicly he had to have consideration for the festival and be careful what he said. The Jews were a source of much needed money and he let it be known privately that his views about anti-Semitism had not changed.[151] After his death in 1930, the Nazis took possession of his papers from Winifred and they ended up in Berlin, where they were captured by the Russians in 1945. They were recently discovered (2001) in Moscow and make mention of his exchanges with a certain Dr. Salomon, the rabbi of Bayreuth.

The rabbi wrote to Siegfried in June 1924, complaining of a rise in "anti-Semitic influences," to which Siegfried replied, "We are against the Marxist spirit, [but] we have nothing against patriotic Jews…" He referred to the fact that many of his father's friends were Jews and that Jewish singers had been hired at the festivals which proved that Richard Wagner was no anti-Semite. Siegfried did mention that the Jews were alleged to be foreigners in Germany and anti-Semitism was a defense against their perceived anti-German feelings. He gave an example of the old Israel and asked what the Jews would have done had a foreign nation settled there

---

149. Hamann, *Winifred Wagner*, 68.
150. Spotts, *Bayreuth*, 154.
151. Hamann, *Winifred Wagner*, 68.

and thereafter derided and undermined their religion and priesthood and institutions of civil society.[152] He continued by saying: "Although I have found regrettable things in my father's handwriting, I have no bad feelings for Jews – that must be understood. Some of them have been of great help to me in my work." Siegfried expressed misgivings against half caste Jews but said he had much liking for pure Jews. The rabbi was persistent and wanted to know exactly where Siegfried stood on Nazism. "Art reaches us through the heart," replied Siegfried evasively, "and God gave hearts to all human beings."[153]

Foreigners took more and more interest in attending and taking part in the festival, a feature that was to irritate Hitler and other Germans. Mention was made of the fact that at the first festival in 1876 a harpist from New York by the name of Orleana Boker was in the pit. French, Britons and Americans were predominant among the theatergoers, though the last mentioned were sneered at and referred to as "Wagnerized Yankees" and came to represent vulgar and commercial philistines. The failure of the American fundraising trip and the commercial success of the New World was partly responsible for the xenophobia. In the 1931 season the *Frankfurter Zeitung* made special mention of an American visitor who slept through three-quarters of *Parsifal* and when she awoke – after the ecstatic applause – joined in the clapping with gusto and said, "wasn't it wonderful?"[154] Hitler had nothing but contempt for Americans. "I feel the deepest hatred and repulsion towards anything American. In its whole outlook America is half-Jewish, half-Negroid society…The German Reich has 270 opera houses and a richer cultural life than is known there. Basically Americans live like pigs in a well-tiled sty."[155]

The fanaticism of the recently released politician was to present peculiar problems for the Wagner establishment. When Hitler proposed living in Bayreuth after his liberation at the end of 1924 the police were outraged and threatened to occupy Wahnfried. Winifred and her Gauleiter friends were keen to challenge the authorities on the point but Siegfried put his foot down, although he relented soon thereafter – Hitler was permitted

---

152. Ibid., 121.
153. "The Wagners and the Rabbi," by Norman Lebrecht, http://www.scena.org/columns/lebrechtindex.htm, April 3, 2002.
154. Spotts, *Bayreuth*, 25.
155. Spotts, *Hitler and the Power of Aesthetics*, 107.

to attend the festival the following year.[156] If the baton was to become a scepter as Wagner had predicted, then anyone anxious to take possession of the latter had to know how to wield the former. Hitler reckoned that this was where the candidacy of General Ludendorff was doomed to failure: he could never be a successful political leader, as he had no ear for music.[157]

There has never been any doubt that Hitler loved and appreciated Wagner's music and acquired considerable knowledge about how it should be properly performed. As a young man he had speculated as to which role Stephanie, his secret love, should sing. Having heard Lucie Weidt as Elsa in *Lohengrin* he had pondered whether his love could equal her vocal skills. Much has been written about his advice to Winifred about productions and he went so far as to make constructive comments to conductors about his not inconsiderable understanding of the score. And yet his hatred of the Jews was so all encompassing that it blinded him and robbed him of all judgment.

At times the merits of the Jewish artists were such that even the anti-Semites were compelled to make mention of their virtues. The music critic of the *Völkischer Beobachter*, the Nazi newspaper, could not but help praise the Wotan of Schorr, though he coupled his comments with a vicious aside. "We, as always, honour the truth and declare that, regrettable as it is that the leading Germanic God should be sung in Bayreuth by a Jew – namely Friedrich Schorr – he offers a performance that in singing as well as acting is of the highest Bayreuth standard."[158] Many reckoned Friedrich Schorr to be the greatest Wotan of all time but Hitler was not even able to muster the compliment of the music critic – he complained that he had been "sickened" by the appearance of "that Jew Schorr."[159]

The same critic evaluated the works as parables; Fafner – the giant, who kills his fellow giant Fasolt, and hoards the gold, including the ring symbolizing world power – represented the indolent upper classes at the time of Wilhelm II, who had been too myopic to see the coming revolution. Hagen, of course, represented politicians who stabbed Germany in the back and Siegfried was the symbol of the young Germany and the

---

156. Wagner, Nike, *The Wagners*, 208.
157. Waite, *The Psychopathic God*, 63.
158. Spotts, *Bayreuth*, 155.
159. Ibid.

new Third Reich.[160] Siegfried again wrote to the Bayreuth rabbi assuring him that, contrary to newspaper reports, he had not dropped a Jewish singer, Friedrich Schorr, because Hitler was in attendance. No Jew would be excluded from Bayreuth. "Anyone who wants can come to the festival, whether Hitler or [the pacifist] Harden," he wrote. He put his money where his mouth was and sent the rabbi a pair of tickets.[161]

At the 1925 festival Hitler was accompanied by Wagnerians Franz von Epp and Ernst Röhm. The last-mentioned said something disparaging about Hitler to Siegfried to the effect that Hitler was the drummer but no statesman and they were still looking for such a man.[162] Little did Röhm know that for Hitler the drummer and the statesman were one and the same person.

Apart from his passionate anti-Semitic and dyspeptic speeches the young politician also put pen to paper to announce his views. In that year he and Dietrich Eckart wrote a pamphlet entitled "Bolshevism from Moses to Lenin" in which they concluded, "one can only understand the Jews when one realizes their final purpose: to master the world and then destroy it...while they pretend to raise mankind up, actually they contrive to drive mankind to despair, insanity and destruction. If they are not stopped they will destroy us."[163] There were very distinct echoes of the Wagner of the regeneration writings. The pamphlet praised Martin Luther for his anti-Semitism and applauded his proposal that all synagogues be burned. But he had not gone far enough and they found that, by splitting the church, he weakened the attack against the Jews. Inevitably they also found his solution of "rooting out" the Jews too mild.[164]

While many wondered when he would marry and who the lucky girl would be – matchmakers had a field day soliciting his approval for a number of girls – Hitler's attitude to women was to remain a mystery to most members of the public and his entourage. Odd incidents baffled his closest associates. Shortly after his release at Christmas of 1924 he was trapped by an attractive woman under the mistletoe and given a good-natured kiss. A

---

160. Ibid., 157.
161. "The Wagners and the Rabbi," by Norman Lebrecht, http://www.scena.org/columns/lebrechtindex.htm, April 3, 2002.
162. Hamann, *Winifred Wagner*, 139.
163. Waite, *The Psychopathic God*, 86.
164. Ibid., 118.

witness recorded the look of horror and astonishment on his face – he then became enraged and when that emotion dissipated, he lapsed into a glacial sulk.[165] Twelve years later he was to be embarrassed in similar fashion. The Berlin Olympic Games was the scene and his day was wrecked when a fanatical Dutch woman who received her medal suddenly embraced him in two hefty arms and tried to kiss him in plain view of a hundred thousand spectators. Hitler could not stand the irreverent guffaws of foreign visitors, and left the stadium in high dudgeon.[166]

Prior to that Hitler had reacted strongly to a production of Paul Hindemith's opera *Neues vom Tage* on the Berlin stage in 1929. The soprano Laura appeared clad only in a flesh-colored bodysuit in a bathtub and Hitler was disgusted.[167] He was clearly intimidated by women and the thought of sexual intercourse. Asked what he thought of intercourse on one occasion he compared it to the experience of a soldier fighting his first battle. In a classic projection of his own anxieties he portrayed women as the cowards. "The encounter with her first man is for a young woman to be compared with the revelation that a soldier knows when he faces war for the first time."[168]

He would on occasion compare the conquest of women with that of the masses. "Like a woman whose psychic feeling is influenced less by abstract reasoning than by indefinable sentimental longing for complimentary strength, who will submit to the strong man rather than to dominate the suppliant…they see only the inconsiderate force, the brutality to which they finally always submit."[169] For Hitler rape seemed a natural consequence of the role taken by women in society, or was this a memory of what he had witnessed as a young child in his parental home?

For the children of the extended Wagner family the reopening of the festival in 1924 was a matter of the greatest excitement. Daniela, the eldest daughter of Cosima and Hans von Bülow, made them costumes depicting the characters in the operas, and a contemporary photograph shows a charming set of junior Valkyries and gods. Daniela was designated by the family to look after her aging father Hans and she helped bring him

---

165. Ibid., 51.
166. Langer, oss *Psychological Report on Adolf Hitler*, 64.
167. Kater, *The Twisted Muse*, 180.
168. Ibid., 52.
169. Waite, *The Psychopathic God*, 53.

back from Egypt where he had been sent to recover from illness.[170] Her life had not been easy and she had an unconsummated marriage to Henry Thode, an art historian and Wagnerite. For him the lure of the printed page exceeded that of the gilded sheets. Writing at the time of his marriage he wondered at his fortune at entering "the house of one of the greatest geniuses who ever walked the earth" but this did not equal the chance of "contact that the house offers with this most magnificent of all women." Had he been speaking of his bride one would have understanding for his hyperbole, but he was talking of Cosima[171] – shades of Chamberlain who had married Eva, while nurturing a secret passion for her mother, which history insists was unconsummated.

The newly wed Thodes provided a home in Frankfurt for a young Richard Strauss and Siegfried during his years at university. The latter described it as a "miniature Wahnfried," with portraits of Cosima; true to form the conversation featured political views that were "arrogant, nationalist, anti-French and anti-Semitic." Thode tired of living with the daughter while still worshipping the mother and fell into the more receptive arms of Isadore Duncan, who had choreographed the seductive bacchanal in *Tannhäuser* and had clearly learned from it.[172]

The residents of Wahnfried agreed to assume the honorary presidency of the recently created "Bayreuth League of Youth," whose credo established "the closest unity…between Bayreuth and National Socialism."[173] Hitler became so much part of the family that six-year-old Wieland declared that he wanted "Uncle Wolf" as his father and Siegfried as his uncle.[174] One can only guess as to how close he came to the truth of the almost totally secret relationship between his mother and the future Führer of Germany.

What Hitler lived on at that time was not particularly clear and his income tax returns indicate that he reported no income for 1924 and the first quarter of 1925. Despite this lack of income he was able to buy a custom-built, supercharged Mercedes.[175] Years later researchers were to search the files in the Munich Finance Office for the years 1925–35 and find evidence

---

170. Wagner, Nike, *The Wagners*, 190.
171. Ibid., 191.
172. Ibid.
173. Ibid., 206.
174. Ibid., 209.
175. Waite, *The Psychopathic God*, 221.

of deliberate and systematic tax evasion. He later resolved the issue by declaring himself not eligible for tax.[176]

When Chamberlain died in 1927 the news was kept away from Cosima, who thought for very good reason that he was too sick to see her. "People do not have to see each other to be together," Cosima told Eva.[177] Siegfried permitted Hitler to attend Chamberlain's funeral and to provide storm troopers as pallbearers. Wagner's only son was never Hitler's favorite and during the war, in one of his interminable table talks, he was to inform the yawning generals, during the small hours, that he was "politically passive" and "somewhat in the hands of the Jews."[178] In the Nazi newspaper Chamberlain was lauded as "one of the great armourers whose weapons have not yet found in our day their fullest use."[179]

The Wagners came to enjoy an intimacy and called Hitler by his nickname Wolf, after which a number of his military headquarters were named.[180] Wotan's alter ego in the Ring cycle, when he went about his nefarious business, siring Valkyries and trying to retain his power, was that of a wolf and the vulpine appellation attached to Hitler's favorite puppy by his last Alsatian, Blondi.[181] Uncle Wolf, according to Wagner's granddaughter Friedelind, told the most exciting stories and they were privy to a number of his intimacies including his attempted suicide and fights with his landlady. The last named might have performed an immense service to mankind had she been more successful when she attempted to kill him with an axe. The bright-eyed youngsters also listened spellbound while he told them the frightening incident when Hitler's driver drove into a ditch at night while Hitler was on one of his numerous visits to Bayreuth.[182]

Articles in the *International Herald Tribune* (Paris) of August 29, 1994 and *Time* magazine of August 15, 1994 (page 56) contained serious and convincing allegations that Hitler sexually abused Wieland.[183] The allegations emanate from author and diplomat Frederic Spotts who told

---

176. Ibid.
177. Marek, *Cosima Wagner*, 263.
178. Spotts, *Bayreuth*, 143.
179. Shirer, *Rise and Fall of the Third Reich*, 144.
180. Wagner and Cooper, *Heritage of Fire*, 37.
181. Köhler, *Wagner's Hitler*, 19.
182. Wagner and Cooper, *Heritage of Fire*, 44, 47.
183. Kater, *The Twisted Muse*, 36.

the international press that family members told him that this happened in the 1920s. The irony of these revelations was that in the early days Winifred was quite happy for her young boys to spend time at Hitler's flat. There is reason to believe she may have had an intuition that something was going on. As a concerned mother on one such occasion Winifred had sent sixteen-year-old Wolfgang to accompany Wieland to Munich. He was also supposed to come back with him. The boys had dinner with Hitler alone, and as the politician had to leave for Berlin at nine in the evening they stayed in his flat.[184]

Friedelind was a firm favorite at that time of Hitler and he was much amused on account of her naivete – she professed total ignorance as to what prostitution was.[185] She was to flee Germany just before the war and write a book about her experiences in Bayreuth. She makes mention in her book of various personalities, including the top brass of the Nazi Party, who visited Bayreuth at the time of the festival. She witnessed the romance between Lieselotte and Hans Frank, who achieved notoriety in later life. Frank acted as Hitler's personal lawyer and was to assist him in tracing his roots and quelling an embarrassing blackmail attempt by his nephew, who later suggested Hitler was a quarter Jewish. Hitler repeatedly had his blood tested and used leeches to purify it, fearing tainting from his Jewish background or the close relationship of his forebears.[186] Finally Frank was to achieve lasting notoriety in his stewardship of an area – renamed the General Government – where he became known as the butcher of Poland. The holding cells at Nürnberg were his last place of residence and he was executed for his part in the extermination of the Jews.[187]

From time to time Friedelind would visit Hitler in Munich and she witnessed his violent temper. On one occasion she lunched with him and he exploded with wrath at Julius Schaub, his general factotum and erstwhile fellow inmate at Landsberg Prison.[188] His wrath encompassed many acts of violence but his cultural heredity dictated that it had to include biting the carpet, while the brass section of the orchestra played the Wagnerian leitmotif of revenge.

---

184. Hamann, *Winifred Wagner*, 311.
185. Wagner and Cooper, *Heritage of Fire*, 83.
186. Wallace et al., *Intimate Sex Lives of Famous People*, 221.
187. Wagner and Cooper, *Heritage of Fire*, 79.
188. Ibid., 86–87.

Hitler settled down after his release from jail and finished *Mein Kampf* in Berchtesgaden and Nürnberg. But it was not all work as Hitler tells us in his autobiography and would have us believe how he and his friends were very keen on visiting the Dreimäderlhaus, where there were always pretty girls. Not that he could have married any of them – the suggestion is that he and they deeply desired that condition – as he was on probation and at the slightest imprudence ran the risk of going back to prison for six years. So there could be no question of marriage.

When Hitler set up house at Haus Wachenfeld in Obersalzberg, the Wagners were at hand to help with donations of linen and china and later sent a set of the Master's complete works, together with a page from the original score of *Lohengrin*.[189] Hitler wondered if the gifts had been made with an ulterior motive when he discovered that Siegfried Wagner was worried about the festival. It was the old dilemma, the clash of cultural excellence and ideology – if no Jewish singers were allowed to participate in the festival, he could not produce the operas. For Hitler the problem was even more difficult and he settled for a compromise – he was prepared to consider exemption for the festival, until other arrangements could be made.

The Nazi party grew slowly in numbers, and in 1926 Hitler successfully established his position against Gregor Strasser, who had built up a rival Nazi movement in north Germany. That same year Josef Goebbels visited Bayreuth and spoke to Winifred whom he described as a "thoroughbred" woman who was "fanatically on our side." He did not have the same to say about Siegfried whom he described as "spineless…feminine…somewhat decadent, rather like a cowardly artist." He then recorded a repetition of her earlier complaint – "a young woman weeps because the son is not what the Master was."[190]

For the annual Nazi Party festival Hitler chose Nürnberg, rich in Wagnerian association, following the success of the opera concerning *Die Meistersinger von Nürnberg*. The first such rally in 1927 attracted 169,000 members and was appropriately named the "Rally of Awakening," inspired by the great chorus "Wacht auf" (Wake up!) from the opera. When the rally was held there in 1929 he was to inform the membership, gathered

---

189. Fest, *Hitler*, 251.
190. Spotts, *Bayreuth*, 144.

under the waving swastikas, that if a million children were born that year in Germany and 800,000 of the weakest and most "unworthy" were killed, the nation would be strengthened.[191] One of the honored guests, applauding and raising her gloved hand in the Nazi salute, was Winifred Wagner, the "Lady of Bayreuth."[192]

The press was warming to the clarion call to the rebirth of the nation and the connection between the Nazis and Bayreuth was being exploited to the benefit of the politicians. In 1928 the *Frankfurter Zeitung* reported that "since the war the right wing has elevated Richard Wagner to its special artistic culture-god."[193] Some saw through the hollow racist shell that constituted Nazi political policy. That same year Hans Stuckenschmidt, the musicologist, very perceptively analyzed the process taking place at the Mecca of Wagnerians. He found a solid ideological substructure to the festival and said: "it stinks of swastika and reaction. Princes and generals come so that they can be reborn by German myths."[194] Ironically that same year saw a Hebrew translation of *Lohengrin* in Palestine based on Wagner's libretto. Little children gathered and listened starry-eyed to a hero who saved a damsel in distress and went back to his kingdom – a hero who was to give birth to the Führer title taken on by Jewry's scourge.[195]

It would be folly to underestimate Hitler's political acumen and during the economic collapse in 1929 he made an alliance with Alfred Hugenberg in a campaign against the Young Plan. Hugenberg's Nationalist Party had nationwide recognition through its organization and the newspapers it controlled. Access was now possible by the Nazis to the magnates of business and industry who controlled political funds and were anxious to use them to establish a strong right wing, anti-working-class government.

The subsidies that accrued from that source enabled Hitler to make effective his emotional appeal to the lower middle class and the unemployed, based on the proclamation of his faith that Germany would awaken from its sufferings to reassert its natural greatness. Rienzi was ready to take on the role he had inherited from Friedrich Barbarossa and Siegfried. Part of the program of preparation of the nation for a war against the Jews, ad-

---

191. Waite, *The Psychopathic God*, 392.
192. Kershaw, *Hitler 1936–1945: Nemesis*, 310.
193. Spotts, *Bayreuth*, 156.
194. Ibid., 157.
195. Sheffi, *Ring of Myths*, 39.

The famous Italian conductor and maestro Toscanini with Wagner's only son Siegfried. Wolf Siegfried Wagner, page 96.

vocated by Wagner, was to portray the latter as aggressors, bent on world domination. Writing in the *Illustrierter Beobachter* on March 30, 1929, Hitler linked the Jews with the Nibelungs, in particular Alberich, just as Wagner had done. "It seems to be possible for the Jews to extend the rule of Alberich from Russia, the only place where it is thoroughly established, to other countries."[196]

That same year saw the start of the Combat League for German Culture, founded by Nazi Party ideologue Alfred Rosenberg, which advocated a new approach to music. An example of the League's activities was the concert in March 1933 in Halle, which included an evening of Brahms sonatas and Wagner's *Wesendonck Lieder* with the aim of sweeping "the last bits of Jewish rot out of our German house, quickly and thoroughly."[197]

In 1930 Siegfried broke with tradition and invited Toscanini to conduct at Bayreuth, an invitation that was provocative to the right wing. He had wanted to do this for many years but had been prevented by domestic

---

196. Köhler, *Wagner's Hitler*, 350.
197. Kater, *The Twisted Muse*, 15.

and national politics. In May 1931 shortly before the beginning of the rehearsals there was a political scandal in Bologna: when Toscanini refused to open a concert with the fascist Giovinezza hymn he was physically assaulted by Mussolini followers who hit him several times in the face. In a long letter to Mussolini he protested about this incident and declared that he would never give in on the issue. Together with many others Winifred quickly assured the maestro of her sympathy but Toscanini's unambiguous worldwide and publicly confirmed political attitude was bound to lead to conflicts in Bayreuth because the festival leadership was in Hitler's camp and were fans of the Italian dictator.[198]

Once invited the Bayreuth spin doctors reworked the script on the great conductor's origins. They now reckoned that Toscanini was from Northern Italy, had a lot of Nordic blood in his veins and – voilà – clearly qualified, whether he liked it or not, as an Aryan. There was excellent precedent for such trans-frontier biogeography. In the manipulative hands of Chamberlain the sophistry had accommodated the designation of Dante, Columbus and St Paul as de facto Germans![199] Siegfried undertook a new production of *Tannhäuser* that year but did not live to see the end of the festival. His heart was not strong and his chain-smoking did not help his condition. A mild heart attack when carrying out a concert tour in England in January 1930 should have convinced him that he had inherited at least one feature from his father. La Scala saw his vast energies bent to produce the *Ring* during the next month and his mother's death in April, added to Toscanini's rampages later in July, provided the cardiac overload.[200]

His will was to lead to much speculation. The provisions directed that his estate be transferred to his young widow Winifred, but an interesting codicil had the tongues wagging as far as Munich. Should Winifred remarry, the estate would automatically devolve on their children. Was this aimed, the skeptics mused, at preventing Hitler marrying her?[201] Had the benign, gay and only son of the legendary composer guessed what was going on behind his back?

As Cosima lay dying a few months before, her thoughts were not of Wagner but of Chamberlain. "How is Houston? Tell him he is often in my

---

198. Hamann, *Winifred Wagner*, 200.
199. Spotts, *Bayreuth*, 153.
200. Ibid., 158.
201. Ibid.

thoughts," she said to her daughter Eva, who was his widow. He had died three years previously but his death continued to be kept from her.[202] On another occasion just before she died she said, "Greet Chamberlain for me, I think we met on another star."[203] That year saw the death of Franz Beidler, Cosima's banished son-in-law and husband of Isolde, the love child of Wagner. It was a good year for undertakers and lest one surmise humorlessness in the Bayreuth Brigade, Beidler's son Franz Wilhelm complained that he did not get out of mourning clothes that year.[204]

Another chain-smoker – Winifred, the widow of Siegfried – was now firmly at the helm of the dynasty and the festival. Freud, himself an inveterate cigar smoker, had decided that smoking, drugs and gambling were substitutes for the "primal addiction" – masturbation.[205] Did her British origins ("We are not amused") make the last-mentioned vice improper and the lack of interest from her unenthusiastic husband, mean that puffing away was her only solace?

Her eldest son, Wieland, who was in particular awe of his mother's rather masculine beauty, had formed a friendship with Gertrud Reissinger but vowed he would never marry her as he would only marry "someone who is as beautiful as my mother."[206] His brother Wolfgang, who had not taken any particular interest in girls at that stage, was a practical lad and loved wrought-iron work. More easygoing than his moody and volcanic elder brother, he was to outlive him by three decades and sit in the midst of a family feud – over the control of the festival – worthy of the dramas Wagner had produced.

Friedelind ("Mausi") was reckoned to be the rebel of the children and as a consequence was sent to boarding schools from the age of twelve. Her mother's gargantuan appetites and the plentiful supply of good Bavarian cooking, including Hitler's own favorite, potato dumplings, did not help her obesity problems.[207] The last daughter, Verena ("Nickerl"), was a capricious,

---

202. Köhler, *Wagner's Hitler*, 120.
203. Marek, *Cosima Wagner*, 272.
204. Wagner, Nike, *The Wagners*, 211.
205. Wallace et al., *Intimate Sex Lives of Famous People*, 178.
206. Ibid., 212.
207. Wagner, Nike, *The Wagners*, 212.

vampish girl, who charmed the Führer and teased him unmercifully, a privilege shared by few.[208]

The Wagner family and staff were firm in their commitment to Hitler's cause and he would share picnics and other social occasions with them. On one such occasion Hitler suddenly phoned and invited Winifred with or without children to a rural restaurant. He was accompanied by five guards from the ss and the Wagner family was mesmerized by his wonderfully beautiful violet blue eyes, which reflected his whole soul and heart.[209]

He was clearly particularly fond of the children who saw him as a god and after the wonderful meal they went back to Wahnfried where Hitler sat on Wieland's bed and beguiled the children with stories. To them he was a wonderful uncle with a wonderful sense of humor.[210]

He clearly had a great political influence on them as well. The Wagner children made their own Nazi propaganda and ordered a text for a puppet play from Wolzogen. Their choice was a puppet show with a Jew in it and Wolfgang had already acquired a Jew as a doll with a big nose. Wieland painted the backdrops, Verena played the women's roles and Wolfgang took over the direction. The play was called Princess Meat Patty and was a Punch and Judy type of show with Punch as a Nazi. In case of any doubt as to his affiliations, in the end Punch lifts his hand in a Nazi salute and says "Heil Hitler" after lambasting the Jew.[211]

Never one to tolerate any competition for power, Hitler soon appropriated a form of papal infallibility. During a closed meeting of the faithful at the Brown House in 1930 he said: "I hereby set forth for myself and my successors in the leadership of the Party the claim of political infallibility. I hope the world will grow as accustomed to that claim as it has to the claim of the Holy Father."[212]

There was still one matter that gnawed away at his repose. Towards the end of that year he called in his private lawyer Hans Frank on a personal matter – a relative who claimed that he had information that Hitler had a Jewish grandfather was blackmailing him. His stepbrother Alois had married an Englishwoman, Bridget, and their son Patrick was extorting money

---

208. Ibid., 213.
209. Hamann, *Winifred Wagner*, 209.
210. Ibid., 210.
211. Ibid., 211.
212. Waite, *The Psychopathic God*, 29.

out of his uncle.[213] Frank duly carried out his mandate and investigated the legitimacy of the claim. When he found out that Frankenberger had been paying maintenance to Hitler's grandmother Maria Anna Schickelgruber, Hitler denied this as an infamous lie, saying that his grandmother only accepted the money because she was destitute.[214]

In 1921 Ernst Ehrensperger, a man who dared to challenge Hitler early in his career, wrote a pamphlet in which he said: "He believes the time has come to introduce disunity and dissension into our ranks at the behest of his shady backers…And how is he conducting this struggle? Like a real Jew."[215] A photograph of the tomb of Hitler's paternal grandfather in the Jewish cemetery in Bucharest appeared in the *Daily Mirror* in October 1933. This photograph found its way into Himmler's file on Hitler and it can be viewed in the Federal Archives. Whatever the truth of the matter it seems clear that Hitler always suspected he had Jewish blood in him. How otherwise can one explain two incidents in his later life? Traveling in rural Austria with Albert Speer and Martin Bornmann in 1942 he was incensed when someone pointed out the small village of Spital and a farmhouse where a sign had been erected: "the Führer lived here in his youth." Hitler raged at Bornmann: "how many times had he said this village must never be mentioned…the sign must be removed at once."[216]

In March 1938 after taking over Austria he had the little farming village of Dollersheim used for a shooting range for heavy artillery. After a tremendous barrage the village was leveled including the cemetery containing the grave of his grandmother. There were hundreds of appropriate acres of rural ground that could have been used and yet he chose to destroy his ancestry.[217]

So great was his power and magnetism that he seemed to be convincing a large number of people of his destiny. For many years eyes had been scanning the horizon for "a new Siegfried who, in company with Wagner and Chamberlain, would emerge as the saviour of the German Volk." These

---

213. Ibid., 132.
214. Ibid., 126.
215. Lewis, *The Man Who Invented Hitler*, 29.
216. Waite, *The Psychopathic God*, 130.
217. Ibid., 130–31.

were the words of Theodor Heuss, later president of the German Federal Republic, in 1932.[218]

A political colleague at this time, Hermann Rauschning, in his 1940 book *The Voice of Destruction*, said that before Hitler came to power, he predicted the end of the great world conflagration that was to come, and for which he would be responsible. Rauschning also wrote about Hitler's propensity to hum motifs from Wagner's operas. He went on to say of Hitler on one occasion when things were not going well in 1932 with the Nazi Party:

> He seemed to me preoccupied and moody. From having been communicative, he fell suddenly into a dry silence. The political movement was in danger. National Socialism was approaching one of its crises. The Party was in a well-nigh desperate position. But Hitler's every word rang with the firm conviction that he would soon be in power, and be able to lead the German people to a new destiny. We spoke of the result of the war, and the tragical turn of all German victories. "We shall not capitulate – no, never," Hitler exclaimed. "We may be destroyed, but if we are, we shall drag a world with us – a world in flames." With that he hummed a characteristic *motif* from the *Götterdämmerung*.[219]

That same year saw Hitler at the side of Winifred Wagner at the festival and in October the Palestinian critic Menashe Rabinovich commented in the literary journal *Moznaim* about the festival: "the swastika can often be seen on the clothing of the critics. Bayreuth, that obscure corner that had only music to bring it fame and glory, threatens to become an impediment to music in its subordination to non-musical purposes."[220]

Using his great skills for mass agitation and unremitting propaganda, Hitler pointed out the failure of the government to achieve any success in internal or external affairs. This resulted in an increase in the electoral strength for the Nazis, who became the second largest party in the country, with more than six million votes at the 1930 election. Part of the new propaganda in the election – put out by the Bayreuth newspaper *Fränkisches*

---

218. Köhler, *Wagner's Hitler*, 15.
219. Hermann Rauschning, "The Voice of Destruction" (London: Thornton Butterworth, 1940), 5.
220. Sheffi, *Ring of Myths*, 44.

Volk – was an exhortation to the people not to buy in Jewish shops. The local Jewish community leaders issued a notice to their fellow citizens not to believe the defamatory and insulting statements they saw and heard; it was an appalling election ploy on the basis that the Jews were to blame for everything. The Jews were people just like everyone else and just as German – no better nor worse. Only internal peace would guarantee the resurrection of the Fatherland, they said.[221]

The election turned into a mudslinging match when a Munich paper revealed Röhm's homosexuality. Recently returned from Bolivia, he was stoutly defended by Hitler who stigmatized the hate campaign as filthy, false and an abuse of power.[222] Röhm had the support of Wahnfried as he was a frequent visitor to the festival and stayed in the Siegfried House with his companion Franz von Epp. Their homosexuality was always known there and was never considered any sort of stigma.[223]

Never a man to let an opportunity slip, Hitler opposed Hindenburg in the presidential election of 1932, capturing 36.8 percent of the votes on the second ballot. With skillful manipulation and intrigue, including *dramatis personae* as disparate as von Papen, General von Schleicher and Meissner, he sought the chancellorship by constitutional methods despite a decline in the strength of the party in November 1932. In January 1933 Hindenburg invited him to be chancellor of Germany, and he took office with the support of Papen and Hugenberg, with Field Marshal Werner von Blomberg as minister of defense. The next month he made a menacing announcement: "There will be no mercy now. Anyone who stands in our way will be cut down. The German people will not tolerate leniency."[224] Edwin Bechstein wrote to Winifred and told her about the overwhelming torch parade of the victorious Nazis through Berlin and said that he had heard that already all the Jews had left Berlin.[225]

With his ascension to high political office he moved quickly to achieve what he had written and spoken about. The musical works of Jews and

---

221. Hamann, *Winifred Wagner*, 228.
222. Ibid., 213–14.
223. Ibid.
224. Lewis, *The Man Who Invented Hitler*, 259.
225. Hamann, *Winifred Wagner*, 231.

moderns were banned, as was the great writer Thomas Mann for his essay "The Suffering and Greatness of Richard Wagner."[226]

The great writer, who was awarded the Nobel Prize for literature, had admired the composer in his youth. A Jewish intellectual, Rabbi Benjamin, wrote articles in Palestine analyzing Mann's work. He described how Mann had listened to a performance of Siegfried's Funeral March from *Götterdämmerung* in the Piazza Colonna in Rome. "His knees give way in his excitement, but he does not applaud, since in the press of the crowd he cannot move his hands; he does not join in the shouts, for his throat is tight; but as the Notung motif builds, tears run down his cheeks, he smiles and his heart beats with the turbulence of youth…"[227]

Later Mann saw the danger in Wagner's philosophy. The power of the subconscious was a feature that he commented on and he must have been thinking of the racist message in the subtext. "On the subject of *Wagner the psychologist* a whole book could be written, dealing with the psychological art of the musician and the poet (inasmuch as one can distinguish between the two in his case). The device of musical reminiscence, already used on occasion in the old operatic tradition, was gradually developed by him into a subtle and masterly system that made music, to a degree never before realized, into *an instrument of psychological allusion*, elaboration and cross-reference."[228]

Mann had been devastated by his first acquaintance with *Tristan* in 1901 and described it via the autobiographical Herr Pfuhl in his book *Buddenbrooks*: "this is demagogy, blasphemy, insanity, madness! It is a perfumed fog, shot through with lightning. It is the end of all honesty in art." Pfuhl succumbed with time and became an acolyte; "with an expression of shamefaced pleasure, he would glide into the weaving harmonies of the leitmotiv."[229]

Hitler wrote to Winifred in January 1933 and addressed her as "honoured and dear Wini," thanking her for her help. He explained that he only appreciated then why he should have said so much more in his youth about Wagner and his destiny as well as other great Germans. It was the

---

226. Spotts, *Bayreuth*, 164.
227. Sheffi, *Ring of Myths*, 43.
228. Ibid., 34.
229. Spotts, *Hitler and the Power of Aesthetics*, 142.

same eternal battle against hatred, envy and a lack of understanding.[230] On February 13, 1933, the fiftieth anniversary of the death of Wagner provided an opportunity for an elaborate ceremony in Leipzig, arranged by Hitler, to which Winifred and Wieland, her eldest son, were invited but none of the "usual Jewish literary crowd."[231]

On the dais were the pantheon of Third Reich gods, including Goebbels, head of the Chamber of Culture and Ministry for Public Enlightenment and Propaganda. As a tribute to the apotheosized Wagner, his opera *Meistersinger*, specifically the wonderful chorus "Awake! Soon will dawn the day," became the party hymn.[232] The opera became the main cultural event at the party rally in Nürnberg that year; soldiers and party officials, unwilling to attend, were herded out of the bars and watering holes and dragooned into the opera house.[233]

Those who were not fortunate enough to be part of the audience in the opera house – many of whom had been pressed into service against their will to show party support for the event – listened to the prelude to the opera at the opening of the rally. The Führer announced the ban on non-Aryans from taking part in the cultural life of the nation.[234] Wagner's prophetic words in his article "Jewry in Music" were finding physical manifestation in the new Aryan Germany. To shouts of jubilation from the serried ranks of flag-waving Nazi members Goebbels pointed out that the composer had called Jews "demons of decadence."[235]

Wagner intruded everywhere. Commemorating the German victory over the Russians at Tannenberg in 1914 at a ceremony in August 1933 Hitler saluted the fallen hero: "dead warlord, now enter Valhalla."[236]

The ascension to the German political throne by Hitler did not go unnoticed in the small town of Bayreuth. The *Bayreuther Blätter* rose to the occasion, applauding the advent of the new Führer and sermonizing that Germany was incredibly blessed. The reasons had been prophesied by the composer and were trumpeted abroad. "Now there is a Chancellor who

---

230. Hamann, *Winifred Wagner*, 230.
231. Spotts, *Hitler and the Power of Aesthetics*, 164.
232. Ibid., 164–65.
233. Ibid., 165.
234. Köhler, *Wagner's Hitler*, 247.
235. Ibid.
236. Spotts, *Hitler and the Power of Aesthetics*, 55.

loves Wagner, understands German culture, and who will not be afraid to deal with the Jewish question."[237]

Was this the "rough beast" of which the Irish poet William Butler Yeats spoke – "its hour come round, slouches towards Bethlehem…?"

---

[237]. Ibid., 165.

Chapter fourteen
Sexual Depravity

It is time to examine Hitler's personal life to see how he related to other people, and especially to women. Initially shy and diffident, with a feeling of social inferiority, particularly in relation to his Austrian accent, he benefited from the assistance he gained from his association with the Bechsteins and the Wagners, most of all the matriarchs. With time he grew more relaxed and confident and the success of the Nazi Party brought him into contact with aristocrats and the captains of industry. His income at this time was derived in a haphazard manner from party funds, from the sales of his book and from writing in nationalist newspapers. He had few social graces and appeared to be indifferent to clothes and food, never smoking or drinking tea, coffee or alcohol.

He also became a vegetarian, though the reasons for his diet are not completely clear. Some said that he believed a vegetarian diet would prolong his life and increase his vitality and stamina. His reasoning was crass and unscientific – elephants outlived lions and horses could easily outrun dogs that tired easily, panted and drooled when exhausted.[1] The real reason falls in with the pattern that had irresistibly dictated his life. "I don't touch meat largely because of what Wagner says on the subject."[2]

Fest has pointed out the parallels in the two figures. "There are striking

---
1. Waite, *The Psychopathic God*, 26.
2. Ibid.

parallels between Hitler and Wagner: the uncertainty about ancestry, the failure at school, the flight from military service, the morbid hatred of Jews, even the vegetarianism which in Wagner ultimately developed into the ludicrous delusion that humanity must be saved by vegetarian diet. Also in both was the violent quality of their moods, the abrupt alternation of depression and exaltation, triumphs and disasters."[3]

According to Wagner, the Jewish God "Jehovah" found Abel's fatted lamb more savory than Cain's offering of the produce of the field. To eat vegetables and fruit showed that one showed no allegiance to a Semitic deity. Both conveniently believed that Jesus was Aryan and the son of a Greek soldier in the Roman army by the name of Pantherus.[4] The adulation of Gustav Mahler for Wagner's music was to lead him and others of his *Leseverein* (a sort of book club) including Hugo Wolf to become vegetarians in the late 1880s, having read Wagner's "Religion and Art."[5]

What sort of man was this cultural heir of Richard Wagner who was determined to travel along the ideological road map drawn by the composer and refined by his quixotic son-in-law Houston Stewart Chamberlain? That he loved the music and the political philosophy was clear, but how would he respond to the clarion call to do something about the race question? He was already making vague threats – and even on some occasions apocalyptic predictions – about what would happen to the Jewish inhabitants, but was he serious or was he just winning votes? Was his anti-Semitism the variety enjoyed by Martin Luther and others or was this a fanaticism that boded ill for his enemies?

As Walter Langer has pointed out in his security report in 1943 Hitler was *not* the sort of figure that made true heroes. "In height he is a little below average. His hips are wide and his shoulders relatively narrow. His muscles are flabby; his legs short, thin, and spindly, the latter being hidden in the past by heavy boots and more recently by long trousers. He has a large torso and is hollow-chested to the point where it is said that he has his uniforms padded."[6] Although his physical attributes were not imposing it was universally accepted that his hypnotic light blue eyes, with a touch of greenish-gray, were his finest feature. The French Ambassador Coulondre

---

3. Fest, *Hitler*, 49–50.
4. See Gutman, *Richard Wagner*, 594.
5. Franklin, *Life of Mahler*, 48–50.
6. Langer, OSS *Psychological Report on Adolf Hitler*, 43.

admired them and the German dramatist Gerhart Hauptmann described seeing them as the "greatest moment in his life." Martha Dodd, daughter of the American ambassador, found them "startling and unforgettable."[7]

Women certainly found him attractive and schoolgirls were reported to have painted swastikas on their fingernails. "Heil Hitler" was the expletive one group of blonder Valkyries uttered when they reached orgasm. One male admirer expressed his admiration as follows: "There is only one thing for me either to win with Adolf Hitler or to die for him. The personality of the Führer had me in its spell."[8]

Doubt has been cast on the evidence of Hitler's sexual perversions and an authority as eminent as Ian Kershaw says that "conjecture that sexual repression later gave way to sordid sado-masochistic practices rests, whatever the suspicions, on little more than a combination of rumor, hearsay, surmise, and innuendo, often spiced up by Hitler's political enemies."[9] It is with considerable diffidence that one challenges so eminent a historian. The sexual act, in most instances, of course, occurs in privacy and is not the sort of activity that is witnessed by a number of unimpeachable sources – the evidence has to come from a participant. What the reader has to consider when evaluating the accounts set out below, is the credibility of the source and the potential and reasons for fabrication. In the end one is not searching for authentic proof of any particular act but a general picture of a lifestyle, garnered from a series of facts and circumstances.

In the summer of 1928 Hitler rented Haus Wachenfeld on the Obersalzburg high up above Berchtesgaden. With the help of Winifred Wagner and Helene Bechstein and masquerading under the name "Wolf," the pseudonym of Wagner's great god Wotan in the Ring cycle, he set up house opposite the mountain where Barbarossa was waiting in his magic sleep to take on his historical mission to conquer the world and annihilate the Antichrist, the Jews.[10]

Hitler had an obsession with wolves as he also believed his name (Adolf) was derived from Athalwolf (noble wolf). All his military headquarters were named after wolves including that in eastern France, schlucht

---

7. Waite, *The Psychopathic God*, 6.
8. Lewis, *The Man Who Invented Hitler*, 9.
9. Kershaw, *Hitler 1936–1945: Nemesis*, 46.
10. Köhler, *Wagner's Hitler*, 283.

A forgery by Konrad Kujau of Hitler's sketch of his niece Geli Raubal in the nude. See Spotts, Hitler and the Power of Aesthetics, page 145.

(Wolf's Fort), and Eastern Prussia, Wolfschlucht (Wolf's Lair),[11] and when he telephoned Bayreuth he would announce himself to Winifred Wagner as the "conductor wolf."[12] He desperately needed a housekeeper and his widowed half sister Angela Raubal agreed to take on the employment, bringing her two daughters Geli and Friedl.

Opinions differed about the attractions of Geli, but what was common cause amongst those who gave an account of her was her infectious humor and most delightful nature. An American journalist interviewed an old woman who had lived in the same street as Geli. "I was walking down the street and I heard her singing. I saw her and I just stopped dead. She was just so tall and beautiful."[13] Ilse Hess, wife of the more famous Rudolf, said that it was not so much that "she was pretty but she had the famous Viennese charm."[14] Konrad Heiden called her "a buxom young country girl from Upper Austria with *fair* curly hair"; Emil Maurice, Hitler's chauffeur said her "big eyes were a poem and she had magnificent *black* hair."[15] Were the observers so bowled over by her personality that they failed to notice the color or did she indulge in the penchant of Mathilde Wesendonck for

---

11. Lewis, *The Man Who Invented Hitler*, 26.
12. Waite, *The Psychopathic God*, 26.
13. Hayman, *Hitler and Geli*, 102.
14. Ibid.
15. Ibid.

dyeing her hair? Hitler took her for walks in the mountains and to all the theatres in Munich. In addition he did something somewhat out of the ordinary for an uncle – he sketched her nakedness.

A fortune-teller once told her that she would die as a result of a bullet and after that she had a pathological aversion to guns and weapons of any nature. When Hitler moved to his apartment in Munich she accompanied him. She had passion and was a woman a man could be proud of – especially a politician who was already winning a significant part of the electorate over to his point of view.

A long trail of incest runs through the Ring cycle but for Hitler there could not be any scandals – he was keenly aware that any relationship with his niece had to remain totally clandestine. Indeed one author has stated that incest was no barrier to sexual relations for either Wagner or Hitler.[16] An American doctor, Fritz Redlich, has written a book in which he examines Hitler's health.[17] He tells of an erstwhile supporter, Otto Strasser, who later broke from Hitler and criticized him for his "capitalist" views. When life became unbearable he fled Germany and spoke to the Office of Strategic Services in Washington and later to officers in Montreal on May 13, 1943. He described the relationship between Hitler and Geli as one that was "very generous with her [Geli] in some respects and very harsh with her in others."

Hitler was obsessively jealous and concerned that he retain total control over all her activities. Strasser went on to describe how Hitler frequently locked her up for long periods of time because she refused to accede to his wishes. After being treated in that fashion Geli had complained to Strasser who had tried to make light of the matter and said to Geli: "Well, why don't you sleep with him? What difference does it make if he is your uncle?"

Her answer was to shake the normally imperturbable Strasser. Geli responded – with many hesitations and blushes – by telling him that she would be very glad to sleep with him if that was all he wanted, but she just couldn't go through with the "other performance" again. "My uncle is a monster, you would never believe the things he makes me do."[18] For obvious reasons Geli was somewhat reticent about divulging what had occurred

---

16. Koch-Hillebrecht, *Homo Hitler*, 74.
17. Redlich, *Hitler: Diagnosis of a Destructive Prophet*.
18. Wallace et al., *Intimate Sex Lives of Famous People*, 220.

Hitler is reputed to have had a perverted relationship with his niece Geli Raubal, who is pictured here swimming. Bishop, Hitler's Third Reich vol. 1, page 5.

but Strasser had persisted. After much urging concerning the nature of this performance, she finally told Strasser what had taken place.

It is as well to note that she had a love/hate relationship with her uncle and was fascinated and overwhelmed by his power and authority in the party and the country. Hitler made her undress and he then lay down on the floor. Hitler ordered her to squat down over his face where he could examine her at close range, and this would make him very excited. When the excitement reached its peak, Geli told Strasser, shaking off tears of embarrassment and shame, Hitler demanded that she urinate on him, and that gave him his sexual pleasure. Geli stressed the fact that it was of the utmost importance to him that she squat over him in such a way that he could see everything of her sexual organs. The noted psychologist Havelock Ellis in his *Studies in the Psychology of Sex* tried to explain this perversion as follows: "The man whose predominant impulse is to subjugate himself to his mistress and to receive at her hands the utmost humiliation, frequently finds the climax of his gratification in being urinated on by her, whether in actual fact or only in imagination. In many such cases, however, it is

Some writers maintain that Hitler shot and killed his niece Geli Raubal because he suspected her of having an affair with a Jew. Few doubted that he had a great love for her and deeply mourned her loss. Hayman, 113.

evident that we have a mixed phenomenon; the symbolism is double. The act becomes desirable because of intimately sexual associations in the act itself, as a symbolical detumescence, a simulacrum of the sexual act, and one which proceeds from the sexual focus itself."[19]

Hitler's reputed love Röhm, in an entirely different connection, once said, "He (Hitler) is thinking about the peasant girls. When they stand in the fields and bend down at their work so that you can see their behinds, that's what he likes, especially when they've got big round ones. That's Hitler's sex life. What a man." Hitler, who was present when his friend spoke, did not stir a muscle but only stared at Röhm with compressed lips.[20]

Other unnamed informants gave similar testimony to the officers about Hitler's perversion.[21] When Strasser asked Geli how she felt about the performance she said it was "extremely disgusting to her." She continued by confessing that, although it was sexually stimulating, it gave her no gratification. Freud was to call this sort of activity "the mechanism of many perversions, which consist in a lingering over the preparatory acts of the sexual process."[22] There were other side effects for her as Hitler was

---

19. Havelock Ellis, *Studies in the Psychology of Sex*, vol. 3 (New York: Random House, 1915), 56.
20. Langer, OSS *Psychological Report on Adolf Hitler*, 186.
21. Waite, *The Psychopathic God*, 238.
22. Freud, *On Sexuality*, 132.

extremely jealous of any man who ever made a pass at her. In addition Geli was keenly aware that if she did not give her uncle what he wanted he would find somebody who would.

Since Hitler refused to let her have any contact with other men, she was in the position of being continually stimulated without any adequate outlet, and that state of affairs couldn't possibly continue. There were other complicating factors. Geli never understood his relationship to Winifred Wagner and she was worried when the media speculated that he might marry her. Geli had attended the 1930 Bayreuth festival and a contemporary photograph showed her there with Helene Bechstein.[23] Spurred on by Hitler, who wanted her to sing Wagner, so that all his fantasies could be fulfilled, she told him she wanted to go to Vienna for singing lessons. Hitler told her that he could never allow that – that was a great disappointment to her.

Other accounts tell of his sado-masochism and witnesses told how Geli sometimes flinched when he hit his leg with his dog whip. He never could understand that, as he believed that pain was but an enhanced state of extreme pleasure. Hitler was fond of quoting the few lines he knew from Nietzsche: "you are going to a woman? Do not forget your whip."[24] There was a strange contradiction in the sexual bondage aspect – he was going to be the master of the universe but he had to be her bonded slave. Nietzsche's own experience at the hands of the countess was to provoke his comments on the joys, to a select few, of masochism.

Geli's death in September 1931 from "suicide" was a great tragedy. The official version put out thereafter by the Nazi Party – Hitler was too distraught to speak for weeks on end – was that she insisted on going to Vienna and, when Hitler refused, she shot herself. Geli, so it was said, was a victim of possessive jealousy that had driven her to commit suicide. Whatever the cause of her death – and the account of Ronald Hayman makes out a strong case for murder – for many years thereafter Hitler was inconsolable.

Otto Strasser told the American and Canadian officers that he believed that Hitler killed Geli and that her death were directly attributable to Hitler's demand that she continue with the perverted practices that have been described. Strasser was satisfied in his own mind that Hitler had de-

---

23. Hamann, *Winifred Wagner*, 185.
24. Waite, *The Psychopathic God*, 54.

manded that Geli go through with this performance again and that she had refused, and that Hitler thereupon became enraged and murdered her.

Otto's brother Gregor, who was also very close to Hitler at the time, also believed this to be the case and it was from this time that his relations with Hitler became strained. Gregor was one of the few people who was called to the house shortly after Geli's death and saw her before the funeral. Gregor was privy to what was a very embarrassing piece of information relating to a politician who needed to have a better reputation than Caesar's wife. Otto Strasser believed that it was this knowledge that led to Gregor's murder during the Blood Purge in 1934.[25] Although Hanfstaengl claimed that Geli had been pregnant by a "young Jewish art teacher from Linz," Hitler rejected this suggestion as preposterous.[26] Another report was to the effect that the postmortem revealed that she was a virgin.[27] Even if Geli had no sexual relations with the Jewish art teacher from Linz it requires little imagination to gauge the extent of Hitler's outrage on discovering that rumor.

Some historians have cast doubt on the veracity of this account – certainly with respect to the sexual perversions discounted by Ian Kershaw – but it has received confirmation from other independent sources. A member of the SA, Wilhelm Stocker, was on guard duty at the Munich flat where Hitler and Geli stayed. Apparently he became her lover and, once she was sure that he would not betray her to Hitler, she whispered to him that "at times Hitler made her do things in the privacy of her room that sickened her."[28] Asked by the astounded Stocker why she did not refuse she explained that "she didn't want to lose him to some woman who would do what he wanted."[29]

Years before the OSS heard the account of Otto Strasser, in the United States of America and Canada, they listened incredulously to what Father Bernhard Stempfele, an anti-Semitic Catholic priest of the order of St. Jerome, told them about the Nazi leader. Father Stempfele had helped Hitler edit *Mein Kampf*, after which they became friends. When Hitler and Geli were not living together they were in regular correspondence, though few of

---

25. Redlich, *Hitler: Diagnosis of a Destructive Prophet*, 81–82.
26. Waite, *The Psychopathic God*, 227.
27. Ibid.
28. Hayman, *Hitler and Geli*, 136.
29. Ibid.

the letters have survived. Hitler's landlady had a son by the name of Rudolf who was an inquisitive and felonious fellow and he would on occasion rifle through the private possessions of the rising political star.

Ever in need of cash the opportunistic Rudolf found a letter during his loitering in Hitler's quarters and pilfered it. To his delight it turned out to be eminently salacious and of great value to those denizens of the underworld who thrive on blackmail. The letter, in the distinctive cursive of the man shortly to be placed at the helm of the country's political affairs, made extensive reference to what he had required her to submit herself. Rudolf exploited the blackmail possibilities of the incriminating document and Hitler became desperate, given his uncertain political future at that time.

There were anxious frowns and deliberations in the Brown House, the headquarters of the Nazi Party, before a plan was conceived, involving a most disreputable and quixotic character. A close friend and confidante of Father Stempfele was a diminutive, pigmy-sized collector of memorabilia named JFM Rehnse. This man sniffed out the esoteric manifestations of moral turpitude and hoarded every sort of document evidencing the times, including the erotic and scandalous.[30] If there was ever an inhabitant of the sewers of Munich society totally suited to this task, it was this diminutive collector. Hitler pondered over his problem very deeply and finally decided to send his party treasurer Franz Schwarz to Rehnse, to try and persuade him to buy the letter. Given his profession – he was an innocent party who had a legitimate reason for the purchase – hopefully no link would be made to Hitler.

Rehnse consulted with the cleric Father Stempfele, who advised him that there was some financial advantage to be gained from the future Führer's quandary. It was to have fatal consequences for the duplicitous cleric. The financial demand on Hitler was exorbitant and extortionate; it required Hitler not only to furnish the purchase price of the letter, but also, in addition, to provide enough money to underwrite Rehnse's entire collection. In the end Hitler may have concluded the money was well spent, but he was very angry.

Father Stempfele acted as the go-between; the letter was recovered and handed to the treasurer for onward transmission to a visibly relieved

---

30. Waite, *The Psychopathic God*, 238.

Hitler.[31] The treasurer Schwarz continued to bask in the favor of his leader and ended up as the sole executor of his private will, but the scheming cleric was not so fortunate. In the purge of Hitler's enemies, he did not forget the trouble the priest had given him, and three bullets through the heart were his reward, fired in the depths of the forest of Herlaching, near Munich.[32]

Any further doubts about the perverted nature of Hitler's sex relationships are put to bed – so to speak – by the account the film actress Renate Müller, star of Ufa, Germany's leading film company, gave to director Adolf Zeissler in 1936. She had starred opposite Emil Jannings in the film *Liebling der Götter* and had met Hitler in 1932, when she was filming on location, near the Danish coast. A fanatical filmgoer, Hitler had watched the filming all day and in the evening he visited the house where she was staying.[33]

It was to be a strange evening for the ill-matched pair. At forty-three, he lacked the necessary social graces when alone with any woman, let alone the most glamorous woman in Germany. Renate described how he just sat there looking at her all the time while she made small talk from time to time. He was truly infatuated with her beauty and intoxicated by her fame and his good fortune in having her pay attention to him. He took her hand in his and stared for some time at the face that was adored by millions of German movie fans. According to Renate, Hitler's conversation – when he abandoned his painful silence – was infantile and, though he talked incessantly, what he said was mostly nonsense.

She clearly made a deep impression on him and Hitler invited Renate to a party at the Chancellery, but he ignored her all evening, until everyone was leaving. He then offered to show her round the building, took her into his apartments and showed her his tail-coated dinner suit, a form of dress that he explained to her he had never worn until he came into power. After this he arranged frequent meetings with her, and showered her with expensive gifts, including perfume and a diamond bracelet of great value. One of the most important displays of his manhood to the incredulous film star was when he assumed the Nazi salute and explained that he could maintain it for hours on end.[34] What would Freud have made of that gesture?

When Hitler eventually made love to Renate she was astounded by

---
31. Ibid.
32. Ibid., 239.
33. Infield, *Hitler's Secret Life*, 79.
34. Ibid., 80.

The German actress Renate Müller, with whom Hitler had a strange and perverted relationship. She later committed suicide after persecution by the Gestapo. Hayman, page 112.

what he required of her. Renate described to Adolf Zeissler how Hitler had invited her one night to the Chancellery and began the evening by going into detail about Gestapo methods of torture, comparing them with medieval techniques. Renate was totally horrified by this, but worse was to follow. She described how they had both taken their clothes off and Hitler had begged her to hit him and kick him. Hitler was into some strange bondage ritual – she assumed. When Renate refused he went on heaping accusations on his own head, saying he was her slave, unworthy to be in the same room as her.

Eventually giving in, she started to kick him, abuse him with obscene words and hit him with a whip. No sexual intercourse took place but Hitler became increasingly excited and started to masturbate. After orgasm, he suggested quietly that they should both put their clothes on. Renate was amazed to find that within moments Hitler behaved as though nothing untoward had taken place. He invited her to drink a glass of wine with him and they chatted about trivialities. Finally he stood up, kissed her hand, thanked her for a pleasant evening and rang for a servant to show her out.[35]

She suffered a similarly tragic end. When she wanted to take a holiday in London, she asked his permission, which was granted. She little knew that the Gestapo kept her under surveillance while she was there, and after

---

35. Hayman, *Hitler and Geli*, 146.

Eva Braun, Hitler's long-standing girlfriend and the woman he finally married in the Berlin bunker, before they both committed suicide. See Hitler and Geli by Hayman, page 112.

spending a lot of time with a former lover, Frank Deutsch, who was Jewish, she found on returning to Germany that she had been blacklisted. She also heard that she would be put on trial for "race defamation." Her life fell apart and she became addicted to morphine.

Eventually she went into a sanatorium and after being discharged asked for an interview with Hitler, who refused to see her. Her addiction continued and she was placed back in the institution. One day she was looking out of the window of the sanatorium, in a state of great depression, when she saw a car pull up in the street below and four SS officers get out. Renate thought she knew exactly why they were visiting the sanatorium; she opened the window and, hesitating for a moment as she looked at the road below, flung herself to her death. She was thirty years of age.[36]

Later a woman was to enter Hitler's life, who was to be with him in the bunker at the end of the war, when he took his own life. Eva Braun, a shop assistant from Munich, eventually became his "mistress," or so he would have his closest aides believe. He had met her in 1930 and, apart from his initial attraction, had paid her scant attention until she twice attempted suicide – in 1932 and 1935. Hitler rarely allowed her to come to Berlin or appear in public with him and would not consider marriage on the grounds that it would hamper his career. Eva was a warmhearted, wholesome and impressionable girl with no real claims to intellectual ability. He even

---

36. Ibid., 146–47.

referred in public to her shortcomings by suggesting how important it was for a "highly intelligent man to take a primitive and stupid woman."[37] Her great virtue in Hitler's eyes was her unquestioning loyalty, and in recognition of this he made her his legal wife at the end of his life.

Little evidence remains of what took place between them, but the fragmentary vignettes give an impression of her life with the chancellor of Germany. From time to time Eva committed her experiences to paper and some of these have survived. She explained in her diary that Hitler loved to undress her and that his strong hands would drive her crazy.[38] That he was crazy about her body goes without saying and it will be recalled that he sketched his niece Geli in the nude. When Hitler and Eva went on the picnics he was so fond of, he ordered the SS to block off an area so that he could watch her swim in the nude.

Otto Skorzeny, who personally led the courageous liberation of Mussolini from Italian partisans in 1943, spoke to her and she explained something that related very directly to what Geli had endured from him. Eva told the flying ace that she did have a sexual relationship with Hitler and the only detail she supplied was that "on the floor he was very erotic."[39] One possible explanation and interpretation of the obscure utterance was that a spirited and unconventional coupling had taken place. But this could not be true because Eva Braun told her hairdresser that no intercourse had ever taken place.[40]

The other alternative interpretation is that the sort of perversions described by Geli and Renata persisted. Apart from the inherent probabilities that his sexual preferences would not suddenly change but would continue, there is some confirmation for this in her own writings. Her diary of the period from February to May 1935 seems to suggest that the perversions continued. "He uses me only for *certain purposes*: nothing else is possible…nonsense…when he says he loves me it is just *in that moment* – like his promises that he never keeps. Why does he torture me but does not finish right now?" Cryptic though the comments may be there is a strong suggestion that the "certain purposes" were the fulfillment of his perverted sexual practices.

---

37. Waite, *The Psychopathic God*, 52.
38. Infield, *Hitler's Secret Life*, 170.
39. Ibid., 171.
40. Redlich, *Hitler: Diagnosis of a Destructive Prophet*, 84.

Eva's friends must have been wildly inquisitive as to what life was like, living with such a charismatic and popular leader. She said to a close friend, who had known her since her schooldays and became the wife of Hermann Esser, "I get nothing at all from him *as a man*."[41] Nothing could be clearer than this. In her diary she says: "the weather is magnificent and I, the mistress of the greatest man in Germany and in the whole world, sit here waiting while the sun mocks me through the windowpanes."[42] Mocks her no doubt for not having any sexual fulfillment from her man. She told Eugen Dollmann in 1938 that Hitler was obsessed with his life's work and neglected her: "…Always the mission, the mission, the mission, self-sacrifice and renunciation."

The old Wagnerian motif that emerged from the depths of the Rhine at the beginning of the Ring cycle, when Alberich renounces love in substitution for the power of the ring, was to be the pretext for not giving her physical love.[43] Eva then went on to describe how Hitler claimed to have created the "authentic masculine Reich." Ruefully she continued, "people naturally believe that my life [at Hitler's] side takes quite a different form; if only they knew!"[44] One would have expected women who lived in close proximity to have shared confidences. His secretary Christa Schröder had the impression that Eva and Hitler did not have sexual intercourse. Eva tried to commit suicide on two occasions and one of Hitler's bodyguards hurled himself from the Kehlstein because he was in love with her but could not trespass on the Führer's domain.[45]

Why did Hitler go through the charade of having a woman in his life if he was really homosexual and wanted a relationship with another man? Fest believes the relationship was to confirm his manhood before his friends.[46] Hitler told Otto Wagener, his SA Chief, in 1929 that he had overcome the need for any woman.[47] Hitler worried that he, as a genius, could never produce progeny that equaled his own talents. It was Karl Kraus who said,

---

41. Waite, *The Psychopathic God*, 233.
42. Hayman, *Hitler and Geli*, 207.
43. Machtan, *Hidden Hitler*, 169.
44. Ibid.
45. Langer, OSS *Psychological Report on Adolf Hitler*, 83.
46. Hayman, *Hitler and Geli*, 207.
47. Ibid.

"The genius can only remedy the drawback of coming from a family by making sure that he doesn't leave one behind him."[48]

Various reasons were tendered over his lifetime as to why he never married. In no special order of merit these included: a fear of syphilis – a morbid fear all his life – and of capitulation, as he regarded intercourse as such. Other reasons included that he also worried that his children might be imbeciles, his only bride was the Motherland, he wanted to marry Geli but she was dead and the earlier Savior from Palestine had never married.[49] The loss of five million women's votes was the most trivial and pragmatic reason advanced, especially irrelevant once he had acquired total power, given his lack of enthusiasm for democracy.[50]

Mention has been made of Hitler's rather unappealing physiognomy but there is little to indicate physical abnormalities or deformities. Hitler, according to the Russian autopsy on his body, had only one testicle (monorchism), which some tentatively suggest could have led to feelings of sexual inadequacy.[51] Those disparaging the strong evidence presented of his perversions and homosexuality point to a form of vocal or mental sublimation. Did he not, they argued, achieve full sexual pleasure from his speeches, which many compared to the sexual act, with gentle introductory foreplay, a gradual move to the denouement and a massive crescendo ending with an "orgasm of words"?[52] Putzi Hanfstaengl had felt the sexual power of his words and succumbed to his oratory.

Dr. Redlich also makes mention of his incessant changing of underwear and bathing, which the doctor attributes to slight leakage after urination. Redlich then comments, "Perhaps the idea of preventing degeneration in other Germans led him to his vulgar Darwinism, eventually to the cruel and inhuman legislation on sterilization, and, ultimately, to euthanasia and elimination of the inferior by genocide." Was the Holocaust a cleansing process initiated by the adulation he had for Richard Wagner?

Dr. Redlich sees something of this in his own analysis and even mentions the Bayreuth composer in his comments. "Hitler saw himself as a redeemer (there is a bit of Wagner and, more precisely, Parsifal in this)

---

48. Wagner, Nike, *The Wagners*, 167.
49. Waite, *The Psychopathic God*, 234.
50. Ibid.
51. Redlich, *Hitler: Diagnosis of a Destructive Prophet*, 303.
52. Waite, *The Psychopathic God*, 53.

who would deliver his people and King through his own suffering."[53] It will be recalled that in the opera Amfortas, the leader of the knights of the Holy Grail, was wounded and the wound refused to heal. Stephen Roberts reports that "in Munich in the early autumn of 1936 I saw coloured pictures of Hitler in the actual silver garments of the Knights of the Grail; but they were soon withdrawn. They gave the show away; they were too near the truth of Hitler's mentality."[54] Only when Parsifal refused the blandishments of Kundry, did he become worthy of winning back the Spear. In other words salvation, redemption and great power were only possible to one who exercised sexual self-restraint. In fact in the opera it is only when Parsifal holds up the sword as a cross that the evil power of Klingsor is defeated and his castle crumbles with a mighty crash in the brass.[55]

At the end of the opera Kundry dies symbolizing the end of the Antichrist (Jewry), whereas Parsifal and Christianity survive.[56] Hitler felt this great need to abstain from women – so he claimed – in order to become worthy of the leadership of Germany and the architect of its cleansing of the Jews. There was historical precedent for it, set out in the most holy text of all. The secret of Wagner's hero Rienzi was that he could never surrender to the love of a mortal woman – his only true love was Rome![57] To a large extent he had modeled himself on the Roman hero and often recalled the evening with Kubizek, when he knew the fact of his destiny. Hitler also had a pathological fear of syphilis and had made mention of his aversion to that disease at great length in his book. Chamberlain told a businessman who came to see him before he died that Hitler was going to be the new Parsifal.[58] The final irony was that in the myths that Wagner pillaged to find his sources, Parsifal contracted a normal marriage and from the union came the great hero Lohengrin, hero of one of Hitler's favorite Wagnerian operas, from which the notion of "Führer" emanates.

Despite Hitler's apparent identification with the sublimated Wagnerian version of *Parsifal*, he did not eschew women entirely. There were other

---

53. Redlich, *Hitler: Diagnosis of a Destructive Prophet*, 230.
54. Langer, OSS *Psychological Report on Adolf Hitler*, 56.
55. Gutman, *Richard Wagner*, 584.
56. On the significance of Parsifal holding up the cross see ibid., 600, as this represents a thwarting of Klingsor the Jew.
57. Köhler, *Wagner's Hitler*, 28.
58. Ibid., 223.

women in his life, who also gave accounts of irregular sexual practices. Mimi Reiter was a sixteen-year-old girlfriend of Hitler's in the late 1920s and she enjoyed woodland walks with him. She was his "woodland sprite" and he was the "wolf." He liked to watch her swimming nude and, although little is known about their other sexual practices, she became intensely frustrated. Such was the level of her personal anguish that on one occasion she tried to hang herself. In 1932 Hitler sent Rudolf Hess to persuade her to visit him and she left the Seefeld hotelkeeper she had married to spend one memorable night with him at his new flat in Prinzregentenplatz. "I let him do whatever he wanted with me," was the way she described the events of that evening.[59] After the war she claimed Hitler's sexual tastes were too extreme.[60] Some years before that, a woman named Suzi Liptauer had hanged herself, after an all-night rendezvous with the man.[61]

Winifred Wagner was reckoned to have been in love with Hitler from the moment her eyes met his unfathomably blue ones. Friedelind is alleged to have said that marriage was always possible – "my mother would like to, but Uncle Wolf wouldn't."[62] Gottfried Wagner, the great grandson of the composer, suggests that it was the other way round. "If my grandmother had accepted Hitler's proposal of marriage I could have been Gottfried Wagner-Hitler."[63] The provisions of Siegfried Wagner's will – that the estate, and in particular control of the festival, would pass over to the other children should she marry – probably added another obstacle to the path of what might be considered a cultural, historical imperative. On one occasion in spite of being quite busy Winifred took time off at a Nürnberg Nazi Party day to speak to Hitler about Siegfried's will. Hitler felt that the prohibition of her remarriage was right.[64]

The stories of the degree of intimacy and other details of the relationship are varied and not always easy to reconcile. Some believed Winifred became his mistress, and from his humble first appearances in the midtwenties, Hitler graduated to staying in the Siegfried Haus next to Wagner's

---

59. Waite, *The Psychopathic God*, 225.
60. Chris Bishop, *Hitler's Third Reich* (London, Midsummer Books Ltd., 1999), vol. 8, 4.
61. Wallace et al., *Intimate Sex Lives of Famous People*, 221.
62. Wagner, Nike, *The Wagners*, 207.
63. Wagner, Gottfried, *Twilight of the Wagners*, 210.
64. Hamann, *Winifred Wagner*, 188.

home, Wahnfried in Bayreuth.[65] The cottage was reconstructed to add a wing in grey marine chalk with a roof terrace and an ornamental basin with a stone sculpture of a fish.[66] The furniture consisted of imitation Chippendale and Sheraton designed to match the Führer's taste as exhibited in Berlin and his Berghof house in the Obersalzburg.[67] The architect was Hans Carl Reissinger, who was the uncle of Wieland's future wife. He was to serve Bayreuth with distinction in his professional capacity after Winifred managed to lure him away from Düsseldorf.[68]

Hitler showered gifts on Winifred Wagner, including an ivory sewing case one year and a small pendant in the shape of a triple swastika, when he saw her at the next festival. A leather vanity case followed quickly on the heels of the Nazi bauble and the last recorded gift rolled majestically into the spacious grounds of Wahnfried in 1938 – the latest model Mercedes Benz.[69] From Winifred's correspondence with Hitler, which escaped the incinerator, it is clear that she consulted him on all important decisions regarding the festivals and even the production of the operas – he was sponsoring them after all.[70] After the performances the two would return to Wahnfried and discuss every detail of the singing, the productions and the future – long into the night the leader of Germany talked to the cultural duchess of the country.[71]

In Bayreuth there was a great deal of gossip about the nature of the relationship between Hitler and Winifred. Albert Speer, who often accompanied Hitler on his trips there, was convinced that he had an affair with her. On their return from a visit Hitler seemed quietly elated and Speer noticed a blissful gleam in his eye. When Hitler was in a bad mood it was thought that he needed the Bayreuth cure.[72]

It was Thomas Mann who expounded the view that Wagner's works were a uniquely explosive mixture of myth and psychology, rousing the

---

65. Hitler sneaked into Bayreuth in the early twenties but later lived in Bayreuth in style in the Siegfried Haus. See Geissmar, *The Baton and the Jackboot*, 206–7.
66. Wagner, Nike, *The Wagners*, 175.
67. Ibid., 176.
68. Ibid., 177.
69. Ibid., 157.
70. Spotts, *Bayreuth*, 188.
71. Ibid.
72. Hamann, *Winifred Wagner*, 312–13.

most sensitive emotions, the deepest primordial passions.[73] Mann wrote a number of stories including *Tristan*, in which a performance on the piano of excerpts from the erotic idyll in *Tristan und Isolde* proves fatal to a patient in a sanatorium. In another story, *The Blood of the Walsungs*, twins, significantly renamed Siegmund and Sieglinde, have passionate intercourse on a bearskin rug, after attending a performance of *The Valkyries*, in which their operatic namesakes do the same in the forest at the end of act 1.[74]

During the small hours in the great mansion reeking with musical history, what happened between the two heirs of that cursed inheritance? Nike Wagner suggests Winifred Wagner was "twenty-seven, sizzling with an erotic energy that was mainly channeled into eating…[but] old enough to desire the whip-cracking authority of the dominating man."[75] It is not clear that Nike was aware of the intimate secrets of the relationship between Wagner's daughter-in-law and Hitler but her metaphor has a Freudian ring about it.

Given the Wagnerian penchant for destroying documents and protecting reputations, little has siphoned through the miasma of secrecy. Corroboration for a perverted relationship with her comes from an unlikely source, given the force of the Hippocratic oath. Interviewed after the war, Winifred's doctor told the US Army investigators that she was terrified of being alone with Hitler. She had visited Dr. Kurt Krüger in Munich, ostensibly to consult him about her daughter Friedelind's problems with obesity. Left alone with the doctor for a while she blurted out how shocked she was by the Führer's unorthodox lovemaking.[76] She told the doctor that she could not control him and he frightened her.

What horrors were perpetrated in Wahnfried and in the adjoining cottage built for Siegfried Wagner and subsequently called the Hitler annex? Winifred's daughter Friedelind must have enjoyed her mother's confidence in those early years; she later told the American authorities that the man disgusted her mother, as he liked to be whipped.[77] Dr. Karl Brandt, a doctor who attended on the Führer from time to time, was of the view that "rela-

---

73. Spotts, *Bayreuth*, 6.
74. See Conrad, "He's Tricky, That Dicky."
75. Ibid.
76. Infield, *Hitler's Secret Life*, 89.
77. See Chris Bishop, *Hitler's Third Reich* (London, Midsummer Books Ltd., 1999), vol. 8, 4.

tions between Frau Wagner and Hitler were [possibly] fostered by her to attain the fulfillment of her objective [the revival of the Bayreuth Festival]."[78] On the surface all was courtesy and good-mannerliness. On January 8, 1933 Hitler wrote to Winifred and said, "Today I understand why in my youth it was Wagner and his destiny that spoke to me more than many other great Germans. It was the same ordeal, the eternal struggle against hatred, envy and incomprehension."[79]

In a report based on what Strasser and others told the OSS, Dr. Walter C. Langer and other American psychoanalysts and clinical psychologists concluded that Hitler was a "neurotic psychopath."[80] His aberrant sexual activity was "an extreme form of masochism in which the individual derives sexual gratification from the act of having a woman urinate or defecate on him."[81] Waite, who subtitles his book on Hitler as *The Psychopathic God*, concludes that his "sadomasochistic tendencies were consistent with coprophilic perversion, for in it masochism and sadism are united."[82]

Freud himself indicated why this form of perversion had arisen. "The coprophilic instinctual components [have] proved incompatible with our aesthetic standards of culture, probably since, as a result of our adopting an erect gait, we raised our organ of smell from the ground."[83] He suggested that psychoneurotics fell ill "when the libido fails to get satisfaction along normal lines."[84]

Walter Langer of the OSS pointed out Hitler's love for pornography. One of his favorite magazines was *Der Stürmer* and he could hardly wait to read the dirty stories and leer at the cartoons. Hitler also had a large collection of nudes and, according to Hanfstaengl and others, he also enjoyed viewing lewd movies prepared by his personal photographer Hoffmann and other purveyors of smut for his benefit.[85]

Perhaps the most accurate analysis of his sexuality comes from a confidant who had reason to know the man more intimately than any doctor.

---

78. Infield, *Hitler's Secret Life*, 89.
79. Spotts, *Hitler and the Power of Aesthetics*, 253.
80. Langer, OSS *Psychological Report on Adolf Hitler*, 17.
81. Waite, *The Psychopathic God*, 237.
82. Ibid., 241.
83. Freud, *On Sexuality*, 258.
84. Ibid., 85.
85. Langer, OSS *Psychological Report on Adolf Hitler*, 85–86.

Hanfstaengl told the American intelligence agency in 1942 that Hitler's "most personal problem" was that he did not have "a normal sex life." He later told historian Fritz von Siedler in 1951: "Hitler's potency was partly limited and partly perverted into abnormality. The basis of that abnormality must have been developed by his experiences in the men's hostel in Vienna. That he had a liaison with Hess…is beyond doubt."[86] From this it seems to be clear that Hitler must have told Hanfstaengl about his experiences in Vienna with the homosexuals he habitually brought home with him. Langer's report in the early forties commented on the pleasure Hitler derived from looking at men's bodies and associating with homosexuals. Strasser made mention of the fact that his personal bodyguards were almost always exclusively homosexuals.[87]

Langer makes mention of remarks dropped by Förster, the Danzig Gauleiter, a known homosexual, in conversations with Rauschning. The remarks deal mostly with Hitler's impotence as far as heterosexual relations go but Hitler called Förster "Bubi," a common nickname employed by homosexuals in addressing their partners.[88] Of course there was a very strong reason for Hitler to want to hide his homosexuality. It will be recalled that homosexual acts even between consenting males were criminal offenses in terms of section 175 of the German penal code. For many years homosexuals were referred to as 175ers.

Rauschning made it clear to Langer that this was an extraordinary man with extraordinary perversions. "Most loathsome of all is the reeking miasma of furtive, unnatural sexuality that fills and fouls the whole atmosphere around him, like an evil emanation. Nothing in this environment is straightforward. Surreptitious relationships, substitutes and symbols, false sentiments and secret lusts – nothing in this man's surroundings is natural and genuine, nothing has the openness of a natural instinct."[89]

Hanfstaengl maintained that Hitler dwelt in a "sexual no-man's-land" where there was no one "who could bring him release" – neither man nor woman. Hitler's stunted sex life was "a sort of bisexual narcissistic vanity." His "excess of male energy" found no normal outlet and he was "neither

---

86. Machtan, *Hidden Hitler*, 277.
87. Langer, OSS *Psychological Report on Adolf Hitler*, 195.
88. Ibid., 194.
89. Ibid., 85.

completely heterosexual nor completely homosexual."[90] Just the sort of personality who would contemplate carrying out the "great solution" suggested by Richard Wagner. The composer had spoken of his own "highly susceptible, intense, voracious sensuality, which must somehow or other be flattered if my mind is to accomplish the agonizing labor of calling a non-existent world into being." Was the warped, perverted "sensuality" of the politician flattering and helping him accomplish his great mission of creating his own nonexistent world – a world without any Jews?

---

90. Ibid.

Chapter fifteen
Absolute Power

Once in power, Hitler proceeded to establish his absolute control over the reins of government and arranged for new elections on the grounds that a majority in the Reichstag could not be obtained. A fire in the Reichstag, the German parliament building, on February 27, 1933, reminded Hitler of the burning of the capitol at the end of *Rienzi*,[1] and provided an excuse for a law trampling on all guarantees of freedom and an intensified campaign of violence by his paramilitary and military thugs. The elections on March 5 secured the Nazis 43.9 percent of the votes. The Reichstag assembled and passed a law giving full powers to Hitler. An ominous note was struck with the establishment of the first concentration camp at Dachau, twelve miles from Munich, on March 22.[2]

One of the first laws passed as part of Hitler's campaign against the Jews was the Law for the Restoration of the Civil Service of April 7, 1933, which provided for the dismissal of all Jewish civil servants. Soon lawyers, doctors, writers, artists, university and schoolteachers and students were to follow. Albert Einstein was one such exile – his work had been assigned the strangest stigma. "And when the physicist Einstein asserts that the principle of the constant speed of light applies only when there is no gravitation that

---

1. Köhler, *Wagner's Hitler*, 3.
2. Kershaw, *Hitler 1936–1945: Nemesis*, 464.

The case that Hitler was homosexual is strengthened by a consideration of the art he loved the most. Arno Breker sculpture in the Reich Chancellery. Homo Hitler, page 270. Zentralinstitut für Kunstgeschichte, München.

is also cultural Bolshevism and a personal favor to Stalin," was the wisdom of Carl von Ossietzky, a Nazi party publicist hack in April 1931.[3]

Further indignities followed in rapid succession; for ease of recognition Jews were required by subsequent legislation to have the first name of "Sara" or "Israel."[4] In 1939 Jews were prohibited from driving motor vehicles or taking part in cultural events. On May 10, 1933, the burning of books of authors unacceptable to the Third Reich took place and twenty thousand books of poets and philosophers were consigned to conflagration. Freud's monumental contribution to psychotherapy was thrown on the literary funeral pyre, stigmatized as "Jewish pornography."[5] The most spectacular burning of his work took place in Berlin where his works were publicly burned.[6] Other authors suffering the same fate included Heinrich

---

3. Spotts, *Hitler and the Power of Aesthetics*, 24.
4. Waite, *The Psychopathic God*, 369.
5. Wallace et al., *Intimate Sex Lives of Famous People*, 177.
6. Freud, *On Sexuality*, 30.

Heine, who had written "where books are burnt, in the end people are also burnt."[7] Did the prophetic poet, who had helped Richard Wagner in his darkest hours in Paris, have the ovens of Auschwitz in mind?

A hundred years before, the Jewish writer and poet Heine wrote that the violence of German writers of his day had "developed revolutionary forces which only await the day to break forth and fill the world with terror and astonishment."[8] Heine maintained that Christianity had restrained the German's "brutal joy in battle" for many centuries but "should the subduing talisman, the Cross, break, then will come roaring forth the wild madness of the old champions, the insane Berserker rage of which the Northern poets sing. That talisman is brittle, and the day will come when it will pitifully break. The old stone Gods will rise from the long-forgotten ruin and rub the dust of a thousand years from their eyes; and Thor, leaping to life with his giant hammer, will crush the gothic cathedrals."[9] The emperor Barbarossa had awakened from his magic sleep in the Obersalzberg and was preparing to embark on his sacred mission.

Once Hitler became chancellor in 1933 Bayreuth became a Nazi festival, festooned with swastikas and awash with ss soldiers.[10] According to Albert Speer, his minister of armaments and erstwhile architect, even during his busiest times as chancellor of Germany Hitler carried on making detailed sketches for all four parts of the *Ring*, on which he worked night after night for three weeks.[11] The festival program that year compared Hitler to Wagner, as the most German of citizens, and hailed the former as the "creator of the new Germany" and the agent of "spiritual and moral renewal of the people."[12]

Anti-Semitism was not restricted to Germans alone. Even foreigners objected to aspects of the production of the *Ring* and offense was found with the most innocent of stage props. In the concluding glorious twenty minutes of *The Valkyries*, the second of the four operas, Wotan orders his daughter Brünnhilde to submit to a magic sleep on a prominent rock,

---

7. Kershaw, *Hitler 1936–1945: Nemesis*, 483.
8. Waite, *The Psychopathic God*, 261.
9. Ibid.
10. Hitler's visit in 1933 to Bayreuth is described with the whole town crawling with ss. See Wagner and Cooper, *Heritage of Fire*, 97.
11. Köhler, *Wagner's Hitler*, 66.
12. Spotts, *Bayreuth*, 174.

The relationship between Hitler and the Wagner family was very close. Here Hitler is shown with Siegfried and Winifred Wagner's two sons, Wolfgang and Wieland. See Wolf Siegfried Wagner, page 123.

from which a hero who knows no fear – Siegfried – will rescue her. Adolf Zinsstag, the leading light and president of the Swiss Richard Wagner Association, vented his spleen on the Valkyrie rock, designed by Preetorius, describing it as "subversive Jewish poison."[13]

Hitler continued to treat Wieland and Wolfgang Wagner, grandsons of Richard Wagner, as his own and gave the former a motorcar for his seventeenth birthday.

The Greek amphitheatre had been an inspiration to the composer as had been the drama and the myths. The adulation continued and Wieland gave his graduation speech in fluent ancient Greek.[14] In Hitler's house in Munich could be found a painting of Sir Adolf on horseback, dressed in shining white armor similar to that worn by the hero in Wagner's opera *Lohengrin*.[15] Of all the portraits painted of him he chose that painting to represent him for the year 1938.[16]

When Leni Riefenstahl made the film *Triumph of the Will* she knew immediately who should portray the part of Lohengrin – Adolf Hitler.[17]

---

13. Wagner, Nike, *The Wagners*, 155.
14. Ibid., 217.
15. Viereck, *Metapolitics*, 136.
16. Waite, *The Psychopathic God*, 101.
17. See Andrew Clark, "A Redeemer Tainted by Purity," *Financial Times*, April 3, 2005.

Hitler often depicted himself as a Wagnerian hero – more particularly as Lohengrin, the main role in his most romantic opera. From Larry Solomon website.

Apart from his moral support Hitler granted the festival fifty thousand marks a year from his private funds and, to the envy of the other theatres, granted tax exemption.[18] According to Fest the supreme expression of opera to him was the finale of *Götterdämmerung*, the fourth part of the *Ring*. In Bayreuth, whenever Valhalla collapsed in flames, he would take the hand of Frau Winifred Wagner and "breathe a deeply moved Handkuss upon it."[19] In the light of what we know about Hitler's sexual practices Winifred must have been relieved that he limited his attentions to such a tranquil move.

During the festival Hitler liked to think he was on holiday and should not be bothered with important matters of state. The children watched fascinated as the Führer consumed vast quantities of sweets and cake. He was reckoned to eat up to two pounds of chocolates a day and Friedelind

---

18. For an account of Hitler and Winifred Wagner see also Skelton, *Wagner at Bayreuth*, 143.
19. Fest, Hitler, 520.

watched intrigued each teatime to see if he would remember to put in the seven spoons of sugar – his favorite number.[20]

For some time it was impossible to run the festival without the Jewish singers and musicians and in 1933 Winifred did ask Hitler for leave to make use of Jewish artists and Hitler reluctantly agreed.[21] In the second Ring cycle during the interval after the second act of *Walküre* Hitler's great election speech was broadcast via loudspeakers. The speech was quite drawn out and the delay was increased when the Brownshirts sang the *Deutschland über Alles* hymn and the Horst Wessel song, which became the official Nazi anthem. The beginning of the mighty third act was postponed by two hours because of these political events, a cause for immense irritation from even the most good-natured old festival guests.[22]

Walter Legge (husband of the famous soprano Elizabeth Schwarzkopf) described in the *Manchester Guardian* the noticeable changes in the Bayreuth atmosphere emphasizing that it had become a Hitler festival. Commerce had also seen the advantages of the politician's love of the composer. In former festivals each shop, regardless of the nature of its business, would have had at least one reproduction of Wagner's portrait whereas now there were dozens of Hitler busts. Booksellers had displayed Wagner's autobiography and now the porcelain shops were full of Hitler miniatures. *Mein Kampf*, Legge said trenchantly, has ousted *Mein Leben*. He commented on the change of bunting as from every flagpole the swastikas were waving and the Brownshirts were the order of the day. While the theatre still played the maestro's music, when you passed the café Tannhäuser or Gasthof Rheingold all you heard was the Horst Wessel *Lied*. This Hitler adulation had an adverse effect on attendance by the traditional audience. The irony was that his presence drove away those he denigrated until he had to support the survival of the festival himself.[23]

During his lengthy diatribes, after the operas at Bayreuth, in the comfort of the old Siegfried Wagner house, Hitler talked about his hopes and dreams for the new Germany. A theme he constantly returned to was his fear of getting old and the tragic loss to Germany of the decade between the

---

20. Waite, *The Psychopathic God*, 8.
21. Wagner and Cooper, *Heritage of Fire*, 82–83.
22. Hamann, *Winifred Wagner*, 259.
23. Ibid.

The conductor Heinz Tietjen ran the Bayreuth Festival for some years and was a lover of Winifred Wagner. He is pictured here with her and the famous German composer Richard Strauss. Wolf Siegfried Wagner, page 114. Foto Lauterwasser, Überlingen.

Beer Hall Putsch and his accession of power that year.[24] The tragedy was compounded by the fact that he reckoned he would need twenty-two years to prepare Germany adequately for his successor. There was something for posterity to look forward to – during his retirement he would write up his achievements, including the bible of National Socialism.[25]

The new mayor of Bayreuth, Karl Schlumprecht, made use of an opportune moment during one of Hitler's visits in 1933 and went to the Parkstrasse wearing an SS uniform and his mayoral chain. Accompanied by local party leaders and the deputy Gauleiter, he gave Hitler official freedom of the town, the "keys to the city," as it were. In the council minutes it was recorded that Bayreuth breathed a sigh of relief and felt the sense of liberation from the conscious oppression and even humiliation of the town through a government that was hostile to the Nazi worldview. The minutes applauded the advent of a new will to remedy the old injustices.[26]

Winifred did not see herself as capable of undertaking the overall artistic direction of the festival and employed Heinz Tietjen, an erstwhile generalintendant of the Prussian theatres in Berlin. Gradually an intimate

---

24. Langer, *The Mind of Adolf Hitler*, 38.
25. Ibid.
26. Hamann, *Winifred Wagner*, 257.

relationship developed between them. The tone between Winifred and Tietjen became more intimate and the Wagner children made fun of the new boss whom they only knew from fuzzy newspaper photographs. They claimed he looked like an orangutan, so he sent them a photograph in order to rehabilitate himself. There was no doubt that there was a beginning of more than a work relationship between Winifred and Tietjen. Soon Winifred was in a hectic state obviously in love and she asked her friend Lenchen and her husband to exercise discretion. She realized that news of such a relationship could jeopardize her whole future if they should even hint at anything.[27]

This love for Tietjen who was difficult to make out and who had so many secrets even from her made Winifred into a bundle of nerves. She was not clear about her own feelings. She complained to Albert Knittel. In Bayreuth she had moments of terribly painful loneliness and sometimes she had to start crying because she missed so much Tietjen's love, goodness and care for her. At other times she wondered what he was there for and she thought she had wasted the best years of her life without purpose. No amount of willpower or distraction helped her to overcome her emptiness when he was not there, though she tried all manner of diversions such as going for walks, writing letters and watching puppet plays. She wondered if these were the occupations for a woman with her abilities but for the time being she felt she could not change it and resigned herself to it.[28]

Tietjen was reckoned a charmer of women, despite his physical drawbacks (his physique was not stereotypically attractive), and kept Winifred on a string, with countless promises of marriage, while indulging in dalliances with a succession of other socialites. She appointed him guardian of her children and his political adroitness made him difficult to classify, though many reckoned his favorite adornment was the swastika.[29]

The Nazi race laws were enacted and enforced with great strictness including Goebbels's decree that every Nordic was to divorce his Jewess.[30] The unhappiness the chancellor endured in permitting Jewish artists to perform was replicated in their reluctance to sing before the vicious anti-

---

27. Ibid., 197.
28. Ibid., 220–21.
29. Wagner, Nike, *The Wagners*, 214–15.
30. As to how this affected certain artists see the anonymously published *The Strange Death of Adolf Hitler*, 254.

Semite. Despite much soul-searching the legendary singers Alexander Kipnis and Emanuel List continued to perform even in the chancellor's presence in 1933. Kipnis had been a favorite of Bayreuth audiences and had sung in the festival since 1927 in a number of roles, including Gurnemanz, Marke, Landgraf, Pogner and Titurel.

Those fortunate enough to attend, rate the performances at Bayreuth of *Tristan und Isolde* of 1927 and the *Tannhäuser* of 1930, with Toscanini at the helm, and Melchior, Kipnis and Maria Müller in the lead roles, as treasured memories.[31] Because the festival constituted the high watermark of operatic production in the world, the artists in early Bayreuth days, including famous conductors Karl Muck (Hitler was not immune to gossip and was known to favor the view that Muck was an illegitimate son of Wagner[32]), Arturo Toscanini and – in later years – Hans Knappertsbusch, refused any remuneration.[33] The honor bestowed upon them in being asked and the privilege of being at the Mecca of all music festivals was reckoned sufficient.

Although Kipnis was reckoned a poor actor his voice was imperious and he learned much about stagecraft from Siegfried Wagner.[34] That year was to provide a particularly embarrassing moment for the legendary singer. Kipnis and his wife received an invitation to attend a function at Wahnfried, where Hitler was bound to be in attendance. He was naturally most anxious not to attend and pondered long and hard as to how he could solve his dilemma. The remedy of Oscar Wilde came to mind; the wit had refused an invitation because of a *subsequent* engagement. Eventually he thought of an excuse; he arranged an invitation to the music biographer Ernest Newman and his wife, who were attending the festival, as they invariably did, to dine with him. He was able to decline the invitation with good grace.[35]

That was to be the legendary singer's last season at Bayreuth and two years later he was to be classified as "undesirable" in Berlin.[36] Not that the performances were uniformly excellent and Newman wrote amusingly about how one of the singers, "Gunnar Graarud, the Siegfried of the

---

31. Skelton, *Wagner at Bayreuth*, 109.
32. Spotts, *Hitler and the Power of Aesthetics*, 250.
33. Ibid., 6.
34. Ibid., 154.
35. Douglas, *Legendary Voices*, 124–25.
36. Ibid.

Götterdämmerung, came so near to complete loss of voice in the last act that probably Hagen saved his life by killing him when he did."[37]

Apart from the reluctance of the Jewish artists to perform, the anti-Semitism drove away Jews and decent operagoers and provided a financial dilemma for Winifred. Into the breach goose-stepped the composer's greatest fan, whip in hand, and the State's coffers were as available as had been those of King Ludwig II of Bavaria. Facing the icy reaches of East Prussia he told his yawning generals, "I considered it to be a particular joy to be able to keep Bayreuth going at a time when it faced financial ruin."[38] At a memorial event in 1933 at Ludwig's monument to Wagner – the fairy tale castle Neuschwanstein, beloved of children and the model for the Walt Disney films – Hitler told the audience with great pride of his mission to complete what Ludwig had started and spoke of financial support for Bayreuth as a "national obligation."[39] No doubt – secreted in his breast pocket – was that love letter.

The dictator financed a number of the productions himself including those designed with Benno von Arent – the *Lohengrin* in 1935 at the German Opera in Berlin, *Rienzi* at the Dietrich Eckart Open Air Theatre in Berlin and *Meistersinger* in 1934. His favorite architect and minister for armaments Albert Speer recorded: "At the chancellery Hitler once sent up to his bedroom for neatly executed stage designs, coloured with crayons, for all the acts of *Tristan und Isolde*; these were to be given to Arent to serve as an inspiration. Another time he gave Arent a series of sketches for all the scenes of *Der Ring des Nibelungen*. At lunch he told us with great satisfaction that for three weeks he had sat up over these, night after night. This surprised me the more because at this particular time Hitler's daily schedule was unusually heavy with visitors, speeches, sightseeing and other public activities."[40] The relationship between Hitler and Speer, according to Dr. Matthias Schmidt in his book *Albert Speer: The End of a Myth*, was "erotic" and while Speer was working on architectural drawings for Hitler's official residence, Adolf invited him to lunch. "At lunch, Speer

---

37. Spotts, *Hitler and the Power of Aesthetics*, 154.
38. Ibid., 169.
39. Ibid., 170.
40. Ibid., 239.

sat at Hitler's side. The conversation became personal and the two men fell in love at first sight."[41]

Hitler still desired the office of president as well and to take it he needed to retain the support of the army and the leaders of industry, provided they served the interests of the Nazi state. One of Hitler's earliest supporters and confederates was Ernst Röhm, a colorful character and masterful organizer of the masses. Röhm was against Hitler's decision to consolidate the political position at that time and advocated a "continuing revolution." The charismatic leadership of Röhm as head of the powerful SA brought him into conflict with the other armed forces and he was greatly distrusted by the army.

Röhm's death on Hitler's orders was to have serious consequences for the dictator's sleep patterns and it is necessary to briefly examine his background. Röhm was a practicing homosexual and cultured bon vivant. A Reichswehr general alleged in 1934 that Röhm's friendship with the chancellor extended much further than comradely affection; in fact he had a sexual relationship with Hitler.[42] The German leader's conduct with fellow soldiers in the First World War and with other males in Munich seems to make a relationship of that nature a real probability. There is corroboration for the Reichswehr General's account from a medical source. A doctor who treated Hitler during the early days of the Third Reich, Kurt Krüger, who also administered to the Wagner family medical problems, was also convinced that the two men enjoyed an intimate friendship.[43]

Röhm's homosexuality was well known in Nazi circles and he and Hitler were immediately attracted. They had a lot in common, including their musical tastes. A contemporary account of Röhm, during a short interlude at a big country house in Wolmirsedt, Thuringia gives a good impression of why he and the Führer saw so much of each other. Thuringia it will be recalled was the area where Tannhäuser met Venus and engaged in lustful follies in the Venusberg. The account described him playing the piano nearly every night and his favorite composer was the one revered by Hitler – the music of Richard Wagner was consequently the main musical diet. He also visited the shrine of Bayreuth and paid homage to their

---

41. See Schmidt, *Albert Speer: The End of a Myth*, 41f.
42. Machtan, *The Hidden Hitler*, 111.
43. Infield, *Hitler's Secret Life*, 197.

Hitler enjoyed a homosexual relationship with Ernst Röhm, whom he later had murdered during what became known as The Night of the Long Knives. Bishop vol. 8, page 23.

mutual god. He described in his own words why a liaison with Hitler at that very venue might have taken place on frequent occasions. "In line with my special predilection and object of veneration, I was privileged to be a frequent guest at Haus Wahnfried in Bayreuth, where I was able to let the overpowering musical creations of our most German of masters affect me in [an atmosphere of] consummate solemnity and beauty."[44]

From time to time party members spoke to Hitler complaining about the openness with which his friend conducted his activities. Hitler's terse riposte was that "his private life cannot be an object of scrutiny unless it conflicts with basic principles of National Socialist ideology."[45] Hitler explained that it was not an "institute for the moral education of genteel, young ladies, but a formation of seasoned fighters," and threatened to expel the complainers. But Röhm wanted total power and when persuasion and the offer of high political office failed to convince Röhm to fall into line, Hitler carried out the suggestions of Göring and Heinrich Himmler.

On June 29, 1934, the occasion subsequently referred to by historians as "The Night of the Long Knives," Ernst Röhm and his lieutenant

---

44. Ibid., 110.
45. Bleuel, *Sex and Society in Nazi Germany*, 98.

The legendary German tenor Max Lorenz as Wagner's hero Siegfried in the Ring of the Nibelung. See Osborne, page 209. Bildarchiv Preussischer Kulturbesitz, Berlin.

Edmund Heines were executed without trial, together with Gregor Strasser, Schleicher and others. Hitler conducted this purge of elements in and out of the Nazi party who were causing him problems, including the bothersome cleric who had knowledge of his perversions. The murders of these erstwhile comrades at arms and street fighters showed that Hitler would not tolerate any opposition and made short shrift of anyone challenging his leadership position.

For the bigoted the fact that Röhm was a homosexual meant an opportunity not to be missed to attack all those of his ilk. Many star artists and assistants at Bayreuth were in jeopardy and the process was to strike megastar Max Lorenz who was caught *in flagranti delicto* behind the scenes with a young man by Wolfgang Wagner and arrested. This was a great embarrassment to Winifred as his employer and Hitler regarded it as unbearable. Winifred knew that without her star singer she might as well close the festival – she could not do without him. He was to sing the major roles Walter von Stolzing in *Meistersinger* and Siegfried in the *Ring*. After a nervous delay the charge was dropped and Lorenz dared to sing in Bayreuth. What was more, his wife and manageress, who did not wish him ill, received Aryan status from Göring in the light of his credo that he determined who Jews were.[46]

The new chancellor showed no undue anxiety when he was confronted by the Jewess Lotte Lorenz. A foreign visitor witnessed how intrigued he was by the mysterious blonde in Berlin and then found out it was the wife of Lorenz. Hitler slapped his thigh and laughed hysterically. When he heard Lorenz he was hypnotized by the beauty of his voice. In some regards his love of music trumped his bigotry. He forgot the blood scandal of the marriage, accepted the Jewish wife and neglected the pompous Winifred.[47]

When Friedelind Wagner heard that when Röhm was killed the assassins found him in bed with another man she was relieved. The young pigtailed daughter of Winifred and Siegfried Wagner remarked naively that it was lucky he was not in bed with a woman. So much did homosexuality permeate society that in his book *The Arms of Krupp*, William Manchester concluded that sodomy was known as "the German vice."[48] As such it formed the title of a book. In *Germany's National Vice* Samuel Igra was forced to conclude that such was especially rife in the higher echelons of government, for "in Germany these unnatural vices became a veritable cult among the ruling classes.…"

Extravagant indeed were the measures some took to obtain pleasure. History records that in 1936, Goebbels threw a party including "torch-bearing page boys in tight fitting white breeches, white satin blouses with lace cuffs and powdered rococo wigs." The Nazi bigwigs quickly succumbed to the temptation and "were so affected by the rococo setting that they hurled themselves upon the bewigged page boys and pulled them into the bushes. Tables collapsed, torches were dimmed, and in the ensuing fracas a number of Party old fighters and their comely victims had to be rescued from drowning."[49]

After "The Night of the Long Knives," a series of mysterious events troubled Hitler; when he opened his correspondence he would find in one corner of the stationery, embossed in red letters the initials "RR." The mystery persisted for some time and on one occasion his peace of mind was in tatters when he found a treaty with a foreign power similarly inscribed.

---

46. Hamann, *Winifred Wagner*, 283.
47. Ibid.
48. Manchester, *The Arms of Krupp*, 232.
49. Grunberger, *The Twelve-Year Reich*, 70.

That the perpetrators had access to his clothing and immediate surroundings became apparent when the same mysterious letters appeared on his trench coat and on his bedroom wall – in blood! Rauschning told Walter Langer that Hitler had a compulsion that his bed was made in a particular way and that a man must make the bed, before he could go to sleep. Langer postulated an extension of his homosexual nature and concluded from his general psychological structure that such a compulsion was possible.[50]

The Gestapo and other agencies had their work cut out finding the culprits; their day-and-night endeavors eventually led them to a sinister and aptly named group known as *Röhm's Revengers*.[51] Some of the members were rounded up and executed; the trail of one – Heinz Formis – led to the city of Prague in Czechoslovakia where this close associate of Röhm, who had sabotaged Hitler's speeches while operating the German radio, met his grisly end in a back street, mutilated beyond recognition.[52]

Throughout his years as leader of Germany Hitler was plagued by insomnia. All the best doctors in Germany suggested cures – though Freud and his ilk were never consulted. Who knows what horrors they would have found had they been privileged to gaze into that troubled psyche. Rauschning claimed that one of Hitler's close associates told him that "Hitler wakes at night with convulsive shrieks; shouts for help. He sits on the edge of his bed, as if unable to stir. He shakes with fear, making the whole bed vibrate. He shouts confused, unintelligible phrases. He gasps, as if imagining himself to be suffocating. On one occasion, Hitler stood swaying in his room, looking wildly about him. 'He! He! He's been here!' he gasped."[53] Was Hitler referring to the ghost of his great friend? The account continues "His lips were blue. Sweat streamed down his face. Suddenly he began to reel off figures, and odd words and broken phrases, entirely devoid of sense. It sounded horrible. He used strangely composed and entirely un-German word formations. Then he stood still, only his lips moving…Then he suddenly broke out 'There, there! In the corner! Who's that?' He stamped and shrieked in the familiar way."

Hitler tried everything to deal with the specters and to fall asleep; from standing on his head before retiring to bed, to watching a film of a

---
50. Langer, OSS *Psychological Report on Adolf Hitler*, 56.
51. Infield, *Hitler's Secret Life*, 53–55.
52. Ibid.
53. Langer, OSS *Psychological Report on Adolf Hitler*, 135.

waterfall – the suggestion of a Swiss psychologist – which had no better result than incessant visits to urinate. The best brains of India, China and Japan were also consulted with less than mediocre success. "Perchance to dream" – the real reason for his insomnia may have been his tortured soul.

Even if Röhm had murdered Hitler's sleep the army was not similarly hampered and the prospect of a weaker SA meant more influence for the generals. When Hindenburg died on August 2 a unique opportunity was presented to Hitler to merge the offices of chancellor and president. Hitler was now in supreme command of the armed forces of the Reich and officers and men took an oath of allegiance to Hitler personally. Hitler took advantage of the world economic recovery and a reduction in unemployment to hold a plebiscite in which 90 percent of voters, encouraged by his paramilitary allies to place their crosses in the right box, found that his regime was doing a fine job.

The stage was now set for the dictator to move. Hitler's objectives as laid down in *Mein Kampf* based on Wagner, Gobineau and Chamberlain were now within his grasp, and he moved to carry out his sacred mission. The accretion of all German speakers had been advocated in speeches and print for many years. Pan-Germanism, as advocated by the Austrian Georg von Schönerer, involved the reunion of the German peoples and this received attention as his first priority. Hand in hand with the acquisition of all Teutons who spoke the German language was the need to acquire living space for them to spread themselves decently. *Lebensraum* (literally: room to live) later required the natural expansion eastward to Poland and the USSR to continue Germany's historic conflict with the Slav peoples – a race regarded by Hitler as inferior to the Teutonic master race, defined by Wagner and Chamberlain.

Hitler showed himself to be a canny politician with a ruthless daring that shocked and bewildered other European and American leaders. In his view – and he brooked no opposition – Fascist Italy was regarded as a potential ally in the fight against the Slavs as was Britain, provided it limited itself to its interests overseas. France was the natural enemy of Germany and had to be dealt with to make possible the rampant territorial ambitions of the Führer.

Always the master of deception, he pretended on the one hand to be a man of peace who wished only to remove the inequalities of the Versailles

Treaty, and yet when the first opportunity presented itself, he withdrew from the Disarmament Conference and from the League of Nations in October 1933. To allay suspicions that he had done so to embark on territorial acquisition, he signed a nonaggression treaty with Poland in January 1934.

When the Austrian Nazis, with Hitler's connivance, murdered Chancellor Engelbert Dollfuss of Austria and attempted a coup d'état in July 1934, the Nazis were confident the neighbor state would quickly fall into their dominion.

On July 25, 1934, Hitler arranged the Dollfuss murder. Ostensibly Dollfuss had opposed the Nazi plan to annex Austria but he also was known to dislike Hitler intensely. The Italian press, in this instance represented by *Il Popolo di Roma*, Mussolini's mouthpiece, suggested that the murderers were "pederasts and assassins" from Berlin. Mussolini even mobilized troops on the Austro-Italian frontier, as a gesture against Hitler's designs on Austria. The reason Dollfuss disliked Hitler was that he had divined his imperial ambitions, which were in fact patently manifest, but Dollfuss's objections to Hitler were given teeth by the fact that he had a range of weapons at his disposal including salacious blackmail material.

Dollfuss was not the only one to have the goods on Hitler, although others managed to avoid paying the ultimate price as he did. Magnus Hirschfeld – a leading campaigner for homosexuals – experienced a less devastating version of Hitler's defensive destruction of those who might challenge him. He was Director of the Sex Research Institute of Berlin, a German version of the Alfred Kinsey Institute. Hitler destroyed the Institute in 1934, some suspect because of evidence held there that incriminated him. A book has been written about Hirschfeld by Charlotte Wolff, M.D., who quotes an institute patient as describing Hitler as "the most perverted of us all. He is very much like a soft woman…"[54] Hitler's deviance in fact seems to have been rather well known. Desmond Seward has recorded that Fascist dictator Benito Mussolini often referred to Hitler as "that horrible sexual degenerate."[55]

Dollfuss himself may have played a large part in the spreading of this knowledge. Samuel Igra has concluded that revenge was Hitler's motive for

---

54. Ibid., 103.
55. Seward, *Napoleon and Hitler*, 148.

the assassination. "For Dollfuss had come into possession of an authentic affidavit which connected Hitler directly with the moral scandals I have spoken of…[H]e had certified copies of the affidavit made and entrusted to the diplomatic representatives of several governments in Vienna…Among others Dr. Hermann Rauschning assured me that he had seen a copy of such a document, which was in the hands of a foreign government. *It declared that Hitler had been a male prostitute in Vienna at the time of his sojourn there, from 1907 to 1912, and that he practiced the same calling in Munich from 1912 to 1914…*"[56]

When Hitler received news of the Dollfuss assassination he was attending the Wagner festival at Bayreuth. He had been attending *Das Rheingold* and was standing in the library downstairs, near the portrait of Cosima in the black dress painted by Lembach. Winifred Wagner told him that he was urgently required in a private room at Wahnfried where two SS officers, Schaub and Bruckner, were waiting.[57]

Winifred was so excited she gave Hitler a big kiss and called him the chancellor of Germany and Austria. She predicted that Hitler would soon be the ruler of the whole world. After receiving this wonderful news a beaming Hitler told her that they had to go to the restaurant and show themselves to the other guests – otherwise people would think that Hitler had something to do with it.[58] Despite the assassination, the attempt by Austrian Nazis to take over Austria failed, and as Mussolini moved troops to the frontier, Hitler disclaimed all responsibility and cynically sacrificed those who had acted with his sanction. He had clearly overplayed his hand but he was confident the mountain state would soon form part of his Pan-German empire.

The festival brochure for that year included a piece by the Nazi mayor of Bayreuth who pointed out that Wagner was a forerunner of Hitler. "Hail Germany! Hail Hitler! Hail Bayreuth art!" and a journalist pointed out how Hitler's *Mein Kampf* had led many Germans to an appreciation of the composer.[59]

Hermann Rauschning, author of *Hitler Speaks*, recalls a conversation in 1934 when Hitler stated that he and only he comprehended the true

---

56. Ibid., 137.
57. Shirer, *Rise and Fall of the Third Reich*, 345.
58. Ibid., 345.
59. Spotts, *Bayreuth*, 174.

meaning of Wagner's idea: "the composer had really proclaimed the eternal tragedy of human destiny and was the supreme prophet of the Germans." Providence or accident had brought him to Wagner early in life and "everything written by that great man that he had read was in agreement with his own innermost, subconscious, dormant conviction."[60]

Apart from the Wagner operas, which always remained his favorites, Hitler saw a number of other operas such as *Friedenstag* (The Day of Peace) by Richard Strauss. Not one of Strauss's most popular operas, the premiere in Munich with Hans Hotter was reckoned by critics as a tour de force but the Führer's ideas were more on the antithesis of peace at that time. Hitler remembered with special affection the festival of 1934 in Bayreuth with Richard Strauss conducting *Parsifal*, the *Ring* and *Meistersinger*. Strauss did have his own worries as his daughter-in-law Alice Strauss was frightened following harassment and threats by the Nazi Party. Strauss was very worried about her and his Jewish grandsons. There was, therefore, much more than physical significance in the fact of the first meeting between Alice and the Führer. Hitler's handshake witnessed by many eyes was meant to warn any overeager party functionaries to be careful in their attitude to her. From now on Alice could point out that she knew the Führer personally.[61]

The impression of a monolithic acceptance of the anti-Semitism is deceptive. An example can be drawn from the schools attended by the Wagner children recounted by Brigitte Hamann in her biography of Winifred. In a sense all the schools were required to provide a similar education, which had an effect on the private schools, especially the church schools that were attended by Friedelind and Verena. In autumn 1934 Elizabeth von Saldern, the mother superior of the Heiligengrabe Convent and the former imperial lady-in-waiting asked Winifred for help. She and three other convent ladies had been denounced by another convent lady and the son of the minister because of hostile statements against the government.

The mother superior is said to have called the Jewish boycott a cultural scandal and she had called prominent Nazi Baldur von Schirach a little upstart, as a result of which he pressed charges against her. In addition one of the pupils at the convent had committed the unpardonable sin of not using the Nazi salute. In response to this an investigation committee

---

60. Windell, "Hitler, National Socialism and Richard Wagner," 219, 227.
61. Hamann, *Winifred Wagner*, 285.

of the Gestapo had arrived unannounced and noted a reactionary spirit. They declared the mother superior to be incapable of taking part in the new order. They recommended that the mother superior should be removed along with those staff members who had backed her, and a Nazi school director employed.

The mother superior defended herself saying that she did adhere to the Nazi principles of Christian values, obedience and patriotism. She pointed to the frequent oppression that the convent had suffered under the Marxist government, as a result of which the convent ladies had greeted the Nazi government with joy. The minister Oestreich who had denounced her, she continued, was a bad teacher and it was very strange that it was specifically children from homes that had been Nazi for a long time like Friedelind who did not like him. None of this helped and the three denounced teachers were dismissed and the mother superior was relieved of her powers. The shortage meant that the higher grades in the school could not be continued and the affected pupils had to leave five months before their matriculation exams.[62] Winifred sent a long plea complaining of the treatment to higher authorities, but to no avail. The end result was a school under Nazi leadership and more influential enemies for Winifred.[63]

Winifred knew she was under the protection of Hitler and never more so than at Christmas 1934 when a large aircraft arrived with a giant portrait of him. Hitler sent his greetings making mention of his friendship and gratitude. The portrait was immediately installed above Winifred's work table where it hung in state until the first American troops arrived in 1945. She wrote a letter to the donor and called him "my dear, dear friend and Führer." She explained how the receipt of the portrait had placed her at a loss for words. She sent unending gratitude and called Hitler the sponsor of unlimited joy. She closed with the salutation, "your Winnie."[64]

As the mother superior Elizabeth von Saldern had discovered, it was not a good idea to be seen as anything but a full and complete supporter of the Führer and his program, and most of the Bayreuth artists in particular took pains to be seen as politically correct. Hotter was one of the few artists to emerge from the sordid saga of collaboration with any dignity and honor.

---

62. Ibid., 294.
63. Ibid., 295.
64. Ibid., 298.

During the Third Reich the Bayreuth Festival became a Nazi cultural highlight. Winifred Wagner, Adolf Hitler and Wieland Wagner are seen entering the theatre ahead of Wolfgang Wagner and some of Hitler's guards. See Gottfried Wagner, page 151.

At the New Year's Eve party of 1934 he participated in a sketch in Prague, still part of the Czechoslovak Republic, in which he compared Hitler to Don Quixote, imitating Hitler's voice, repeating that he only wanted world peace. Prague was awash with anti-German refugees who wept with laughter at his artistry, while the German embassy staff scowled and took notes. Hotter's passport was threatened and only intervention by the professor of medicine at Charles University secured his rights again. Despite this Hitler loved his voice and could quote to him chapter and verse of all his performances. "He is the great baritone of the future," was the dictator's comment in May 1942.[65]

Hitler found it very pleasant to relax at the Wagner home Wahnfried, far from his political struggles. He showed a reverence for the house more befitting a cathedral or sacred site. He visited Wagner's bedroom with the chintz-covered chairs, situated next to the nursery. Nearby the balcony looked over the back garden, the fountain with the rose beds around it and the slab of unmarked grey marble marking the great composer's grave.

---

65. Kater, *The Twisted Muse*, 70.

People commented on how different they found him when in holiday mood. He made a point of meeting all the artists and insisted that they treat him just like a normal citizen and disciple of the great Wagner, paying homage at the shrine. Later he would ride in an open Mercedes to the theatre along the main street – now aptly renamed Adolf Hitler Strasse.[66] Music lovers from the furthest reaches of the world gathered at this sanctuary to read the scores of the great works and talk about the music. They sipped tea and Bavarian beer and watched the Daimlers, Mercedes Benz and Rolls Royce motor vehicles thronging the narrow streets. After the operas, performed at a leisurely pace, with hour-long intervals of time to stroll in the gardens, kings, queens, princesses, grand dukes and duchesses supped in the restaurant with the artists.

Hitler said that he was aware that people perceived him as a very serious person who could never see the funny side of life. But on occasion there was laughter and jokes were told. Hitler's humor was more in the nature of *Schadenfreude*, that indefinable German word indicating joy in the discomfort of others. His favorite joke was the sort of quip a standard pupil would beguile his class with. Why does a swan have such a long neck? Answer: otherwise it would drown.[67]

One year Professor Schultze-Naumberg, the man who remodeled the Nürnberg Opera House, was there. Never an even-tempered man, he was very upset that the rival architect Frau Troost was given the contract to design the interior of the Munich buildings. Apart from his design of buildings, Professor Schultze-Naumberg was a dabbler in racial genetics and had written a book on the characteristics of the Aryan, which really impressed Winifred's sons Wieland and Wolfgang. He had published a second book, *Art and Race*, in 1928 which carried on Nordau's degeneracy principles.[68] One feature of his theory particularly attracted them. The learned professor indicated that the nipples of Aryan women had to be a certain color. "The Aryan woman has full prominent breasts with nipples of a rosy Nordic pink…" With mock serious interest Wieland and Wolfgang questioned the professor about his fieldwork in that regard and who had taken the photographs for the book.

---

66. Spotts, *Bayreuth*, 171.
67. Waite, *The Psychopathic God*, 14.
68. Spotts, *Hitler and the Power of Aesthetics*, 24.

Hitler specially remembered the roles played by Herbert Janssen, the Dutch bass-baritone, who had a beautiful voice and sang the parts of Amfortas and Gunther that year. He had a good sense of humor and told all sorts of stories about the stage and the operas he had sung in. The principal victim of his pranks was Josef van Manowarda, who sang the role of Fafner the dragon. The latter's wife earned the dislike of Janssen as she played a rather different role – offstage – assisting the Nazis to ferret out all their Austrian enemies.

She was a big and rather plain woman and she really worshipped Hitler. The Führer on one occasion gave her a kiss on her wrist and she wore a huge swastika bracelet to mark the position. She did talk too much and at best one had to describe her as a loud-mouthed bore. Herbert Janssen remarked that he wished the Führer had kissed her on the mouth. Janssen became totally disenchanted and boycotted Bayreuth after 1939. His return to his mother country was to present a Wagner with an opportunity to polish a rather weather-beaten marble in the late forties. Winifred – facing a denazification tribunal after the war – alleged that she had assisted his escape.

Amongst the distinguished guests that Hitler met at the festival was the greatest contemporary composer Richard Strauss, who was the president of the German Music Federation and had helped out by conducting at Bayreuth when Toscanini declined. So important did Winifred regard Toscanini's presence at the festival that she prevailed upon Hitler to send him a telegram telling him how as chancellor he would like to greet the great conductor at Bayreuth. A man of principle, Toscanini had little respect for elected heads of state, let alone dictators, and declined – he was never forgiven for standing up for the Jewish conductors Bruno Walter and Klemperer.[69]

The situation was exacerbated when news came of Toscanini's press interviews in New York where he quoted passages from his last letter to Winifred and declared that he would not return to Bayreuth anymore. Winifred was incensed about this indiscretion and all the more so because the newspapers spent a lot of time describing the political differences that

---

69. Mention is made of Toscanini's refusal to work at Bayreuth because of the treatment of Jewish colleagues and Hitler's intervention. See Wagner and Cooper, *Heritage of Fire*, 89.

had caused the alienation between them. One paper quoted the Italian maestro as saying he refused to submit Wagner's genius to the service of Hitler's propaganda. Little did he know! He went on to say that he had left Italy in the spring of that year because hooligans had seriously attacked him when he refused to bow down before Mussolini. He had then sought refuge at Richard Wagner's place but to his disgust had realized that Wagner's daughter-in-law put a lot of effort into propagating National Socialism.[70]

Many Jewish musicians left Germany, including Arnold Schoenberg, who nevertheless maintained his respect for Wagner; he described the Bayreuth Maestro as "the eternal phenomenon" and his greatest work *The Gurrelieder* bears the deep imprint of the Wagner style. Schoenberg saw no future in Germany for himself and fled to the United States.[71]

Hitler was most scathing about the Italian conductor leaving so suddenly and pretending it was because of the treatment of Jewish artists. When Mussolini insisted that the new fascist hymn be sung after the first performance of Puccini's opera *Turandot* Toscanini was horrified and refused point blank. After a vicious standoff during which *Il Duce* huffed and puffed and threatened all sorts of measures against the world-renowned conductor, the dictator beat a tactical retreat. The baton was mightier than the sword – for the time being.

Never the bravest opponent of Nazism, Strauss could on occasion utter acerbic comments on the excesses of the new government. At Bayreuth he was at his sycophantic best and floated the idea that the government should levy one percent on all Wagner performances in Germany and pay the money to Bayreuth. In making the suggestion to Adolf Hitler he was preaching to the most converted but nothing came of the idea because of the factions operating in the world of music and opera. ReichsFührer Goebbels, who was in charge of all theatres except the State Opera, which fell within the jurisdiction of the rotund, bemedaled ReichsFührer Göring, led one faction.

Despite the championship by Hitler of Bayreuth, which soon came to be regarded as his private fiefdom, the wishes of the Führer did not carry the day. Goebbels told his diary "with a woman in charge poor Bayreuth! The Führer is her greatest protector." And Winifred was eternally grateful

---

70. Hamann, *Winifred Wagner*, 205.
71. Richard Wagner Museum brochure, "About Richard Wagner."

for the support: "you know that nothing happens in Bayreuth that is not at the Führer's initiative or in keeping with his explicit approval," she wrote to Richard Strauss in June 1935.[72]

Some of his suggestions included having the flower maidens dance naked round Parsifal, the Norns sitting on a globe of the world in the first act of *Götterdämmerung*, and introducing golden stars in the second act of *Tristan*. Never his strong feature, Hitler's humor was ponderous and cutting and frequently consisted of attacks on his enemies. He told the guests at Bayreuth that he had created two new units of measure – a Goebbels, which was the amount of rubbish a man can talk in an hour, and a Göring, which was the amount of metal one man can carry on his chest. Sycophantic laughter of course accompanied his jests, with artists and diners slapping their thighs in feigned amusement.[73]

Some made courageous stands against the xenophobia and anti-Semitism. The set designer employed by Winifred during the thirties, Emil Preetorius, friend of Thomas Mann and the Jewish conductor Bruno Walter, led a charmed life and made courageous protests as a member of the Union to Combat Anti-Semitism. Had his incredible artistic talents not been in short supply he would have gone the way of all the other protesters – to a concentration camp for the duration of the war, or worse. He survived because Winifred needed him.

There was one problem that was no laughing matter – for Hitler and his anti-Semitic cronies, at any rate – which was the preponderance of Jews singing at Bayreuth. Mention has been made of the concessions made for a number of years in this regard. Hitler worshipped Frida Leider who sang Brünnhilde in the Ring cycle and Kundry in *Parsifal*. The role of Kundry, who represented the Wandering Jewess, ought to have been taken by a Semitic singer, according to Hitler, but he would not permit them to play the role. He regarded Kundry as a defiled woman who tried to seduce and pollute decent Christians. The legendary Lotte Lehman was a Jewess and the dictator remarked cruelly that she should have taken the part, but she had long since been banned from setting foot in Bayreuth.

Always gallant with women, Hitler, who had elements of the toady, was thrilled to again greet Frau Leider at one of Winifred's functions at

---

72. Spotts, *Hitler and the Power of Aesthetics*, 258–59.
73. Langer, *The Mind of Adolf Hitler*, 85.

Wahnfried. As he was about to meet Frau Leider's husband Professor Deman, who was formerly concertmaster of the Berlin Staatsoper, an aide whispered to him that he was a Jew. Pulling back his partially extended hand Hitler deliberately refused to greet the guest and looked pleased with himself that everybody noticed.

This vicious and unnecessary slight might have served his short-term interests but for Winifred it was a tremendous blow – Leider boycotted the festival after 1938.[74] Leider's very close friend and confidante in the Wagner family was Friedelind, the rebellious daughter of Winifred, who started reevaluating the merits of the Führer. She had shown a keen interest in politics from a young age and her book *Heritage of Fire* portrays her journey from Hitler acolyte to anti-Nazi. In this account she tells of her early visits to the Reich chancellery and her proud possession of a silver swastika pendant.[75] Hitler's treatment of her friend and other incidents served to dampen her ardor for the Third Reich and she started recognizing the evils in the regime.

During the mid to late thirties visitors to Bayreuth were privileged to hear the ringing tones of tenor Franz Volker, singing the parts of Siegmund and Parsifal. The Führer had no trouble with his ancestry and was very proud to give him a firm handshake. As the festival had become the cultural highpoint of National Socialism a large contingent of high-ranking politicians were to be counted attending the operas. Hitler spoke to Sepp Dietrich about ensuring the security at Bayreuth, as a number of attempts had been made on his life. For weeks before the festival, sinister looking Gestapo agents prowled around the small town, questioning the bartenders and chefs about strangers or suspicious characters. Bayreuth was declared a prohibited area for aircraft, and batteries of artillery were set up all round the city. Passes were issued to the singers and any person with a legitimate interest in being present.

Once the festival commenced the place swarmed with ss guards and Hitler marched to the theatre through an armed guard of the best soldiers in their uniforms. The whole town was decked with banners and bunting of National Socialism – the swastika flapped from the flagpoles and all was black and red. The streets echoed to the pounding of goose-stepping

---

74. Spotts, *Hitler and the Power of Aesthetics*, 171.
75. Wagner, Nike, *The Wagners*, 222.

soldiers, who stared fixedly ahead. The hotel rooms were crammed with Nazi memorabilia, including a big book in three languages, from which Ernest Newman read with an ever-deepening frown on his noble forehead that the Jews were being treated very well.[76]

Walking up to the theatre opera lovers would crane their necks outside the theatre to try to catch a glimpse of the Führer.[77] Once he appeared a thousand hands shot out in the Nazi salute, while the Aryan god languidly acknowledged their homage before entering the shrine for divine service. After the opera performances Hitler and members of the Wagner family dined with the singers and the artists and were served by ss guards in their black trousers and white linen jackets. There they were subjected to a monologue, combining Wagnerian folklore with racial hygiene and genetics – the reincarnation of Richard Wagner was home.

Apart from Hitler's fanatical attendance at Wagner operas he plied the sycophantic dinner guests with his own interpretations of the ideology behind the more controversial music dramas. Conventional wisdom, especially the sanitized postwar variety, would have it that *Parsifal* was about love and redemption, with respect for animals – witness the concern for the slain bird in act 1 – and a flowery meadow, representing universal toleration. The love feast, with the eucharist portrayed through the wine and bread – so the authorized version goes – was but the outward manifestation of what was reckoned an opera about the sins of fornication (physical love out of marriage) of which Wagner, ironically (witness Mathilde Wesendonck, Jessie Laussot, Judith Gautier plus countless small bit players) was the best example.

Hitler explained *Parsifal*, for instance, as follows: "we must interpret *Parsifal* in a totally different way…Behind the absurd externals of the story with its Christian embroidery and its Good Friday mystification, something altogether different is revealed as the true content of this most profound drama. It is not the Christian-Schopenhauerist religion of compassion that is acclaimed, but *the noble blood in the protection and glorification of whose purity the brotherhood of the initiated have come together.*"[78]

The "brotherhood of the initiated" began to look more and more like

---

76. Spotts, *Hitler and the Power of Aesthetics*, 171.
77. Ibid.
78. Windell, "Hitler, National Socialism and Richard Wagner," 229, quoting the 1940 work *The Voice of Destruction* by Hermann Rauschning.

the Gauleiters of the Nazi party and the thugs of the SS and SA. Needless to say the theme of the purity of the blood was to refer to his new laws defining racial stereotypes, notably the *Herrenvolk* falling within the broad category of Aryans. These knights of the grail would be the very same SS officers who would preside over the final ritual – the mass destruction of all those who did not qualify for the title of Aryan, especially the Jews. This could all take place without conscience, as that quality, according to the homespun Nazi philosopher, was "an invention of the Jews like circumcision."[79] The corollary of this, of course, was that true Teutons did not have a conscience to bother them and were moved by the Will to Power as expressed by Wagner and Nietzsche.

"Only a *pure* race can produce high culture," said Hitler at the party rally of 1934 in Nürnberg under the slogan of *"Unity and Strength,"* and he again pursued the hardy annual of the tyranny of Jewish penetration and invasion of European culture since the Middle Ages.[80] An American journalist described how "Hitler rode into the medieval town at sundown past solid phalanxes of wildly cheering Nazis who packed the narrow streets that once saw Hans Sachs and the *Meistersinger.*"[81] He went on to paint a picture of the hordes of swastika flags blotting out the "Gothic beauties" of the place, the facades of the old houses and gabled roofs.

Once business was over the leader retired to his accommodation to rest after an exhausting day. "About ten o'clock tonight I got caught in a mob of ten thousand hysterics who jammed the moat in front of Hitler's hotel shouting 'We want our Führer.' I was a little shocked at the faces, especially those of the women…They reminded me of the crazed expressions I saw once in the backcountry of Louisiana on the faces of some Holy Rollers who were about to hit the trail. They looked up at him as if he were a Messiah, their faces transformed…"[82] The account was by William L. Shirer, author of the outstanding account of the rise and fall of the Third Reich.[83]

The similarities to the Wagnerian oeuvre were not missed. Ludwig Marcuse, an eminent German exile, said, "what he learned from Wagner he inserted in his speeches – the pompous and the nebulous, brutality and

---

79. Waite, *The Psychopathic God*, 16.
80. Köhler, *Wagner's Hitler*, 247.
81. Waite, *The Psychopathic God*, 4.
82. Ibid.
83. Spotts, *Hitler and the Power of Aesthetics*, 49.

innocence; these are what give his speeches such resonance for Germans."[84] The annual party rally was planned and choreographed down to the finest details. The Nazi filmmaker Leni Riefenstahl's film *Triumph of the Will* documented the Nazi convention of that year and Wagner's music provided the subconscious message in key passages of the dialogue.[85]

The author Louis Lochner has described how Hitler had mastered the art of highlighting his role as the leader of the new Germany. "A searchlight plays upon his lone figure as he slowly walks through the hall, never looking to right or left, his right hand raised in salute, his left hand at the buckle of his belt. He never smiles – it is a religious rite, this procession of the modern Messiah incarnate. Behind him are his adjutants and secret service men. But his figure alone is flooded with light. By the time Hitler has reached the rostrum, the masses have been so worked upon that they are ready to do his will…"[86]

Not that the women at the Nazi rallies were the only ones to show awe and reverence to the new phenomenon. David Lloyd George, the British politician, was at that stage a great admirer of Hitler and described him as the George Washington of Germany. "The old trust him and the young idolize him."[87] He pointed out how he had saved the country from her oppressors and said, "Hitler reigns over the heart and mind of Germany."[88] Hitler had earlier praised George and his "psychological masterpieces in the art of mass propaganda" which had made his people "serve his will completely."[89]

The adulation of the intoxicated masses gave their leader fresh hope and new boldness – the territorial demands of the Führer continued. In January 1935 a plebiscite in the Saarland returned that territory to Germany – Pan-Germanism was rampant. To push the frontiers of his empire further Hitler needed more men in arms. Conscription was introduced in March of that year and despite the united opposition of Britain, France and Italy his duplicitous diplomatic skills persuaded the British to negotiate a naval treaty in June 1935, recognizing Germany's right to rearm. The visit of the

---

84. Ibid., 49–50.
85. Sheffi, *Ring of Myths*, 48.
86. Langer, *The Mind of Adolf Hitler*, 65.
87. Ibid.
88. Ibid.
89. Spotts, *Hitler and the Power of Aesthetics*, 44.

British foreign secretary to Berlin that year saw the mistress of Bayreuth in another role – Winifred Wagner was invited to be his partner at a dinner. Her cultured English, Wagnerian pedigree and fanatical adherence to the ideology of the Third Reich made her a formidable diplomat and table companion.[90]

Once the bugles called forth the warring instincts of the nation the qualities of rationality and moderation were hurriedly packed away in the attic. Mention has been made of Strauss's opera *Friedenstag* (The Day of Peace) which celebrated the end of the Hundred Years War. The cold reception that opera was given was in part due to its Jewish collaborator Stefan Zweig and the message of the text as explained by him: "one can always call the notion of peace among the peoples of the world despicably pacifist if one wants, but here it seems to me to be completely tied to all that is heroic." In addition Strauss himself was compromised as his daughter-in-law and grandchildren were Jewish. They were declared "honorary Aryans."

As the nation prepared for further expansion, the Wagnerian denial of the intellect and clarion call to the emotions were themes to be quickly taken up by Hitler's propaganda minister Goebbels who said the Nazi mission was "to cause outbreaks of fury, to set masses of men on the march, to organize hate and suspicion with ice-cold calculation, to unchain volcanic passions."[91] The "emotionalisation of the intellect" advocated by Wagner was at work.[92]

The nation was gearing up for war and the glories of struggle were themes constantly repeated in the media. Writing in the early thirties of that century the German intellectual Spengler explored the same theme when he said "War is the prime fact of Life, is Life itself…The beast of prey is the highest form of mobile Life…In the Faustian Kultur the proud blood of the beast of prey revolts against the tyranny of pure thought."[93] Nietzsche had been correct when he prophesied the way ahead, as his tormented soul fought insanity and syphilis in the sanatorium in Weimar.

The Nürnberg "Rally of Freedom" that year saw the introduction of the race laws, banning intermarriage, hiring of Aryan girls by Jews and the flying of flags. The notion that Jews were thronging the shops in long

---

90. Ibid., 166.
91. Goebbels in his *Background for War*, 2.
92. Franklin, *Life of Mahler*, 161.
93. So said Oswald Spengler, *Man and Technics*, 1932.

During the Third Reich there were many measures taken against Jews, including a commercial boycott of their shops and businesses. "Don't buy from Jews." From Martin Gilbert, page 289.

lines to buy swastikas and Nazi memorabilia was a bizarre one. An immense "cathedral of light," made up of searchlights turned into the night sky, accommodated the throngs of torch-bearing ss soldiers and party members, waving swastikas, military standards and banners from which golden eagles glowered and searched the east for prey. The transformation was complete – Wagnerian opera had transcended art and entered the battlefield; the knights of the Grail were preparing for conquest.

As Francis King says in *Satan and Swastika*, "Hitler's public appearances, particularly those associated with the Nazi Party's Nürnberg Rallies, were excellent examples of this sort of magical ceremony. The fanfares, military marches and Wagnerian music all emphasized the idea of German military glory."

Apart from the race laws the biological hygienists and geneticists turned their attention to the scavengers of the ocean. In a strange contradiction – given the vicious nature of the anti-Semitic proclamations – Hitler issued decrees for the protection of lobsters and crabs that were designed to prevent pain and cruelty. "Crabs, lobsters, and other crustaceans are to be killed by throwing them in rapidly boiling water. When feasible, this should be done individually."[94] There was a ruthless, political and ideological logic to all this as these denizens of the deep are not on the list of appropriate food on the Semitic table. In Bayreuth Gauleiter put up weatherproof metal

---

94. Waite, *The Psychopathic God*, 41.

boards with the inscription that Jews were not welcome there and distributed a list of still remaining Jewish shops at which Bayreuth citizens were not supposed to buy any more.[95] Winifred showed some courage in this regard and did what she wanted. She kept in contact with her old friends whether they were Jews or of mixed races, homosexuals or ministers and she did not honor the boycott. She gave donations to the church, she bought from Jewish shops and she did it in her own brash way. This behavior irritated the local Nazis and with time under the cover of a purely external politeness eventually a real battle started.[96]

While he was extending mercy to unfeeling creatures of the deep, those reckoned a little lower than the angels by the churches from time immemorial were to be treated with terror. As he told an associate at the same time: "Do I intend to eradicate whole races? Of course I do…Cruelty is impressive. And brutal strength…the masses want it. They need the thrill of terror to make them shudderingly submissive. I do not want concentration camps to become old age pensioners' homes. Terror is the most effective way of politics."[97]

In March 1936 he used the excuse of a pact between France and the Soviet Union to remilitarize the Rhineland against the advice of his own general staff. On March 7, 1936 German troops occupied the Rhineland. Hitler returned from a triumphal ride in his special train to the reoccupied zone. He described his state of mind in a most peculiar figure of speech: "I follow my course with the precision and security of a sleepwalker."[98] As the proud conqueror of fresh German territory passed through the Ruhr he asked for Wagner's music. After listening to the prelude to *Parsifal* Hitler volunteered a further interpretation. "I have built up my religion out of *Parsifal*…Divine worship in solemn form without pretences of humility…One can serve God only in the garb of the hero."[99] In this instance the hero wore jackboots and a cruel glint in his eye.

On the same trip he listened to the funeral march from *Götterdämmerung* and mentioned his first hearing of it. "I first heard it in Vienna at the Opera. And I still remember as if it were today how madly excited I

---

95. Hamann, *Winifred Wagner*, 306.
96. Ibid., 309.
97. Ibid.
98. Langer, *The Mind of Adolf Hitler*, 29.
99. Fest, *Hitler*, 499.

Hitler at the 1936 Bayreuth Festival with (from left to right) Verena Wagner, Fritz Deiss, Winifred Wagner, Max Lorenz and Friedelind Wagner. See Spotts, Hitler and the Power of Aesthetics, page 84. Richard Wagner Museum, Bayreuth.

became on the way home over a few yammering Yids I had to pass. I cannot think of a more incompatible contrast…This glorious mystery of the dying hero and this Jewish shit…"

Clearly for Hitler the hero was the man who would cleanse Germany of any Semitic bloodlines. In other ways the details of the operas gave the Gestapo and ss ideas for their treatment of the Jews and other political dissidents. In the first music drama of the Ring tetralogy, *Das Rheingold*, Alberich the Nibelung makes a ring out of the gold that he has stolen that gives him the power to rule the world. He also makes a magic helmet, the Tarnhelm, which enables him to assume any shape he wishes or become invisible. When Alberich turns himself into another creature or becomes invisible he always whispers the secret code "Nacht und nebel" (night and fog) to describe the darkness into which he disappears. "Nacht und nebel" decrees were to become much favored by the ss to spirit away political opponents and Jews, whose families never discovered their whereabouts.[100]

Hitler's daring had paid off despite his generals' misgivings and the Rhineland was his. Three months later he was taking time off to be with

---

100. For details of this method of causing terror, see Shirer, *Rise and Fall of the Third Reich*, 1139–40.

his "family" at Bayreuth. Of special significance to Hitler was the beautiful *Lohengrin* in 1936 with Furtwängler conducting – Maria Muller sang Elsa and Franz Volker the title role. Of special significance to the conquering leader were the following lines from the opera:

> *Now is the time to guard our Reich's honor.*
> *From east and west, all men count equal in this.*
> *Place armies wherever there is German land.*
> *So that none shall disparage again the German Reich.*

The relationship between Furtwängler and Winifred had been a troubled one especially because the conductor's secretary Berta Geissmar was Jewish. Winifred inferred from this that the conductor was friendly towards Jews. She referred to Geissmar as a "full-blooded" Jewess and also emphasized their differing attitudes to the Jewish dominated press.[101]

Hitler had few regrets that the legendary tenor Lauritz Melchior had left Bayreuth in 1931 with Toscanini. Hitler consoled the Bayreuth team that they did not need the prima donna foreigners, especially the Jews. He was moved to tears by many of the productions and afterwards met the – now exclusively Aryan – singers backstage; the compliant newspapers carried photographs of the Führer, shaking hands with the cast.[102] These singers were among the 773 artists whose income tax was cut by as much as 40 percent in 1938 and included Rudolf Bockelmann, Josef von Manowarda, Helge Roswaenge, Erna Berger, Maria Müller and Margarete Slezak.[103] Hitler had clearly never forgotten his days of suffering in Vienna. His sexual perversions were never far from the surface and he told Goebbels at the Bayreuth festival the next year of his preference for large women after seeing Resi Iffland in the role of Brünnhilde.[104] Maybe that was the reason Winifred stuffed her face with dumplings and did little to inhibit the growth of adipose tissue on her massive thighs and stomach.

In an interesting cultural exchange the London Philharmonic Orchestra played to full houses in Berlin. One incident during the visit of the conductor of the orchestra to Wagner's shrine was to turn out terribly badly for

---

101. Hamann, *Winifred Wagner*, 200.
102. See Geissmar, *The Baton and the Jackboot*, 216–17.
103. Spotts, *Hitler and the Power of Aesthetics*, 80.
104. Kershaw, *Hitler 1889–1936: Hubris*, 856.

Hitler. After three decades the Englishman Sir Thomas Beecham revisited a very different Bayreuth, though the literature he must have read at the turn of the century would have given him premonitions of the way matters would play themselves out. Hitler's territorial exploits and his treatment of political opponents and the Jews had earned him a lot of bad press. The presence of Sir Thomas in Bayreuth presented a glorious opportunity for some good propaganda and Goebbels's team of image manipulators set to work to capture photographs of the visit.

Although Beecham refused point blank to be seen with Hitler the latter's spin doctors made use of modern photographic techniques to insinuate Beecham's figure into the company of the German leader. They faked a photograph of Sir Thomas in Hitler's box at Bayreuth and when the truth finally leaked out the British were understandably terribly indignant.[105] But Beecham's courage did not extend to protecting the interests of one of the greatest composers of all time, Felix Mendelssohn. He bowed to pressure from Hitler and withdrew performance of the composer's Scottish Symphony at a concert by the London Philharmonic Orchestra in the dictator's presence in Berlin in 1936.[106] What was worse was that Hitler's bully boys had destroyed the beautiful statue of Mendelssohn in Leipzig in the same year.[107]

Hitler had always been a great admirer of the British Empire and his territorial ambitions were an attempt to achieve a similar sphere of influence. In some quarters in England pockets of admirers developed, who never failed to emphasize the percentage of German blood in the English royals and the merits of the new policies. Hitler called Unity Mitford, who held the ominously Wagnerian middle name of Walkyrie, "the perfect Germanic woman," to the chagrin of Eva Braun. She was the daughter of Lord Redesdale – who must have been a Wagnerite to burden his offspring with such an appellation – and fell for the blue-eyed boy of Nazism, while her sister Diana, who shared the same ideological predilections, eventually married the fascist leader Sir Oswald Mosley.[108]

Unity sought out Hitler like a lovesick loon and sat dejectedly in

---

105. The faked photograph of Beecham with Hitler is shown in Geissmar, *The Baton and the Jackboot*, 237.
106. Spotts, *Hitler and the Power of Aesthetics*, 271.
107. Radcliffe, *Mendelssohn*, 55.
108. Waite, *The Psychopathic God*, 232.

The English rose – Unity Mitford – fawned over Hitler and tried unavailingly to marry him. She attempted to commit suicide at the commencement of the Second World War. See Bishop, Hitler's Third Reich vol. 8.

restaurants that he frequented in the hopes of seeing him. So abject was her doglike devotion that a witty journalist nicknamed her "Mitfahrt" (hitchhiker) and speculated whether Hitler would break his sexual fast by invading English territory – but Winifred had been proof positive of his steadfastness in that regard.[109] Hitler had met Unity with Sir Oswald Mosley at a diplomatic function and joked that the English wanted him to marry "Unity Mitford, the English rose." After the war the press speculated whether that mismatch would have prevented the conflagration that resulted.

On one occasion Unity had confounded the British Ambassador Sir Neville Henderson by greeting him with a "Heil Hitler" and a Nazi salute. The diplomat responded patriotically with a British Army salute and, perplexed as to what to say, blurted out "Rule Britannia."[110] Unity was a tragic figure in many ways; quite attractive with ash-blond hair, grey eyes, very much like a Botticelli, until she smiled and betrayed a set of very ugly teeth. It was at the Bayreuth festival that year that Hitler met up with these English female admirers Unity and Diana and spoke to them of the

---

109. Wagner, Nike, *The Wagners*, 163.
110. Waite, *The Psychopathic God*, 232.

dangers of Jews and Bolshevism. Unity said that sitting next to Hitler was like "sitting beside the sun."[111]

Some believed that Hitler was temporally infatuated with her but another attempted suicide by Eva Braun restored her to his favor. His strange notions of lovemaking, coupled with his busy political schedule, made for tragic relationships with the fairer sex – five of the six women he was intimate with either committed suicide or came within a whisper of it.[112] The version put out by Hitler was that he could not marry her because she, like Winifred Wagner, was an Englishwoman and had to remain unmarried, like a queen – presumably he had in mind the virgin queen Elizabeth 1.

Unity's sister Diana had also not been lucky in love and was divorced from Lord Guinness; she was more beautiful than Unity, in a pale but insipid way. The second year Unity visited the Bayreuth festival she sought to ingratiate herself with the dominant ideology of the festival – she dyed her hair a Nordic gold. In other ways she drew attention to herself and hoped Hitler would notice. After developing severe bronchitis she was caught by the doctor who attended to her pouring her medicine out of the window, standing in a draft courting pneumonia. This brought about the desired results as Hitler had to bring her to Berchtesgaden to be attended by his physician – but he would not marry her.

The noted psychologist Carl Jung had been at pains in the early thirties – unlike Freud – to state that, though the artist might well have his own personal problems, these were insignificant to the "essential nature of the work of art."[113] A witty man, he once said "show me a sane man and I'll cure him for you."[114] Initially a follower of Hitler, he described him as "a spiritual vessel," but he must have reconsidered this view when he characterized Nazism in the *Neue Schweizer Rundschau* as the first outbreak of epidemic insanity.

In a succession of trenchant images and phrases Jung summed up the heady broth that the Third Reich was dishing up to the supine citizenry. "The emphasis on the Germanic race (vulgarly called 'Aryan'), the Germanic heritage, blood and soil…the ride of the Valkyries…the devil as an international Alberich in Jewish or Masonic guise…all this is the indispensable

---

111. Kershaw, *Hitler 1936–1945: Nemesis*, 13.
112. Waite, *The Psychopathic God*, 21.
113. Vetter, "Wagner in the History of Psychology," 54.
114. Wallace et al., *Intimate Sex Lives of Famous People*, 245.

scenery for the drama that is taking place and at bottom it will mean the same thing; a god has taken possession of the Germans and their house is filled with a 'mighty rushing wind.'"[115] There is no mistaking the reference to Richard Wagner and the political and racial effect of his art. "The mighty rushing wind" was sweeping all before it and Europe and Jewry waited trembling for it to lash out and rip apart the foundations of civilization. Freud had earlier defined civilization as requiring the repression of aggressive, brutish instincts[116] and discovered that "the culminating point of the paranoid's delusional system is his belief that he has a mission to redeem the world and to restore mankind to their lost state of bliss."[117]

During a performance of *The Valkyries* at Bayreuth that year, Hitler received an urgent phone call from General Franco, who requested military assistance at the commencement of the Spanish Civil War. Hitler approved covert assistance to his fellow fascist and set about finding a name for the operation. During the closing scenes of that opera, Wotan surrounds Brünnhilde with magic fire, through which only the world's greatest hero, Siegfried, would be able to pass. The temptation to reach out again to the Wagner legerdemain was too great, and Hitler called the secret operation by the same name – "Operation Magic Fire." The last half hour or so of the opera, reckoned by many (including the author) to be the greatest music ever composed, clearly had a subliminal message of cooperation between the dictators.[118]

The Fascists in Italy were soon in an alliance with the Nazis as predicted in *Mein Kampf*, facilitated by the sanctions imposed by Britain and France against Italy for Mussolini's attack and conquest of Ethiopia. Formally in October 1936 the Rome-Berlin axis was established and links to the east were forged in the Anti-Comintern Pact with Japan. The next year Hitler beseeched Winifred to find a way to persuade Edward VIII to attend the festival that year.[119]

During the Bayreuth festival that year Goebbels returned to the subject of the *Meistersinger*, which he had addressed over the radio during the

---

115. Spotts, *Hitler and the Power of Aesthetics*, 175–76.
116. Ibid., 65.
117. Sigmund Freud: *Psychoanalytic Notes on an Autobiographic Account of a Case of Paranoia*, Standard Edition, vol. 12.
118. Spotts, *Hitler and the Power of Aesthetics*, 167.
119. Ibid., 166.

The Nazis quickly appropriated Wagner's operas and interpreted the underlying anti-Semitism in them. A placard advertising Die Meistersinger with a swastika. Wagners Welten, page 252. Theaterwissenschaftliche Sammlung Schloss Wahn, Köln.

1933 festival. "Richard Wagner taught us what a Jew is," Goebbels opined. "Let us pay heed to him – we who have at last freed ourselves through the words and deeds of Adolf Hitler from slavery at the hands of a subhuman race."[120] Close to the truth in evaluating that opera were the comments of the French writer Romain Rolland after attending the first Alsace-Lorraine music festival in 1905: "its most striking characteristic, since Wagner, is the cult of force. While listening to the end of *Die Meistersinger* I felt how such arrogant music, that imperial march, reflected this military, middle-class nation, weighed down with health and glory."[121] It is, indeed, not surprising that when Hans Sachs commences the musically magnificent but politically poisonous last great monologue to German Art, singing, "Evil deeds are threatening us…That which is German and true will no longer be recognized, unless it lives on in the honor of German Masters…"

---

120. Köhler, *Wagner's Hitler*, 252.
121. Franklin, *Life of Mahler*, 156–57.

the audiences at Bayreuth in the thirties stood up and spontaneously gave the Nazi salute.[122]

In two revealing entries in his diaries on November 15 and 30, 1936, Goebbels recorded Hitler's views on the Jews. "The Jews must get out of Germany, yes out of the whole of Europe. That will take some time. But it will and must happen. The Führer is firmly decided on it."[123] An official publication the next year maintained that Hitler's Nürnberg race laws brought "Wagner's philosophical ideals concerning the universal campaign against the Jews to their triumphant fulfillment."[124]

Admiration, in retrospect, was to come from a strange quarter indeed. In 1937 Winston Churchill reviewed Hitler's accomplishments and called them "among the most remarkable in the whole history of the world."[125] If only he had died before World War II, one German historian speculated, he might have gone down as "Adolf the Great, one of the outstanding figures of German history."[126]

"Adolf the Great" was casting rapacious eyes towards his German-speaking neighbor and in February 1938 Hitler invited the Austrian chancellor von Schuschnigg to Berchtesgaden and pressurized him to sign an agreement giving the Austrian Nazis wide powers in that country. The harangues directed at persuading the Austrian leader to cede over his country to Germany concluded with a thundered rhetorical question. "Do you realize that you are in the presence of the greatest German of all time?" he asked the terrified political leader.[127] When von Schuschnigg returned from the limestone crags he repented of his decision and attempted to repudiate the agreement. He announced a plebiscite on the question of an annexation to Germany, which so infuriated Hitler that he immediately ordered the occupation of Austria by German troops. With many memories of his lonely, miserable times in Vienna he entered to a reception that convinced him to settle the future of Austria by outright annexation.

The annexation was disastrous for many. The legendary German singer Lotte Lehmann was playing the role of the Marschallin in Strauss's

---

122. Osborne, *World Theatre of Wagner*, 100.
123. Kershaw, *Hitler 1936–1945: Nemesis*, 1.
124. Köhler, *Wagner's Hitler*, 253.
125. Waite, *The Psychopathic God*, 5.
126. Ibid.
127. Langer, *The Mind of Adolf Hitler*, 29.

Der Rosenkavalier at Covent Garden when she received the news. Urged to hope for the best about her family and continue singing she moaned, "I can't, I can't," and rushed sobbing from the stage. Luckily Viennese soprano Hilde Konetzni happened to be in the audience and completed the role. Lehmann's husband, who was Jewish, was in a sanatorium in Switzerland and her stepchildren, with paternal Jewish heritage, were trapped in central Europe as were a number of her friends.[128]

The Wagner pilgrimages by the Führer and his ss entourage were repeated that year as they had been every previous one since 1923. The musical leadership of the festival was continuing in its fidelity to the political ideology of its main sponsor and patron. Of interest is an article in the official festival handbook of Bayreuth 1938 urging a conductor to "bring to our consciousness with unexampled clarity in the *Ring the terrible seriousness of the racial problem*…" and, if he cannot, never to raise his baton in German lands.[129] So Alberich, Mime and Hagen, the Nibelungs pitting their wits against the Aryan Siegfried and his Teutonic parent Wotan, were Jews after all, as Gustav Mahler had so emphatically declared.

That year saw an amusing prediction from the singer Marta Fuchs who sang Kundry in *Parsifal*. Her performances were much admired by Hitler and Goebbels and she approached the two after the performance. She half-jokingly accused Hitler of going to start a war and he stated that he had enough of wars having been gassed in the First World War. The next year Hitler chided her and asked if he had started any war and allegedly in her broad Swabian accent she replied, "Herr Hitler, I just don't trust you!"[130]

Less influential persons could have courted imprisonment in a concentration camp for not calling the leader Mein Führer, but Hitler loved his Wagnerians.

Winifred continued in her role as cultural ambassador and plenipotentiary – she graced receptions for Mussolini that year when the Italian dictator met with Hitler in Munich and Berlin.[131] When she stayed over in Munich she was treated to the Führer's bizarre lifestyle, involving rising at lunchtime and going to bed shortly before dawn. Hitler loved movies

---

128. Douglas, *Legendary Voices*, 149.
129. Skelton, *Wagner at Bayreuth*, 144. For the singers and productions during the Hitler era see pages 218 and 221 and following.
130. Kater, *The Twisted Muse*, 223.
131. Spotts, *Hitler and the Power of Aesthetics*, 166.

and would often watch two in an evening, and the same film on countless occasions, his favorites being Walt Disney's *Snow White* and *King Kong*.[132] Hopefully now that he had the scepter in his grasp he left his whip behind when Winifred slept over in the Bavarian capital. She would have felt completely at home in his Berlin quarters – his office was decorated with scenes from the *Ring of the Nibelungs*.[133]

That year saw the establishment by Hitler of the German Richard Wagner Research Centre in Bayreuth and its first task was to check and disprove that Richard Wagner's real father Ludwig Geyer was Jewish.[134] Hitler's successes in Austria resulted in much diplomatic head-shaking but little economic or military response from Britain and France. Hitler had secured Mussolini's support, a debt that was to be repaid less than half a decade later when *Il Duce* was captured by the partisans.

The hunger for land for the Reich continued – Czechoslovakia was next on the list and Konrad Henlein, leader of the German minority in that country, was secretly instructed to agitate for impossible demands on the part of the Sudetenland Germans, thereby enabling Hitler to justify annexation. The pusillanimous attitude of Britain and France and pressure on the Czech government to cede the Sudetenland areas to Germany presented Hitler with an unusual dilemma – not inconsiderable gains by diplomacy or the whole country by force of arms. When Hitler invited the regent of that country, Admiral Horthy, to Germany for discussions about the surrender of his country he chose a performance of *Lohengrin* to entertain him. The following year Prince Paul of Yugoslavia was entertained with *Meistersinger* when Hitler was on the brink of invading Poland.[135] Wagner and German expansionism seemed to go hand in hand.

The Nazi Party rally and celebration in Nürnberg in August 1938 saw the fulfillment of a deep-seated desire of the racists, as the synagogue in the city, which had so offended Wagner nearly a hundred years before, was demolished. Julius Streicher, prominent in the anti-Jewish paper, chose the command from *Meistersinger* "Fanget an" (commence) to set the bully boys and their torches on to the building.[136] Hitler gave a lengthy oration

---

132. Waite, *The Psychopathic God*, 9.
133. Sheffi, *Ring of Myths*, 36.
134. Spotts, *Hitler and the Power of Aesthetics*, 175.
135. Ibid., 230.
136. Köhler, *Wagner's Hitler*, 254.

on how he regarded music which he described as "the greatest animator of feelings and sensibilities that move the mind; yet it seems to be the least able to satisfy the intellect…a world of feelings and moods that is difficult to describe in words is revealed in music…this type of expression…reached its absolute summit in the works of the great Bayreuth Master."[137]

An event occurred in Paris on November 7 which gave vent to the irrepressible anti-Semitic wrath of the rampant Nazis. A seventeen-year-old Polish Jew, Herschel Grynspan, entered the German Embassy in the French capital and shot the Third Legation Secretary Ernst vom Rath. The killer's family had been deported without notice or trial from their home in Hanover, together with eighteen thousand other Polish Jews, over the borders to Poland. Their lives were miserable and the injustice rankled in the mind of the young man. In a further strange irony Grynspan alleged – apparently credibly – that he had had a homosexual relationship with vom Rath and that prevented a show trial being held. Prior to the killing, Grynspan had repaired to a bar – a well-known haunt of homosexuals – where he had loaded his revolver and then asked for the legation secretary.[138]

After the assassination of vom Rath, "spontaneous" demonstrations took place in Bayreuth which were described in the local press as "immediate outbreaks of national rage." The local synagogue was saved as a result of the fear for the neighboring baroque opera house.[139] This was one of the few that survived in the country but the inside was demolished and plundered. Sixty of the 120 Jews still living in the city were dragged out of their beds, mishandled and arrested; twenty-three were placed in prison.[140]

On November 9, later known as *Kristallnacht* for the breaking of Jewish homes and shop windows, all the remaining synagogues in Germany were razed to the ground.[141] Toscanini was to have conducted the overture to *Meistersinger* in Palestine and he willingly replaced it with the overture to *Oberon*. From that time on the Jews in Palestine and elsewhere began to cease speaking of pogroms and mentioned for the first time the horrifying

---

137. Spotts, *Hitler and the Power of Aesthetics*, 278–79.
138. Kershaw, *Hitler 1936–1945: Nemesis*, 881–82.
139. Hamann, *Winifred Wagner*, 378.
140. Ibid., 379.
141. Ibid.

advent of a *shoah* ("a holocaust").[142] Sigmund Freud was ransomed with twenty thousand English pounds by Princess Marie Bonaparte of Greece, a former patient and friend, and he escaped unscathed to London to die the next year of cancer of the jaw and palate.[143]

The inventor of psychoanalysis had explained the potential havoc that can occur when sexual abstinence is practiced especially in a deviant such as Hitler. The latter had found it more difficult, given his high public profile, to carry out his former liaisons. Freud concluded that every perversion corresponds to an earlier phase of development. In addition he referred to patients suffering from dementia praecox and schizophrenia who exhibited two characteristics, the first of which was to carry a menacing warning for the world and Jewry. Freud concluded that a natural consequence was megalomania and a turning away from the world. The latter characteristic is really the abandonment of erotic relations to people in the world, without their replacement by corresponding relations to objects in fantasy. When the libido has been withdrawn from external objects, Freud concluded that the patient's megalomania carried the day as it expresses – and also conceals – an erotic attachment to the ego.[144]

With notable exceptions the churches gave very little opposition to the attacks launched on the Jews. A typical example was the book written by Bishop Martin Sasse of Thuringia who applauded the burning of the synagogues on Luther's birthday. He called Luther the greatest anti-Semite of them all and recorded that Luther had outlined a plan of action to deal with the Jews. There was now perilously little opposition to the "great solution" proposed by Richard Wagner. Criticism of any sort of the regime was repressed with the utmost severity. Hans Pfitzner, the famous composer of the opera *Palestrina*, sarcastically told Göring (who was officially the head of the Prussian State Opera) that in Germany "any criticism is forbidden, indeed abolished, so that you cannot write it if a soubrette sings badly, even when it is really so."[145]

On November 12, 1938 an exhibition entitled "The Eternal Jew" commenced in Berlin and other major German cities including Munich to show Germans how to identify their enemies. In Munich alone 412,300

---

142. Sheffi, *Ring of Myths*, 47.
143. Wallace et al., *Intimate Sex Lives of Famous People*, 177.
144. Wollheim, *Freud* (London: Fontana Collins, 1971), 177.
145. Kater, *The Twisted Muse*, 11.

The exhibition on The Eternal Jew in Berlin. This picture depicts the stereotype advocated by Nazis of Jews and follows that of Wagner in his characters Alberich (from the Ring of the Nibelung) and Klingsor (from his last opera Parsifal) very closely. See Kershaw vol. 2, page 211. Corbis/Bettmann.

visitors saw the show, which was put on to raise the anti-Jewish fever in the country.

From November 12, 1938 Jews were no longer permitted to attend cinemas, theatre and concerts and three days later the children were prohibited from attending school. On December 3 they were ordered to surrender their motor and driving licenses and hand all shares and securities to a specified bank. The outwardly untouched but inwardly destroyed Bayreuth Synagogue was sold under forced sale to the Bavarian State. On December 7 the *Bayerische Ostmark* proudly announced that there were no more Jewish shops open in the city.[146]

On February 21, 1939 the Jews were deprived of jewelry, precious metals and cutlery. Capital levies and mortgage defaults meant that Jews lost all houses and immovable property. They lost tenant protection after April 30, 1939 and could be ejected at any time from their residences.[147]

On November 21, 1938 Hitler told the South African economics and defense minister that in the event of war, the Jews would be killed.[148] Three

---

146. Hamann, *Winifred Wagner*, 380.
147. Ibid., 381.
148. Goldhagen, *Hitler's Willing Executioners*, 142.

days later he was talking to him again about international cooperation in securing the emigration of the Jews.[149] The intervention of his old friend Mussolini persuaded him to accept the Munich Agreement on September 30. The partial acquisition rankled with him and he wasted little time in finding reason to annex the whole of Czechoslovakia. After fostering Slovak discontent he achieved his objective and on March 16, 1939 he proclaimed the dissolution of the state. Memel on the northern frontier of East Prussia followed soon into the Nazi fold and Hitler now set his sights on Poland, which had powerful treaty friends in Britain and France.

The dictator of Germany loved to realize his great building plans; in the basement of the Reich's chancellery he played endlessly with blocks, which he formed into the buildings of his cities of the future. A minister of finance found him lying on his stomach intent on erecting his Berlin of the future.[150] His alliance with Italy was forged, much as Siegfried had forged his sword "Needful," into a "Pact of Steel" in May 1939. The friendship with Mussolini had endured for many years and they shared a delight in the joys their mutual hatred for democracy and human rights brought.

In the basement Hitler had another favorite toy: a small cannon with a thirty-inch barrel, which he would load and discharge at some of the buildings he had erected. Toy soldiers, painted to reflect warriors from the enemy nations of France, England, Poland and Russia, woodenly faced the onslaught from the cannon and when they fell Hitler and Mussolini cheered like schoolboys.[151] All too soon the wooden soldiers would be replaced by flesh and blood as Europe's finest manhood faced the megalomaniacs. To shore up the east a nonaggression pact was concluded with the Soviet Union on August 24 and Hitler was able to contemplate further land aggression to satisfy his long felt quest for *Lebensraum* – expressly and specifically articulated in *Mein Kampf*.

Earlier, on April 20 of the same year, on the occasion of his fiftieth birthday, the Confederation of German Industry had presented Hitler with priceless original Wagner scores at Bayreuth.[152] After receiving them he embarked on an intricate analysis of each work, showing his expert knowledge of the music and factual background. As usual the festival theatre

---
149. Kershaw, *Hitler 1936–1945: Nemesis*, 151.
150. Waite, *The Psychopathic God*, 12.
151. Ibid.
152. Köhler, *Wagner's Hitler*, 13.

The Bayreuth Festspielhaus on Hitler's birthday – April 20, 1939. The Nazi influence during the Third Reich presented huge political problems for Wagner's grandsons, Wieland and Wolfgang Wagner, after the war when they were anxious to disown that disgraceful era. Nike Wagner, page 141.

at Bayreuth was festooned with swastikas to mark the occasion, but the military made up a far larger proportion of the audience.[153] Shortly before his invasion of Poland he paid a visit to Wagner's grave in Bayreuth and remembered that fatal attendance at *Rienzi* in Linz. "That was when it all began."[154] Rienzi was ready for his sacred task.

The rift between Friedelind and her mother became noticeably wider and the former saw no future for herself in a Germany under the Third Reich. The festival of 1938 was the last Friedelind was to attend – a further quarrel with her mother determined her to emigrate to America in 1939.[155] In a last desperate bid to prevent the escape to the land of the free Winifred was sent by Himmler to Zurich to try and bring back her "traitorous" daughter, who was also described by her brothers Wieland and Wolfgang

---

153. Wagner, Nike, *The Wagners*, 161.
154. Köhler, *Wagner's Hitler*, 3.
155. Wagner and Cooper, *Heritage of Fire*, page 213.

Siegfried and Winifred's daughters Verena and Friedelind Wagner with Hitler in 1938. Friedelind was to flee to America at the commencement of the war in protest at Nazi excesses. Her mother threatened her with extermination for broadcasting anti-Nazi propaganda. See Gottfried Wagner, page 151.

as a disgrace to her family.[156] Friedelind was determined to leave and nothing would change her mind.

Assistance for her escape was forthcoming from the legendary Italian conductor Arturo Toscanini, who had enjoyed his own share of misgivings about the Thousand Year Reich and had shaken the dust of a Nazi Bayreuth from his neatly turned Italian shoes.[157] After Friedelind fled Winifred Wagner became so fanatical in her support of the Führer that she threatened her own daughter with extermination, if she broadcast anti-Nazi propaganda on American radio.[158]

In March of 1940 Friedelind slipped through Europe, avoiding the rampant Blitzkrieg, and made it to London where she published a series of twelve articles in the *Daily Sketch* describing life under the dictator's whip. Goebbels told his diary that "the fat, little Wagner girl divulges revelations about the Führer in London. What a little beast! This could be somewhat embarrassing."[159] In the articles she described Hitler as a bumbling fool, a demented fanatic, a man possessed by demons and the greatest liar of all time.

The Friedelind matter did sour the relationship with Hitler, who saw her defection as the supreme betrayal by a member of a family whose loyalty

---

156. Wagner, Nike, *The Wagners*, 222.
157. Ibid.
158. Wagner and Cooper, *Heritage of Fire*, 224.
159. Spotts, *Hitler and the Power of Aesthetics*, 253–54.

meant so much to him. He raised it with Wieland and Goebbels commented on the "terrible scandal that this stupid bumpkin is causing."[160] The propaganda minister then noted that Hitler was deeply "shaken by Friedelind Wagner's mean spiritedness" and called her a "traitor to her country." In 1942 a senior SS officer from the Ministry of Public Enlightenment and Propaganda reassured Winifred that her daughter was redeemable and she was not "rotten to the core." If she was brought back under "German influence" he felt sure she could be persuaded to forsake her foolish ways.[161]

The possibility of war between Germany and Britain had always been a prickly pear between Hitler and Winifred. His attitude to that country had always been mediated by secret envy of the great empire that had been built up and a notion that the British fell into his category of Aryans, who deserved to inherit and rule the earth. On occasion he would comment on their foreign policy in his table talk – his solutions to their colonial problems were often practical and brutal. When problems arose in the Indian subcontinent Hitler's answer as to how to deal with the "upstart" Gandhi was ludicrously simple. "Shoot Gandhi and if that does not suffice to reduce them to submission, shoot a dozen leading members of Congress; if that does not suffice, shoot two hundred more and so on until order is restored."[162] Hitler clearly felt threatened by the Indian leader's enlightened views on race, where he linked anti-Semitism with the pariahs in his culture. "The Jews have been the untouchables of Christianity. The parallel between their treatment by Christians and the treatment of untouchables by Hindus is very close. Religious sanction has been invoked in both cases for the justification of the inhuman treatment meted out to them."[163]

When war threatened, Winifred agreed to see Sir Neville Henderson, the British ambassador, during the festival in Bayreuth, in late July 1939. Carrying a bulging briefcase and the hopes of a nervous world, the diplomat was seeking some way to prevent the conflagration that threatened to consume Europe. Shown into the lounge at Wahnfried the ambassador quickly came to the point – he needed an urgent meeting with the German leader to try to persuade him to hold back. The British were anxious to persuade Hitler not to invade Poland. The message was conveyed to a

---

160. Ibid., 255.
161. Ibid., 223.
162. Waite, *The Psychopathic God*, 13.
163. *Harijan* by Mohandas K. Gandhi, September 1, 1946.

belligerent Hitler, who was staying, as was his custom, in the cottage next door to Wahnfried, and was due to see *The Valkyries* that evening. Hitler refused to see Henderson or share the family box with him – clearly opera came before world peace.[164]

Through the cheering crowds the dictator moved to the holy shrine of music. Doubtless as the angry Wotan punished his daughter Brünnhilde for her disobedience and the mighty chords enveloped the auditorium, Hitler must have felt affirmed in his decision. He still disclaimed any quarrel with Britain, but to no avail, and the invasion of Poland on September 1 was followed two days later by a British and French declaration of war. Speaking to his commanders and fixing them with his cold blue eyes, Hitler told them how to act in the conflict that was to destroy more than fifty-five million soldiers and civilians: "close your hearts to pity...act brutally."[165]

Despite the cruelty observers commented that Hitler's gait was not that of a soldier. One observer described it as "a very ladylike walk. Dainty little steps. Every few steps he cocked his right shoulder nervously, his left leg snapping up as he did so." Mention has been made of the fact that just before the beginning of the Second World War Carl Burckhardt, League of Nations Commissioner for Danzig, met Hitler and described him as "the most profoundly feminine man he had ever met...there were moments when he was almost effeminate." Burckhardt would then imitate the movements of his white flabby hands. He also commented on his dual personality, "the first being that of the rather gentle artist and the second that of the homicidal maniac."[166] He was now deeply involved in his second career; the flabby hands were clenched in a stranglehold on half the civilized world.

Some historians believed that he gambled on the European powers holding back and not backing Poland and that he was not expecting a European war. One of his generals kept a private diary and the entry for August 14, 1939 records his reaction to the prospect of a general war. "Why should England fight? One does not die for an ally."[167]

When he entered the Second World War, Hitler records that the sword motif of Wagner's *Ring* rang continuously in his ears and he felt that he

---

164. Spotts, *Hitler and the Power of Aesthetics*, 166–77.
165. Waite, *The Psychopathic God*, 289.
166. Spotts, *Hitler and the Power of Aesthetics*, xiii.
167. Waite, *The Psychopathic God*, 386.

was "Siegfried setting forth to slay the dragon…"[168] Not that he was totally upbeat about the prospects of victory. He spoke of his "approaching death" and in his Reichstag speech of September 1, 1939 suggested that for him this war was Wagner's fourth part of the Ring cycle *Götterdämmerung* "with the whole of Europe afire as a funeral pyre for Adolf Hitler."[169]

In his speech on that occasion he spoke of two things: firstly, that since the war had been forced upon the Germans, no array of weapons and no passage of time would bring them to defeat, and secondly, that because Jewry had plotted another world war in order to exterminate the Aryan peoples of Europe, it would not be the Aryan peoples which would be exterminated, but Jewry. "At one time, the Jews of Germany laughed about my prophecies. I do not know whether they are still laughing or whether they have already lost all desire to laugh."

Apart from the European conflagration that ensued, a personal tragedy of bizarre proportions played itself out in the English Garden in Munich. In a kitchen sink drama worthy of the cheapest thriller Unity Mitford saw the dream of her life destroyed and, taking a small revolver in her gloved hand, shot herself in the head. As wayward as her political acumen, her marksmanship resulted in nothing more than a swift visit to hospital and the attention of the best physicians Hitler could command. Despite the frantic state of the invasion of Poland, she was favored with a visit from the Führer himself, armed with a great bouquet of flowers and a signed portrait of himself. The last-mentioned adorned her bedside table until she was escorted to Switzerland. She recovered only to be finally taken off in 1948 to Valhalla to be with the Valkyries and the other fallen heroes.[170]

Hitler was also aware of the possibility that the war gave him to carry out his race cleansing and set up the extermination camps of the future. The blueprints so carefully drawn by Wagner, Gobineau and Chamberlain could now be put into execution. Also set down for implementation on September 1 was the sinister sounding *Order for the destruction of lives that are unworthy of being lived.* "Reichsleiter Bouhler and Dr. Brandt are commissioned with the responsibility of extending the authority of specified doctors so that, after critical assessment of their condition, those judged

---

168. See B. Lansing, "Adolf Hitler," *Life*, New York, Sept 25, 1939. A similar quote is to be found in Fest, *Hitler*, 724.
169. Viereck, *Metapolitics*, 136.
170. Waite, *The Psychopathic God*, 232.

incurably ill can be granted mercy-death."[171] In this decree Hitler said as "the father of his people" he had to make sure that unworthy members of the great family of life were destroyed.[172] In all probability 180,000 died in this program.[173]

The greatest family of life were the twenty thousand artists who were exempted from service in the armed forces.[174] Wieland Wagner was the firm favorite and earlier in 1936 he had found a compulsory labor camp too arduous and had been moved to more comfortable surroundings. Apart from that concession Hitler gave the eldest Wagnerian grandson the sole right to market photographs and articles on Hitler's visits and attendance at Bayreuth, a privilege Wieland turned into a handsome profit.[175]

The objectives laid out in *Mein Kampf* were now to be carried out with ruthless efficiency. Momentarily awed by his bravado in invading Poland and anxious over the entry of Britain and France into the war, the Supreme Commander of the Third Reich watched success after success and became persuaded of his invincibility. One of the soldiers taking part in the invasion of that country and facing the brave cavalry was Wolfgang Wagner, who unlike his elder brother, had not been exempted from military service. When his girlfriend Gertrud had expressed sympathy for the "poor Poles," whose country had been so brutally invaded, Wolfgang is reported to have sneeringly mocked her for it.[176]

He was wounded in the hand and rushed back for treatment at the Charité Hospital in Berlin, where he received the attention of the best surgeon in the Reich, the famous Professor Sauerbruch. There the Führer regularly visited him and he was later discharged from further service. Wagners were born and bred to serve Germany in other ways.[177]

Hitler hoped for peace with Britain after conquering Poland, but on being rebuffed he proceeded with his plans in the west. He decided to occupy Denmark and Norway in April 1940 when bad weather in the west spared Belgium, the Netherlands and France. Next his attack through the

---

171. Kershaw, *Hitler 1936–1945: Nemesis*, 253.
172. Waite, *The Psychopathic God*, 392.
173. Kershaw, *Hitler 1936–1945: Nemesis*, 261.
174. Spotts, *Hitler and the Power of Aesthetics*, 86.
175. Ibid., 255.
176. Ibid., 227.
177. Wagner, Nike, *The Wagners*, 219.

Ardennes on May 10 caught those countries off guard and soon continental Europe lay at his feet.

On June 10 Mussolini entered the war on the side of Germany, and by the end of June Hitler tasted the sweet flavor of vengeance on the deeply hated Treaty of Versailles by signing the peace treaty at the same place. The Luftwaffe turned to Britain and dropped its unwholesome hardware on military and civilian targets. Britain failed to surrender and in the summer of 1940, preparations were begun for the invasion of the Soviet Union. The wily old fox Josef Stalin watched enviously as Hitler extended his territories and soon joined the hunting party, eating up territory to the east, including eastern Poland and Bessarabia.

During the war the festival at Bayreuth continued with the operas being produced for Hitler's guests, organized by the "Strength through Joy" party recreation organization.[178] They were transported to the festival in the Reich Music Train, and given meals and cigarettes and lectures; contemporary photographs showed the soldiers marching to the performance under banners welcoming them to Richard Wagner's town.[179] Wagner was now a form of relaxation from the rigors of war and the dream of the composer had become reality – there were free performances for the citizenry. There were rewards for carrying out his political ambitions after all.

Twenty to thirty thousand guests attended the five wartime festivals, and with the passage of time more and more of the guests were the walking wounded or severely crippled. After imbibing from the great ideological fountain of life they then went off to the front the next day to face the enemies of the Reich, who had been stirred up – so Goebbels's radio told them – by the Jewish warmongers. Later when the absence of numbers made the choruses too small, members of the "Viking" division of the SS swelled the ranks of Nürnbergers who hailed "holy German art."

The Wagner curative worked wonders for a stuka bomber pilot in one of the wartime German propaganda films *Stukas*. The hero had distinguished himself on many a daring mission in the subjugation of France but the boredom of inactivity thereafter rendered him psychologically inert in a clinic and every physician pondered how to bring him back to his pristine health. An enterprising nurse took him off to Bayreuth where

---

178. Spotts, *Hitler and the Power of Aesthetics*, 189.
179. Ibid., 190.

a performance of *Götterdämmerung* restored him to sufficient health to enable him to take part in the bombing of London.[180]

In an ironic psychological twist the propaganda spin doctors of the BBC broadcast repeatedly the themes from that same opera on the basis that the hidden text informed the Germans that their gods were destined to fall and their Reich like that of Wotan would tumble in flames. Whether the German masses were sufficiently sophisticated to appreciate the ploy is not known – but if the subliminal text had caused them to abandon reason and cleanse Europe it seemed worthwhile reversing the process.[181]

The Viking brigade took part in every facet of musical life at the wartime festivals and played the fanfares from the balconies to summon the theatergoers to the next act.[182] Hitler himself attended the festival in July 1940, after ordering his train to go back to Berlin via Bayreuth, to see *Götterdämmerung*.[183] He saw his old pal Kubizek on this occasion for the last time and they spoke about his building and other plans he had so fervently articulated years before. "I did not become Chancellor of the Great German Reich in order to wage war," he told his erstwhile friend and the latter believed him. It was compulsory of course.[184] They reminisced for a while and Hitler said, "poor students, that's what we were. And we were hungry, God knows."

Hitler left Bayreuth through a crowd of cheering people and recognizing Kubizek on the side of the road he stopped the fleet of cars and once more shook his hand.[185]

Later only *Meistersinger* was produced, as the other operas – especially *Tristan* – had too much of the Wagner melancholy and pessimism; the troops needed to be filled with that Nürnberg optimism. What was needed was something cheerful, Winifred told the Führer – the cries of anguish of the wounded Tristan in the third act were too close to the bone for the soldiers, gazing blankly at the stage.[186] Most would have preferred home leave and a night or two in their own beds.

---

180. Ibid., 262.
181. Sheffi, *Ring of Myths*, 36–37.
182. Spotts, *Hitler and the Power of Aesthetics*, 193.
183. Ibid., 198.
184. Kershaw, *Hitler 1936–1945: Nemesis*, 306.
185. Hamann, *Winifred Wagner*, 53.
186. Wagner, Nike, *The Wagners*, 223.

One performance that would never be forgotten by the legendary conductor Herbert von Karajan was held in Berlin in 1940. Rudolf Bockelmann was singing the role of Hans Sachs, but unfortunately was drunk on the evening in question and missed his entry. Von Karajan, who memorized the score and conducted without one, saved the situation but the false entry was noted by Hitler who was outraged. In von Karajan's own words "someone told Hitler this came to pass because that man Karajan has to conduct music by heart. I think it was Minister Goebbels who then had somebody tell me that from now on I was to conduct from the score. Sure enough, next time there was a score on the conductor's stand. I just turned it over and continued as usual."[187]

The common soldier was imbued with a patriotic fervor that had been carefully nurtured by the word manipulators of the Third Reich. The war was preordained and the long promised savior was at the helm. When Berlin was bombed in August it came as something of a shock to the Germans. Göring had been so confident of the might of his air force and their control of the skies that he had made a pronouncement that should British planes ever reach Germany his name was not Hermann Göring but Hermann Meier. Wags in the country would snigger and refer to him as Herr Meier.[188]

Hitler had some years previously rebuilt his cottage Wachenfeld, which he renamed Berghof, in Berchtesgaden, and this home lay – fortuitously, some people believed – opposite the very place where the emperor Barbarossa lay in his sleep waiting to be called to his holy mission. A large picture window revealed the site and Hitler was very conscious of the significance.

When his personal photographer Heinrich Hoffman reflected on the link the Führer said, "It is not a matter of chance, it is a reflection of my mission."[189] Apart from Berghof the other members of the higher echelons of the Nazi regime also expropriated or stole the remaining properties in the Berchtesgaden area for themselves; the area became a Nazi playground, with immense security to keep out the world. Eight miles of electrified fence,

---

187. Kater, *The Twisted Muse*, 60.
188. Kershaw, *Hitler 1936–1945: Nemesis*, 309.
189. Köhler, *Wagner's Hitler*, 283.

pillboxes and anti-aircraft batteries were set up in the hills surrounding his home.[190]

Part of the building work in that marvelously beautiful part of the world was the cloud-embracing Eagle's Nest built at Kehlstein for Hitler to entertain guests and hold his famous tea parties with fancy cakes and sweetmeats. The French Ambassador François-Poncet was one of few foreigners ever invited to visit it. "The approach is by a winding road about nine miles long, boldly cut out of the rock…the road comes to an end in front of a long underground passage leading into the mountain, enclosed by a heavy double door of bronze. At the far end of the underground passage a wide lift, paneled with sheets of copper, awaits the visitor."[191]

The grandiose architectural dreams that had occupied the mind of the young Hitler when he roamed the streets of Vienna with Kubizek were being put into execution. The French Yellow Book records further that the lift rises "through a vertical shaft of 330 feet cut through the rock, to the level of the Chancellor's dwelling place. Here is reached the astonishing climax. The visitor finds himself in a strong and massive building containing a gallery with Roman pillars, an immense circular hall with windows all around…"

Pillars are universally accepted as phallic symbols and give an indication of the size and masculinity of Hitler's vision; in all probability also the magnitude of his inferiority complex.[192] The French ambassador concludes: "[the hall] gives the impression of being suspended in space; an almost overhanging wall of bare rock rises up abruptly. The whole, bathed in the twilight of the autumn evening is grandiose, wild, almost hallucinating. The visitor wonders whether he is awake or dreaming."[193] Walter Langer wondered if this was the mausoleum that the dictator had built for himself and where he would finally commit suicide.

When Kehlstein was being built the workers found a piece of rock shaped like a hand that intrigued the Führer. True to the vision he held of myth and religion he named it the "Hand of Wotan" after the chief god in Wagner's Ring cycle.[194] More and more the fanatical leader was turning

---

190. Langer, *The Mind of Adolf Hitler*, 94.
191. Ibid., 169.
192. Ibid., 202.
193. Ibid.
194. Waite, *The Psychopathic God*, 6.

to Germany's ancient mythical roots to find gods who would sustain his vision of the new world order.

It was thither in February 1941 that Hitler called his generals for strategy discussions. The generals whispered amongst themselves for a while before Hitler joined them and expectations were that he would authorize Operation Sea Lion – the planned invasion of Britain. A big surprise awaited them all, however, and Hitler's minister of armaments production spoke to his architect Hermann Giesler. "You know about the decision – Russia. Things will be hard. But look at the Führer, calm and composed and in the background – the Untersberg. You know the story – for a thousand years the hopes of Germany have been linked with this mountain. Is that not strange?"[195]

On that fatal day – February 3, 1941 – the small man with the glittering, fanatical blue eyes gazed across at the holy site and spoke. "When Barbarossa arises the world will hold its breath."[196] Like an Old Testament prophet the emperor dusted off his medieval armor, mounted his horse and led the twentieth century Teutonic hordes into the Soviet Union in fulfillment of the prophecies of Wagner and Chamberlain. Siegfried was taking up his sword Nothung (needful) and creating *Lebensraum* for a superior race. In his rearguard was a new phenomenon – the *Einsatzgruppen* killing squads sent out to kill Jews and other civilians – the first executors of the Wagnerian testament and "great solution." Not surprisingly the discussions were taking place within a few paces of a large bust of Richard Wagner by Third Reich sculptor Arno Breker, adorning a central position in the grand salon of the Berghof, a statue described by Frederic Spotts as "arrogant, cold and contemptuous – Wagner a Nazi, Wagner a Hitlerite."[197]

The existence of a nonaggression pact with Russia had little influence on his decision. Hitler's humor returned as he commented to his generals: "Treaties will be honored only as long as they are useful…Treaties exist for the purpose of being broken at the most convenient moment." That this contradicted an earlier promise, swallowed hook, line and sinker by the gullible English, to honor the treaties "blindly and faithfully" had no impact. "I am the greatest actor in Europe," he boasted, and the word had a second

---

195. Köhler, *Wagner's Hitler*, 284.
196. Ibid.
197. Spotts, *Hitler and the Power of Aesthetics*, 185.

meaning that was to have fatal consequences for fifty-five million soldiers and noncombatants.[198]

In adopting this policy he was clearly following his great mentor the gay Friedrich the Great who said something very similar. "Never be ashamed of making alliances, and of being yourself the only party that draws advantage from them. Do not commit that stupid fault of not abandoning them whenever it is in your interest to do so."[199] On another occasion Friedrich said, "the world is like a game in which there are honest and dishonest players, so that a prince who plays in this game must learn how to cheat, not in order to do it, but in order not to be the dupe of others."[200] Another hero of Hitler's, Napoleon Bonaparte, engaged in the same sort of cynical disregard for international pacts. "Governments keep their promises only when they are forced to do so, or when it will be to their advantage."[201]

One small matter distracted Hitler from his grand plan – his deputy Hess decided to try to achieve peace with Britain on his own and parachuted into Scotland, and into jail for the rest of his life. Fräulein Anna, as he was called because of his homosexual relationship with Hitler dating from the early twenties, including the Landsberg prison episode when *Mein Kampf* was written, had embarked on a frolic of his own to the embarrassment of his famous lover. British humor would have it that Churchill interviewed Hess and asked him if he was the madman. "No, only his Deputy" was the obvious reply.[202]

Operation Barbarossa, the planned invasion of the Soviet Union, was launched on June 22, 1941, and the German army advanced swiftly into the terrain that had defied Napoleon, one of Hitler's great heroes, one hundred and thirty or so years previously. History would not repeat itself, the small man with the Charlie Chaplin moustache predicted. Victory was certain. On the anniversary of the Munich Beer Hall Putsch Hitler embarked on one of his long diatribes and referred to the First World War and the revolution that followed. The news of deaths of German soldiers was filtering through

---

198. Waite, *The Psychopathic God*, 35.
199. *The Confessions of Friedrich the Great*, ed. Douglas Staden, 1915.
200. *Anti-Machievel*, by Friedrich the Great, trans. Paul Sonnino, 1981.
201. Gourgaud, Gaspard, *Talks of Napoleon at St Helena with General Gaspard Gourgaud*, 1904.
202. Kershaw, *Hitler 1936–1945: Nemesis*, 375.

and he needed scapegoats; inevitably he pointed a finger at his old foe: "the search for those ultimately responsible for these events leads to those who have always profited from conflicts between nations – the Jews."[203]

As Hermann Göring said: "this war is not the Second World War. This is the great racial war. In the final analysis it is about whether the German and Aryan prevails here, or whether the Jew rules the world, and that is what we are fighting for out there."[204] He had earlier called anti-Semitism the state religion of the Third Reich and likened the persecution of the Jews to a holy war. It was clear now that the crusaders were on the march.

---

203. Köhler, *Wagner's Hitler*, 273.
204. Burleigh, *The Third Reich*, 571.

Chapter sixteen
The Holocaust

To that end the leader of the Third Reich turned his attention with a vengeance. Ominously enough – the use of innuendo being the mode of communication – Hitler directed Himmler to prepare the ground for the "new order" in Europe. Much has been written about the Holocaust and it is not necessary to repeat the details. The gruesome catalogue of Hitler's fulfillment of his life's work is contained in the magnificent scholarship of, among many others, Martin Gilbert's *The Holocaust*, Daniel Goldhagen's *Hitler's Willing Executioners* and Michael Burleigh's *The Third Reich: A New History*. These scholars built on the wonderful research conducted by thousands of contributors throughout the world. Some mention has to be made of the sinister campaign to exterminate European Jewry but our emphasis here will be on the process that was initiated by Wagner, and Hitler's preoccupation with the composer during the execution thereof.

The propaganda war against the Jews had been going on for years and in November 1940 its most sinister manifestation in film form – *The Eternal Jew* – showed Jews to be less than human and quoted from Wagner's first anti-Semitic essay "Jewry in Music." Hitler was instrumental in a number of aspects of the movie and Goebbels told the filmmaker that Hitler wanted the Jews from the Polish ghettos depicted in it to be removed to Madagascar.[1] Another film, *Jew Suss*, compared the purity of German *Lieder*

---

1. Kershaw, *Hitler 1936–1945: Nemesis*, 911.

The Nazis used every means to vilify and demonize the Jews. Typical of this campaign was the film The Eternal Jew which used Wagner's music and words to impart the murderous anti-Semitic message. Bishop, Hitler's Third Reich vol. 8.

with the inarticulate mutterings in the synagogue – a theme that had the purest Wagnerian roots in that pernicious essay.[2]

From the beginning there were a few voices of dissent in the German armed forces. One such was that of Colonel-General Johannes Blaskowitz whose report spoke of the "criminal atrocities, maltreatment, and plundering carried out by the SS, police, and administration." He referred to what he called the "animal and pathological instincts" of the SS, which caused the slaughter of tens of thousands of Jews and Poles, and such forces were impossible to control "since they can well believe themselves officially authorized and justified in committing any act of cruelty."[3] Hitler's response was predictable: "you can't fight a war with Salvation Army methods."

The extermination campaign commenced with the most sinister instruction ever penned, handed in at the Nürnberg trials, in the veiled lan-

---

2. Sheffi, *Ring of Myths*, 49.
3. Kershaw, *Hitler 1936–1945: Nemesis*, 247.

guage that men of that ilk habitually use. On July 31, 1941, Göring instructed Heydrich in writing as follows: "I herewith commission you to carry out all preparations with regard to…a *total solution of the Jewish question* in those territories of Europe which are under German influence…I furthermore charge you to submit to me as soon as possible a draft showing the…measures already taken for the execution of the *intended final solution of the Jewish question*."[4]

The similarity to Wagner's admonition in his 1881 paper "Know Thyself" is devastating. There he stated that only when his countrymen awakened and ceased party bickering, would there be no more Jews, a "*great solution*" he foresaw as uniquely within the reach of the Germans, if they could conquer false shame and not shrink from ultimate knowledge.[5] As has been alluded to, Wagner's certainty that greatness would be thrust upon him persuaded him to record his life in great detail in a Red book, a Brown book, sundry other articles and finally in his autobiography. In similar vein Hitler worried that posterity might be denied some comment or thought of his and ordered that notes be made of every word he said at the table – these have indeed subsequently been published.[6]

Professor Schramm, a medievalist of international distinction, was called up as a reserve officer and appointed war diarist in the Supreme Headquarters of the Wehrmacht. In an essay summarizing his six-volume edition of the War Diary he said of Hitler: "There was not simply executive ability of a very high order indeed – a photographic memory, a keen brain, the capacity to take on experts and out argue them in their own fields – but two qualities of yet greater importance. He had quasi hypnotic powers of persuasion, with individuals as well as with masses. It was this that enabled him to retain the support of all but a handful of his entourage, to say nothing of the German people as a whole, long past the moment when defeat was clearly inevitable. And he possessed will-power of complete inflexibility; of a massive, primeval strength which reduced all debate and opposition to impotent chirping of grasshoppers. Together with this went a complete and icy ruthlessness. It was as though in his soul several

---

4. Shirer, *Rise and Fall of the Third Reich*, 1147.
5. Gutman, *Richard Wagner*, 602, 603.
6. Trevor-Roper, *Hitler's Table Talk*, 241.

strings were missing which even in the most hardened and violent men can at least now and then be heard reverberating."

The memories of the wonderful times enjoying Wagner would reoccur from time to time. So fanatical had Hitler become at that stage of his life in his idolatry that on one occasion he divided the world into those who were Wagnerians and those who had no special name.

On October 25, 1941 Hitler supped with ReichsFührer ss Himmler and ss General ObergruppenFührer Heydrich, the leading Gauleiters placed in charge of the extermination program. Hitler's monologue traversed a number of solutions to the Jewish problem and cast doubts on the creation of Israel. He is reported to have said: "From the rostrum of the Reichstag I prophesied to Jewry that, in the event of war's proving inevitable, the Jew would disappear from Europe. That race of criminals has on its conscience the two million dead of the First World War, and now already hundreds of thousands more. Let nobody tell me that all the same we can't park them in the marshy parts of Russia. Who's worrying about our troops? It's not a bad idea, by the way that public rumour attributes to us a plan to exterminate the Jews. Terror is a salutary thing. The attempt to create a Jewish state will be a failure."[7]

Hitler must have been thinking of his Bayreuth mentor because it was the same evening when he mentioned how poor he was during the Viennese period of his life that he had to restrict himself to seeing only the finest spectacles. Thus he heard *Tristan* thirty or forty times and always from the best companies.[8] That Wagner and his Jewish composer enemies were never far from his thoughts is clear from a discussion he conducted on the evening of November 5. After expounding on the racial inferiority of the English lower classes he said that the most idiotic war the English had ever begun would lead to an unprecedented flood of anti-Semitism in that country and the "fall of the Jew." Apart from the fields of lying and cheating, in which they excelled, the Jews lacked any ability and creativity: "they don't have a true musician, thinker, no art, nothing, absolutely nothing. They are liars, forgers, deceivers."[9] Wagner, it will be recalled, had

---

7. Ibid., 87.
8. Ibid., 333.
9. Kershaw, *Hitler 1936–1945: Nemesis*, 489.

started the whole racist debacle with an allegation that Meyerbeer was a pickpocket who stole music from more worthy composers.

In December 1941 the Russians regrouped and led a ferocious counter-attack that made it clear that Napoleon's folly was to be Hitler's nightmare. The same month saw the Japanese attack on the American port of Pearl Harbor and the entry into the war of the largest industrialized country in the world. While Hitler did not hesitate to commit fresh troops to the field, either his own or those dragooned from conquered territories, he was not so naïve as to believe victory was possible. General Jodl's diary shows that by early December 1941 Hitler had realized he could not win the war and decided to concentrate his energies on exterminating the Jews.[10]

Hitler's love of Wagner continued and he often harped back on the wonderful days at Bayreuth. Less than two days later on December 13, 1941, Hitler was back to his old themes. He gave his rather morbid views of heaven and pronounced again the lineage of the Savior from Palestine. "Christ was an Aryan and St Paul used his doctrine to mobilise the criminal underworld and thus organise a proto-bolshevism. What is this God who takes pleasure only in seeing men grovel before him? I can imagine people being enthusiastic about the paradise of Mahomet, but as for the insipid paradise of the Christians... In your lifetime, you used to hear the music of Richard Wagner. After your death it will be nothing but hallelujahs, the waving of palms, children of an age for the feeding, and hoary old men."[11]

Mention has been made of the "unique opportunity" the soldiers – "the captive audience," some of whom said they preferred to face the Russian guns – had to visit Bayreuth free of charge during the war, to hear the composer's masterpieces.[12] The national soul needed refreshment from the only authentic wellspring of culture. On December 17, 1941, Hitler explained to his generals that he had several original Wagner scores in his possession – a disclosure that was to confuse music historians and puzzle the Wagner family when they later attempted to recover them.[13]

On December 28, 1941, he was again speaking about the composer and he touched on a subject that was close to his own heart – the attacks on his favorite composer as a homosexual. Without saying as much the

---

10. Waite, *The Psychopathic God*, 409.
11. Trevor-Roper, *Hitler's Table Talk*, 143.
12. Köhler, *Wagner's Hitler*, 8.
13. Trevor-Roper, *Hitler's Table Talk*, 147.

German leader was coming as close as he dared, in the company of rough military men, to defending Wagner. "No man can pass through a sieve. Richard Wagner was attacked because he wore silk pyjamas." The hundreds of yards of satin ordered by the composer must have been common knowledge at the time.

In the small hours in Eastern Prussia Hitler summarized the failings of the Bayreuth prophet: "prodigality, insensate luxury, no knowledge of the value of money…" and went on to explain why an artist needed license – or was it licentiousness? – to create the great works. With a merry laugh as the cold sun rose Hitler told them that Wagner's contemporaries accused him of madness – but he remained a genius, a god.[14]

On January 13, 1942, he was back on a theme that Wagner would have enjoyed – attacking Jewish composers. "Jewry had raised Brahms to a pinnacle. He exploited effects of the hands, effects of the beard and hair… Wagner also had the feeling for gesture, but with him it was innate. Wagner was a man of the Renaissance…"[15] He was pulling together the threads of the whole narrative; from the early struggle of Wagner with Meyerbeer and the other Jewish composers to the fulfillment of the mission.

The sinister instruction regarding the "final solution" galvanized the recipients into convening the most apocalyptic gathering of all time. Shirer records how, at the conference held in the leafy, comfortable Wannsee suburb of Berlin, on January 20, 1942, Heydrich gave instructions to an assembly of some fifteen high officials. While streetcars swept by in the fresh snow and pig-tailed, flaxen-haired children shouted in delight as they ice-skated on the lake, he spelled out the implications. "In the course of this final solution of the European Jewish problem, approximately eleven million Jews are involved…"

Heydrich then called out the numbers of citizens from his list who were to be murdered. In Germany there were 131,800 Jews left, in Russia five million, in the Ukraine three million, in Poland two and a quarter million, in France three quarters of a million and in England a third of a million.[16] The process was systematic and merciless and the innuendo not lost on the group of officials, who pondered the gravity of their task. "The

---

14. Ibid., 155.
15. Ibid., 206.
16. Shirer, *Rise and Fall of the Third Reich*, 1148.

Jews should now in the course of the Final Solution be brought to the East… for use as big labour gangs, with separation of sexes, the Jews capable of work are brought to these areas and employed in road building, in which task undoubtedly *a great part will fall* through natural diminution. *The remnant* that finally is able to survive all this – since this is undoubtedly the part *with the strongest resistance – must be treated accordingly*, since the people, representing natural selection, are to be regarded as the germ cell of a new Jewish development."[17]

"The remnant with the strongest resistance must be treated accordingly." It was reminiscent of Cosima's veiled speech and innuendo fifty years previously. In executing this ruthless plan the first method involved the use of execution squads known as *Einsatzgruppen*.[18] Heydrich addressed the commanders of these squads on two occasions and Walter Blume, the head of Sonderkommando 7a, described how they were informed of Hitler's decision to exterminate Soviet Jewry. "Heydrich himself explained that the Russian campaign was imminent, that partisan war was to be expected, and that in this region many Jews lived who had to be exterminated through liquidation. When one of those assembled called out 'How are we supposed to do this?' He said 'you will find out.'"[19]

Three days later on January 23, 1942, the mastermind of the plan, who avoided signing any documents himself, gave reasons for his extermination plan. The psychopath did not even believe that what he was doing was wrong. "One must act radically. When one pulls out a tooth one does it with a single tug. And the pain quickly goes away. The Jew must clear out of Europe. When I think about it I realize that I'm extraordinarily humane. For my part I restrict myself to telling the Jews they must go away. But if they refuse to go voluntarily I see no solution but extermination… why did the Jew provoke this war? A good three or four hundred years will go by before the Jews set foot in Europe again."[20]

The concentration camps were expanded, and there were added to them extermination camps such as Auschwitz and Mauthausen, as well as mobile extermination squads. Wagner's works were played in concentration

---

17. Ibid., 1149.
18. Ibid., 1164.
19. Goldhagen, *Hitler's Willing Executioners*, 149.
20. Trevor-Roper, *Hitler's Table Talk*, 235–36.

Rounding up Jews. Once the war began Hitler and his forces gathered together as many of the Jews of Europe as they could and transported them to the east to camps for forced labor and gassing. See Martin Gilbert, 673.

camps, in line with Hitler's pronouncement that "whoever wants to know National Socialist Germany must first know Wagner."[21]

The Jews of Germany, Poland and the Soviet Union were the most numerous among the victims but he planned the extermination of all Jewry; he sought them out in countries he had no intentions of colonizing. "The Nazis actively sought out Jews in countries with which they had no connection, and which Germans had neither settled nor had any desire to settle, transporting them hundreds and thousands of miles to their deaths in extermination camps in Poland."[22] The "final solution," in Hitler's view of the Jewish problem, encompassed an attempt to destroy the whole religion. The sufferings of other races were only less when measured in numbers

---

21. Hooper, "Israel Bans Wagner Opera Despite Plea by Barenboim."
22. Burleigh, *The Third Reich*, 573.

killed. Such barbarism was indiscriminate, even where, as in the Ukraine, Hitler might have encouraged nationalist feelings to his own advantage. That the euphemism permeated the whole death structure is established by a signal intercepted by Walter Eytan, a Jew working at Bletchley Park and recorded in *Codebreakers*.[23] "…[I]n late 1943 or early 1944 we intercepted a signal from a small German-commissioned vessel in the Aegean, reporting that it was transporting Jews, I think from Rhodes or Kos, en route for Piraeus *zur endlösung* ('for the final solution'). I had never seen or heard this expression before, but instinctively I knew what it must mean and I have never forgotten that moment."[24]

Four days after the Wannsee conference the Führer was back to his operatic reveries. That the Jewish "final solution" must have also been discussed that same night is proved by the presence of Heinrich Himmler, who was in charge of the whole process. "What joy each of Wagner's works has given me," Hitler exclaims, on the evening of January 24, 1942, soon after the first disastrous defeats in Russia, to his generals and party cronies, in the depths of the underground shelter of Wolfschanze at Rastenburg in East Prussia. He went on to explain that it was at a performance of *Rienzi* in Linz in 1906 that he first resolved to enter politics as "a tribune of the people."[25]

Juxtaposed with a discussion of arguably the greatest tragedy and crime of all time we have Hitler slipping into his maudlin reveries, recalling his happy days at Bayreuth. "I remember my first emotion the first time I entered Wahnfried. To say I was moved is an understatement. At my worst moments, they never ceased to sustain me even Siegfried Wagner… I was on Christian name terms with them… I loved them all, and I also love Wahnfried. The ten days of the Bayreuth season were always one of the blessed seasons of my existence and I rejoice at the idea that one day I shall be able to resume the pilgrimage… On the day following the end of the Bayreuth Festival… I am gripped by a great sadness – as when one strips the Christmas tree of its ornaments…"[26]

His table talk revealed that the boycott of attending Bayreuth by Jewish

---

23. *Codebreakers*, ed. F.H. Hinsley and Alan Stripp (Oxford: Oxford University Press, 1994), 60.
24. Cornish, *The Jew of Linz*, 284.
25. Köhler, *Wagner's Hitler*, 2.
26. Trevor-Roper, *Hitler's Table Talk*, 241–42.

music lovers from 1933 onwards had meant that Hitler had to take up block bookings for his friends and the party and he later conceded that he had financed productions with government funds.[27]

The "extremely humane" plans of Hitler included any Jew irrespective of his position. Emil Preetorius, the wonderful set designer at Bayreuth during the thirties, tried together with Winifred to secure the release of a prominent Dutch Jew, who was the head of the Wagner Society of Amsterdam. That, in any event, was the account Winifred gave when trying to persuade an American tribunal, after the war, that her stewardship of the festival had been untainted by the Third Reich.

A letter written by Winifred with regard to the Dutchman revealed the extent of her knowledge of the "final solution" advocated by her father-in-law and executed by her favorite politician. In her brilliant biography of Winifred Wagner, Brigitte Hamann says that "she certainly knew what was happening in the East." Moreover she used the same old anti-Semitic Wahnfried jargon always when she was dealing with the misfortunes of the Jews. She wrote to her friend Lene and mentioned the Dutch Jew (Louis Wijsenbeek) and the fact that she had written to Rauter about him. She continues by saying that the heightened measures against Jews should be interpreted as retaliation for terrorist attacks and behind them international Jewry skulked. The individual had to expiate or make amends for that although she did not believe that Wijsenbeek should be killed as he was not up to mischief or did not give that impression.[28] She managed to have him freed from the Gestapo jail in The Hague.

During the following years Preetorius – designer of the famous Semitic rock in *The Valkyries* – was harassed by the Gestapo and found to be politically unreliable; all that probably saved him from the extermination camps was his connection to the Wagner establishment.[29]

When the tide turned against Germany and his generals insisted on 800,000 more men Hitler would not relent and release the artists from their exemption. When Ulrich Roller, son of the legendary set designer Alfred, was shot dead in Russia Hitler was furious and ranted: "what is served by sending an artist to war? Some Russian idiot simply shoots down

---

27. Spotts, *Hitler and the Power of Aesthetics*, 169.
28. Hamann, *Winifred Wagner*, 457–58.
29. Spotts, *Hitler and the Power of Aesthetics*, 169.

such a man!…A man of this sort is irreplaceable."[30] Throughout a period when Hitler was convinced that the war *could not be won*, and he therefore was concentrating all his energies and resources on his war against the Jews, he returned time and again to Wagner. A perennial theme was the depth of his passion. In 1942 (the precise date is uncertain) he said: "for me Wagner is a god, his music is my religion. I go to his operas as others go to church."[31] On January 24, 1942, he was talking of Wagner's lover Mathilde Wesendonck and her influence on his compositions. "Whatever one says *Tristan* is Wagner's masterpiece and we owe *Tristan* to what the love Mathilde Wesendonck inspired in him."[32]

Less than a week later on January 30, 1942, Hitler, at his apocalyptic best, addressed the masses in the Berlin Sportpalast. "The result of this war will be the annihilation of world Jewry…and for at least a thousand years the most villainous demon of all time will be powerless to raise its head."[33] On the evening of February 22, 1942 Hitler had Himmler again as his special guest, who must have reported back on his sacred "mission." He spoke out about the "Jewish virus." "The discovery of the Jewish virus is one of the greatest revolutions that have taken place in the world. The battle in which we are engaged today is of the same sort as the battle waged, during the last century, by Pasteur and Koch. How many diseases have their origin in the Jewish virus? Japan would have been contaminated, too, if it had stayed open to the Jews. We shall regain our health only by eliminating the Jew. Everything has a cause, nothing comes by chance."[34]

This is not a far cry from what Wagner said in his article "Jewry in Music" in 1850. Jews dominated a degenerate society whose "body is dead and the Jews lodge in it like a swarm of insects corrupting it." In his first draft of the Ring cycle he describes the Nibelungs as "feverishly, unrestingly they burrow through the bowels of the earth *like worms in a dead body.*"

By March the gas chambers were in full operation and reports were pouring in of the successes at Belzec. Goebbels told his diary that Hitler remained "pitiless" on the Jewish question and he was using "the most brutal means." He spelled this out in a further entry a week later: "from

---

30. Ibid., 86.
31. Köhler, *Wagner's Hitler*, 137.
32. Trevor-Roper, *Hitler's Table Talk*, 240–41.
33. Köhler, *Wagner's Hitler*, 75.
34. Trevor-Roper, *Hitler's Table Talk*, 332.

More than six million Jews were exterminated in the worst racial cleansing in history. Hungarian Jews with 20 minutes to live await their turn in the gas chambers and incinerators. Bishop, Hitler's Third Reich vol. 1, page 9.

the General Government, beginning with Lublin, the Jews are now being deported to the East. A fairly barbaric procedure, not to be described in any greater detail, is being used here, and not much more remains of the Jews themselves. In general, it can probably be established that 60 percent of them must be liquidated; while only 40 percent can be put to work...A judgment is being carried out on the Jews which is barbaric, but fully deserved. The prophecy which the Führer gave them along the way for bringing about a new world war is beginning to become true in the most terrible fashion. No sentimentality can be allowed to prevail in these things. If we did not fend them off, the Jews would annihilate us. It's a life-and-death struggle between the Aryan race and the Jewish bacillus. No other government and no other regime could produce the strength to solve this question generally. Here, too, the Führer is the unswerving champion and spokesman of a radical solution..."[35]

---

35. Kershaw, *Hitler 1936–1945: Nemesis*, 494–95.

In April 1942 Hitler had received the latest tape recording equipment and was commenting on the latest orchestral and operatic performances. He regarded the strings of the Berlin Philharmonic as better than those of the Vienna Philharmonic and talked of a number of singers he regarded as in decline. He also took advantage of the occasion to engage in gossip about Wagner and his descendants.[36] Hitler's insomnia meant that staff had to stay up and play records of his favorites including Beethoven symphonies, Hugo Wolf's *Lieder* and of course the music of the master of Bayreuth. So frequently would he request the same selections that the staff knew the serial numbers and unerringly plucked them from their sleeves.[37] At last peace would descend on the troubled dictator, tormented by a world in which he had adopted the unwilling role, as he claimed, of racial purifier, as opposed to that of artist, and even more importantly as composer and spiritual heir of Richard Wagner.

A film about Friedrich the Great entitled *The Great King* gave Hitler great satisfaction, and Goebbels's comparison of him with the monarch enhanced the standing of the propaganda minister, especially when emphasis was placed on the ultimate triumph of the king against all his mighty foes.[38] As the end of the war approached and defeat was staring the Germans in the face, resort was to be had to the miraculous reversal of Friedrich's fortunes in his battles. The conversations oscillated between Wagner and the extermination of the Jews. Hitler was also keen to show that he was not alone in his hatred of them and, despite calling the Americans and British pawns of the international Jewish conspiracy, he rather paradoxically stigmatized them as anti-Semitic as well. Wagner's attendance at Lessing's play *Nathan the Wise* had resulted in a further anti-Semitic tirade and Hitler returned to this theme in 1942. "Beneath the surface anti-Semitism is far more pronounced among the British and the Americans than among the Germans, who in spite of all their unpleasant experiences persist in clinging to their sentimental image of 'the decent Jew.' And there is a tradition in this. It was, after all, a German dramatist, Lessing, who idealized the figure of the Jew in his play *Nathan the Wise*."[39]

That same year was to see the death of one of Hitler's favorite singers

---

36. Spotts, *Hitler and the Power of Aesthetics*, 12.
37. Kershaw, *Hitler 1936–1945: Nemesis*, 500.
38. Ibid., 501.
39. Köhler, *Wagner's Hitler*, 289.

at Bayreuth, Josef von Manowarda. He had established a great friendship with Hitler and the latter flew into a great rage for the rest of the day when the funeral did not receive the banner headlines it deserved. A state funeral was arranged and Goebbels and Göring forced to attend, despite the war reaching a critical stage with the army suffering reverses at Stalingrad.[40]

Nobody told of the actual process of extermination better than Lucy Davidowicz who described in such simple but horrifying language the process when the Jews arrived at Auschwitz, Belzec, Chelmno, Majdanek, Sobibor and Treblinka. There was a standard procedure "at camps maintaining labour installations, like Auschwitz, 10 percent of the arrivals – those who looked the fittest – were selected for work. The remainder were consigned to the gas chambers. They were instructed to undress; the women and the girls had their hair cut. They were then marched between files of auxiliary police (Ukrainians usually) who hurried them along with whips, sticks or guns, to the gas chambers…these were identified as showers. The Jews were rammed in, one person per square foot. The gassing lasted from ten to thirty minutes, depending on the facilities and technique used. In Belzec, according to an eyewitness, it took thirty-two minutes and finally all were dead, like pillars of basalt still erect, not having any space to fall. To make room for the next load, the bodies were right away tossed out, blue, wet with sweat and urine, the legs covered with faeces or menstrual blood. Later the bodies were burned, either in the open air or in crematoria…a worker at Auschwitz said that the stench given off by the pyres contaminated the surrounding countryside. At night the red sky over Auschwitz could be seen for miles."[41]

Different views were sometimes expressed as to the advisability of maintaining silence about the fate of the victims of the extermination camps. On October 7, 1942 the Commandant of the Chelmno extermination camp Odile Globocnik visited Hitler. He was an odious man – a part-Slovene Austrian policeman – who headed the camp at Lublin from November 1939 before moving on to higher things. After explaining the method of extermination to Hitler the latter shouted "faster, get the whole thing over with faster!" Dr. Herbert Linden of the Ministry of the Interior

---

40. Spotts, *Hitler and the Power of Aesthetics*, 83.
41. Lucy Davidowicz, *The War against the Jews 1933–45*.

Adolf Hitler as painted by Richter from Waite (Cover). The above portrait was described by the art critic of Die Zeit as "the only really authentic portrait of Hitler...perhaps the most important historical portrait that any German artist has ever had the opportunity to paint." Painted in 1941 from a concealed position; Richter was not impressed with Hitler's face until someone said "Jew."

asked: "would it not be better to burn the corpses rather than bury them? Perhaps another generation will think differently of the matter…"

Globocnik then replied: "But gentlemen, if a generation, coming after us should be so cowardly and so corrupt as not to understand our deeds, which are so beneficial and so necessary, then, gentlemen, the whole of National Socialism will have been in vain. Rather, we should bury bronze plates with the corpses on which we should write that it was we who had the courage to accomplish this gigantic task!" Hitler then commented, "Yes my dear Globocnik, that is the truth of the matter. I entirely agree with you."[42] At Hitler's insistence Professor Pfannenstiel, who had witnessed numerous gassings, explained the reactions of the witnesses. He noted that when the people were in the gas chambers at first nothing happened and then he heard wailing as was done in the synagogues as he pressed his ear closer to the wooden door to hear better.[43]

The notion that these sinister figures, discussing the fate of millions

---

42. Hilberg, *Destruction of the European Jews*, 628.
43. Ibid., 627.

The Final Solution. A crematorium in which Jews were burned after being gassed. Kershaw vol. 2, page 74. Ullstein Bilderdienst, Berlin.

of innocent men, women and children, were convinced that they were involved in meritorious work, is difficult to credit. If it was the position they adopted at that meeting it did not seem to be consistent with their subsequent practice – they spent considerable time and effort in disguising their death factories and in covering up all traces of their iniquity. In fact they erected the most extensive crematoria that were ever created and burned the bodies, to prevent identification being effected. The Jewish composer Igor Stravinsky described Bayreuth as "lugubrious" and said it looked like "a crematorium, and a very old fashioned one at that."[44]

It is difficult to understand that such bestiality ever existed. Although the majority of extermination centers were disguised as showers and ablution blocks Treblinka had an added refinement. The gas chambers were designed to look like a synagogue with a giant Star of David beneath the gable and at the entrance a dark heavy curtain, stolen from a Jewish holy

---

44. See Spotts, *Bayreuth*, 1.

place, was hung with the legend "This is the gate through which the just shall pass."[45]

As his tremendous death machine was steaming ahead, Hitler's table talk was often concerned with entirely different matters. In late April 1942 he was at the Berghof and deploring the lack of top Wagnerian tenors in Germany and the failings of Jewish conductor Bruno Walter and even the tall, blue-eyed "Aryan" Hans Knappertsbusch. Walter had been one of the world's finest conductors to ever grace the podium – he left his position as director of the Bavarian State Opera and Leipziger Gewandhaus in 1933 – but Hitler called him an "absolute non-entity." He had also ruined the Vienna State Opera to such an extent that it could no longer play the divine music emanating from Bayreuth, but was good only for "beer music." On the other hand Wilhelm Furtwängler had the right credentials and was the only man worthy of picking up the baton in the cause of proper music.[46]

The work of carrying out exterminations was psychologically distressing not only for the victims, but also for the executioners, as Himmler pointed out. On October 4, 1943 he made a speech in Posnan to those responsible for this cruel and grisly work. It is interesting to see how he equates the sense of duty in killing Jews to that required in killing fellow Germans during "The Night of the Long Knives" in 1934 when Röhm and other political enemies were disposed of.

The chilling words have been recorded. "We Germans, who, alone among nations, have the proper attitude towards animals, will also adopt a proper attitude towards these beasts in human form…take care that these sub-humans always look up to you, they must always look their superior in the eye. It is just the same as for an animal. As long as it looks its tamer in the eye, it does nothing. But always bear clearly in mind that you are dealing with a beast. This approach has enabled us to get the better of the Russians. This approach will always give us the mastery over the Slavs…just as we did not hesitate on 30 June 1934 to do our duty as ordered and to put those comrades who had failed us up against a wall and shoot them, so we did not speak about it afterwards, nor will we ever speak about it."

It was clear then that Himmler was aware that what was being asked of these murderers was something that had to be kept secret. Once the Allies

---

45. Köhler, *Wagner's Hitler*, 287.
46. Kershaw, *Hitler 1936–1945: Nemesis*, 512–13.

started approaching attempts were made to hide the camps and destroy or bury the bodies. Himmler continued with his talk. "Thanks be to God that the discretion which has become second nature to us has stopped us talking about such things, even amongst ourselves. It sent a shudder through every one of us, but it was still perfectly clear to each of us that he would do the same again next time, if he were ordered to do so and if it were necessary. Most of you know what it means when a hundred corpses are lying next to each other, or five hundred, or a thousand. To have to endure this and, apart from a few inevitable examples of human frailty, to have remained decent men, that has made us hard. This is a glorious page in German history, which has never been written down and is never to be written."[47]

A glorious page in German history. The officials had difficulty taking orders of this horrific nature from Himmler and Gauleiter of Danzig-Westprussia Albert Forster was heard to say, "If I had a face like Himmler, I wouldn't speak of race at all."[48] Amongst the persons of whom Himmler was speaking must have been the 261 Jews registered in 1933 as living in Bayreuth.[49] Some of these would have been families who contributed to the festival when Siegfried Wagner approached them for donations after the First World War. On November 10, 1938, their beautiful synagogue, built in 1760, was destroyed and the bullyboys of the SA plundered shops and offices occupied by Jewish families.[50] At that time in Bayreuth about seventy of the original 260 Jews remained. On November 27 they were sent on a three-day journey to the concentration camp Kaiserwald near Riga. That city had hosted Richard Wagner for some years. It was there that he wrote his opera *Rienzi* that so inspired Hitler and where he obtained his ideas for the sunken orchestra pit and the Roman amphitheatre type of seating. On January 16, 1942, eleven Bayreuth Jews over sixty years, including the highly respected senior advocate Berthold Klein and his wife, were taken to an old age home, "The White Dove" near Bamburg, for which they had to pay five times the normal amount. From there they were transported to the concentration camp at Theresienstadt and thereafter to Lithuania and Auschwitz. None of them survived.

---

47. Hilberg, *Destruction of the European Jews*, 648. See also Shirer, *Rise and Fall of the Third Reich*, 1150.
48. Kershaw, *Hitler 1936–1945: Nemesis*, 316.
49. Wagner, Gottfried, *Twilight of the Wagners*, 227.
50. Ibid.

The last seven Bayreuth Jews lived under wretched conditions, one family in an unheated Jewish mortuary. Two committed suicide and four died. Lastly Justin Steinhäuser, a combat veteran of the First World War who had won the Iron Cross, was sent in November 1944 to a labor camp in Thüringen and thereafter to a concentration camp at Flossenbürg. Miraculously he survived.[51]

At the end of 1942, the defeat of the German troops under Rommel at el-Alamein and the relief after the long siege of Stalingrad brought about the turning point in the war. Victory was now impossible and Hitler became reclusive and was only interested in good news from the front. Keeping the strange hours he had always kept – he stayed up until two and three in the morning and rose about lunchtime – he refused to visit bombed cities or to read reports of setbacks.

Mention has been made of his mortal fear of the dark and since he was a boy he was afraid to be left alone at night. As an adult he would order a guest or staff member to stay up with him until the first light. As Eva Braun recorded him saying, "I really shudder at the thought of being alone at night."[52] Was it the nightmares that petrified him, when he was alone with his subconscious? Freud was to deal with children's fear of the dark and especially those "with a sex instinct that is excessive." Adults too, according to him, were also subject to fear of the dark especially those "who have become neurotic, owing to their libido being unsatisfied. [They] behave like children and begin to be frightened when they are alone…"[53] Martin Bormann, Hitler's secretary, blocked visitors and reports that might distress him and he grew sick with a shake in his hand and eyes that watered. Injections from his physician, Theodor Morell, often left him drowsy and indecisive.

From time to time he assumed his old manic dynamic self and was galvanized into action. When his fascist comrade-at-arms Mussolini was captured by partisans in July 1943 and his Italian ally surrendered, he conceived an effective rescue plan. He personally directed the German occupation of positions, inadequately held by the Italian army, and ordered the kidnapping of Mussolini from his prison. On the eastern front, his

---

51. Hamann, *Winifred Wagner*, 450.
52. Waite, *The Psychopathic God*, 13.
53. Freud, *On Sexuality*, 147.

fanatical refusal to allow his commanders to surrender led to huge losses and he would never acknowledge that there was little hope of holding up the Red Army advance.

Inevitably, his generals lost faith in him and attempts were planned to assassinate him. As Hitler interpreted every event in life in Wagnerian terms this proved to be no exception. Hitler said: "My own friends will one day stab me mortally in the back…and it will be just before our last and greatest victory, at the moment of supreme tension. Once more Hagen would slay Siegfried."[54] Tensions arose amongst his commanding officers and he quickly exchanged those who questioned his orders with more compliant leaders. His favoritism was a source of discontent and he gave disproportionate importance to the ss divisions, directly responsible to him alone. All around him his forces were suffering reverses. The heroes of the Atlantic were now no longer so effective and the failure of the U-boat campaign and the bombing of Germany meant that defeat was inevitable.

To negotiate peace became paramount and the leadership of the army questioned his sanity. The most well known attempt on his life, a bomb blast on July 20, 1944, orchestrated by Col. von Stauffenberg at a conference at Hitler's headquarters in East Prussia, failed to kill him and he concluded that he was indestructible. Included in the plot was Karl Goerdeler, an erstwhile mayor of Leipzig, who had protested the removal of the statue of Mendelssohn in the city.[55] Those implicated in the plot were executed in the most hideous manner, by slow strangulation on butcher's hooks in the Ploetzensee Prison; their deaths filmed and watched several times by the madman. The sexual perversions and sadism that had manifested themselves earlier in his life had now assumed a more macabre garb. The irony of the sordid exercise was that the conspirators recast an operational plan code-named Valkyrie, designed to mobilize the reserve army in the event of internal unrest, and attempted to remove the dictator and mass murderer.[56]

The failure of the plot finally convinced Hitler of his role as Messiah of the German people. "These criminals who wanted to do away with me have no idea what would have happened to the German people…I am the

---

54. Langer, *The Mind of Adolf Hitler*, 210.
55. Kater, *The Twisted Muse*, 229.
56. Kershaw, *Hitler 1936–1945: Nemesis*, 669.

only one who knows the danger, and the only one who can prevent it."[57] Ian Kershaw quotes the last-mentioned comment in his magnificent two volume biography of Hitler and then goes on to identify the psychological process. "Such sentiments were redolent, through a distorting mirror, of the Wagnerian redeemer-figure, a hero who alone could save the holders of the Grail, indeed the world itself, from disaster – a latter day Parsifal."[58]

The Wagnerite always snatched any opportunity to visit Wahnfried and pay homage to the shrine. Not long before this event Hitler had visited Bayreuth and told Winifred that he was hearing "the rustling of the wings of the victory goddess," but she was too much of a realist to believe him and thought he was high on drugs, administered by his quack Dr. Morell.[59]

During the visit they chatted about the old days and walked about Wahnfried in the warm spring weather. News from Winifred was that her eldest son Wieland had successfully created stage sets for a Ring cycle to be produced in Nürnberg and Altenburg and was designing a new production of Weber's *Der Freischütz*.[60] Wieland had married Gertrud two years earlier at Nussdorf, on Lake Constance, but there was to be no honeymoon for the eldest Wagner boy, who fled back to his easel, while his new bride took to her heels to Italy to learn the language.

His brother Wolfgang had met and married Ellen Drexel, a pretty dancer he met while working with the Berlin State Opera.[61] The topsy-turvy and bubbling Verena, the fourth child – the third, Friedelind, was never mentioned after her defection to America – disappointed all by marrying an older man named Bodo Lafferentz, who had led parties of festival goers under the wartime "Strength through Joy" scheme. Her new husband had been instrumental in setting up the new Volkswagen factory at Wolfsburg (another vulpine appellation) and he wore his swastika with the greatest pride of all the husbands at Wahnfried.[62] In Israel it was interesting to note the public response to the sale of that vehicle in the decades after the Second World War, given its tainted origins.

In December 1944 Hitler made one last bold move. Having moved

---

57. Ibid., 695.
58. Ibid.
59. Spotts, *Bayreuth*, 198.
60. Wagner, Nike, *The Wagners*, 219.
61. Ibid., 221.
62. Ibid.

his headquarters to the west, he launched an offensive in the Ardennes, the venue of his great advances earlier in the war. But the forces ranged against him were too mighty and his own depleted and demoralized. His new weapons did not have the impact he desired and his troops were overwhelmed by the superior weaponry and willpower of the Allies. Hitler still wallowed in his false hope and told Goebbels that the Bayreuth festival would continue as usual in July and August 1945. Goebbels noted in his diary, "I can easily foresee once the war is over he will once again devote himself with the most passionate enthusiasm to such matters."[63]

---

63. Spotts, *Hitler and the Power of Aesthetics*, 39.

Chapter seventeen
Last Will and Testament

Hitler's own end is well documented – from January 1945, save for a few isolated instances, he never left the chancellery in Berlin or its bunker. He returned to the capital city on January 15 with his entourage of secretaries, orderlies and staff officers. The city was convenient, as one humorist would have it, as he could reach the eastern and western fronts by suburban railway.[1] He heard with great dismay of the four bombing raids on the fifth, eighth, tenth and eleventh of April on Bayreuth and the destruction of part of Wahnfried, including Wagner's grand piano and many of the decorations on the walls. Ironically the Führer block remained unscathed, as did Winifred, her daughter-in-law Ellen, and the children's nurse, who lay terrified in the bomb shelter under the cottage.[2] Caught unawares by the raid, and unable to return home to help the womenfolk, Wieland and his brother-in-law had hidden under a bridge in Bayreuth and thereby escaped the wrath of the American bombers.[3]

Mention has been made of the priceless original Wagner scores that Hitler boasted were in his possession – Wieland and his wife Gertrud visited Hitler and tried to recover them. They lunched with Hitler who had his arm in a sling following the attempt on his life. They were assured that

---

1. Kershaw, *Hitler 1936–1945: Nemesis*, 768.
2. Wagner, Nike, *The Wagners*, 177.
3. Ibid.

the scores were safe in the bunker but went away shaking their heads and rightly so – the scores were never recovered.[4]

In the final days of the war Wolfgang managed to smuggle the valuable collection of art and scores from Wahnfried past ss patrols and the invading Americans to a temporary resting place and, thereafter, to their final home at Oberwarmensteinach.[5] On April 14 Wolfgang's first child was born and named Eva after the heroine of *Meistersinger.* Amidst the ruins of Wahnfried he found his grandfather's spectacles, which had occupied the interest of the young Hitler when he visited the shrine in 1923. He could not have been wearing them in later life when he disavowed all connection with the Third Reich. "We had no reason to put on sackcloth and ashes or to beat our breasts in repentance…we did not have to seek any justification for what we did or failed to do."[6] Wieland and his family later fled to the Wagner's timber family home on Lake Constance from which they were only to return in 1949.[7]

A pall of smoke covered Berlin and the approaching Russians were the Führer's main concern. Lives meant nothing to the beleaguered leader and he enlisted old men and boys to defend a city that was being bombed on a daily basis by American and British bombers. He abandoned a plan to lead a final resistance in the south and instituted his scorched earth policy – on the basis that Germans had proved unequal to the elevated status as the *Herrenvolk*, chosen for them by Wagner, Gobineau and Chamberlain. The *Vöelkischer Beobachter* expressed his wishes in the following manner: "not a German stock of wheat is to feed the enemy, not a German mouth to give him information, not a German hand to offer him help. He is to find nothing but death, annihilation and hatred…"[8] But even his faithful spaniel and architect, fellow planner of the new Germany, did not heed him any longer; his commands to destroy the economy were disobeyed by his minister of war Albert Speer, who realized that all was lost.

On March 10, 1945 Hitler drafted his political will in a small room under the Reich Chancellery.[9] To get there you had to walk down a flight

---

4. Ibid., 224.
5. Ibid., 225.
6. Ibid.
7. Ibid.
8. Langer, *The Mind of Adolf Hitler*, 237.
9. A plan of the Berlin bunker is found in O'Donnell, *The Berlin Bunker*, 70–71. At

of stairs at the bottom of which was a steel-reinforced door guarded by two ss men. After this door there were more stairs that led to a corridor called Kannenbergallee after the butler Artur Kannenberg. At that time it was a foot deep in water and was covered by duckboards. A short flight of stairs led to the upper level of the bunker, which had twelve small rooms opening onto a small vestibule that served as a general mess hall.

The Führer bunker was even lower down and contained eighteen cubicles separated by an entrance hall that was divided into a waiting room and a conference room. On the left of the conference room was a small map room, a rest room for a bodyguard and a six-room suite. On the right were the quarters for his personal physician Dr. Theodor Morell and his surgeon Ludwig Stumpfegger. The bunker was protected by a twelve-foot-thick reinforced ceiling and was topped by thirty feet of concrete. The famed German engineering was successfully resisting the approaching guns of the Russians and yet the end was inevitable.

The conference room was the biggest of the rooms and the furniture consisted of a table with ten chairs around it. Apart from these there were also a few comfortable chairs and smaller tables. A gramophone with a handle for winding was placed on a table in the corner. On one wall was a city plan of Linz, which Hitler had planned to rebuild since those carefree days with his friend August Kubizek. Hitler was in pitiful shape; after he had a bad case of flu in 1942 Dr. Morell had given him all sorts of injections. Since then his left eye had run uncontrollably and people mistakenly thought he was crying. Further complications emerged; numbness appeared in his left leg and left arm, so he made a habit of placing his left hand in his pocket.

His secretary Frau Junge wrote down the will at his dictation. As he spoke he cast his mind back on the period since he became chancellor on January 30, 1933, and his twelve years of power. He began with his political will. "The situation is serious, very serious. It seems even to be desperate. We might very easily give way to fatigue, to exhaustion, we might allow

---

p. 205 O'Donnell includes a photograph of the outside of the bunker. The scorched earth policy is set out in O'Donnell, 96–99. The political will is set out in O'Donnell, 190, and Hilberg, *Destruction of the European Jews*, 635. Much of what is said on the question of the scorched earth policy is set out in Shirer, *The Rise and Fall of the Third Reich*, 1311–12.

ourselves to become discouraged to an extent that blinds us to the weaknesses of our enemies. But these weaknesses are there, for all that."

He must have thought back to how he had exploited those weaknesses – Austria, Czechoslovakia, the Sudetenland, France, Belgium, Norway – half the civilized world had been within his grasp. "It is untrue that I or anyone else in Germany wanted the war in 1939. It was desired and instigated exclusively by those international statesmen who were either of Jewish descent or worked for Jewish interest." It was the old theme, without any variations.

Some years previously Dr. Erwin Giesing, an ear, nose and throat specialist, had examined him and had given a report to Dr. Karl Brandt. The news was deeply disturbing; he told Hitler that the drug prescribed by Dr. Morell – Dr Koester's Anti-gas Pills – contained strychnine and belladonna. Morell was slowly poisoning him. Hitler's mind was so confused he fired Brandt and replaced him with Stumpfegger. But he could not concentrate for long. He could not even raise a glass of water to his lips without spilling it, such was the trembling in his hands.[10] He was haggard, shuffling along, dragging his legs, and yet still the maniacal stare never dimmed. He continued dictating the political will. "After six years of war, which in spite of all setbacks will go down one day in history as the most glorious and valiant demonstration of a nation's life purpose, I cannot forsake the city which is the capital of the Reich...I do not wish to fall into the hands of an enemy who requires a new spectacle organized by the Jews for the amusement of their hysterical masses..."

The reference was to Mussolini and his mistress, Clara Petacci, who had been hanged upside down in a square, to be publicly ridiculed. The obsession with the Jews was to remain there until his last breath was drawn. Assuming the mantle of a prophet, staring into the future, with eyes glazed by madness and drugs, he foresaw that future generations would visit their wrath on the persons responsible – the Jews. "Centuries will pass away, but out of the ruins of our towns and monuments the hatred against those finally responsible, whom we have to thank for everything, international Jewry and its helpers will grow. I also made it quite plain that if the nations of Europe were once more to be regarded as mere chattels to be bought and sold by these international conspirators in money and finance, then

---

10. Kershaw, *Hitler 1936–1945: Nemesis*, 780.

that race, Jewry, which is the real criminal of this murderous struggle, will be saddled with the responsibility."

He must have realized the destruction he had sowed upon the Aryans and wondered if he had been a tad cruel in his "final solution." Ironically enough his words echoed in part those of the Hebrew prophet Isaiah of three thousand years before who foresaw a man "who made the earth quake to such a degree that kingdoms trembled and who made the world into a wilderness and destroyed the cities thereof."

The political will continued. "Furthermore, I left no one in doubt that this time not only would millions of children of Europe's Aryan peoples die of hunger, not only would millions of grown men suffer death, and not only would hundreds of thousands of women and children be burned and bombed to death in the cities – but also the real criminal would have to atone for his guilt, even if by more humane means…"

Hitler turned his attention to the political succession of that rotten regime – why he thought his successor would enjoy any significant period of rule is difficult to understand. Himmler was rejected as a possible successor for a reason that had a hideous logic, given Hitler's idolatry of Richard Wagner – Heinrich had been a tower of strength, especially as far as the final solution was concerned; but he was not musical enough![11] He also suspected Himmler and Göring of treason; they were trying to negotiate peace terms with that gang of international Jews and bandits – the Allies.

"Before my death, I expel former Reich Marshal Hermann Göring from the party and withdraw from him all the rights that were conferred on him by the decree of June 20, 1941…I hereby appoint Grand Admiral Karl Dönitz as my successor as President of Germany. Goebbels is to be Chancellor. Before my death, I expel the former Reichsfüehrer of the ss and the Minister of the Interior Heinrich Himmler from the party and from all his state offices. My personal property I leave to the party."

As the morning sun rose over the bomb-strewn, burning Berlin there was one last instruction to the new government – it was the old refrain. "Above all, I enjoin the government and the people to uphold the racial laws to the limit and to resist mercilessly the poisoner of all nations, international Jewry."

More than a year previously on March 24, 1944, the president of the

---

11. Waite, *The Psychopathic God*, 63.

United States of America Franklin Roosevelt had given a press conference in which he described the wholesale systematic murder of the Jews of Europe as one of the blackest crimes of all history. Roosevelt proclaimed the determination of his country to punish anyone who knowingly took part in the deportation of the Jews to their death in Poland. More than six million Jews perished in a phenomenon now known as the Holocaust, largely at the instance of the man with the weeping eye, dictating his will in that Berlin Bunker, while the Soviet guns roared menacingly in the near distance.

There was, of course, time for one more concert on April 13 by the Berlin Philharmonic and the lugubrious choice had to include Wagner's music[12] – the funeral march of Siegfried from *Götterdämmerung*, plus Bruckner's Romantic Symphony, provided part of the fare. As the brass growled out the magnificent themes, the serried ranks of uniformed, grim-faced Nazi leaders must have pondered their futures, with defeat days away. Where ushers would normally stand to assist patrons, members of the Hitler Youth handed out free cyanide capsules.[13] The American and British firebombs meant the city was ablaze and the artillery bombardment, cratered streets and skeleton buildings, courtesy of General Zukhov, provided a mise-en-scène any director would ache for.

Scurrying back to the bunker, the man who once commanded half the civilized world was escorted inside by the remains of his ss elite guard and a handful of grime-faced teenage boys with First World War rifles. Once out of range of the bombs he slumped down and stared at the concrete cave that had become home to him and a handful of officials and servants. In a final bid to prove his heterosexual manliness he decided to accede to Eva's plea to get married and they found Herr Walter Wagner – appropriate enough – of the awful stutter, to conduct the service.[14] The marriage officer was from the German form of the Home Guard – the *Volkssturm* – a motley assortment of old men and young boys who were mercilessly rounded up and forced to fight the Russians.

Despite the virginity that clung unwillingly to her person, Eva eschewed white and wore her black silk taffeta dress with the gold clasps,

---

12. Köhler, *Wagner's Hitler*, 18.
13. Spotts, *Hitler and the Power of Aesthetics*, 87.
14. For an account of the marriage of Hitler and Eva Braun, see O'Donnell, *The Berlin Bunker*, 187–88.

which was Hitler's favorite. It seemed more appropriate for a funeral – but then that was only a few days away. Hitler's favorite henchmen to the last, Bornmann and Goebbels witnessed the ceremony and no doubt they put on the record of the bridal chorus from Wagner's *Lohengrin*, which had accompanied millions of couples since it was first heard in the middle of the nineteenth century. A secretary of his, Christa Schröeder, recalled him saying, "Wagner's music sounded in his ear like a revelation of the divine."[15] Mendelssohn's *Wedding March* would have been sacrilege.

The marriage official asked if he had to ask all the questions required by law for a valid German marriage and, on being reassured, he asked Hitler if he was a third generation Aryan! Given Hitler's ancestry this was not an easy question. But Hitler regarded it as impertinence and the couple were quickly inducted into the blessed but short institution of matrimony. The ceremony stretched past midnight and the date on the marriage certificate was changed from April 28 to April 29, 1945.

In those last days the beleaguered Führer sought solace out of anything. Goebbels believed that it was written in the stars that the second half of April would be a turning point for the Nazis. Of special importance to those bent on summoning the occult to their assistance, when the Tiger tanks and V1 and V2 rockets had failed, was Friday April 13. That date stood out as particularly auspicious, according to certain horoscopes Hitler had ordered. These notoriously unreliable barometers of prescience had been used with singular success on previous occasions. The first one, relied on by the Nazis, was drawn up on the day Hitler took office on January 30, 1933, and the other one had been concocted on November 9, 1918 during the Weimar Republic, by an unknown astrologer.

As the desperate Nazis huddled round the small tables in the bunker, they recalled how the horoscopes had correctly predicted the outbreak of the war in 1939, the victories until 1941, and the subsequent series of reversals, with the hardest blows during the first months of 1945, particularly during the first half of April. In the second half of April, Goebbels reported, after gazing once again into their gloomy depths, there would be a temporary success; then there would be stagnation until August and – voilà – peace that same month. The compliant oracle projected a rosy

---

15. Spotts, *Hitler and the Power of Aesthetics*, 237.

future – for the following three years Germany would suffer misfortunes, but commencing with 1948 she would rise again.

One factor the horoscopes failed to account for was the arrogant disregard for auguries shown by the advancing tanks and heavy artillery. As the Russian guns belched and offloaded their unwholesome communist hardware on their beloved capital city of Berlin and the earth trembled, the Nazi leaders listened to their crackly radio and suddenly erupted in cheers. Their chief persecutor and avenging angel, President Roosevelt, had died. With eyes shining triumphantly Goebbels assured Hitler that the war would now turn in their favor. He had been reading to Hitler from Carlyle's *History of Friedrich the Great*, one of his favorite books. This was the same work Cosima Wagner quoted when she pondered the obscurity of the lives of the famous, and why it was important for her to note down, in her virulently anti-Semitic diary, every aspect in the composer's life.

In Goebbels's tortured mind Roosevelt's death seemed to be historically analogous to the death of the Czarina Elizabeth of Russia, the implacable enemy of Friedrich the Great. One of the few pictures in the bunker – apart from the chief architect of his racial policies, the Master of Bayreuth – was Anton Graff's portrait of Friedrich, bought by Hitler in 1934, showing the great man in his powder blue uniform. This likeness showed off his "startling blue eyes," which Hitler believed were the equal of his own and proclaimed why he was the legitimate heir of the Prussian leader.[16] "When bad news threatens to crush my spirit I derive fresh courage from a contemplation of this picture," he is reported to have said.[17] It will be recalled that Friedrich the Great had a very cavalier attitude to alliances and treaties and the mores of the day favoring heterosexual relationships.

In those earlier years, in circumstances that appeared similar to the plight of the desperate Nazis, the Russians had beleaguered the Prussian forces who stood at the threshold of defeat and death. Elizabeth's death brought to the throne Peter III, who was a friend of Friedrich the Great, and there was a reversal of alliances. And as history had shown, through the erudite pen of Carlyle, thus ended the Seven Years War. But there was not to be any repetition of that chance circumstance in Berlin in April 1945, as the Allies approached the capital city in a great pincer movement.

---

16. Waite, *The Psychopathic God*, 256.
17. Kershaw, *Hitler 1936–1945: Nemesis*, 776.

Despondency set in again when reality finally dawned on the Nazi leaders that the death of Roosevelt would result in no reversal of alliances there. The thoughts of an alliance between the West and Germany against the Communist beast Stalin were doubtless contemplated in Whitehall and Berlin, but dismissed. While it was a close call, fascism and Nazism outranked communism in the British and American hall of ogres. After the total destruction of Dresden Goebbels demanded the execution of tens of thousands of Allied prisoners of war but reason finally prevailed and Hitler realized there would be immediate retaliation in equal or greater measure by the dominant forces surrounding his capital. Guderian was shocked when Hitler expressed his views on how to achieve the best results in the military field. "The soldiers on the eastern front fight far better. The reason they give in so easily in the west is simply the fault of that stupid Geneva Convention which promises them good treatment as prisoners. We must scrap this idiotic convention."[18] Once the frustrated artist became a politician there were no limits on his brutality.

The end was near but the dictator was to have one final swipe at his enemies. In a memoir dictated shortly before he committed suicide he claimed that the world "would be eternally grateful to me and to National Socialism for having exterminated the Jews in Germany and in Central Europe."[19]

Gerda Bornmann wrote a letter to her husband illustrating the levels of make-believe the top Nazis had reached in their maniacal euphoria. "One day the Reich of our dreams will emerge. Shall we, I wonder, or our children, live to see it? In some ways, you know, this reminds me of Götterdämmerung in the Edda. The monsters are storming the bridge of the Gods…the citadel of the Gods crumbles, and all seems lost; and then, suddenly a new citadel arises, more beautiful than ever before…We are not the first to engage in mortal combat with the powers of the underworld, and that we feel impelled, and are also able, to do so should give us a conviction of ultimate victory."[20]

Hitler's end came on the simple blue and white velvet sofa in his small lounge.[21] Next to it was a small table with a vase of greenhouse tulips and

---

18. Ibid., 779.
19. Köhler, *Wagner's Hitler*, 8.
20. Kershaw, *Hitler 1936–1945: Nemesis*, 789.
21. O'Donnell, *The Berlin Bunker*, 250.

white narcissi that Eva had somehow managed to find. Hitler had made all the arrangements for his own and Eva's cremation with Linge, his valet. There was historical precedent: Rienzi, and Siegfried the greatest hero in the world, who had been stabbed in the back by Hagen, the Nibelung (Jew). Outside the world was ablaze – doubtless the madman saw that as appropriate – and the fire was reaching to the gods in Valhalla. It was *Götterdämmerung* – no doubt in his fervid imagination the great tetralogy was being reenacted – the Rhine was overflowing its banks and Valkyries were waiting with their winged helmets and chain mail, to carry the fallen hero to heaven.

Hitler had urged Linge to join the breakout group and serve the man who succeeded him. In all probability, as he prepared to take his life, the great music theme of the Volsung race was majestically rising in the orchestra. Swirling around and punctuating the crashing brass had to be the death motif as Hitler saw his whole life expressed in those mighty chords. After that the sword theme followed by the Siegfried motif would have blazened out on the horns, trumpets and trombones – with the specially made Wagner tubas growling ominously in the lowest reaches of the orchestra.

Magda Goebbels had urged the Führer to flee to continue the struggle from Berchtesgaden but Hitler had decided to stay on with his people. He sat on the sofa with Eva Braun and they each held a pistol – a standard Walther 7.65 and a smaller Walther 6.35 – in their hands. The plan was that as they bit into the cyanide capsules they were to pull the trigger. Once they were dead their bodies were to be carried to the chancellery garden and burnt.[22] The capsules had been tested on the Alsatian Blondi and her puppies with success. Tornow the Führer's vet had seen to that and the same fate had befallen his pet Dachshund.[23]

In Hitler's demented mind the Berlin Philharmonic orchestra had by this stage gathered all its forces for that apocalyptic climax. With the death motif swirling and threading its way through the brass, they simultaneously pulled the triggers and bit into the fatal capsules. All heaven and earth and hell broke loose – the sound and fury was, however, orchestrated by the Russians, who broke into the chancellery garden and seized the burnt

---

22. Ibid., 250–58. See also Shirer, *The Rise and Fall of the Third Reich*, 1346.
23. The death of Blondi is set out in O'Donnell, *The Berlin Bunker*, 199.

bodies of the evil man and his wife. The winged Valkyries were nowhere to be seen – Valhalla was no more.

When Walter Langer and the other psychiatrists prepared the OSS report on Hitler, they had reckoned that suicide was the most plausible outcome. "Not only has he frequently threatened to commit suicide, but from what we know of his psychology it is the most likely possibility…" They also foretold of his neuroses as the end approached. "Whatever else happens, we may be reasonably sure that as Germany suffers successive defeats Hitler will become more and more neurotic. Each defeat will shake his confidence still further and limit his opportunities for proving his own greatness to himself. In consequence he will feel himself more and more vulnerable to attack from his associates and his rages will increase in frequency. He will probably try to compensate for his vulnerability on this side by continually stressing his brutality and ruthlessness."

Although they failed to predict his tomb they were not far wrong in the historic inevitability of the site they chose. He would choose that holy site in the holy mountain long established as the resting place of heroes. "His public appearances will become less and less for, as we have seen, he is unable to face a critical audience. He will probably seek solace in his Eagle's Nest on the Kehlstein near Berchtesgaden. There among the ice-capped peaks he will wait for his 'inner voice' to guide him. Meanwhile, his nightmares will probably increase in frequency and intensity and drive him closer to a nervous collapse. It is not wholly improbably that in the end he might lock himself into this symbolic womb and defy the world to get him."

The psychiatrists clearly knew their Wagner – the fate of Rienzi and Siegfried was to be shared by their most fervent admirer. "In any case, his mental condition will continue to deteriorate. He will fight as long as he can with any weapon or technique that can be conjured up to meet the emergency. The course he will follow will almost certainly be the one which seems to him to be the surest road to immortality and at the same time drag the world down in flames."[24]

On May 1, 1945, German radio announced a brief message. "Our Führer Adolf Hitler, fighting to the last breath against Bolshevism, fell for Germany this afternoon."[25]

---

24. Langer, OSS *Psychological Report on Adolf Hitler*, 248–49.
25. Waite, *The Psychopathic God*, 411.

Chapter eighteen
Denazification

The famed German novelist Thomas Mann had become a refugee, after writing an essay on Wagner in the early thirties. The thought of culture flourishing in the Third Reich was anathema to him and he wrote in 1945: "it was not right, it was impossible, to go on producing culture in Germany while all the things we know of were taking place. To do so meant palliating depravity, extenuating crime…Strangely, no one seems to have felt there were more honourable occupations than designing Wagner sets for Hitler's Bayreuth."[1]

The American Counter Intelligence Corps occupied the Führer block – previously the Siegfried Wagner house – for some time after the war and gave the Wagner children their first taste of chocolate.[2] The festival theatre was used for religious services, plays and – God forbid – operettas and musicals. Grace Moore and Martini were the first to grace the sacred precincts on May 31 and their debut was followed by two musicals – *Ten Little Indians* and *Anything Goes*. Fifty shows were put on in all by the American forces, including appearances by the Rockettes of New York Radio City Music Hall, the Billy Rose Revue, the Diamond Horseshoe Revue, Jack Bennie and his Broadway show.[3]

---

1. Spotts, *Hitler and the Power of Aesthetics*, 188.
2. Wagner, Nike, *The Wagners*, 240.
3. Bauer, *Forty Years of New Bayreuth*, 31.

Later the famed acoustics of the house that Wagner built echoed to the ultimate desecration – Italian opera – as the haunting beauties of *La Traviata* and *Madame Butterfly* introduced the stolid Bavarians and troops to the southern musical diet. Some solace would have been felt when Beethoven's *Fidelio* and Mozart's *Die Entführung aus dem Serail* elevated the level of harmonic delinquency.[4] If that sacrilege was not enough there were reports of American soldiers "jitterbugging" on the grave of the great composer. The Wagners and their illustrious successors could never be faulted for omitting a prejudice and Winifred complained about "black soldiers dancing with blonde German girls" and that "black soldiers plundered the Festspielhaus."[5]

The first postwar Bayreuth mayor, Oskar Meyer, tried to make contact with Friedelind Wagner at the end of 1945 "in order to persuade her to return to Bayreuth and continue the Bayreuth idea" but she did not reply. The German people were quick to turn on the most rabid Nazis and their sympathizers and fellow travelers. According to the *Fränkische Presse* of February 15, 1946, "the members of the Wagner family living in Germany had forfeited the right to continue the Festival's time-honoured tradition as a result of their friendly dealings with Hitler."[6]

After the war Winifred was nothing if not constant. She fled to a cabin in the Fichtelbirge Mountains and named her retreat "exil" – not a far cry from Wagner's "Asyl" – with the Wesendoncks.[7] Klaus Mann visited Germany and Winifred was the only self-confessed National Socialist he came across, in his numerous interviews.[8] She appeared before a tribunal set up to assess her implication in Nazi war crimes. She spoke to the press before her hearing in 1947 and identified the real cause of the war. She said: "I often said to [Hitler] in a reproachful tone that his bachelor existence was not the right thing for him. If he'd had a home and a sensible wife, there would have been no war."[9] She appeared dressed to represent simplicity and innocence and was defended by a "fellow traveler," who made his own

---

4. Spotts, *Bayreuth*, 202.
5. Ibid., 201.
6. Bauer, *Forty Years of New Bayreuth*, 32.
7. Wagner, Nike, *The Wagners*, 179.
8. Ibid., 159.
9. Ibid., 226.

admiration for the Führer apparent during his presentation of her case, to the dismay of the tribunal.

She was accused of a number of transgressions including, firstly, having been one of Hitler's most fanatical supporters, and secondly, having turned over Richard Wagner's legacy to the Nazi party for propaganda purposes.[10] She told the American and British authorities in answer to the first charge that "Hitler never interfered with any artistic questions concerning the Festival but conversely backed any of my decisions which might not agree with the party programme." In her memorandum for her trial she explained that Hitler had saved the Bayreuth festivals from their demise in 1933 and she asked for understanding for this. She went on to state that it would have been irresponsible to refuse the offer of financial support for the festival from Adolf Hitler and it would also have been impossible during the Third Reich to refuse, as anyone in their right mind would have to admit. In addition Hitler had protected the festivals from the negative attitude of the party against Wagner. For a people hailing the ideal of a Nordic hero the thought of being saved by the devoted love of a woman was not acceptable.[11]

Inherent in their philosophy was the expectation of the "Superman" advocated by Nietzsche who had to cope with life completely on his own. Winifred also had to counter the criticism of Wagner's music as an offshoot of baroque and having an intoxicating, almost drug-like quality. Hitler's annual pilgrimage was the greatest security against undermining the cultural importance of the festival and an erosion of the philosophy Richard Wagner had advocated.[12]

What a pity the authorities did not know the real truth. In fact Winifred was eternally grateful for the support of Hitler. "You know that nothing happens in Bayreuth that is not at the Führer's initiative or in keeping with his explicit approval," it will be recalled she told Richard Strauss in June 1935.[13]

A third charge touched a tender spot; it alleged that she had asked the head of the ss in Prague, Karl Frank, to give her valuable furniture confiscated from Czech Jews, who had been sent to the concentration

---

10. Spotts, *Bayreuth*, 203.
11. Hamann, *Winifred Wagner*, 251.
12. Ibid., 261.
13. Spotts, *Hitler and the Power of Aesthetics*, 258–59.

camps.[14] The report of her activities recorded her membership of the Nazi Party and her holding the Golden Party Badge and that "as a woman of high intellectual standing and international reputation, she must have known that, through her actions, she would become a model for countless lesser individuals of lesser intellectual gifts."[15]

Other charges related to her silence, despite knowledge of the murders of the Scholl siblings, the pianist Karlrobert Kreiten and a Munich music critic. She wrote to a friend in 1947 loudly protesting her innocence. "I have done nothing wrong in my life. I more or less remained faithful until the bitter end, only because I knew this man [Hitler] to be kind, noble and helpful. It was the man and not the Party that held me."[16] She looked for a loophole and in the letter she speculated whether she could escape prosecution by marrying a suitable candidate from her country of origin. "I am looking for an Englishman who is the right age for me. I am not that old and not that ugly, not to have an even chance."[17]

It is a pity that no one found the letter Winifred wrote in 1923 in which she stated her "greatest inner sympathy and approval [for] the uplifting work of Adolf Hitler, this German man who, filled with ardent love for his fatherland, is sacrificing his life for his idea of a *purified*, united, national greater Germany…" Evidence was brought on her behalf about help given to Jewish musicians. The irony of it all was that she had tried to help two Jewish singers – both also homosexuals – Lorenz and Janssen, and others, and had been successful in some instances. She claimed the Festspielhaus had never been bombed because she had insisted to the army that it was not to be used for military purposes. "In order to avoid doing anything that might have resulted in the risk of an air raid on Bayreuth, I refused point blank to allow the Festspielhaus to be used for military purposes during the war – there were plans, for example, to use the building as a Luftwaffe depot and to install an observation post on the roof. To cap it all [Werner von Fritsch, the chief of Army Command] wanted all news bulletins broadcast from a central transmitter in Bayreuth, or, to be more precise, from the Festspielhaus."[18]

---

14. Ibid.
15. Bauer, *Forty Years of New Bayreuth*, 41.
16. Spotts, *Bayreuth*, 203.
17. Ibid.
18. Bauer, *Forty Years of New Bayreuth*, 29–30.

Eventually she managed to wriggle out of most of the most serious charges – the evidence was difficult to gather, given the circumstances after the war. She was found guilty of "Category Three lesser incriminated" for "having thrown the weight of one of the most famous names in cultural history into the balance in Hitler's favour."[19] The question of sentence was a difficult matter for the tribunal, given her age and the enormity of the crimes her great hero had committed. To her relief she was not placed in a labor camp but was prohibited from speaking about Nazism and forced to hand over the control of the festival to her two sons. After considerable haggling she was prevailed upon to transfer the reins in 1949 – her denazification was then deemed complete. Apart from blemishes, here and there, she kept silent until 1976 when – at the Bayreuth festival centenary celebrations, to the shock and chagrin of all her family – she showed the extent of her contrition and repentance.[20] How different were the feelings of the man who painted a large sign in the Feldherrnhalle in Munich, scene of the abortive putsch, witnessed by a younger Winifred, then in the first fine careless rapture of her love for Hitler. "I am ashamed to be German."[21]

In 1949 a Society for the Friends of Bayreuth was founded and assisted the Wagner brothers to resurrect the festival, on the condition that silence was maintained about the past. No repentance for the close association with the Third Reich was forthcoming and the appearance of Winifred at the society's first plenary session was cause for an ovation.[22] When Winifred returned to Bayreuth she moved into the Führer cottage and quickly fell back into her bad ways; she supped and drank tea with her old friends Edda Göring and Ilse Hess.[23]

Wolfgang had served in the armed forces and escaped censure but Wieland faced the tribunal, emerging with the stigma of a "fellow traveler." To his chagrin his sole accuser was his old teacher Kurt Overhoff, who branded him rather unspecifically as a beneficiary of Hitler.[24] While the brothers were quick to throw off the mantle of adopted sons of Hitler, Winifred's fiery fidelity to the Führer irked them and measures had to be

---

19. Ibid., 228–29.
20. Ibid.
21. Kershaw, *Hitler 1936–1945: Nemesis*, 840.
22. Spotts, *Bayreuth*, 206.
23. Ibid.
24. Ibid., 228.

taken to signify the new Wagner approach. Wieland built a wall between Wahnfried and the cottage to keep away any memories of the bad times and to persuade the world that he had nothing to do with it. His only utterances on political issues were laconic in the extreme and were limited to shamed confessions such as – "after Auschwitz there can be no more discussion of Hitler."[25]

The festival reopened in 1951 with a simple production of *Meistersinger*. It was followed by *Parsifal* and the *Ring*, with a panoply of distinguished conductors, including Herbert von Karajan and Hans Knappertsbusch on the podium.[26] Wieland took over as producer from Winifred after the war and his productions were to set new standards of excellence. Wolfgang specialized in the administration and his ventures into directing were less successful than those of his elder brother, which led to tension between the families.

Try as the brothers might to bury the past it had a habit of rearing its head from time to time – mostly via the utterances of Winifred Wagner. Winifred later told the media that "as far as Wolfgang is concerned, it is undesirable for such matters to be mentioned again."[27] Not that she set much store by his sentiments. Dietrich Fischer-Dieskau sang Wolfram in the *Tannhäuser* of 1954 and listened to Winifred criticizing her son Wieland and Picasso and extolling the virtues of the mastermind behind the extermination of the Jews.[28] The old guard was not welcome and when Hans Ziegler fondly remembered the close relationship between Hitler and the festival Wieland accused him of "having done the Festival a grave disservice…undermining my efforts to bury *this lethal subject* for good and all."[29]

There was support from distinguished quarters. Albert Schweitzer wrote to the brothers and told them that "Bayreuth is not music, but the experience of emotion and exaltation through ideas above earthly existence."[30] The problems lay with the ideas of Wagner that had taken root on

---

25. Ibid., 208.
26. Ibid., 235.
27. Köhler, *Wagner's Hitler*, 133.
28. Spotts, *Bayreuth*, 229.
29. Köhler, *Wagner's Hitler*, 134.
30. Skelton, *Wagner at Bayreuth*, 164.

mother earth, predominantly in the geopolitics of Europe in the previous twenty years.

The brothers determined that the best way to deal with political debate and discussion was to ban it at the festival. Just as Siegfried Wagner had prohibited the singing of *Deutschland über Alles* after the First World War in the 1924 festival, so his sons repeated the quote from *Meistersinger*: "it is art that matters here." If that was not explicit enough the notice went on to say, "in the interests of a smooth operation of the festival we request visitors kindly to refrain from conversations and discussions of a political nature on the Festspielhaus hill."[31]

The performances under Wieland, influenced by the monumentality of the ideas of Appia, reached new heights of excellence, with the emphasis on space, a sparing use of props, and depth psychology. Twenty members of the lighting staff conveyed the emotions, nuances and subtleties of the music and theatre in a kaleidoscope of colors. Some reckoned the muted shades in certain performances so extreme that the program credits should not accrue to the lighting crew but those who provided the "darkening."[32]

Though the productions were recognized for their own worth, as outstanding cultural experiences, the conservatives were appalled. Opponents formed a *Society for the Performance of the Dramas of Richard Wagner as He Intended Them* and pressured the festival organizers to return to the ideas of the originator of the operas. When persuasion of both the muted and vehement varieties failed, the courts were approached to determine the issue. The suit resulted in defeat for the conservatives, who retreated with their swallowtails between their legs.[33]

The festival struggled initially and times were hard. Wolfgang and his family lived in the gardener's cottage until 1954, the main house Wahnfried – the Mecca of all Wagner pilgrims – suffering a further indignity. The American forces used it as a casino until 1957, and the political hegemony of the erstwhile Nazi redoubt was manifest via an immense American flag flying overhead. After living through the war in the US Friedelind Wagner returned to the festival in 1953 but was firmly told that

---

31. Wagner, Nike, *The Wagners*, 236.
32. Spotts, *Bayreuth*, 236.
33. Richard Wagner Museum brochure, "About Richard Wagner."

the festival was not hers. She would be allowed to conduct master classes but otherwise she should keep away.[34]

Two years later she returned and posed with her mother in what appeared – on the surface – to be reconciliation, but a photograph of a tight-lipped smile from both betrayed the festering antagonism. Too much water had flowed under the bridge. Friedelind had become thoroughly Americanized and she sported new generation blonde hair and dramatic dark lipstick, reminiscent of the smoldering screen idols who were fascinating the postwar filmgoers. That trademark of the family – the Wagner nose – together with her perennial weight problem kept her off the silver screen.[35] Wieland and Wolfgang had outmaneuvered her and she never again secured a foothold on the festival.

Mention of Wagner in America cannot be concluded without brief reference to Chuck Jones's hilarious 1957 cartoon film *What's Opera, Doc?* In this send-up of the majestic tetralogy Bugs Bunny and Elmer Fudd ascend to Nibelheim, where they gambol and play catch with the Nordic gods and subterranean dwarfs of the *Ring*. If that did not win you back to the Wagner cause – somewhat in decline, given the unsavory Third Reich relationship – the year before, Republic, a two-bit studio that specialized in westerns, made a film dripping with sentimental slush called *Magic Fire*. The production steered clear of the operas and concentrated on a far more salacious topic – the affairs of the composer. Hollywood idol Alan Badel, playing Wagner, strutted round the courts of Europe and cuddled the voluptuous muses mentioned in previous dispatches – so Mathilde Wesendonck, Jessie Laussot, Cosima Liszt and Judith Gautier finally found immortality on the silver screen.[36] The film was no doubt based on the racy, fictionalized book of the same title, written and published in 1954 by Bertita Harding.

Wagner's erotic heat was the theme for the movie that proclaimed that "His passion for beauty set the world aflame!" The studio even featured a crooner chanting: "Magic fire, you are my heart's desire." For *Magic Fire*, the operas were drastically abbreviated by the Jewish composer Erich Wolfgang Korngold, ironically a great admirer of Wagner, who had fled Germany

---

34. Spotts, *Bayreuth*, 248.
35. Wagner, Nike, *The Wagners*, 223.
36. Conrad, "He's Tricky, That Dicky."

because of anti-Jewish feeling and composed a number of outstanding operas in his own right.[37]

Back in Bavaria the Wagner grandsons were to start asserting their authority on the productions and the legacy. With time the baying of the conservatives, opposing the new reforms in Bayreuth, died down and in 1965 Wieland Wagner won the *Pour le Mérite* award, instituted by Friedrich the Great, and presented to Germans who contributed most to cultural life in the country. His contribution was to demythologize and liberate Wagner from Hitler.[38] The next year he died[39] and his widow Gertrud's claim to the festival was quickly trumped by a signed agreement between the brothers, bequeathing the *damnosa hereditas* to the survivor of the two. When Gertrud complained to her mother-in-law Winifred about her exclusion, she received short shrift – Winifred told her that the "forester's family [had] to leave the forester's house" when the guardian of the woods died.[40]

Wolfgang took over the festival to tell the world two years later, to great applause from patrons longing for real absolution, that "Bayreuth's political past has been confronted and the matter is now closed."[41] While posterity, the Nürnberg Trials, and countless books depicted Hitler as a megalomaniac and mass murderer, Wolfgang seemed to distance himself from this and said that the dictator presented himself to Bayreuth as "an Austrian gentleman of the old school."[42] Having lurked in his brother's cultural and artistic shadow too long he lost no time, however, in stigmatizing his deceased sibling as a Nazi.

Wolfgang did not see his grandfather as anti-Semitic – in fact he was the "very opposite" – and his authority for this remark was Wagner's comment that "if I were to write about the Jews again, I would say that there is nothing to object about them, except that they arrived too soon."[43] The problem was, the cynics observed, that whatever time the Jews arrived, it was too soon for Richard Wagner. Many would have seriously challenged his assertion that a religion had relevance in one age but not in another.

---

37. Ibid.
38. Spotts, *Bayreuth*, 247.
39. Marek, *Cosima Wagner*, 275.
40. Spotts, *Bayreuth*, 249.
41. Köhler, *Wagner's Hitler*, 135.
42. Ibid.
43. Ibid., 119.

Wolfgang had clearly not dusted off and read the literary legacy – in particular the regeneration writings – nor bent an inquisitive ear to the hidden subconscious message in the music.

Just when the political waters seemed safe for the festival the old shark bared the serried ranks of its racist teeth again. In a filmed interview in 1975 Winifred Wagner said, "If Hitler were to walk in the door today, I would be just as pleased, just as delighted to see him as I was back then."[44] She went on to describe what she found attractive in him. "He had this Austrian delicacy of the heart and this warmth…I knew him for twenty-two years and was never disappointed in him as a human being."[45] Gone were her fears of being alone with him and she told the worldwide audience, "the part of him I know…I treasure as much today as before."

Winifred was never to publicly divulge what happened when the whip-cracking politician with the blue-grey eyes discussed the operas, after evenings of magic and musical enchantment at Bayreuth. Nor was she to mention whether he had ever discussed with her his plans for the Jews. She did acknowledge that much was secret about him. "And everything that is dark about him, I know that exists, but for me it doesn't exist, because I don't know that part…that will perhaps remain incomprehensible forever, *you must leave it to a psychoanalyst to explain my relationship with Hitler*…and I think if it remains a mystery to anybody who may listen, then let it remain one, in God's name."[46]

That much of their relationship remains a secret and a mystery is the result, in no small part, of her large-scale destruction of documents.[47] She had clearly inherited the instincts of her mother-in-law and Chamberlain, with respect to the needs of posterity and the sanctity of the truth. That Winifred had become a huge liability was clear from the fact that Wolfgang had broken off relations with her, banning her from performances of the 1975 festival. In the film she is reported to have said: "I am basically a totally unpolitical person and I was astonished when the denazification tribunal accused me of political involvement. I said that I hadn't been involved in politics, and they all laughed…but I wasn't involved in politics."[48] Her

---

44. Marek, *Cosima Wagner*, 238.
45. Wagner, Nike, *The Wagners*, 165.
46. Ibid., 166.
47. Machtan, *The Hidden Hitler*, 22.
48. Ibid., 160.

National Socialism, she claimed, was only connected to Hitler and she was grateful for what he had done with his money to protect the festival.[49] "I will always remember him with gratitude, because he literally tended the flowerbeds here in Bayreuth and helped me in every way."

The film *Hitler*, directed by Hans Jurgen Syberberg, opened dramatically with the mass murderer and dictator arising from the grave of Richard Wagner at Bayreuth.[50] A blatantly evasive Winifred laid all the horrors of the Third Reich at the door of others. The murder of six million Jews was Streicher's work – films of the concentration camps were "falsified' and misrepresented; the murder of Röhm and others on "The Night of the Long Knives" was not Hitler's work, but his cruel political associates; the bombing of London was the work of the military, who forced his hand.[51]

The much repeated question if she did not think that the final solution was what Richard Wagner contemplated elicited a firm denial. Wagner's opposition was to the spiritual, cultural and political influences of the Jews. "He never contemplated personal extermination of the Jews." The Jews had played an important role in politics and theatre in the twenties. She referred to Wagner's many Jewish friends and said that his article "Jewry in Music" was a small part of his huge output.[52]

There was also secretiveness about her pact with the past that only occasionally revealed itself. For those in the know her Delphic utterances had meaning and the code words were interpreted. When she referred to USA, those ignorant of the mysterious ciphers might have thought she spoke of the United States of America. In truth and in fact she was referring to "Unser seliger Adolf" (our blessed Adolf), the acronym she and her cronies used to identify the man the whole world reviled, but they kept in their hearts.[53] She often signed her correspondence with the numerals "88," which referred to the eighth letter of the alphabet (H) and meant "Heil Hitler," a convention that clearly indicated how deeply the whip-handling pervert had penetrated her heart.

The horrors of the Holocaust meant little to her and she stuck to her guns in her rampant anti-Semitism. Asked about the refusal of Toscanini to

---

49. Wagner, Nike, *The Wagners*, 164.
50. Spotts, *Hitler and the Power of Aesthetics*, 244.
51. Ibid., 164.
52. Hamann, *Winifred Wagner*, 617.
53. Wagner, Gottfried, *The Twilight of the Wagners*, 29.

conduct in 1933 she blamed the New York Jews. "You know, when Toscanini was to conduct here, the Jews of New York worked on him to such an extent, urging him not to come here, that in the end he gave in; they told him that if he stayed in New York and didn't go to Bayreuth, he'd get blank cheques for his conducting in New York – he could write his own cheques in that case. That's how it was. I mean that, basically, the New York Jews – as you know the entire musical life in New York takes place in Jewish circles. Wherever you look – and these people worked on him, quite certainly."[54]

Others were more honest in their appraisal of the darkest era of the festival. The centenary year of the founding of the festival in 1976 saw celebrations with Walter Scheel, president of the Federal Republic, making mention that Bayreuth became "an instrument for evil policies" and recognizing that even modern Germans could not "erase the dark chapter of German history and of Bayreuth's history." Wolfgang Wagner decided against making his prepared speech and Karl Böhm – himself a fervent supporter of Hitler – proceeded with the musical tribute to the instigator of the evil.[55] Winifred also appraised the production of the *Ring*, during that centenary year, by Frenchman Patrice Chereau, praised by some, castigated by others. Her comments were worthy of her greatest hero – she threatened to kill him if she met him – Wagner's Francophobia had been passed on to his daughter-in-law.

At the end of her life Winifred no longer saw fit to suppress her anti-Semitism and on one occasion did not spare Yehudi Menuhin when he was awarded the Peace Prize of the German book trade. She said that in spite of his many services she deplored the fact that a Jew had won the prize. She went on to deprecate that people still had to kowtow to Jews and asked plaintively if people had any pride and how long one had to put up with this.[56] In April 1979 she entered the lists concerning the possible cancellation of the prescription of Nazi atrocities. In other words some felt there should be no termination date for such heinous crimes and that Nazi criminals should be hunted down irrespective of how much time had elapsed. She saw this as only in the interests of Germany's enemies who were intent on ensuring worldwide hatred for Germans and out of

---

54. Wagner, Nike, *The Wagners*, 162.
55. Spotts, *Bayreuth*, 269.
56. Hamann, *Winifred Wagner*, 638.

revenge and incompatibility were seeking to undermine every friendly compromise.[57]

Winifred died on March 5, 1980, aged eighty-two years. When she was gone no doubt Wolfgang, the surviving heir to Bayreuth, must have felt he had *finally* rid himself of the ghastly Nazi past. In his autobiography, published in 1994, Wolfgang Wagner says that "there are no skeletons in the Wahnfried cupboard."[58] In a further manifestation of Freudian wish-fulfillment, Wolfgang said that his grandfather Richard Wagner was a harmless operatic composer "whose views existed *uneasily* alongside the philosophy of National Socialism."[59]

Perhaps the truth was too ghastly to contemplate. There were further attempts to downplay the anti-Semitism in the life and work of the composer. In 1985 the Richard Wagner Museum in Bayreuth staged a photographic illustrated exhibition entitled *Wagner and the Jews*. The director Manfred Eger claimed that it was a plea, not for Wagner, but for the truth.[60] Eger conceded that "Wagner's anti-Semitism throws a considerable shadow over his person and his work" but maintained that "there are also remarks in which he retracts some of his earlier pronouncements. Moreover, several of his colleagues and friends were Jews."

In rebutting that Hitler's anti-Semitism had its origins in Wagner, Eger points to Wagner's appreciation of Jewish composers such as Mendelssohn and Halévy, his friendships with Jews such as the choirmaster Heinrich Porges and the conductor Hermann Levi. That he should have included the unfortunate conductor as a recipient of friendship from Wagner betrays a less than zealous knowledge of the facts, but Wagner did tolerate Jews who were useful to him. Eger also makes mention of his affair with the French writer Judith Gautier, daughter of author Théophile Gautier and Jewish singer Giulia Grisi.[61]

Eger emphasizes Wagner's jealousy over the operatic triumphs of Meyerbeer and points out that as a Jew-hater he was in good company with Voltaire, Marx, Luther, Napoleon and others. Despite the checkered past the festival had purged itself, he said, as "these days there is not a trace of

---

57. Ibid., 637–38.
58. Köhler, *Wagner's Hitler*, 133.
59. Ibid., 134.
60. Eylon, "The Controversy over Richard Wagner."
61. Ibid.

anti-Semitism in Bayreuth: in 1983 alone, the Bayreuth Festival had three Jewish conductors."

The presence of Jewish conductors, singers and musicians did not mean that the operas were universally admired by the critics, as Friedelind Wagner, in her role as critic and teacher, was quick to point out. Her nose might be bulbous but her tongue had inherited the Wagnerian sharpness. She called the English producer Peter Hall's 1983 production of the *Ring* the "worst amateur show I have ever seen in the theatre" and then spent time condemning the Allied bombing of Germany.[62] Had she already forgotten the excesses of the regime she fled in 1939 with loud protests? The press – in particular the *Frankfurter Allgemeine Zeitung* – followed up her scathing comments by pointing out that Hall was the son of a railway stationmaster and grandson of a housepainter and a rat exterminator. Clearly to properly produce Wagner, pedigree was all-important – or was it that to design the productions you had to be able to extend your arm at forty-five degrees and hold it there virtually indefinitely.

---

62. Spotts, *Bayreuth*, 295.

Chapter nineteen
Wagner in Israel

Because of the accusations of anti-Semitism and the use of his music by the Third Reich, Wagner has been outlawed in concerts in Israel for half a century or more. No one has described the agonizing debate in that country more objectively and dispassionately than Na'ama Sheffi in her book *The Ring of Myths: The Israelis, Wagner and the Nazis*. Prior to the Second World War there were isolated instances when Jews heard portions of the works. The Palestine Orchestra, under the hand of Arturo Toscanini, played his music in 1938 in Haifa some half a year before *Kristallnacht*, the night Jewish businesses were destroyed.[1] There was a ban on the music in Palestine after that fateful night.[2]

Since the creation of the new state of Israel not a note of Wagner's music was heard for many years for reasons that are easy to understand. For many Jews and Israelis the debate on the topic has raged over the last fifty years and many have differentiated between the musician and the ideologist. Much of what was said in that country would not have enjoyed the benefit of the research that has been conducted over the last decade.

In November 1952 the conductor of the Israel Philharmonic Orchestra, Igor Markevitch, suggested the banned music be played. "I love Israel, and yet – I am an outsider among you. And the view of the outsider is: Play

---

1. Kater, "The Twisted Muse", 107.
2. See Mazelis, "Daniel Barenboim Conducts Wagner in Israel."

Wagner and Strauss." The idea was stopped in its tracks with a broadside from the newspaper *Herut*.[3] There was also a ban on public performances of any work in German, which had a most unfortunate consequence as it affected Jewish composer Gustav Mahler's wonderful *Das Lied von der Erde*. Mezzo-soprano Jennie Tourel got away with it through the agency of Jewish conductor Leonard Bernstein, but her singing partner Ernest Garay sang in Hebrew.[4]

The debate raged on sporadically throughout the half-century that followed. The first flautist of the IPO Uri Toeplitz wrote in a concert program in Israel in 1966: "We speak of music to emphasize that we can only accept Wagner as a composer, not the ideologist of the 'total work of art,' even less so the theoretician, the writer of inflammatory works on cultural or political subjects, the unprincipled, egoistic, ambiguous revolutionary, friend and exploiter of kings, friend of Jews and arch Jew-hater – in short, the man who acted out all the contradictions of his complex personality. We do not want people to forget what the Nazis made of him, namely one of their spiritual ancestors, but we should also bear in mind that we can never know what Wagner would have said about it, because he had been long dead when National Socialism emerged."[5]

He went on to advocate playing the music. "We feel the time has come for a change, not only because of the paramount demands of artistic freedom, but also because the opposition to Wagner has become a mere gesture. Why should we go on denying ourselves some of the greatest music by forbidding the playing of Wagner, a loss that cannot be replaced by the works of any other composer, while a mere convenience like the German Volkswagen, with all its associations from the Hitler era, is allowed to crowd our streets?"[6] The passages I have quoted were highly controversial but the first night audience were shocked and outraged to read a passage, deleted thereafter, where the flautist explained that "a change has taken place in the nation's attitude to the exterminators of our people." Toeplitz made the obvious point that long, boring operas were easier to boycott than consumer goods and that the Federal Republic of Germany was not

---

3. Sheffi, *Ring of Myths*, 54.
4. Ibid., 56.
5. Wagner, Gottfried, *Twilight of the Wagners*, 191.
6. Sheffi, *Ring of Myths*, 73.

the heir apparent to the Third Reich.⁷ The timing was not right and the idea was squashed.

The reference to the wholehearted acceptance of the commerce of Germany was not entirely correct. Yael Ben-Yehuda, an announcer on the Voice of Israel Radio, refused to read out an advertisement for Volkswagens in February 1966.⁸ At one level the comparison is odious: the motor vehicle remained an inanimate object that had not and could not have propagated anti-Semitism. It remained a symbol and somewhat far removed from the contribution of the composer from Bayreuth.

In June 1974 the IPO announced that a work by Richard Wagner would be played shortly before the end of the season. Resistance grew by the hour, the most emphatic being from the workers' committee of the Mann Auditorium, a group of ushers who described themselves as handicapped workers, including concentration camp survivors, partisans, resistance fighters and veterans of the Israeli Defense Force. "We learned with great sorrow and grieving hearts that the management of the Israel Philharmonic Orchestra has agreed to the suggestion of the conductor Zubin Mehta…Shame! Woe to the Jew in the State of Israel who agrees to play the music that accompanied the six million, the children, women, men, and babes, to the death camps."⁹ Understandably the plan was immediately abandoned.

The notion that Jews had been marched off to the gas chambers to the music of Richard Wagner does not stand up to closer scrutiny. In his book, musician Moshe Hoch disclaims such a notion: "the members of the Jewish orchestra played mainly Viennese waltzes…" Former inmates of Auschwitz, including Fania Fenelon, testified to the fact that the music of Richard Wagner was never played as the inmates were going to their deaths.¹⁰

In 1981 Zubin Mehta, the chief conductor of the Israel Philharmonic, tried to play Wagner's music – a short excerpt from *Tristan und Isolde* – as an encore to a concert of the music of other composers. The audience was outraged and caused mayhem in the Mann Auditorium in Tel Aviv. Before taking up the baton Mehta spoke to the concertgoers and tried to convince them to forget the sins of the composer and give the music

---

7. Ibid., 74.
8. Ibid., 159.
9. Ibid., 89–90.
10. Ibid., 51.

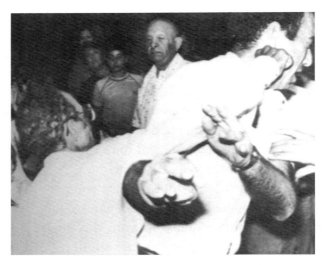

The furious fight that broke out in the Mann Auditorium in Israel when Zubin Mehta tried to play an excerpt from Wagner's Tristan and Isolde in 1981. See Osborne, The World Theatre of Wagner, page 89. Associated Press.

a chance, emphasizing that Israel was a democracy in which all music should be played. If anyone was offended they were free to leave, he assured them. In fact two orchestra members had been excused from playing the encore and some older members of the audience took up his offer to leave and went home without protest. Those who remained were persuaded to sample the Wagnerian diet. Some of those remaining continued protesting noisily, even intruding aggressively onto the stage, but the orchestra played on…to the end.[11]

One of the concert ushers bared his scarred belly and cried out in anguish as the first notes were played. Ben-Zion Leitner, a Holocaust survivor who had been awarded a medal for his heroism in Israel's War of Independence, was not going to allow the performance to continue if he had anything to do with it.[12] One of the musicians who had declined to play, violinist Avraham Melamed, told the press about some of his feelings about Wagner's music. "Some time ago I saw the film *Apocalypse Now*, and in one of the scenes helicopters came down and bombed to the sound of music that made my stomach turn over. At first I didn't understand what

---

11. See Eylon, "The Controversy over Richard Wagner."
12. Sheffi, *Ring of Myths*, 105.

was wrong with me, but afterwards I suddenly realized that it was Wagner's music."[13] "The Ride of the Valkyries" – it was so appropriate to show Wagner's messengers of death, sowing destruction in Vietnam.

Dov Shilansky, the deputy minister in the prime minister's office, suggested that Mehta return to his native land of India; this was interpreted by many as racist even though he later explained it away by stating that Mehta should leave it to Israelis to solve their own problems.[14]

The director of the classical music division of Israel's state radio, Avi Chanani, said: "I am opposed to any ban on culture. Zubin Mehta risked playing Wagner in one fell swoop, but I believe in introducing him gradually, and that is what I have been doing. Wagner was a revolutionary in music. His work is central to the development of European music. Without Wagner it is difficult to understand the history of music. That is one important consideration for playing his music. But what I feel is cardinal in my decision to present Wagner on the radio is my belief that in a democracy, the public has a right to know; it must be exposed to all information."

One of the strongest voices against performances of Wagner's music was the government attorney general Gideon Hausner, who asserted that the issue raised by Mehta was a public Jewish one and not a musical one. In his opening speech in the Eichmann trial, the accused having been captured in South America and brought back for trial, he thundered: "When I stand before you here, judges of Israel, to lead the prosecution of Adolf Eichmann, I am not standing alone. With me are six million accusers."[15]

When a survey was conducted some years later 50 percent were against playing Wagner, 25 percent for, and 25 percent had no firm convictions on the subject. In 1992, the Philharmonic conducted a poll among its subscribers that showed a majority in favor of playing Wagner's music, while 30 percent were against. The size of the minority and their sensitivities inclined the authorities to discontinue playing Wagner until matters changed. There have been tentative steps to introduce the music since then. Wolfgang's estranged son Gottfried Wagner – the composer's great grandson – records that Wagner's music was played over Israeli radio in

---

13. Ibid.
14. Ibid., 7.
15. Ibid., 83.

1990[16] and some five years later in August 1995, Wagner's opera *The Flying Dutchman* was broadcast, during prime time on a Saturday evening.[17]

Ruth Jordan, an Israeli author, has described in her autobiography the favorable audience reaction to prewar performances of Wagner's works by Toscanini with the Palestine Orchestra. Paul Johnson points out a further enigma in an article in the *Spectator*: the founder of modern Zionism, Theodor Herzl, was a passionate admirer of Wagner.[18] He had been a student in Vienna at the time of Wagner's death in 1883 and was present at a meeting of the students to commemorate his life. What started as a "fervent demonstration of nationalist German sentiment" on that occasion, according to a local newspaper, deteriorated sadly into "an exhibition of anti-Semitism" with the depressing concomitant violence.[19]

While writing his great work *Der Judenstaat* Herzl frequently heard Wagner at the opera house and claimed it inspired him. "Only on the nights when Wagner was not performed did I have doubts about the correctness of my idea." Herzl made great plans for the creation of a Zionist state, including a coronation of the ruler, a Rothschild, and incorporated Wagner's music into the grand opening. His views seem to be gaining ground.

A vociferous grouping continues to oppose the playing of the music in Israel. No one can quibble with an aversion by a nation to the music of a man so centrally linked with a regime that attempted to destroy whole nations. The topic is one that belongs properly to the views of the descendants of the victims of the Holocaust.

After a thorough analysis of the modern view of the playing of the music in that country Johnson proffers a conciliatory solution. He concludes that "Israel itself is a huge risk, a great adventure, embarked upon by men and women who put their ideals, their vision, above their comfort and safety, and so far the risk has proved abundantly worth it. Playing Wagner is a further, tiny hazard that Israel and its brave people ought to be able to take in their stride."[20]

---

16. Wagner, Gottfried, *Twilight of the Wagners*, 220.
17. Eylon, "The Controversy over Richard Wagner."
18. Johnson, Paul, "Should the Valkyries Ride over Jerusalem?" *Spectator*, January 4, 1992, 20.
19. Köhler, *Wagner's Hitler*, 67.
20. Johnson, Paul, "Should the Valkyries Ride over Jerusalem?" *Spectator*, January 4, 1992, 23.

Those wishing to take strides forward have not had it very easy in recent times. On May 30, 2001 the organizers, including Holocaust survivors, of an Israeli arts festival cancelled a performance of act 1 of Wagner's opera *The Valkyries*. The production was to have been held less than two months later on July 7 and the world-renowned tenor Placido Domingo had been booked for the performance.[21] Schumann's Fourth Symphony and Stravinsky's *The Rite of Spring* were played instead. Clearly the organizers had either forgotten or were not aware of Schumann's intemperate attacks on Meyerbeer, at the time Wagner crossed swords with him in Dresden.

Daniel Barenboim, an Israeli citizen, presently (2002) the conductor of the Chicago Symphony Orchestra, as well as the State Opera in Berlin, was to have been on the podium. An illustrious career had previously seen him in charge of the Orchestre de Paris and the Opéra de Paris. He was incensed by the cancellation and said that actions such as that would further the cause of neo-Nazism. Earlier that month he told the German magazine *Focus* that he saw the outcome of the affair as a test for Israeli democracy.[22]

Barenboim is a controversial personality with regard to championing Wagner's music, as is James Levine, who has also conducted a number of Wagner operas around the world, including at Bayreuth. Levine speaks highly of Wagner's Mecca: "For a conductor Bayreuth has the advantage of being able to conduct unseen. And the audience is able to give itself entirely over to the music, and this creates a different mood. Wagner's works need this intensive concentration."[23]

The author was present when Levine conducted a performance of *Parsifal* at Bayreuth in 1991, a production with four enormous crystalline stalactites, which represented, after rotation, the forest and the temple of the grail. Rescued by the magnificent singing of Waltraud Meier and Hans Sotin, the critics panned the rest of the opera – the tempi were so slow they were described as "limp and boring," with no particular reference to Winifred's appreciation of Siegfried's libido.

Barenboim, whose parents were Russian Jews who had emigrated to Argentina, left for Israel at an early age. As the husband of renowned cellist

---

21. Hooper, "Israel Bans Wagner Opera Despite Plea by Barenboim."
22. Ibid.
23. Spotts, *Bayreuth*, 13.

Jacqueline du Pré, his name became well known to filmgoers and readers of her biography. A versatile and able pianist and conductor, his interpretation of Mozart is world-renowned. More controversial is his role as Wagner conductor, especially at Bayreuth. He did not share Levine's enchantment at appearing at Bayreuth and described conducting in the pit of the theatre there "like being 150 feet under water without a diver's helmet."[24]

Barenboim's Wagner has had mixed reviews – his 1981 conducting of *Tristan* was described as "saccharine" by some and others maintained that Ponnelle's production had changed the couple into Pelleas and Melisande. The leading opera magazine *Oper und Konzert* was overwhelmed by his reading of the score and went into raptures – "at last Bayreuth has found a great Wagnerian conductor."[25] His *Ring* of 1992 was widely praised – "a triumph," said *Figaro* – and the critic from the *Observer* confessed that he had never heard better playing at Bayreuth.[26]

Barenboim's background in conducting Wagner illuminates, to some extent, his passionate defense of the controversial production, in which many looked forward to hearing Placido Domingo as Siegmund in Israel. The tenor has sung many of the Wagnerian roles but abstained from the taxing role of Siegfried, apart from excerpts – it has a long catalogue of victims. The organizers of the festival cancelled the performance of *The Valkyries* after requests by the Israeli president, the culture and sports minister, the mayor of Jerusalem and citizens of that city. Although only seventeen deputies attended the session the Israeli parliament said that as long as a single Holocaust victim was still alive in Israel no music by Wagner should be publicly performed in the country.

The intensity of the opposition to the performance is illustrated by the fact that the Simon Wiesenthal Center in Jerusalem – famous throughout the world for its courageous work hunting down Nazis – approached the courts for an interdict. Not all music lovers were so committed in their opposition to the favorite composer of the Third Reich. That some music lovers were prepared to overlook the dubious political reputation of the composer is illustrated by the fact that all the concert tickets were sold out weeks in advance.

---

24. Ibid., 15.
25. Ibid., 291.
26. Ibid., 302.

When the festival took place in Jerusalem on July 7, 2001,[27] Barenboim returned for a second encore and asked the audience if they wanted to hear Wagner. One would have expected him to take cognizance of the earlier contretemps. "Despite what the Israel festival believes, there are people sitting in the audience for whom Wagner does not spark Nazi associations," Barenboim told the audience. "I respect those for whom these associations are oppressive. It will be democratic to play a Wagner encore for those who wish to hear it. I am turning to you now and asking whether I can play Wagner."

A lively thirty-minute debate followed – interrupted at times by shouts of "fascist" – and many walked out, banging doors behind them. Barenboim took the criticism on the chin. "If you're angry, be angry with me, but please don't be angry with the orchestra or the festival management," he barked back. The great majority stayed, and gave a standing ovation to the visiting Berlin Staatskapelle orchestra for its performance of the prelude to *Tristan und Isolde*.

Barenboim has recounted how strongly people feel in Israel. While in Tel Aviv during the debacle I have described a lady came up to him and said: "How can you play that? I saw my family taken to the gas chambers to the sound of the *Meistersinger* overture. Why should I have to listen to that?"[28]

The right-wing politicians, including Israeli Prime Minister Ariel Sharon, Jerusalem Mayor Ehud Olmert, President Moshe Katsav and other figures quickly denounced Barenboim for meddling in Israeli culture again. Olmert, a leading member of the right-wing Likud Party, said Barenboim was "brazen, arrogant, insensitive and uncivilized," and should be banned. The Knesset committee on culture and education "urged Israel's cultural bodies to boycott the conductor…for performing music by Hitler's favorite composer at Israel's premier cultural event until he apologizes."[29]

As a Jew Barenboim had been criticized from time to time outside Israel. His website records a conversation with the well-known Arab academic Edward Said – considered a black mark against him – and his views are similar to those of the late Yehudi Menuhin, whose father was

---

27. Mazelis, "Daniel Barenboim Conducts Wagner in Israel."
28. Guzelimian, *Parallels and Paradoxes*, 104.
29. Ibid., 176–77.

a noted anti-Zionist. Barenboim's position regarding Wagner, however, is that politics are irrelevant. He is careful to distinguish the various facets that go to make up Richard Wagner. "First of all, there is Wagner the composer. Then there's Wagner the writer of his own librettos – in other words, everything that is tied to the music. Then there is Wagner the writer on artistic matters. And then there is Wagner the political writer – in this case, primarily the anti-Semitic political writer. These are four different aspects to his work."[30]

While acknowledging that Wagner was "an open and terrible anti-Semite," Barenboim has defended his role by saying that the operas do not reflect his prejudice against Jews and that the Jewish public should still listen to the music. Barenboim's performances and recordings of Wagner at Bayreuth and elsewhere have received widespread critical acclaim and he has made large sums of money.

When he spoke at Columbia University a questioner from the audience indicated that he had been present at Bayreuth in 1991 when Barenboim conducted. He attacked the conductor maintaining that the production perpetuated the stereotypes devised by Wagner. "This production of *Das Rheingold*, which was directed by Harry Kupfer, had the most appalling anti-Semitism in it that I've ever encountered. In the production, the Alberich character is a blatant copy of the kinds of caricature of Jews that were put in *Der Stürmer*, the Nazi newspaper, and to see this man gallivanting on stage as such a caricature of a Jew, and then, near the end of the opera, when he's captured by Wotan and Loge – they not only capture him, but take a metal pole and stick it between his legs and twist it and he's tortured on stage, ends up completely bloody – to see this in Bayreuth, where there's already been this experience with Nazis and this kind of torture, I couldn't understand how a Jewish conductor could take part in such a production."[31]

Barenboim maintained that this was a mistaken and very personal interpretation which the conductor did not share. "I can assure you; I worked very carefully with Harry Kupfer on the production of this. We spoke openly about every subject that was treated in this staging. Never was there an intention; never was there an idea on Kupfer's side to make a Jewish character out of Alberich, or anybody else. Therefore, I'm afraid

---

30. Ibid.
31. Ibid., 106–7.

I have to tell you this: it really says more about how you saw it than what it really was."

While captivated by the magical charm of the music, the maestro from Bayreuth was not the sort of character Barenboim had much sympathy with. His preference, as a personality, was for the little genius from Salzberg, Wolfgang Amadeus Mozart, named the composer of the millennium. "I'd love to follow Mozart around for twenty-four hours; I'm sure it would be very entertaining, amusing and edifying, but Wagner…I might invite him to dinner for study purposes but not for enjoyment. Wagner, the person, is absolutely appalling, despicable, and, in a way, very difficult to put together with the music he wrote, which so often has exactly the opposite kind of feelings…noble, generous, etc."

The vociferous opposition of Holocaust survivors and other sensitive Jews has presented an immense problem to Barenboim and other conductors, including non-Jews. As a solution Barenboim has suggested that Wagner be performed at non-subscription concerts, so that objectors could stay away without feeling that their subscriptions were financing the music.[32] Barenboim has other problems from right-wing politicians. While Barenboim was running the Berliner Staatsoper, Klaus Landowsky, the leader of the Christian Democratic Union in the Berlin senate, raised the hackles of decent people when he talked about the difficulty of finding the right person for the job. In the presence of a reporter Landowsky said: "On the one hand, you have the young Karajan, Christian Thielemann. On the other, you have the Jew Barenboim."[33]

A journalist, Fred Mazelis, writing on the World Socialist Website on August 1, 2001, had a different take on the whole debate. He maintained that the ban on Wagner's music was part of a nationalist agenda, which had been fostered by the Zionist establishment for its own political purposes.

The views of other individual musicians on the playing of Wagner's music in Israel are also interesting. "I don't believe in tying music to racism. If we did, we would have to stop playing Chopin in Israel – he too was a rabid anti-Semite." That was the view of Nechama Rosler, a violinist with the Jerusalem Symphony Orchestra. She goes on to qualify her approval. "But, because Wagner's music arouses such deep emotions, I feel strongly

---

32. Ibid.
33. Ibid., 169.

that as long as it disturbs anyone who associates it with the Nazis, with his own or his family's suffering in the Holocaust, Wagner's music should not be played publicly. The function of music, after all, is to soothe, to make the listener feel good, to stimulate or pacify his or her soul. Whoever wants to hear Wagner's music can listen to it in private."[34]

Yaakov Mishori, a leading Philharmonic musician, is in favor of playing Wagner. "After all," he says, "Wagner died fifty years before Hitler came to power. Moreover, he was a kind of private anti-Semite, refusing to sign any public declarations against the Jews. He actually worked with many Jews. Wagner's public relations man was a Jew named Neumann, Hermann Levi conducted Wagner's works at the time, and a musician named Rubenstein finished the orchestration of some of his operas."

Motti Schmidt, leader of the Jerusalem Symphony Orchestra, states: "Wagner was a genius. His was a complicated personality – he was like a many-layered cake – but he was not a good man. If his music still hurts the feelings of people in this country, we should respect the rights of the minority and not play Wagner."

Military hero Reuven Dafni, an ex-diplomat, who parachuted into Nazi-held Yugoslavia, makes a number of important points. "Even though Zubin Mehta once told me that no orchestra can be a real orchestra without playing Wagner, I would wait until the last of the Holocaust survivors is no longer with us." He points out that hypocrisy has to be avoided. "Nevertheless, I think we are being hypocritical in that we play Carl Orff without compunction – Orff, who was a self-declared, card-holding Nazi."[35]

Dafni points out other inconsistencies in the application of the cultural ban. "When, in the 1940s, the ban on Wagner was imposed, it included the music of another Richard – Strauss. About thirteen years ago, conductor Igor Markevitch was eager to conduct Strauss with the Jerusalem Radio Orchestra (today the Jerusalem Symphony Orchestra). This was denied him. But he did make a studio recording of *Til Eulenspiegel*. Ever since then, radio listeners have been hearing the music of Richard Strauss."

Lili Eylon in her article *The Controversy over Richard Wagner* points out that while Wagner was a "theorist whose ideas were meant for posterity,

---

34. Eylon, "The Controversy over Richard Wagner."
35. Ibid.

Strauss was a compliant pragmatist." Mention has been made of early attempts of the latter to undermine the work on the podium of Levi and obtain the same post himself at Bayreuth. Posterity has not looked with favor at his betrayal of Jewish musicians, when he stepped into the breach vacated by Toscanini's boycott of the festival.

Strauss had been appointed head of the *Reichsmusikkammer* in 1933 and Eylon maintains that in his two years in this position "he managed to get all performing Jewish artists removed from public view." It is not clear how fervent his anti-Semitism was and he still had immense respect for his Jewish collaborators. Despite the ban on Jewish artists he tried to continue his association. Eylon concedes that "in 1935, Nazi censors came upon a letter of his to Stefan Zweig – who, together with another Jew, Hugo von Hofmannstahl, wrote many of his libretti – stating that he wanted to continue working with him."

Other cultural contradictions persist in Israel. The music of Carl Orff is frequently performed in Israel, including the world famous *Carmina Burana*, composed in 1937, expressly for the leaders of the Nazi regime, including the Führer. Orff has not emerged with much credit in relation to the music of another of the Bayreuth maestro's enemies, the Jewish composer Felix Mendelssohn, whose best-known work was the wonderful *Midsummer Night's Dream*. How many couples have walked out of their wedding service as man and wife to the stirring strains of *that march*? The qualities of the music were such that the Nazis were anxious that it be preserved, whereas all other "decadent" music was suppressed. The Nazis asked Strauss to rewrite the music, which he regarded as an insult – but Orff agreed. Fortunately for him and posterity the project was never carried out.[36]

Those against playing the music of Wagner in Israel include a number of significant members of society. Moshe Landau, a retired Supreme Court judge and presiding judge at the Eichmann trial, says: "I have the same opinions today that I held in the 1940s. It was enough for me to have read "Jewry in Music." No, I don't think Wagner's music should be played here." Eylon concludes that for Holocaust survivors, "Wagner's music represents a vivid reminder of that regime. The argument that music must be separated

---

36. Ibid.

from politics is not cogent in general, and certainly not in this case. If anybody introduced politics into music, it was Richard Wagner himself."[37]

It is not difficult to understand why Jewish people and Israelis still have difficulty liking the music of Richard Wagner and permitting it to be performed in their country. Joachim Köhler, in his wonderfully erudite study, is quite unequivocal in his conclusion. "And there was a second heartfelt desire of Wagner's, [the first was the opening of Bayreuth to all persons free of charge] seldom openly expressed but raised to the status of doctrine by Wagner's son-in-law Houston Stewart Chamberlain, which Hitler later fulfilled as a chilling monument to his memory – the annihilation of the European Jews."[38]

Wagner is in no danger of being sanctified or beatified. His malign influence will endure for the foreseeable future. An example of this is the character chosen by Batya Gur as the murderer in her thriller *Orchestrated Murder: A Musical Murder*. Does it come as a surprise to the reader that the person chosen for this role is an eccentric Israeli conductor working abroad, who – despite vehement opposition from the people of Israel – insists on playing the musical works of Richard Wagner![39]

Gottfried Wagner visited Israel in 1990 and regularly lectures on a large number of topics, including the anti-Semitism of his great grandfather. He is of the view that "as a listener, I consider *Tristan und Isolde* a masterpiece of nineteenth century music, but I am at the same time repelled by Wagner's *Weltanschauung*. I cannot just sit and enjoy his music. I never put on Wagner's music in my home…Richard Wagner's anti-Semitic writings will always overshadow my life. I cannot separate the operas from his theoretical work. His writings and his music form a unified whole…He always considered himself a philosopher first, and a composer only second."[40] In 1993 Gottfried wrote about the subconscious message designed to indoctrinate the world. "Wagner himself misused music as a vehicle of propaganda. Where arguments about Wagner are concerned, Germans quickly lose their sense of humor. With Wagner the German soul becomes exalted! Woe betide anyone who questions Wagner…" Nor did he ever shrink from linking his great grandfather with the Holocaust. "Richard Wagner, through his

---

37. Ibid.
38. Köhler, *Wagner's Hitler*, 8.
39. Sheffi, *Ring of Myths*, 138.
40. Eylon, "The Controversy over Richard Wagner."

inflammatory anti-Semitic writings, was co-responsible for the transition from Bayreuth to Auschwitz."[41]

Gottfried has set up the Post-Holocaust Dialogue Group, composed of survivors of the victims and the perpetrators. A six-point plan identifies their objectives and includes recognizing the Holocaust as "a unique rift in Western civilization" and the starting point of a new morality. Full exposure is advocated of all the evil of the Holocaust and action is planned via conferences and publications. The group opposes totalitarian dogmatism in all its manifestations and pledges itself to influence nations to prevent a future repetition of the Holocaust. The ultimate goal is a world living in peaceful tolerance and "appreciative of all diverse humanity."[42]

Meanwhile the controversy rages on in Israel. Attempts to enforce a television boycott could never last given the advent of cable television; Channel 8, a science and culture channel, was a pioneer in the broadcasting of the operas of Richard Strauss and later in 1997 the Wagner operas from the Bayreuth festival.[43] Still, many are not ready for the public broadcasting of Wagner; there were angry reactions when the artistic adviser of the New Israeli Opera, Asher Fisch, tried to play a tape of Wagner's music during a public debate in that country in 1998. That same year saw a conference on "Wagner and the Jews" at Bayreuth which was condemned by Israelis.[44] To some extent of course the whole controversy has become a question of public perceptions. Compact discs are freely available in stores and the public is at liberty to purchase whatever music appeals to it. If concerts are not available in Israel the moneyed aesthete can travel and hear the "forbidden composers" in any country in the world. So the debate has become whether it is sensitive and politic to give public approval to composers who advocated anti-Semitism or lent support to the Third Reich.

In a little known incident the French writer Guy de Maupassant wrote about a visit of his to the Hotel de Palmes in Palermo, some years after Wagner had stayed there. As he opened the door of a wardrobe, "a powerful and delicious perfume came from it, like the caress of a breeze blowing over a bed of roses." The proprietor informed him that the great composer had stored his linen there and that, following his penchant for

---

41. Wagner, Gottfried, *The Twilight of the Wagners*, 239, 256.
42. Ibid., 286–87.
43. Sheffi, *Ring of Myths*, 8.
44. Ibid., vi.

Apotheosis: Wagner finally ascends to Heaven (Valhalla) after his earthly life at Bayreuth has ended. Prawy, 223.

strong perfumes, he had sprinkled it liberally with *essence de roses*. De Maupassant was stunned by the good fortune that had brought him to stay in the same room as the genius. "I drank in this breath of flowers and I seemed to discover something of Wagner himself, of his desire, of his soul, in this trifling matter of the secret and cherished habits that go to make up the inner life of a man."[45]

For many the notion that the soul and secrets of Richard Wagner would smell of roses would be anathema. Let us never let the sorcery of his music divert us from our will to eschew the subconscious text. Even one of his most dedicated enemies, the Jewish music critic Hanslick, whom he had pilloried mercilessly as Beckmesser, allowed himself to succumb to the narcotic effects. He hinted at the godhead the composer had assumed on himself when he said after his death in 1883: "We have yet to encounter a musician sufficiently purblind or vehement to fail to appreciate Wagner's brilliant talent and amazing art, to underrate his enormous influence, and, even in the case of an avowed antipathy, to gainsay the greatness and genius of his works…And if one were to remind us of his mortal frailties and violent emotions, we would find no trace of them in our memory, for with Grillparzer we say that 'death is like a bolt of lighting which transfigures what it consumes.'"[46]

---

45. Newman, *Life of Richard Wagner*, vol. 4, 698.
46. Gutman, *Richard Wagner*, 636.

Lest we sink forever in the quagmire of racism, sexual perversion, depravity and anti-Semitism, it is salutary to conclude with a note of sanity and reason in a world still reeling from the aftereffects of Hitler's Wagnerian idolatry. The slogan of the Post-Holocaust Dialogue Group is the words of Jewish judge and Holocaust survivor Samuel Gringauz who said in 1947, "Our tragedy must become the starting point of a new humanity."[47]

The narrator's closing words in a Swedish film on the Holocaust made in 1961 provide an imperative no person can ever afford to ignore: "It must never happen again – never again."

---

47. Wagner, Gottfried, *The Twilight of the Wagners*, 286.

Select Bibliography

Bauer, Oswald Georg. "Forty Years of New Bayreuth." Bayreuth: Bayreuth Festival program notes, 1991.

Beckett, Walter. *Liszt*. Rev. ed. Master Musicians Series. London: J.M. Dent and Sons, Ltd., 1963.

Bedford, Herbert. *Schumann*. London: Keegan Paul, 1933.

Bentley, Nicolas, and Evan Esar. *The Treasury of Humorous Quotations*. London: Aldine Paperbacks, 1967.

Bishop, Chris. *Hitler's Third Reich*. London: Midsummer Books, Ltd., 1999.

Bleuel, Hans. *Sex and Society in Nazi Germany*. New York: Lippincott, 1973.

Burleigh, Michael. *The Third Reich: A New History*. London: Pan Books, 2001.

Burk, John N., ed. *Letters of Richard Wagner: The Burrell Collection*. New York: Macmillan, 1950.

Chamberlain, Houston Stewart. *Lebenswege Meines Denkens*. Munich: Bruckmann A-G, 1919.

Christiansen, Rupert. "Kultur Clash." *The Daily Telegraph*, April 22, 2000, Arts and Books Supplement.

Cohn, Norman. *The Pursuit of the Millennium; Revolutionary Millenniums and Mystical Anarchists of the Middle Ages*. 2nd ed. London: Oxford University Press, 1970.

Conrad, Peter. "He's Tricky, That Dicky: Even Wagner virgins needn't feel intimidated by a fresh appraisal of the world's most controversial composer." *The Observer*, Sunday, October 27, 2002.

Cooke, Deryck. *I Saw the World End*. London: Oxford University Press, 1979.

Cornish, Kimberley. *The Jew of Linz: Wittgenstein, Hitler and Their Secret Battle for the Mind*. London: Century Books Ltd., 1998.

Cross, Colin. *Adolf Hitler*. London: Hodder and Stoughton Ltd., 1974.

DiGaetani, John Louis, ed. *Penetrating Wagner's Ring: An Anthology*. New York: Fairleigh Dickinson Press, 1978.

Douglas, Nigel. *Legendary Voices*. London: Andre Deutsch, 1992.

Ellis, Havelock. *Studies in the Psychology of Sex*, vol. 3. New York: Random House, 1915.

Evans, Edwin. *Tchaikovsky*. London: J.M. Dent and Sons, 1957.

Eylon, Lili. "The Controversy over Richard Wagner." Israeli Foreign Ministry: The American-Israeli Cooperative Enterprise, 2002.

Fest, Joachim C. *Hitler*. London: Weidenfeld and Nicolson, 1973.

Fischer-Diskau, Dietrich. *Wagner and Nietzsche*. New York: Seabury Press, 1976.

Frank, Leonard. *Quotationary*. New York: Random House Webster, 2001.

Franklin, Peter. *The Life of Mahler*. Musical Lives Series. Cambridge: Cambridge University Press, 1997.

Freud, Sigmund. *On Sexuality: Three Essays*. Pelican Freud Library, vol. 7. Ed. James Strachey, with Angela Richards. London: Pelican Books, 1977.

Geissmar, Berta. *The Baton and the Jackboot*. London: Hamish Hamilton, 1945.

Gilbert, Martin. *The Holocaust: The Jewish Tragedy*. New York: Harper Collins, 1987.

Gobineau, Count. *Essai sur l'inegalite des races humaines* (1853–1855). Trans. Adrian Collins as *The Essay on the Inequality of the Human Races*. Paris: Firmin Didot, 1853–55.

Goldman, Albert, and Evert Sprinchorn, arrangers. *Wagner on Music and Drama*. London: Victor Gollancz Ltd., 1970.

Goldhagen, Daniel Jonah. *Hitler's Willing Executioners: Ordinary Germans and the Holocaust*. Abacus, 1997.

Gregor-Dellin, Martin. *Richard Wagner: Eine Biographie in Bildern*. Munich: R. Piper and Co. Verlag, 1982.

Grunberger, Richard. *The Twelve-Year Reich*. New York: Ballantine, 1971.
Gutman, Robert W. *Richard Wagner: The Man, His Mind and His Music*. Harmondsworth: Pelican Books, 1971.
Guzelimian, Ara, ed. *Parallels and Paradoxes: Daniel Barenboim and Edward W. Said – Explorations in Music and Society*. London: Bloomsburg, 2003.
Hamann, Brigitte. *Hitler's Vienna: A Dictator's Apprenticeship*. Oxford: Oxford University Press, 1999.
———. *Winifred Wagner oder Hitlers Bayreuth*. Munich: Piper Verlag, 2003.
Hanfstaengl, Dr. Ernst F.S. "My Leader." *Collier's*, August 4, 1934.
Harding, Bertita. *Magic Fire*. London: George G. Harrap and Co., 1954.
Hasan-Rokem, Galit, and Alan Dundes, eds. *The Wandering Jew*. Bloomington: Indiana University Press, 1986.
Hayman, Ronald. *Hitler and Geli*. London: Bloomsbury Paperbacks, 1998.
Hilberg, Raul. *The Destruction of the European Jews*. New York: New Viewpoints, 1973.
Hinsley, F.H., and Alan Stripp, eds. *Codebreakers: The Inside Story of Bletchley Park*. Oxford: Oxford University Press, 1994.
Hitler, Adolf. *Mein Kampf*. London: Hurst and Blackett Publishers, 1939.
Hooper, John. "Israel Bans Wagner Opera Despite Plea by Barenboim." *The Guardian*, Thursday, May 31, 2001.
Hurn, Philip Dutton, and Waverley Lewis Root. *The Truth about Wagner*. London: Cassell and Co., 1930.
Hussey, Dyneley. *Jakob Liebmann Meyerbeer*. The Music Masters, vol. 2. Harmondsworth: Pelican Books, 1958.
Icke, David. *...and the truth shall set you free*. Cambridge: Bridge of Love Publications, 1995.
Igra, Samuel. *Germany's National Vice*. London: Quality Press, 1945.
Infield, Glenn B. *Hitler's Secret Life*. New York: Stein and Day, 1979.
Jackson, John E. "Baudelaire and Wagner, or the Meeting of Two Modern Minds." Bayreuth: Bayreuth Festival program notes, 1991, part 7, page 36.
Jacobs, Arthur. *Arthur Sullivan: A Victorian Musician*. Oxford: Oxford University Press, 1986.
Johnson, Paul, "Should the Valkyries Ride over Jerusalem?" *Spectator*, January 4, 1992, 20.

Jones, Ernest. *The Life and Work of Sigmund Freud.* Edited and abridged by Lionel Trilling and Steven Marcus. Los Angeles: Pelican Books, 1964.

Kater, Michael H. *The Twisted Muse: Musicians and Their Music in the Third Reich.* New York: Oxford University Press, 1997.

Kershaw, Ian. *Hitler 1889–1936: Hubris,* vol. 1. New York: Penguin, 1999.

Kershaw, Ian. *Hitler 1936–1945: Nemesis,* vol. 2. New York: Norton, 2001.

King, Francis. *Satan and Swastika.* London: Mayflower, 1976.

Koch, H.W., ed. *Aspects of the Third Reich.* London: Macmillan Education, 1987.

Koch-Hillebrecht, Manfred. *Homo Hitler: Psychogramm des deutschen Diktators.* Munich: Wilhelm Goldmann Verlag, 1999.

Köhler, Joachim. *Wagner's Hitler: The Prophet and His Disciple.* Cambridge: Polity Press, 2000.

Kolbe, Jürgen, et al. *Wagners Welten.* Munich: Münchner Stadtmuseum, Edition Minerva, 2003.

Kubizek, August. *Young Hitler.* London: George Mann Ltd., 1973.

Langer, Walter. *The Mind of Adolf Hitler: The Secret Wartime Report.* New York: Basic Books, Inc., 1972.

———. *The OSS Psychological Report on Adolf Hitler.* http://www.nizkor.org/hweb/people/h/hitler-adolf/oss-papers/text/profile-index.html. July 25, 2004.

Lewis, David. *The Man Who Invented Hitler: The Making of the Führer.* London: Headline Book Publishing, 2004.

Lively, Scott, and Kevin Abrams. *The Pink Swastika: Homosexuality in the Nazi Party.* Keiser, Oregon: Founders, 1997.

Lomas, Herbert. "A Nietzsche of Sweetness and Light." *The Spectator.* August 1, 1992.

Machtan, Lothar. *The Hidden Hitler.* New York: Basic Books, 2001.

Manchester, William. *The Arms of Krupp.* Boston: Little, Brown, 1968.

Marek, George R. *Cosima Wagner.* London: Julia MacRae Books, 1981.

Mazelis, Fred. "Daniel Barenboim Conducts Wagner in Israel." World Socialist Web Site, http://www.wsws.org/articles/2001/aug2001/wagn-a01.shtml. August 1, 2001.

Muller-Hill, Benno. *Murderous Science.* London: Oxford University Press, 1988.

Newman, Ernest. *The Life of Richard Wagner*. Four Volumes. New York: Alfred A. Knopf Inc., 1946.

———. *Wagner as Man and Artist*. London: Jonathan Cape Paperback, 1969.

———. *Wagner Nights*. London: Putnam and Company, 1968.

O'Donnell, James P. *The Berlin Bunker*. London: Arrow Books, 1979.

Osborne, Charles. *The World Theatre of Wagner*. New York: Macmillan, 1982.

Pachl, Peter P. *Siegfried Wagner: Genie im Schatten*. Munich: Nymphenburger, 1988.

Petzet, Michael, and Gerhard Hojer. "Neuschwanstein Castle." Official brochure. Munich: Bavarian State Castles, 1998.

Poliakov, Leon. *The History of Anti-Semitism from Voltaire to Wagner*, vol. 3. New York: Vanguard Press, 1968.

Porter, Andrew, trans. *The Ring of the Nibelung by Richard Wagner*. German text with English translation. London: Faber Paperbacks, 1977.

Poznansky, Alexander. *Tchaikovsky: The Quest for the Inner Man*. New York: Schirmer Books, 1991.

Prawy, Marcel. *Richard Wagner: Leben und Werk*. Munich: Wilhelm Goldmann Verlag, 1982.

Radcliffe, Philip. *Mendelssohn*. The Master Musicians Series. London: J.M. Dent and Sons, 1976.

Ravenscroft, Trevor. *The Spear of Destiny*. York Beach, ME: Samuel Weiser, 1982.

Redlich, Fritz, M.D. *Hitler: Diagnosis of a Destructive Prophet*. New York and Oxford: Oxford University Press, 1999.

Richard Wagner Museum Brochure, sixth ed. Bayreuth: Richard Wagner Foundation, 1990.

Rose, Paul Lawrence. *Wagner: Race and Revolution*. London: Faber and Faber Ltd., 1990.

Russell, Lord, of Liverpool. *The Scourge of the Swastika*, ninth ed. London: Cassell and Co. Ltd., 1955.

Schmidt, Dr. Matthias. *Albert Speer: The End of a Myth*. New York: St. Martins Press, 1984.

Schramm, Percy Ernst. *Hitler, The Man and the Military Leader*. Trans. from the German by Donald S. Detwiler. London: Allen Lane the Penguin Press, 1972.

Shakespeare, William. *The Complete Oxford Shakespeare*, vol. 2, The Comedies. Oxford: Oxford University Press, 1994.

Sheffi, Na'ama. *The Ring of Myths: The Israelis, Wagner and the Nazis*. Brighton, East Sussex: Sussex Academic Press, 2001.

Shirer, William L. *The Rise and Fall of the Third Reich*. London: Pan Books Ltd., 1960.

Skelton, Geoffrey. *Wagner at Bayreuth*. London: Barrie and Rockliff, 1965.

———. *Cosima Wagner's Diaries*. London: Pimlico, 1994.

Solomon, Larry. "Wagner and Hitler." http://solomonsmusic.net/WagHit.htm. July 21, 2003.

Spotts, Frederic. *Bayreuth: A History of the Wagner Festival*. New Haven: Yale University Press, 1994.

———. *Hitler and the Power of Aesthetics*. London: Hutchinson, 2002.

Stang, Alan. "Hitler and Homosexuality: Nazism Is Just One Version of Homosexuality." http://www.talkaboutgovernment.com/group/alt.politics.communism/messages/32828.html.

The Strange Death of Adolf Hitler. New York: The Macaulay Company, 1939.

Taylor, Ronald. *Richard Wagner: His Life, Art and Thought*. London: Panther, 1979.

Toland, John. *Adolf Hitler*. New York: Ballantine Books, 1976.

Trevor-Roper, H.R. *Hitler's Table Talk 1941–44: His Private Conversations*. 2nd ed. London: Weidenfeld and Nicolson, 1973.

van Rjndt, Philippe. *The Trial of Adolf Hitler*. London: Futura Publications Ltd., 1980.

Vetter, Isolde. "Wagner in the History of Psychology." Bayreuth: Bayreuth Festival program notes, 1991.

Viereck, Peter. *Metapolitics: From the Romantics to Hitler*. New York: Alfred A. Knopf, 1941.

Viles, Ann. Introduction to brochure. Richard Wagner Collection. New York: Curtis Institute of Music, 1978.

Wagner, Friedelind, and Page Cooper. *Heritage of Fire*. New York: Greenwood Press, 1945.

Wagner, Gottfried. *Twilight of the Wagners: The Unveiling of a Family's Legacy*. New York: Picador, 2000.

———. *The Wagner Legacy*. London: MPG Books, Bodmin, 1997.

Wagner, Nike. *The Wagners: The Dramas of a Musical Dynasty*. Princeton, NJ: Princeton University Press, 1998.

Wagner, Wolf Siegfried. *The Wagner Family Albums*. London: Thames and Hudson Ltd., 1976.

Waite, Robert G.L. *The Psychopathic God: Adolf Hitler*. New York: Da Capo, 1993.

Wallace, Irving, et al. *The Intimate Sex Lives of Famous People*. London: Arrow Books, 1981.

Weiner, Marc A. *Richard Wagner and the Anti-Semitic Imagination*. Lincoln, NE: University of Nebraska Press, 1997.

Wilhelm, Kurt. *Richard Strauss: An Intimate Portrait*. London: Thames and Hudson, 1989.

Windell, George C. "Hitler, National Socialism and Richard Wagner." In DiGaetani, John Louis, ed. *Penetrating Wagner's Ring: An Anthology*. New York: Fairleigh Dickinson Press, 1978.

Winworth, Freda. *The Epic of Sounds: An Interpretation of Wagner's Nibelungen Ring*. London: Simpkin and Co. Ltd., Novello and Co. Ltd., 1898.

Wollheim, Richard. *Freud*. London: Fontana Collins, 1971.

Yan, Mark. "King Ludwig II of Bavaria: His Life and Art." Sydney, Australia: http://www.geocities.com/Paris/LeftBank/4080/home.htm. July 20, 2003.

Index

A

A Communication to My Friends (Wagner) 50, 73, 112, 183
Aachen 15
Adorno, Theodor 80
Adso of Montier-en-Der 161
adulation of Hitler 303, 347, 351, 352–53, 360, 361
Ahasuerus 49–50, 51, 65, 150, 154, 184
Ahna, Pauline de 206
Aign, Walter 248
Albert, Prince 85
Alsace-Lorraine music festival 363
Also Sprach Zarathustra (Nietzsche) 16
Amann, Max 236, 237
America 275
Americans, attitude toward 282
Amsterdam 10–11
Andreas-Salomé, Lou 175–76
Antichrist 161
Anti-Comintern Pact 362
anti-Semitism 4, 6, 7, 10, 11, 20, 21, 27, 30, 31, 33, 41–72, 77, 82, 94, 108, 111, 120, 121, 136, 143, 145, 147, 154, 156, 159, 162, 164, 170, 171, 184, 198, 200, 202, 204, 205, 212, 222, 229, 230, 239, 242, 243, 244, 245–46, 247, 249, 254, 256, 266, 275, 280, 281, 284, 327–28, 334, 343, 349, 383, 388, 394, 397, 427, 429, 430, 431–32, 442, 445, 446–47
Hitler's beer cellar speech advocating 242
Apel, Theodor 53
Appia, Adolfe 135, 197, 425
Apponyi, Count 137
Arent, Benno von 334
Arnim, Harry 145
Art and Revolution (Wagner) 73
The Art Work of the Future (Wagner) 73
artists, artistic activity 6, 8, 9, 22–23, 46, 61, 62, 64, 66, 68, 73, 74, 77, 87, 107–8, 115, 119, 120, 126, 131, 141–42
arts (singers, musicians, composers, conductors), Jews in the 63, 64, 67, 93, 155, 157, 167, 204–5, 206, 258, 273, 283, 289, 330, 332, 348, 349, 358, 388, 390, 422, 432, 445
banning works of 298, 299.
See also Levi; Mahler; Mendelssohn; Meyerbeer
Aryan race 4, 14, 80, 81, 147, 162, 163, 174, 227, 234, 242, 261, 266, 271
Asyl (cottage) 87, 88
Auden, W.H. 19
Auf Gut Deutsch 253

Auschwitz 3, 391, 398
Austria 17, 153, 341, 410
    annexation of 364–65, 366
Austrian Postal Savings Bank 13
Autobiographical Sketch
        (Wagner) 52, 56, 112, 183

B

Bach, Johann Sebastian 32–33
Bad Ems 91
Badel, Alan 426
Bakunin, Michael 68, 69, 70
Bantock, Granville (composer) 208
Barbarossa, Friedrich (emperor) 15,
        63, 160–61, 274, 290, 327
Barenboim, Daniel 26, 125, 126, 439–443
Basel 113
Baudelaire 94
Bavaria 258
Bayreuth 3, 5, 9, 10, 11, 25, 41, 42, 80, 109,
        123–24, 133, 135, 137, 138, 141, 146,
        149, 156, 157, 158, 175, 185, 187,
        188, 200, 201, 202, 203, 205, 206,
        207, 220, 233, 256, 258, 264, 269,
        271, 279, 282, 284, 288, 292, 296,
        299, 304, 319, 327, 331, 367, 376,
        378, 393, 402, 405, 407, 419, 423
    Jewish community of 256
    synagogue 367, 369
Bayreuther Blätter 159, 166, 180
Bayreuth Festival 33, 41, 125, 135, 136,
        158, 180, 181, 185, 197, 198, 200,
        203, 208–9, 227, 247, 248, 249,
        250, 251–52, 257, 268, 275, 280,
        282, 283, 284, 285, 289, 296, 327,
        329, 330, 333, 334, 342, 343, 347,
        349–350, 356, 364, 365, 377, 393,
        402, 406, 421, 423, 424–26, 427,
        429, 430, 431–32, 439, 440, 442
    Festspielhaus 125–26,
        371, 419–20, 422
Bayreuth Festival Foundation 280
Bechstein 101, 301
Bechstein, Edwin 253, 297
Bechstein, Helene 253–54, 303, 308
Beecham, Sir Thomas 209, 359

Beethoven, Ludwig von 37, 42, 193
    Hammerklavier 137
Beidler, Franz Wilhelm 109, 293
Belgium 376, 410
Belloni (Liszt's secretary) 82
Belzec 395, 398
Ben-Yehuda, Yael 435
Berchtesgaden 63, 161, 238, 253, 254,
        289, 303, 361, 364, 379–80
Berger, Erna 358
Berghof 379, 401. *See also* Obersalzberg
Berlin 59, 60, 147, 148, 188, 205, 254, 297,
        313, 326, 379, 407, 408, 414
Berlin Olympic Games 285
Berlin Philharmonic 397, 412
Berlin Staatskapelle orchestra 441
Berlioz, Hector 26, 56
Bernhardt, Sarah 202
Bernstein, Leonard 434
Bertling, Richard 192
Biebrich 97
Bismarck, Otto von 135, 145–46, 158, 264
Blaskowitz, Johannes 386
Blech, Leo 250
blindness, Hitler's psychological 238–39, 270
Bloch, Dr. 216, 220
Blomberg (minister of war) 273
Blume, Walter 391
Bockelmann, Rudolf 358, 379
Böhm, Karl 430
Boker, Orleana 282
Bologna 292
"Bolshevism from Moses to Lenin"
        (Hitler and Eckart) 284
Bonaparte, Princess Marie (of
        Greece) 368
Bonfantini Stuckert, Thekla 113, 195
Bonfantini (printer) 113, 190
Borchmeyer, Dieter 82
Bordeaux 75, 193
Bormann, Gerda 415
Bormann, Martin 295, 403, 413
Börne, Ludwig 44
Bouhler, Reichsleiter 375
Boulogne 44

Bracher, Karl 6
Branau am Inn 211
Brandt, Dr. 375
Brandt, Karl 320–21, 410
Braun, Eva 229, 313–14, 359, 361,
    403, 412–13, 416
Brecht, Bertolt 225
Breker, Arno 326, 381
Britain 353–54, 362, 366, 373, 376, 377, 390
Brockhaus, Hermann 114
Brockhaus, Ottilie 114
Brown book 112, 150, 183, 387
Bruckmann (firm) 185
Bruckmann, Elsa 275
Bruckner (SS officer) 342
Bruckner, Anton 124, 133
Bryce, James
    The Holy Roman Empire 161
Buchner, Frau 254
Bullock, Alan 7
Bülow, Daniela von 285
Bülow, Eduard von 60
Bülow, Hans von 55, 74–75, 88–89, 90,
    93–94, 101, 102, 103, 104, 109–11,
    113–14, 118, 122, 195, 285
Bulwer-Lytton 48
Burckhardt, Carl 216, 374
Burleigh, Michael
    The Third Reich: A New History 385
Burrell, Mary 9, 48, 112, 113, 188,
    190, 191, 194, 195
Burton, Richard 9
Busch, Fritz 280

C

Carlyle, Thomas
    History of Friedrich the Great 414
Carolsfeld, Schnorr 101
Chamberlain, Houston Stewart 6,
    8, 13, 16–17, 157–58, 179–84,
    185–87, 193, 197, 257, 258–63,
    266, 269, 270, 271, 287,
    292–93, 317, 340, 375, 408
    Das Drama Richard Wagner 182
    *Foundations of the Nineteenth
        Century* 186, 259, 260, 266
    Notes sur Lohengrin 182
    Pathways of My Thoughts 259
Chamberlain, Neville Bowles 179,
    229, 238
Chanani, Avi 437
Chelmno 398
Chereau, Patrice 430
Christianity 4, 45, 136, 151, 153, 155, 327
churches, responses to attacks
    on Jews by 368
Churchill, Winston 364
Ciceri (designer) 83
Clark, Andrew 10, 22
Clarke, Mark 13
Clewing, Carl 255
Collins, Adrian 146
Combat League for German Culture 291
composers, Jewish. *See* arts
concentration camps 391
conductors, Jewish. *See* arts
Confederation of German Industry 370
Constantin, Prince 27
Cornelius, Peter 90, 99, 190
Coulondre (French ambass.) 302–3
Crailsheim, Count von 198
culture, Jews and 64, 65, 122, 164,
    165, 167, 183, 186, 222. *See
    also* arts, Jews in the
Czechoslovakia 366, 370, 410

D

d'Agoult, Marie 89–90, 138
D'Annunzio 19
Dachau 325
Dafni, Reuven 444
Dannreuther, Edward 139
Danzig 67
dark, Hitler's fear of 35, 403
Darwin, Charles 147
    The Descent of Man 169
David (king) 15
David, Leah 33
Davidowicz, Lucy 398
Davison, J.W. 84, 86, 139
death, Wagner's 172–73, 174
Debussy, Claude 202, 203

Degas, Edgar 19
Delius (composer) 208
Deman, Prof. 350
Denazification Tribunal 269, 347, 428
Denmark 376
Deutsch, Frank 313
Deutschland über Alles 280, 330, 425
Devrient, Eduard 159
Dietrich, Sepp 350
Dinter, Arthur
    The Sins Against the Blood 254
Dodd, Martha 303
Dollersheim 295
Dollfuss, Engelbert 341–42
Dollman, Eugen 315
Dom Pedro II, Emperor 133
Domingo, Placido 439, 440
Donington, Robert 189
Dönitz, Karl 411
Dorothea (mother of Johanna
    Wagner) 27
Dresden 32, 48, 55, 58, 59, 60, 67, 68,
    69, 90, 183, 192, 205, 415
    uprising (1848/9) 67, 71,
    87, 187, 191, 192
Drexel, Ellen 405, 407
Drexler 277
Dühring, Eugen 166
Duncan, Isadora 286

E

Eagle's Nest (at Kehlstein) 380, 417
Eckart, Dietrich 253, 254, 284
Edward VIII 362
Eger, Manfred 431
Egusquiza, Roger de 157
Ehrenfels, Christian von 92
Ehrensperger, Ernst 295
Einsatzgruppen 381, 391
Einsiedel, Ernst von 38
Einstein, Albert 325
Eisner, Dr. 168
Elgar (composer) 208
Eliot, George 138–39
Eliot, T.S.
    The Waste Land 19

Ellis, Ashton 179, 187, 193, 194
Ellis, Havelock 306
Engel, Carl Dr. 12
Engels, Friedrich 134
England 84, 260
Epp, Franz von 284, 297
Epstein family 230
Eternal Jew, The (film) 385
"Eternal Jew" "The (exhibition) 368–69
Eulenburg, Philipp von 248
Ewers, Hanns 277
extermination camps 391
Eylon, Lili
    *The Controversy over Richard
    Wagner* 444–45
Eytan, Walter 393

F

fascism 45, 240, 348
Fascists 362, 340, 341
father, issue of Wagner's 28–31,
    190–91, 212
Fatherland Society 67, 164
Fenelon, Fania 435
Fest, Joachim 3, 4–5, 7, 301, 315, 329
Fetis (critic) 83
Feuerbach, Ludwig 73
Final Solution 10, 166, 274–75, 317, 323,
    356, 368, 369, 375, 386, 390–91,
    392–93, 394, 401, 411, 429, 446
fire, Hitler's notion of 77, 227, 362
First World War 62, 233–38, 253,
    259, 260, 273, 335
Fisch, Asher 447
Fischer, Franz 209
Fischer-Dieskau, Dietrich 424
Fliess, Wilhelm 168
Ford, Henry
    *The International Jew: the World's
    Foremost Problem* 275
Formis, Heinz 339
Förster, Albert 322, 402
Forster, Edmund 238–39
France 42, 49, 362, 366, 376, 410
Francis of Assisi (Saint) 16
Franco, General 362

François-Poncet (ambassador) 380
Frank, Hans 288, 294
Frank, Karl 421
Frankenberger (Hitler's alleged
 grandfather) 212, 295
Frankfurt am Main 15, 29, 80
Franks 162
Franz Joseph (emperor) 17
Freischütz, Der (Weber) 34, 405
Freud, Sigmund 7, 87, 88, 107, 120,
 141, 150, 168, 176, 191, 212, 213,
 214, 215, 220–21, 237, 244, 293,
 307, 321, 326, 339, 362, 368
 *Creative Writers and
 Day-Dreaming* 221
Freudenfeuer, V. (pseud. of
 Richard Wagner) 54
Friedell, Egon 125
Friedrich II 15, 16, 68, 161
Friedrich August 57
Friedrich August II 10
Friedrich the Great 265, 269,
 278, 382, 397, 414
Friedrich Wilhelm IV (k. of Prussia) 57
Fritsch, Werner von 422
Fuchs, H. 131
Fuchs, Marta 365
Führer, concept of 159, 160–62, 167,
 203, 238, 253, 266, 272, 274,
 280, 299, 317, 404–5
Furtwängler, Wilhelm 358, 401

G

Gandhi, Mohandas Karamchan 373
Garay, Ernest 434
gas chambers 395–400
Gauguin, Paul 19
Gautier, Judith 47, 141, 252, 351, 426, 431
Gay Science, The (Nietzsche) 23
Geissmar, Berta 358
German Workers' Party 239
Germany 5, 16, 17, 21, 22, 44, 48, 57, 62,
 63, 69, 93, 94, 116, 119, 121, 123,
 153, 203, 227, 238, 239, 244–45,
 253, 256, 258, 259, 390, 392
Gevaert (composer) 83

Geyer, Ludwig 28–29, 30–31,
 32, 34, 190, 366
Gielgud, John 9
Giesing, Erwin 410
Giesler, Hermann 381
Gilbert, Martin
 The Holocaust 385
Glasenapp, Carl Friedrich 8,
 179, 190, 193, 199
Globocnik, Odile 398–99
Gobineau, Joseph Arthur de 146–49,
 184, 271, 340, 375, 408
Goebbels, Magda 416
Goebbels, Paul Jozef 249, 252, 289,
 299, 348, 354, 359, 362, 364,
 372, 373, 379, 385, 395–96,
 398, 406, 413, 414, 415
Goerdeler, Karl 404
Goethe, Johann Wolfgang
 von 27, 35, 115, 170
 The Sorrows of Young Werther 22
Goldhagen, Daniel
 Hitler's Willing Executioners 385
Göring, Carin 268
Göring, Edda 423
Göring, Hermann 258, 266, 268,
 336, 337, 338, 348, 368,
 379, 383, 387, 398, 411
Graarud, Gunna 333
Graff, Anton 414
Gray, Dorian (fictional character) 140
The Great King 397
"great solution." *See* Final Solution
Greenblatt, Robert 132
Grieg, Edvard 133
Gringauz, Samuel 449
Grober, Professor 220
Gross, Adolf von 198, 248
Grosz, Georg 267
Grunsky, Hans 280
Grynspan, Herschel 367
Guderian 415
Gulbranson, Ellen 207–8
Gur, Batya
 *Orchestrated Murder: A
 Musical Murder* 446

Gurnemanz 150
Gustrow, D. 214
Gutman, Robert W. 11, 91, 93, 188

H

H.V. (initials used by Wagner) 54, 60
Halévy, Jacques 431
Hall, Peter 432
Hamann, Brigitte 11, 343, 394
Hamburg 204
Hamburg State Opera 10
Hamilton, Eddie 139
"Hand of Wotan" (a rock) 380
Hanfstaengl, 'Putzi' [Ernst] 8, 276,
    277–78, 309, 316, 322
Hanfstaengl, Egon 279
Hanfstaengl, Helene 277, 279
Hanisch, Reinhold 225, 231
Hansel and Gretel (Humperdinck) 201
Hanslick, Eduard 115, 133, 206, 448
Hanussen (speech teacher) 241
Harden, Maximilian 248–49, 284
Harding, Bertita 426
Harnack, Alfred von 260
Harris, Clement 202
Hauptmann, Gerhart 20, 303
Hausner, Gideon 437
Hayman, Ronald 244, 308
Hebrew translation of *Lohengrin* 290
Heiden, Konrad 8, 183, 241, 260, 304
    Der Führer 184
Heine, Ferdinand 55, 57, 65
Heine, Heinrich 44–45, 52, 61,
    62, 264, 326–27
Heine, Mathilde 45
Heine, Thomas 236, 274
Heines, Edmund 336–37
Henderson, Sir Neville 360, 373, 374
Henlein, Konrad 366
Heroism and Christendom
    (Wagner) 162–63
"Heroism" (Wagner) 162, 163–64
Herrenvolk (master race) 120,
    262, 352, 408
Herzl, Theodor 438
Hess, Ilse 304, 423

Hess, Rudolf 255, 266, 270, 318, 322, 382
Heuss, Theodor 296
Heydrich, Reinhard 386, 388, 390, 391
Himmler, Heinrich 17, 336, 371, 385,
    388, 393, 395, 401–2, 411
Hindemith, Paul
    Neues vom Tage 285
Hindenburg, Paul von 297, 340
Hirschfeld, Magnus 131, 341
Hitler, Alois 211, 212, 216, 294
Hitler, Paula 213
Hobbes, Thomas 3
Hoch, Moshe 435
Hofburg Imperial Palace (Vienna) 13, 18
Hoffmann (photographer) 321
Hofmannstahl, Hugo 445
Hofmuseum (Vienna) 14, 17
Hogarth, George 85
Hohenlohe-Langenberg, Prince 198, 202
Hohenschwangau, Castle 101, 103
Holocaust 9, 18, 24, 385–406
Holzinger, Emil 256
homosexuality and homosexuals 8,
    127, 131, 193–94, 202, 212, 229,
    235–36, 240, 243, 244, 248,
    249, 252, 265, 273, 278, 297,
    315, 322–23, 335, 337, 338, 339,
    341, 367, 382, 389–90, 422
Horning, Richard 127
Horst Wessel lied 330
Horst, Anna 180
Horthy, Admiral 366
Hotter, Hans 343, 344–45
Hugenberg, Alfred 290
Huguenots, The (Meyerbeer) 53
Humperdinck, Engelbert 201
Hymn to the Beloved (Hitler) 228

I

Iffland, Resi 358
Igra, Samuel 341–42
    Germany's National Vice 338
Infield, Glenn B. 7–8
influence of Wagner on Hitler 225, 243,
    256–57, 260, 265, 266, 269, 271,
    272, 274, 299, 316, 325, 329, 340,

342–43, 352–53, 355, 362, 371, 374–75, 386, 388, 393, 395, 404
insomnia, Hitler's 339–40, 397
Invincible, The (List) 14
Irish people, the 148
Isaiah (prophet) 211
Israel, approach to Wagner in 6, 11, 20, 24, 433–49
Israel Philharmonic Orchestra 433, 435, 437
Italy 162, 172, 362, 370

J

Jahoda, Rudolf 222
James, Henry 138
Janssen, Herbert 346–47, 422
Jericho 15
Jesus Christ 15, 20, 50, 150, 152, 160, 389
Jew Süss (film) 385
Jewish boycott 343
Jewish problem and solution 166, 242, 243, 244–45, 388. *See also* Final Solution
"Jewish Question as Race Pestilence" (Dühring) 166
Jewish question 50, 272, 300, 387, 395
Jewish race 4, 155, 184, 275, 363. *See also* racism
"Jewry in Music" (Wagner) 63, 78, 122, 123, 163, 164, 184, 255, 273, 299, 385, 395, 429, 445
Jews. *See* antisemitism; culture; Final Solution; racism; singers
Jodl, General 389
Johnson, Paul 77, 438
Jones, Chuck
 What's Opera, Doc? 426
Jones, Ernest 107
Jordan, Ruth 438
Joshua 15
Jostenoode, Harald von 16
Joukowsky, Paul von 148
Joyce, James 19
Judaism 45, 64, 65, 230, 280
Jung, Carl 141, 361–62
Junge, Frau 409

K

Kaiserwald 402
Kaltenbrunner, Ernst 17
Kannenberg, Artur 409
Karajan, Herbert von 379, 424
Karlsruhe 155
Karpath, Ludwig 202
Katsav, Moshe 441
Kehlstein 380
Keplinger, Herr 216
Kershaw, Ian 7, 217–18, 268, 309, 405
Kietz, Ernst 47
Kietz, Gustave 124
Kind, Alfred 131–32
King, Francis
 Satan and Swastika 355
Kipnis, Alexander 332–33
Kirchmeyer 69
Klein, Berthold 402
Klein, Hermann 115
Klemperer, Otto 250, 347
Klindworth, Karl 101, 249–50
Knappertsbusch, Hans 333, 401, 424
Kniese, Julius 198, 199
Knittel, Albert 332
"Know Thyself" (Wagner) 81–82, 121, 165, 387
Köhler, Joachim 11, 65, 167, 446
Konetzni, Hilde 365
Königsberg 42
Königswarder, Moritz 231
Konwitschny, Peter 10
Korngold, Erich Wolfgang 426–27
Kranich (set designer) 257
Kraus, Karl 247–48, 315–16
Kreisler, Fritz 277, 278
Kreiten, Karlrobert 422
Kristallnacht 265, 367, 433
Krüger, Kurt Dr. 320, 335
Kubizek, August 14–15, 217–18, 219, 221, 222–26, 227, 228, 229–30, 235, 378
Kuntze, Otto 180
Kupfer, Harry 442
Küstner, Court Intendant 60

L

La Grange, Henry-Louis de, 79
La Spezia 84
Lafferentz, Bodo 405
Lammers (officer) 235
Landau, Moshe 445
Landowsky, Klaus 443
Landsberg prison 268, 270, 275
Langer, Walter C. 7–8, 212, 214, 232, 268, 302, 321, 322, 338–39, 380, 417
Laussot, Eugene 75, 76, 193, 351, 426
Laussot, Jessie. *See* Taylor
Lawrence, D.H. 19
leader. *See* Führer
Lebensraum 340, 370
Legge, Walter 330
Lehman, Lotte 349, 364–65
Lehmann, Lilli 205
Lehrs, Samuel 47
Leider, Frida 349–50
Leipzig 25, 26, 29, 32, 34, 80, 299, 359
  Am Brühl 33, 171
Leitner, Ben-Zion 436
Leonding 17, 214, 227
Lesimple, August 47
Lessing, Gotthold Ephraim
  Nathan the Wise 166, 397
Leubald und Adelaide (Wagner) 35
Levi, Hermann 93, 145, 155–56, 157, 172, 174, 198, 199, 205–7, 431, 444, 445
Levine, James 439
Levy, Lippert 33
Lewes, George Henry 138
Lichtenberg, Reinhold von 247
Linden, Herbert 398–99
Linderhof 105
Linge (Hitler's valet) 416
Linneman, Richard 280
Linz 212, 217, 218, 220, 225, 235, 409
Liptauer, Suzi 318
List, Emanuel 332, 333
List, Guido von 14
  Invincible, The 14
  Secret of the Runes, The 14
Liszt, Cosima. *See* Wagner, Cosima
Liszt, Franz 61, 66, 69, 72, 80, 84, 89, 95, 111, 124, 125, 132, 133, 136–37, 200, 205
Lloyd George, David 353
Lochner, Louis 353
Lohengrin (poem) 59
Lohr, Fritz 204
Lombroso, Cesare 131
London Philharmonic Orchestra 358–59
London 84, 136, 137, 187, 429
Longinus 15
Lorenz, A.O. 189
Lorenz, Lotte 337–38
Lorenz, Max 337, 422
Louis XIV, King 127
Lucerne 93, 142
Lüdecke, Kurt 277
Ludendorff, Erich 258, 267, 269, 275, 283
Ludwig II (king of Bavaria) 10, 32, 56, 80, 94, 98–101, 102–6, 109, 126–27, 128–30, 135, 156, 172, 176, 183, 198, 238, 257, 258, 277, 278
Luther, Martin 27, 264–65, 284, 368
  On the Jews and Their Lies 265
Lüttichau, Baron von 48

M

Machtan, Lothar
  The Hidden Hitler 237–38
Madagascar 385
Magdala 58
Magdeburg 37, 41
Magee, Brian 19
Magic Fire (film) 426
Mahler, Ernst 153, 173
Mahler, Gustav 78–79, 153–55, 204–5, 221–22, 250, 302, 365
  Das Lied von der Erde 434
Maier, Mathilde 97, 131
Majdanek 398
Manchester, William
  The Arms of Krupp 338
Manheit, Jacques 173
Mann, Klaus 240–41
  "The Left and Vice" 240
Mann, Thomas 11, 21, 93, 98, 253, 319–20, 419

The Blood of the Walsungs 320
Buddenbrooks 298
"The Suffering and Greatness of Richard Wagner" 298
Tristan 320
Mannheim 80
Manowarda, Josef von 347, 358, 398
Marcuse, Ludwig 352–53
Mariafeld 99
Markevitch, Igor 433–34, 444
Marseilles 106
Martini 419
Marx, Karl 71, 134–35
Marxism and Marxists 238, 268, 269, 272
masturbation 168–69, 191, 194
Maudsley, Henry 169
Maupassant, Guy de 447–48
Maurice, Emil 304
Mauthausen 391
Maximilian II 132
Mayr, Karl 239
Mazelis, Fred 443
Mehta, Zubin 435–36, 437, 444
Meilhaus, Baroness 94
Mein Kampf (Hitler) 14, 212, 213, 239, 243, 270, 271, 272, 273, 274, 279, 289, 330, 340, 342, 362, 370, 376
Meissner 297
Melamed, Avraham 436–37
Melchior, Lauritz 358
Memel 370
Mend, Hans 236
Mendelssohn, Felix 56, 57, 63, 86, 359, 431, 445
  A Midsummer Night's Dream 66
  The Fair Melusina 84
  Wedding March 413
Menuhin, Yehudi 430, 441
Meyer, Friederike 97–98, 131
Meyer, Oskar 420
Meyerbeer, Giacomo 37, 42–43, 44, 45, 46, 48, 53–54, 56, 57, 59–61, 63, 65, 66, 69, 70, 80, 82, 85–86, 94, 102, 139, 145, 164, 273, 389, 431, 439
  Les Huguenots 59
  Le Prophète 59, 70

Mildenburg, Anna von 219
Millington, Barry 78
Mishori, Yaakov 444
Mitford, Diana 359, 360, 361
Mitford, Unity 359–60, 375
Mohr, Wilhelm 133
Moltke, General von 17
Montez, Lola 132–33, 136, 137
Moore, Grace 419
Morell, Theodor 403, 405, 409, 410
Moscow 281
Mosley, Sir Oswald 359, 360
Mozart, Wolfgang 26, 53, 103, 443
  Il Nozze di Figaro 172
Muck, Karl 333
Müller, Maria 333, 358
Müller, Max 1
Müller, Renate 229, 311–312
Munich 93, 98, 99, 103, 104, 105, 108, 109, 121, 122, 188, 205, 233, 235, 239, 243, 253–54, 258, 266, 267, 276, 288, 305
  opera 94, 101, 198
Munich Agreement (1938) 370
music, Hitler's knowledge and appreciation of Wagner's 217–19, 223, 225, 227, 232, 234, 270–71, 273, 283, 317, 319, 334, 351, 356–57, 367, 370, 389, 393. *See also* Bayreuth Festival
musical works (texts, music, performances, discussion regarding), Wagner's
  Ban on Love, The 41, 43
  Columbus 53
  The Fairies 37
  The Flying Dutchman 25, 42, 46, 48–49, 50, 51–52, 57, 65, 68, 137, 153, 191, 219, 438
  Götterdämmerung 76, 154, 208, 219, 298, 329, 349, 356–57, 375, 378, 412
  Lohengrin 10, 23, 25, 66, 67, 68, 70, 94, 101, 104, 115, 191, 222, 272, 283, 289, 290, 328, 334, 366, 413
  Die Meistersinger von Nürnberg 10, 18, 25, 33, 80, 90, 95, 108, 109, 115, 116, 122, 142, 155–56, 164,

206, 208, 209, 218, 222, 225,
  257, 273, 274, 279, 280, 289,
  299, 334, 337, 343, 362–64,
  366, 378, 424, 425, 441
Parsifal 4, 10, 16, 25, 77, 126, 136,
  141, 145, 149–53, 155, 156, 157,
  158–59, 169–70, 173, 174, 180–81,
  183, 198, 199, 201, 206, 208, 209,
  220, 247, 257–58, 268, 270, 282,
  317, 343, 349, 351, 356, 424, 439
played in concentra-
  tion camps 391–92
Das Rheingold 21, 45, 76,
  77–78, 80, 84, 87, 94, 122,
  259, 342, 349, 357, 442
Rienzi 36, 42, 44, 47, 55–56, 57, 59,
  60, 225–26, 325, 334, 371, 393
Ring des Nibelungen, Der (*Ring of the
  Nibelungs*; tetralogy) 10, 14, 20,
  25, 62, 76, 77–78, 80, 84, 101, 106,
  120, 121, 122, 133, 140, 147, 189, 197,
  198, 205, 207, 208, 209, 247, 257–
  58, 271, 292, 327, 328, 334, 337, 343,
  365, 366, 374, 424, 430, 432, 440
Siegfried 76, 87, 107, 148
Siegfried's Death 73, 76 (poem)
Tannhäuser 2, 10, 25, 36, 58, 68,
  84, 94, 105, 115, 139, 140, 186,
  191, 218, 286, 292, 333, 424
Tristan and Isolde 25, 35, 75, 87, 88, 91,
  92, 93, 94, 101, 102, 114, 115, 118,
  119, 121–22, 139, 197, 219, 222, 223,
  234, 276, 279, 298, 320, 333, 334,
  349, 388, 395, 435, 440, 441, 446
The Valkyries 76, 81, 87, 88, 94, 122,
  135, 138, 140, 148, 227, 263, 320,
  328–29, 362, 374, 437, 439, 440
Wesendonck Lieder 291
musicians, Jewish. *See* arts
Mussolini, Benito 275, 292, 341, 348,
  365, 366, 370, 377, 403, 410
My Life (Wagner) 112, 113, 167,
  183, 190, 195, 272
myth 5–6, 21, 26, 32, 35, 45, 50, 62, 63,
  65, 73, 74, 82, 119–20, 121, 125,
  150, 232, 317, 328, 380–81

N

Napoleon Bonaparte 20, 382
nationalism 47, 67, 108, 254
National Socialism 4, 5, 9, 11, 271, 331, 348,
  350, 392, 399, 415, 429, 431, 434
National Socialists 62, 187, 240
Nattiez, Jean-Jacques 80
Nazi Party 3, 14, 142, 224, 241, 242,
  243, 253, 269, 275, 276, 280,
  289, 301, 318, 351, 355, 421
  1938 Nürnberg rally 366
Nazism and Nazis 12, 21, 282, 290, 434
  and Bayreuth 280, 290
Netherlands, the 376
Neue Zeitschrift, 1842 article
  by Wagner in 54
Neuschwanstein (castle) 105
Newman, Ernest 7, 11, 12, 20, 35, 113,
  152, 177, 189, 191, 199, 333, 351
  The Life of Richard Wagner 188
Nibelungs 6, 76, 78, 80, 82, 109, 120, 125,
  135, 141, 160, 219, 243, 263, 280,
  291, 395, 416. *See also* musical
  works: *Ring des Nibelungen, Der*
Nietzsche, Elizabeth 117, 175
Nietzsche, Friedrich 4, 12, 13, 19, 31, 74,
  77, 109, 114, 115–21, 122, 135, 136,
  167–70, 171–72, 173–74, 175, 176,
  185, 190, 191, 203, 209, 225, 254,
  274, 276, 280, 352, 354, 421
  Also Sprach Zarathustra 16, 118
  *The Birth of Tragedy from the
    Spirit of Music* 118
  The Case of Wagner 74
  The Free Will 209
  Gay Science 23
  My Sister and I 116, 169
  Towards a Genealogy of Morals 22–23
  "Die Unschuld des Werdens" 174
"Night of the Long Knives" 336–37,
  338, 401, 429
Nilsson, Birgit 2
Nordau, Max 20, 346
Norway 376, 410
Nürnberg 3, 13, 15, 16, 17, 18, 108, 134,
  142, 153, 288, 289, 299, 364

Nürnberg trials 386

O

Obersalzberg 63, 272, 274, 319, 327
    Haus Wachenfeld on 289, 303
Oberwarmensteinach 408
Olivier, Laurence 9
Olmert, Ehud 441
Opera and Drama (Wagner) 73, 74
operas, Hitler listening to
    Wagner's 270–71
Operation Barbarossa 382
"Operation Magic Fire" 362
oratory, Hitler's 241, 277, 279,
    366–67, 375, 381, 395
Order for the destruction of lives that are unworthy of being lived 375–76
Orff, Carl
    Carmina Burana 445
Ossietzky, Carl von 326
Overbeck, Franz 173
Overhoff, Kurt 423

P

Palestine Orchestra 433, 438
Palestine 367–68
Palladilke
    Patrie 202
Palmer, Tony 9
Pan-Germanism 208, 340, 342, 353
Papen, Franz von 297
Paris 43–44, 46, 47, 49, 54, 56, 69,
    70, 71, 94, 141, 202, 367
"*Parisian Fatalities for the German*"
    (Freudenfeuer [Wagner]) 54
Parry (composer) 208
Parsifal (Wolfram von Eschenbach) 14
Patton, George 13
Paul (prince; Yugoslavia) 366
Pecht, Friedrich 47
Penzing 99
Petacci, Clara 410
Pfannenstiel, Prof. 399
Pfistermeister, Herr 99
Pfitzner, Hans 368
philandering, Wagner's 6, 76, 186, 192–93

Phineas 15
Planner, Minna 37, 42, 55–56, 57, 58,
    59, 60, 66, 68, 75, 85, 88, 90,
    91, 103, 106, 112–13, 131, 195
Planner, Natalie 37, 112, 192
Poland 341, 370, 371, 373–74,
    376, 390, 392, 412
Pollent, Karoline 42
Ponte, Lorenzo da 172
Porges, Heinrich 98, 145, 431
pornography 321
Post-Holocaust Dialogue Group 447, 449
Praeger 8
Praeger, Ferdinand 84, 187, 193
    Wagner as I Knew Him 187
Prague 344, 345
Preetorius, Emil 349, 394
Prevatsky-Wendt, Josef 220
Prinz (Hitler's godfather) 212
prostitutes 273
Protocols of the Elders of Zion 275
Pudor, Heinrich 131
Puringer, August 280–81
Puschmann, Theodor 174–75
Pusinelli, Anton 98, 106
putsch 255, 266, 278

R

Rabbi Benjamin 298
Rabinovich, Menashe 296
race laws, Nazi 332, 354, 355, 364
racism 11, 20, 21, 66, 77, 78–79, 82, 88,
    111, 120, 121, 122, 124, 136, 147–48,
    149, 171, 172, 206, 245, 255,
    260–62, 271–72, 290, 346, 388
    racial hygiene 163
rallies, Nazi 289–90
Rally of Freedom" (Nürnberg) 354–55
rape 285
Rastenburg 93, 393
Rath, Ernst vom 367
Rathenau, Walther 245
Raubal, Angela 304
Raubal, Friedl 304
Raubal, Geli 7, 118, 229, 304, 314

Rauschning, Herman 235–36,
    322, 338, 342
  The Voice of Destruction 296
The Red Book (Wagner) 112, 183, 387
Redern, Count 60
Redgrave, Vanessa 9
Redlich, Fritz 305, 316–17
Rée, Paul 175
Regeneration Writings (Wagner); regeneration writings 159,
    167, 171, 174, 272, 284, 428
Rehnse, JFM 310
Reich Music Train 377
Reissinger, Gertrud. *See* Wagner, Gertrud
Reiter, Mimi 229, 318
"Religion and Art" (Wagner) 302
Renoir, Auguste 19, 149
Restoration of the Civil Service act 325
restrictions against Jews 297, 369
Rhineland, occupation of the 356, 357
Richardson, Ralph 9
Richard Wagner Museum (Bayreuth) 431
Richard Wagner Research Centre,
    German (Bayreuth) 366
Richter, Hans 206, 209, 248
Richter, Jean Paul 25–26, 123, 124, 202, 211
Ride of the Valkyries, The 10
Riefensthal, Leni
  Triumph of the Will 328, 353
Rienzi (hero) 226–27, 235, 255, 274,
    275, 290, 317, 371, 416, 417
Riga 42, 54
Ring cycle 10, 37, 54, 73, 76, 82, 99,
    106, 148, 160, 243, 257, 259,
    287, 395. *See also* musical
    works, Wagner's: *Ring*
Ritter (family) 75
Ritter, Frau 75
Ritter, Karl 90, 194
Roberts, Stephen 317
Röckel, August 67, 68, 69, 70, 87, 187, 192
Roger (tenor) 60
Röhm, Ernst 35, 242, 243, 268, 284,
    297, 307, 335–36, 401, 429
Röhm's Revengers 339
Rolland, Romain 52, 363

Roller, Alfred 219, 220
Roller, Ulrich 394
Roman Catholicism 136
Roosevelt, Franklin 412, 414, 415
Rose, Paul 152–53
Rosenberg, Alfred 266, 291
Rosler, Nechama 443–44
Rossini, Gioacchino 2, 53, 58–59
Roswaenge, Helge 358
Rothschild 54
Rousseau, Jean Jacques
  Confessions 214
Rubinstein, Herr 148
Russia 53, 389, 390

S

SA (Sturmabteilung) 243
Saarland 353
Said, Edward 80, 116, 126, 441
Sainton, Prosper 84
Saint-Saens, Camille 133, 208
Saldern, Elizabeth von 343–44
Salomon, Dr. (rabbi of
    Bayreuth) 281–82, 283
Sand, George 80
Sartre, Jean-Paul 246
Sasse, Martin 368
Sauerbach, Prof. 376
Saul (king) 15
Scaria, Emil 198
Schaub (SS officer) 342
Schaub, Julius 288
Scheel, Walter 430
Schemann, Ludwig 62, 204
Scheubner-Richter, Erwin von 268
Schickelgruber, Maria Anna 295
Schickelgruber. *See* Hitler, Alois
Schiller, Friedrich 182
Schiller, Johann C.F. 35
Schleicher (Nazi) 336
Schleicher, General von 297
Schlumprecht, Karl 331
Schmedes, Erik 219
Schmidt, Ernst 236–37, 239
Schmidt, Matthias
  Albert Speer: The End of a Myth 334

Schmidt, Motti 444
Schoenberg, Arnold 348
Scholl siblings 422
Scholz, Dieter David 3
Schönerer, Georg von 340
Schopenhauer, Arthur 87, 119, 148, 234
Schorr, Friedrich 283, 284
Schramm, Percy 6, 387–88
Schröder, Christa 315, 413
Schröder, Leopold von
    The Consummation of the Aryan
        Mystery in Bayreuth 234
Schröder-Devrient, Wilhelmina 36–37
Schultze-Naumburg, Prof. 346
    Art and Race 346
Schumann, Clara 55
Schumann, Robert 53, 54, 56, 58, 83, 274
Schure, Edouard 168
Schuschnigg, Kurt von 364
Schwarz, Franz 310, 311
Schwarzkopf, Elizabeth 2
Schweitzer, Albert 185–86, 208, 248, 424
scores, Hitler's possession of
    Wagner 289, 370, 389, 407–8
Secret of the Runes, The (List) 14
Sehulster, Jerome 225
Semper, Gottfried 68, 231
Seward, Desmond 341
sexual affairs, Wagner's 75–76,
    87–88, 92, 107, 130–31
sexuality 7, 8, 71, 127, 131–32, 141,
    176, 213, 215, 254, 285, 321
    perversions and depravity 7, 8,
        24, 190, 223, 229, 232, 235–36,
        239, 244, 273, 305–10, 311–16,
        318, 320–23, 338, 341, 358
Shakespeare, William, works
    set to music 25, 35
Sharon, Ariel 441
Shaw, George Bernard 19, 92,
    134, 189, 207
Sheffi, Na'ama 5
    The Ring of Myths: The Israelis,
        Wagner and the Nazis 433
Shilansky, Dov 437
Shirach, Baldur von 343

Shirer, William L. 271, 352, 390
Siedler, Fritz von 322
Siegfried (hero) 4, 62–63, 73, 140–41,
    218, 219, 227, 235, 243, 267,
    283, 290, 295, 328, 362, 370,
    381, 404, 412, 416, 417
    linked to Christ 160
Siegfried Idyll (Wagner) 251
Siegfried, Walther 186
Sievers, von (head of Nazi
    Occult Bureau) 17
Sigismund (emperor) 17
Silling (teacher) 32
Simon Wiesenthal Center
    (Jerusalem) 440
singers, Jewish. *See* arts
Sipp, Robert 33
Skorzeny, Otto 314
Slezak, Margarete 358
Smyth, Ethel 208
Sobibor 398
Society for the Friends of Bayreuth 423
Society for the Performance of the
    Dramas of Richard Wagner
    as He Intended Them 425
Solti, Georg 9
Sorrento 171
The Sorrows of Young Werther
    (Goethe) 22, 115
Soviet Union 377, 381, 392
    non-aggression pact with 370
Spartacist movement 267
Spear of Destiny 13–18, 150–51,
    152–53, 161, 183–84, 317
Spear of Herod Antipas. *See*
    Spear of Destiny
Spear of Longinus. *See* Spear of Destiny
Speer, Albert 295, 319, 327, 334, 408
Spengler, Oswald 354
Spielmann, Julius 79
Spital 295
Spitzer, Daniel 130
Spontini (composer) 56–57
Spotts, Frederic 5, 20, 166, 287–88, 381
Stalin, Josef 377, 415
Stalingrad 398, 403

Stanford (composer) 208
Starnberg 103, 106, 110, 122, 195
Stauffenberg, Col. von 404
Stein [author of Wagner book] 189
Stein, Walter Dr. 14, 16
Steinhäuser, Justin 403
Stempfele, Bernhard 309–10
Stern, Julius 109
Sternfield, Richard
    Richard Wagner and the Holy German War 233
Stocker, Adolf 202
Stocker, Wilhelm 309
Strasser, Gregor 289, 309, 336
Strasser, Otto 241, 305–6, 308–9
Strauss, Alice 343
Strauss, Richard 205–6, 207, 247, 286, 343, 347, 348–49, 421, 444, 445
    Friedenstag 343, 354
    Der Rosenkavalier 365
Streicher, Julius 245, 266, 366, 429
Streseman 258
Stuckenschmidt, Hans 290
Stuka (film) 377–78
Stumpfegger, Ludwig 409, 410
Stürmer, Der 245, 321
Stuttgart 99
the Sudentenland 67, 366, 410
Sullivan, Arthur 115, 208
Switzerland 105, 175, 191
Syberberg, Hans (director)
    Hitler (429)
Symphony in C Major (Wagner) 37
syphilis, Hitler's fear of 273, 316, 317

T

Tandey, Henry 238
Tausig, Karl 98, 145
Taylor, Jessie Laussot 74–76, 91, 113, 131, 194
Taylor, Ronald 188
Tchaikovsky, Peter 133
Teplitz 29, 30
Third Reich 3, 5, 9, 11, 20, 64, 284, 326, 379, 383
Thode, Henry 286

Thor, god of Thunder 44
Thuringia 335, 368
Tichatschek, Joseph 68
Tietjen, Heinz 331–32
Toeplitz, Uri 434
Tornow (Hitler's vet) 416
Toscanini, Arturo 206, 291–92, 347, 348, 358, 367, 372, 429–30, 433, 438
Tourel, Jenni 434
Towards a Genealogy of Morals (Nietzsche) 22–23
Treblinka 398
Trevor-Roper, H.R. 11, 93, 223
Triebschen 106
Troost, Frau 346
Twain, Mark 1, 205
    "Some Thoughts on the Science of Onanism" 169

U

Uffing 278
Uhlig, Elsa 191
Uhlig, Theodor 61, 68, 191
Ukraine 390, 393

V

Vaisseau Fantôme, La (opera) 46
Valentino, Henri 53
Valkyries (Wagner) 21
vegetarianism 301–2
Venice 25, 90, 91, 93, 94, 172, 268
Verdi, Giuseppe 28, 173
    Aida 223
Verlaine, Paul 177
Victoria, Queen 85, 137, 139
Vienna 7, 13, 14, 15, 16, 17, 80, 94, 97, 153, 154, 182, 205, 219, 220, 221, 222, 228, 261, 322, 358
Viereck, Pieter 5
Villa Pellet (Lake Starnberg) 103
Vogl, Therese 208
Volk 266, 271–72
Völkischer Beobachter 244
Volker, Franz 350, 358
Voltaire 127–28, 278

W

Wagener, Otto 315
Wagner (Palmer) 9
Wagner and the Jews (photo exhibit) 431
"Wagner and the Jews" (conference) 447
Wagner, Adolf 35
Wagner, Albert 29
Wagner, Blandine 202
Wagner (née Liszt), Cosima von Bülow 8, 9, 55, 76, 89, 94, 103, 105, 106, 108, 109–11, 113, 119, 120, 122, 123, 131, 135, 136–37, 138, 141, 142, 148, 155, 157, 162, 164, 165, 166, 175, 181, 182–83, 185–86, 188, 190, 192, 193, 194, 195, 197–200, 202, 203, 205, 206, 207, 208, 222, 233, 247, 248, 250, 255, 257, 258, 262, 275, 280, 286, 287, 292–93, 391, 414, 426
Wagner, Eva (d. of Wolfgang) 408
Wagner, Eva 6, 108, 109, 131, 187, 190, 192, 293
Wagner, Friedelind 11, 251, 287, 288, 293, 318, 320, 338, 343, 350, 371–73, 405, 420, 425–26, 432
   Heritage of Fire 350
Wagner, Friedrich 28–29, 30, 190
Wagner, Gertrud 293, 405, 407, 427
Wagner, Gottfried 3, 29, 135, 318, 437, 446–47
Wagner, Isolde 109–10, 131, 249
Wagner, Johanna 27, 28–29, 30, 190
Wagner, Klara 34, 90
Wagner, Luise 31
Wagner, Nike 112, 135, 320
Wagner, Rosalie 31
Wagner, Siegfried 30, 101, 108, 109, 100, 131, 142, 197, 200–3, 208, 209, 247–48, 249, 250–54, 255, 257–58, 263–64, 266, 267, 268, 269, 271, 275, 276, 280, 281, 283, 286, 287, 289, 291–92, 318, 333, 393, 402, 425
   Der Bärenhäuter 247
   Wahnfried Idyll 250–51
Wagner, Verena 251, 293–94, 343, 405
Wagner, Walter 412
Wagner, Wieland 135, 250, 251, 286, 287, 293, 294, 299, 328, 346, 371, 373, 376, 405, 407, 423, 424–25, 426, 427
Wagner, Winifred Williams 11, 101, 118, 206, 220, 229, 250, 254–55, 256, 257, 258, 263, 266, 268–69, 270, 275, 276, 279, 281, 282, 283, 288, 289, 290, 292, 293, 296, 297, 298, 303, 304, 308, 318, 319, 321, 330, 331, 332, 337, 338, 342, 343, 344, 347, 348–49, 350, 354, 356, 358, 365, 371, 372, 373, 394, 405, 407, 420–23, 424, 427, 428–31
Wagner, Wolfgang 251, 252, 288, 293, 294, 328, 337, 346, 371, 376, 405, 408, 423, 424–25, 426, 427, 428, 430, 431
Wahnfried (house) 9, 30–31, 125, 147, 157, 187, 188, 200, 207, 250, 252, 255, 256, 258, 282, 286, 294, 345, 393, 405, 407, 425
Waite, Robert G.L. 7–8, 321
Walter, Bruno 259, 347, 401
Walton, William 10
Wandering Jew 49–50, 51–52, 58, 65, 150, 153
Wannsee conference 390
Want (poem; Wagner) 71
War Diary (Schramm) 387–88
Wasner, Stefan 214–15
Weber, Carl Maria von 26, 57, 61, 83
Weidt, Lucie 228, 283
Weimar 69, 70
Weiner, Marc 11, 23–24, 80, 121, 152
Weinert, Susanne 188
Weingartner, Felix 200, 250
Weininger, Otto
   Sex and Character 120
Weinlig, Theodor 36
Werder, Professor 57
Wesendonck, Mathilde 87, 90, 91–93, 131, 193, 194–95, 255, 304, 351, 395, 426
Wesendonck, Otto 85, 93, 194
Wesendoncks 420
"What is German? (Wagner) 164

Wibelungen, Wagner's essay on the 62–63, 159, 160, 272
Wieland the Smith (Wagner) 75, 215, 223
Wijsenbeek Louis 394
Wilde, Oscar 2, 132, 140, 248
Wilhelm II, Kaiser 259
will, Hitler's political 408–11
Wille, Eliza 255
Wille, General 255
Wille family 99
Williams, Winifred. *See* Wagner, Winifred
Wolfram Von Eschenbach
    Parsifal 14
Wolf (Hitler's nickname) 279, 286, 287, 303–4
Wolf, Hugo 154, 302
Wolf's Lair 21
Wolff, Charlotte 341
Wolfschanze (Rastenburg) 393
Wolzogen, Hans von 203–4
    Der Jude im Dorn 250
Wotan (operatic figure) 4, 21, 76, 78, 80, 120, 134, 140, 160
Wulf, Amalie 53
Würzburg 37

X

xenophobia 108, 111, 274, 282, 349, 337

Y

Yeats, W.B. 108
Young Siegfried (Hitler) 232
Yugoslavia 366

Z

Zeissler, Adolf 311
Ziegler, Hans 424
Zola, Emil 19
Zurich 70, 73, 193, 255, 371
Zweig, Stefan 354, 445